"The subject of this book is very timely and relevant, a
ence recently, especially with the rise of the Islamic-ori
Turkey. The writing style, the presentation of the mat......, organization, and the
conclusion were clear, reasonable, and well documented. This book will fill the void
in the literature and I recommend it very highly to students and scholars that are
interested in the region, its culture, and Islam."

Tareq Y. Ismael, *University of Calgary, Canada*

"The Arab Middle East has a long and complex history, an understanding of which
is necessary for a full appreciation of the current situation. This book makes an
important contribution to that process and gives important new insights."

Fraser Taylor, *Carleton University, Canada*

"By analyzing the legacy of the Ottoman Empire, Özay Mehmet—a distinguished
emeritus research professor of international affairs at Carleton University in
Canada—presents an original perspective on the origins of the modern Middle
East. Thus, this study offers a valuable complement to works that instead emphasize
the heritage of Western imperialism. Stylistically well written and smoothly flowing,
Professor Mehmet's wealth of insights range from earlier centuries up to the new
Silk Road Economy, extending from Beijing to Istanbul, Turkish-EU relations, the
war in Ukraine, and failures of democracy, among others. Highly recommended."

Michael M. Gunter, Professor of Political Science,
Tennessee Technological University, United States

ISLAMIC IDENTITY AND DEVELOPMENT AFTER THE OTTOMANS

Exploring themes of identity and development in the post-Ottoman Arab world, this book updates the author's earlier *Islamic Identity and Development* (Routledge, 1990) to analyze the root causes of chaos, civil war, and conflict in the Islamic Core today.

Adopting a neo-Ottomanist framework, and using the latest scholarship on the Middle East, the author traces the historical development of the current crisis to the World War I (WWI), when the West instigated invasions, coup d'états, civil and proxy wars. It is argued that Western powers have facilitated the dispossession of the Arab people in their overarching aim to gain control of the oil fields. A range of historical case studies are provided as evidence, from the Balfour Declaration and the Sykes-Picot Agreement to the creation of Israel and the displacement of Islamic refugees. Individual nations are also analyzed, including Iran, Saudi Arabia, Iraq, Syria, Libya, and Egypt. Ultimately, the author suggests that artificial countries and unsustainable frontiers are the root causes of the Islamic crisis. However, a realistic (and long-term) solution may lie in the evolution of a new Silk Route Economy.

This book will appeal to graduate-level students in political economy, area studies, international affairs, and Middle East studies generally.

Özay Mehmet is Distinguished Research Professor of International Affairs at Carleton University in Ottawa, Canada. He was educated in Cyprus, the London School of Economics (1959–1962) and he received his MA and PhD in Economics at the University of Toronto. He has taught at various Canadian universities (Windsor, York, Toronto, Ottawa, and Carleton), and is the author of more than 20 academic books and over 100 articles in academic journals.

Routledge Studies in Middle Eastern Politics

For a full list of titles in the series: www.routledge.com/middleeaststudies/series/
SE0823

ISLAMIC IDENTITY AND DEVELOPMENT AFTER THE OTTOMANS

The Arab Middle East

Özay Mehmet

Routledge
Taylor & Francis Group

LONDON AND NEW YORK

First published 2023
by Routledge
4 Park Square, Milton Park, Abingdon, Oxon OX14 4RN

and by Routledge
605 Third Avenue, New York, NY 10158

Routledge is an imprint of the Taylor & Francis Group, an informa business

© 2023 Özay Mehmet

British Library Cataloguing-in-Publication Data
A catalogue record for this book is available from the British Library

ISBN: 978-1-032-21567-9 (hbk)
ISBN: 978-1-032-21569-3 (pbk)
ISBN: 978-1-003-26899-4 (ebk)

DOI: 10.4324/9781003268994

Typeset in Bembo
by Newgen Publishing UK

CONTENTS

TABLES

PREFACE

The COVID-19 has claimed, as at August 8, 2022, 6.59 million (WHO, 2022). In the last two decades alone, conflict, due to invasion and civil war, in the Post-Ottoman Middle East has killed, wounded, and uprooted no less than 30 million (Table 2.3). The oil-rich Muslim Core, the Arab Middle East,[1] is far removed from a just and humane world, totally at variance with the grand promise of Islam, a perfect Social Contract initiated by the Prophet himself.

The Muslim Ideal State was a historical fact. It existed under the leadership of the Prophet and lasted four decades, from 622 AD to 661 AD. This Golden Age was Islamic governance in accordance with the Islamic Social Justice created in real time by the Prophet in the seventh century (II&D, 1990, 11). After the death of the Prophet came the rule of his disciples, the Four Righteously Guided Caliphs (Esposito, 1988, 8).

The Golden Age of Islam began when the Prophet migrated in 622 AD from Mecca to Medina, not as a preacher or Prophet, but as reformer and a judge for the entire community, Muslim, and non-Muslim. Medina then was a prosperous trading center, a multiethnic city, Muslims and Jews, and Muhammed set up a government delivering good governance to all. Mohammed began by drafting a written constitution, the Charter of Medina (II&D, 1990, 53–54). It was a brilliant, man-made example of problem-solving document, dealing with the social and economic life of the community. It provided for trade regulation, dispute settlement, including blood money, and private property. The Prophet eliminated the old ways and replaced them with new regulations. The Prophet was both messenger of God, political head of Medina, its chief judge, and commander in chief. What he did and said became the core of Islamic traditions (*hadith*), in addition to *Suras* (God's words as revealed in 600 verses, *ayats*, in the Quran), and they were passed on in oral and written form for later generations (Esposito, 1988, 14). Sadly, the precedent of man-made, problem-solving legislation was not sustained; instead, arbitrary governance emerged as the norm.

In 624 the decisive Battle of Badr was fought, the first and decisive "victory for the forces of monotheism over those of polytheism" (12). But warfare continued with attacks by Meccans and Bedouin who clung to the old ways. Finally, Muhammed marched into Mecca, leading a *Jihad*, God's army of 10,000, and the Meccans capitulated. They converted to Islam and were incorporated within the growing *Umma*, brotherhood of believers. In 632 Mohammed led the first pilgrimage to Mecca. When he died three months later, all Arabia was united under the banner of Islam. He chose no successor, nor did he show any preference for anyone among his inner circles. This was a major gap, intentional or not, and it shaped subsequent Islamic history.

The Caliphate, the Prophet's deputy, began in 632 with Muhammed's successor chosen by seniority. Four Rightly Guided Caliphs followed: Abu Bakr (632–634), Umar (634–644), Uthman (644–656), and Ali (656–661). During their rule, *Sunni* Islam emerged as the normative model. Ali, the Prophet's cousin, and son-in-law, ruled as the fourth Caliph, but many believed that by right, as the beloved of the Prophet, he should have followed Muhammed. Civil war ensued and *Shi'a* Islam emerged.

This study updates my earlier one, *Islamic identity and Development* (II&D)[2] using a Neo-Ottomanist perspective. This makes the study quite original in the literature on the making of the modern Middle East, which generally has ignored the Ottoman legacy. Recently there has been renewed interest in the demise of the Ottoman Empire, even critical books on the imperialist plans in the making of the Middle East, utilized in this study (Chapter 3), but none of which pays due attention to the Ottoman legacy, especially its good governance in the classical period, derived from the Circle of Equity (II&D, 64), that is, the idea that all organs of the government must rest on Justice and that the ruler is answerable to God, but is responsible for the social harmony of society to ensure good governance. In the Ottoman statecraft, welfare of the subjects was vital, as demonstrated in the Circle of Equity, embodied, for example, in the laws of Sultan Süleyman. People's welfare was of little concern in European imperialism.

European imperialism in the WWI period was ruthless, it penetrated the Ottoman lands, drew boundaries in the sand, and created new countries for one purpose: oil. Through several invasions, coup d'états, and civil and proxy wars, imperial powers have made sure that oil was delivered to the West to fuel cars, factories, and the military–industrial complex, while the subject people suffered oppression, conflict, and disunity.

Imperialisms: European versus Ottoman

Imperialism[3] is a major theme in this study. It is a negative, pejorative term implying domination of other nations or countries for economic gain. Our concept is close to Edward Said's: Imperialism rested on "doctrines of European superiority," racist in theory, and embraced by "policymakers, government officials, institutional economists, intelligence experts" to justify ruling a distant territory and people on 'colonialist' ideology (1979, 8–9). Western or Ottoman powers shared this feature. Ottomans, however, were more interested in territorial expansion, than economic gain. In European imperialism, economic gain was driven by investment in resource exploitation, which could be monetized, as in the case of hydrocarbons (oil), minerals (gold), or natural resources (plantations) but also as infrastructure (Suez Canal). Investment came first; gunboats and invasions followed to protect investments. In economic imperialism, territorial expansion was rarely the aim; strategic trading cities (e.g., Singapore, Hong Kong, Goa) as financial hubs were adequate to facilitate capital flows, investment in one direction, and surplus value or profit extraction in the reverse. In the Spanish case, the Aztec/Maya gold was the paramount objective, by any means possible. Although sanctioned by the Pope, ethics was the last thing in the minds of the Conquistadors.

Power over adversaries, no doubt, shaped the Ottoman penetration into the Balkans and Central Europe. In the Muslim Core, however, the Ottomans, from beginning to the end, viewed themselves as part of, indeed, the guardians of *Dar ul Islam*, the land of the faithful, in contrast to *Dar ul Harb*, the land of unbelievers. They regulated trade and markets, maintained peace in the *millet* system, with a sense of Muslim social justice. In WWI, they fought for Islam, expecting Arabs and all Muslims to join in a global *jihad*. In Western imperialism, religion often had a racist connotation: White/Christian supremacy, as in the days of Conquistador; Slavery, Apartheid or in such literary terminology as the White Man's burden, which continue to this day in different manifestations, as, for example, Islamophobia or Southern Confederacy in the USA.

Islamic Core and Periphery

There is a further originality in the present study. II&D focused on the Islamic periphery, (Malaysia and Turkey), two modernizing Muslim majority countries at opposite ends of the Islamic world. The present study deals with the more complex Muslim Core and the Arab Middle East. Written almost 40 years ago, well before religious terrorism hijacked Islam, II&D is still substantially valid, particularly in predicting the crisis of Islam, which on 11 September 2001 plunged Islam into the age of terrorism. But it needs updating in the light of developments that have occurred since and many important contributions to the literature that have been made since.

The present study uses scholarship on the making of the modern Middle East, particularly following WWI, when European imperialism drew lines in the sand creating artificial boundaries. It argues that the demise of the Ottoman Empire has been a disaster for Islamic unity. From Sykes-Picot to the murder in Istanbul of the Saudi dissenter/journalist Jamal Khashoggi, and to the present, the Islamic Core has been in turmoil. With the end of the Ottomans, the *Caliphate* and *Ummah* (Muslim brotherhood) were gone. Imperialism fragmented the Arab world in pursuit of oil wealth. Dynastic regimes, installed by imperialists, soon turned into brutal military dictatorships, squandering national wealth in warfare. Many false prophets emerged, all claiming to be the new Caliph, using terror and brutality as their instrument, but inflicting untold misery and nonquantifiable human loss and suffering. The Islamic crisis needs to be studied realistically; this study is intended as a small contribution in that direction.

Outline of the Study

This study is focused on identity and development in the post-Ottoman Arab world. It is a story of failed states, torn by coups, civil wars, military dictatorships, and invasions in search of oil. Chapter 1 begins with winners and losers centered on the question of why some cases of nation-building have been successful, while others have not. Chapter 2 briefly examines state failure, highlighting the chaos in the Arab world after the Ottomans, using the latest estimates of human toll from war and conflict. Chapter 3 uses recent literature on the making of the modern Middle East to document the role of Western imperialism. Chapter 4 emphasizes the critical role of historical continuity and the historical roots of the long decline of the Muslim world, from the rise of mercantilism to neo-imperialism. Historical continuity sets the stage for Chapter 5, which is devoted to the elusive quest for Islamic Social Contract and the contest between nationalism and neo-imperialism. The chapter summarizes six case studies: Iran, Saudi Arabia, Iraq, Syria, Libya, and Egypt. Historical continuity is sustained in Chapter 6, which attempts to link the Sykes-Picot legacy to the failure of socioeconomic development, latest wave of neo-imperialist invasion, finally erupting in the rise of Islamic terrorism.

In the post-pandemic world, a new Silk Route Economy (SRE) is emerging, extending from Beijing to Istanbul. This potentially new world order is the focus of Chapter 7. Several Central Asian countries are booming with new infrastructure and economic development, although progress is far from a linear path. SRE is a new, sometime fragile long-term opportunity; it offers a ray of hope, a way out of the current chaos in the Muslim Core. As the Western frontier of the new SRE, Turkey is situated at the confluence of Asia and Europe. There is a chance that Turkey may play a cultural bridging role, promoting peace and cooperation between the Muslim world and Christian Europe. Accordingly, Chapter 8 examines relations between Turkey and the EU. Turkey may never gain EU membership, but good relations between Brussels and Ankara are unavoidable to deal with Islamophobia and the changing geopolitics, now experiencing the shock of war in Ukraine. Chapter 9 uses the latest statistics, however imperfect, to examine the Muslim refugee crisis, death tolls, and the collective moral failure in Middle East in sharp contrast to the plight of the Ukrainians. Chapter 10 will offer a historical evolution of Arab nationalism and the failure of democracy to take root in the Arab Core. Finally, Chapter 11 will conclude with a long-term prospect of Islamic revival, possibly within the emerging SRE, given the impossibility, anytime soon, of a Modern Caliphate as proposed in the precursor study (II&D, 232–233). Chapter 12 highlights the principal conclusions of the study.

Notes

1 Iran is not an Arab country, so in this study Arab Core and Muslim Core have been used as appropriate.
2 The 1990 monograph will be cited throughout the present study as (II&D, 1990), the original date of its publication, even though it has gone through several editions.
3 Lenin's concept of monopoly capitalism (Baran and Sweezy, 2010) is relevant, but in this study, imperialism is wider mirroring a state-private enterprise partnership, as in military–industrial complex. Mathematically, it has been explained as *capitalization* (Mehmet, 1999, 17–32).

References

Baran, Paul. A. and Paul Sweezy, 2010, Notes on the Theory of Imperialism, https://mronline.org/2010/06/24/notes-on-the-theory-of-imperialism/, accessed on 10 Feb. 2022

Esposito, John L., 1988, *Islam: The Straight Path*, New York: Oxford University Press.

Mehmet, Ozay, 1990, (II&D), *Islamic Identity and Development: Studies of the Islamic Periphery*, London: Routledge.

Mehmet, Ozay, 1999, *Westernizing the Third World, The Eurocentricity of Economic Development Theories*, 2nd ed., London: Routledge.

Said, Edward, 1979, *Orientalism*, Vintage Books: New York.

WHO, 2022, WHO Coronavirus (COVID-19) Dashboard, https://www.google.ca/search?q=who+global+covid+mortality+data&sxsrf=ALiCzsZUYqM0vAyMfKF7G8rvKyRsrtDuFQ%3A1667124886803&source=hp&ei=lk5eY9OeLo6r5NoPuviKqAE&iflsig=AJiK0e8AAAAAY15cpmeNaQt2Zeb1QC-oTVeyh1JY5v9x&oq=WHO+global+covidmortality+data&gs_lp=Egdnd3Mtd2l6uAEB-AEBKgIIADIEECCEYCsICBBAjGCfCAgQQABhDwgIFEAAYkQLCAgsQLhiABBixAxiDAcICCxAAGIAEGLEDGIMBwgIHEC4Y1AIYQ8ICBhAAGAoYQ8ICBRAAGIAEwgIIEAAYgAQYsQPCAgUQLhiABMICBhAAGBYYHsICCBAAGBYYHhgKwgIIEAAYgAQYyQPCAgoQABiABBiHAhgUwgIFEAAYhgPCAgUQIRigAcICBxAhGKABGArCAgcQABiABBiHhiiBMICBRAAGKIESObMAlAAWMyyAnAHeADIAQCQAQCYAWqgAZoXqgEEMzUuMg&sclient=gws-, accessed on 30 Oct. 2022

ACKNOWLEDGMENTS

Several academic friends have contributed to this study, and it is my pleasure to acknowledge them all. I owe special thanks to the following colleagues in particular: Professor Tareq Ismael and his wife Jacqueline, longtime friends, have enthusiastically encouraged my work from the start. As specialists of the subject themselves, their support has been both an inspiration and confidence. Professor Fraser Taylor, my colleague, with whom, for many years, I taught international development at the Norman Patterson School, Carleton University, has been most helpful, reading various parts of the earlier drafts. Dr. Leslie McDonald, formerly of the Social Sciences Council of Canada, and his wife Gwen, have read the entire manuscript and provided valuable editorial input.

I also wish to thank my editors at Routledge with whom I have had a long relationship, extending back over 30 years, going to the first publication of my II&D (1990): Joe Whiting and Euan Rice-Coates. Joe has supported me all along and Euan provided meticulous editing in the final stages.

Last, but not least, I would like to acknowledge the moral support of my family, particularly my wife Karen Ann, to whom I dedicate this work, for her constant dedication. My brother-in-law Georges Chiha, originally from Lebanon, and I had many informed discussions.

Finally, I thank to all the authors, agencies, and sources of information, in books, articles, and, of course, on the internet, which I utilized. I am particularly grateful for permissions granted to use sources as indicated in the relevant parts of the book.

All remaining errors, and especially on matters of interpretation, are my responsibility, as the author, and mine alone.

Extensive use has been made in this study of current internet websites. While these are gratefully acknowledged, the author states that they are valid as of access dates given. He bears no responsibility for altered or expired websites.

1

WINNERS AND LOSERS IN NATION-BUILDING IN THE POST-OTTOMAN MIDDLE EAST

On 29 October 1914, in a reckless attack on Russia, the Ottomans entered World War I (WWI). Official declaration of war followed on 10 November 1914 (Aksakal, 2008, 182–183). After a costly four-year fighting on several fronts, it accepted defeat in 1918, and in 1922 the Sultanate was dissolved to make way for the Turkish Republic. In 1914 the party in control of the *Devlet-i Aliye-i Osmaniye*, the Sublime Ottoman State, was the Young Turks party, the Committee of Union and Progress (CUP), an inexperienced group of ambitious politicians who had come to power a few years earlier through revolution. Aksakal has argued that the Young Turk elite believed war was the only way to restore national pride, so badly damaged in recent wars in the Balkans and Libya. In the party, power belonged to a triumvirate of the pro-German War Minister Enver, the Prime Minister Talat, and the Marine Minister Djemal. The Sultan was insecure and powerless (Ahmad, 1969). Germany, under Kaiser Wilhelm II, took advantage of the Young Turks' weakness, and grossly miscalculated the value of a "Global *Jihad*" by the Sultan-Caliph to knock Britain out of India and Egypt. Essentially an intra-European imperial struggle for world supremacy, WWI resulted in 15–22 million deaths and a further 13 million wounded (Wikipedia).

Why did the Ottomans declare war? It was political suicide by the inept Young Turk leaders who were ignorant of the strategic value of oil, signing away the precious commodity to imperialist interests. These leaders understood that the world was changing rapidly under expanding European imperialism; they understood that modernization was necessary, and following a pseudo-Darwinian logic, they assumed that survival depended on "the demonstration of military power" (Aksakal, 2008, 2). However, their response was patriotic and emotional rather than rational. They took an "all-in" gamble to regain lost reputation and restore the Ottoman state to its past glory. Throughout the summer of 1914, the CUP leaders went to great lengths to stay out of the imminent war, but when it became clear

DOI: 10.4324/9781003268994-1

that the offer of German alliance could wait no longer, they embarked on war, confident that "only the battlefield could bring the unifying and liberating experience it so desperately needed … military power alone could prevent dismemberment and colonial status" (Aksakal, 2008, 2–3). In fact, they committed diplomatic and military suicide, falling into the trap of European imperialism.

Germany then was under the influence of warmongers. Backed by a wide circle of German scholars and politicians, the Kaiser and his advisors had an inflated idea of the power of the Ottoman Caliphate. The German general and reformer of the Ottoman army, Colmer von der Goltz, for example, believed that "Old Turkey now has the opportunity … in one fell swoop, to lift itself up to the heights of its former glory" (17). In the Young Turks party, Enver was obsessed with the German military might. He knew virtually nothing of the oil politics, the US domestic politics, the influence of the British and American Zionism, or the power of the Raj. In the end, the Young Turks lost everything, bringing down with them, the House of Osman. The dynasty was replaced by a brand-new Turkish homeland, modern Turkey, based on the ethnocentric ideology of Turkism: "Turkey for the Turks." Ottoman multiculturalism was buried in history.

The Ottoman Empire was not a purely Turkish Empire. Its mission was good governance in accordance with Islamic justice. In its classical age (Inalcik, 1973), the conquering Sultans were not *Jihadists*, forcing Islam on the conquered people. In Serbia, Hungary, and much of the Balkans, they relied on indirect rule, employed local leaders, and granted the conquered people freedom to practice their religion and enjoy self-government. So long as taxes were paid, peace prevailed. At the headquarters, at the *Bab-ı Aliye*, the Sublime Porte, the ruling establishment was, at best, only part-Turk by blood, as they were conceived in the *harem*, typically of non-Turkish concubines. At the top of the civil government, the majority of 272 *Sadrazams* (prime ministers) were non-Turks.

During the first three centuries, the ruling class of the Ottoman State was dominated by Turkoman families, but afterward non-Turks, converted to Islam, rose to prominence under the system known as *Devşirme* (levy on Christian families to provide the eldest son to the state) (Shaw and Shaw, 1976, 113). It is worth quoting Shaw and Shaw (114) fully:

> It is easy to decry a system that required separation from one's family, home and religion for advancement, but the practice should be evaluated in the context of sixteenth century conditions and values. In Ottoman society, as in Europe at the time, religion was not merely an expression of individual or even group viewpoints of life and the position of man in relation to his maker but also a definition of human behaviour and position in all aspects of life.

The system was functionally flawed; it generated division and tension between the non-Turks and Turkoman families and played a significant role in the decline of the Empire, which became evident in the 17th century. In the end, in the last half century before WWI, the House of Osman was a strange family torn asunder from within.

In the expansion period, the majority of the population of the Empire, the majority population was Christian, and the Ottoman Empire was the Sultanate of Rum, a tradition originating from the Selcuk Empire (Köprülü, 1992, 116; Wittek, 2012, 34). Only after the conquest of Egypt in 1517 did the Empire become Muslim-majority. This fact may also explain why there are only four or five Arabs on the list of 272 *Sadrazams* (Wikipedia, 2021), far fewer than Albanians, for example. As part of the Muslim *millet*, perhaps the Arabs did not feel ethnically distinct in the Empire. Turks, however, developed an ethnic consciousness much earlier.

Turkism, a new ideology formulated by the first Turkish sociologist Ziya Gökalp (II&D, 13–14), emerged in the second half of the 19th century, following the *Tanzimat* reforms. These were reforms at the top, intended to arrest and reverse the decline of the Ottoman fortunes primarily in the military establishment, to regain power on the battlefields. In legal and constitutional fields, mostly alien ideas were imported from Europe, which, because they aimed at centralizing a multi-national Empire, accelerated its decline. The problem went deeper: the Empire, after 600 years, was tired, like an old oak, and rotten to its core. Dynastic loyalty was ill-suited to compete in an age of aggressive imperialism and the Empire fell victim to European capitalist penetration. The death of the Ottoman dynasty was inevitable because of chronic decay from within; the entry into the WWI was a last desperate act of the "Sick Man of Europe."

Young Turks, Social Darwinism, and Oil Politics

The greatest folly of the Young Turk leadership, which pushed the Ottoman Empire into WWI, was its relative ignorance of oil politics. This leadership joined the Germans, driven by passion and rhetoric, not realpolitik. In Europe, on the other hand, a new ideology was spreading: Social Darwinism, mixed with a racist ideology, declared the supremacy of the white man, justifying expansionism, all backed by gunboat diplomacy. Herbert Spencer, who coined the phrase "survival of the fittest," published his major work, *Progress: Its Law and Cause* (1857), three years before the publication of Darwin's *On the Origin of Species* (1860). As an ideology social Darwinism advocated that the strong should see their wealth and power increase, while the weak should see their wealth and power decrease, offering a convenient justification to European imperialism. Of course, imperialism preceded Spencer and Darwin, but their writings popularized an ideology that finally erupted into WWI. Parallel literary warmongering occurred in Germany.

With respect to the Ottoman Empire, the imperialist powers of Europe at the time pursued two parallel agendas: One was the "Eastern Question" to expel the Turks out of Europe, once and for all, and partition its vast territories. At the same time, they were engaged in a wild, competitive drive for oil. At the turn of the 20th century, the Automobile Age had begun. Geologists and diplomats already were in possession of strategic knowledge from the field that the Arab lands were rich in oil, and the capitalists, German and British, were already engaged in a bitter diplomatic war to gain control of the hydrocarbons, which drove cars, powered factories, and fueled navies. Again, academics trained in such places as Oxford and Cambridge, including Lawrence, Bell, and Hogarth, were at the forefront of empire-building.

In the Sultan's capital, the Young Turks, a revolutionary Ottomanist party, was in power. Created and active for much of its life in Europe to escape the repressive Hamidian regime, its leaders put all their eggs in one basket, the ideology of Ottomanism (Kushner, 1977, 38–39): how to make the Ottoman state great again? The entire Young Turk agenda was imported from Europe with little understanding of the long historical struggles since Luther to achieve democracy and liberty. Freedom, Reform, and Identity became their guiding principles, but each one of these principles had European, not (Turkish) endogenous roots. It was a futile project: While the Ottoman elite was attempting to reform a multinational Empire, the ethnic minorities everywhere were in revolt for independence. Even the Muslims in the Arab provinces were aspiring for home rule.

Ziya Gökalp, the pioneer ideologue of Turkism, hailed from the Kurdish town of Diyarbakir. His ideas were shaped by sociologists like Weber, Durkheim, and Comte (II&D, 13). Freedom, for Young Turks, meant the end of the oppressive rule of Sultan Hamid and the restoration of the Constitution; it was, theoretically achieved, at least temporarily in 1908, but, amid great controversies over rank and experience (Ahmad, 1969, 16), it fell into chaos. Reform meant rebuilding the institutions of the State on laws, as in Europe, guaranteeing equality of all Ottomans, regardless of religion, language, or ethnicity. Thus, they extended an olive branch to Christian minorities and embraced even the revolutionary Armenians, not because they were democratic (one man, one vote), but more for the sake of preserving the Sultanate. Half-baked ideas led to tragic results. Even the question of identity was shaped with reference to Europe, influenced by such quasi-scholars as Armenius Vambry (Kushner, 1977, 9) pushing theories of "one great 'Touro-Aryan' race." The Young Turks were passionate secularists, paying little or no attention to the Islamic heritage of the Ottomans. Islamist thinkers, like Afghani and Abdu, were in a spiritual world (II&D, 65–66) far removed from the realpolitik of Europe.

The Young Turk revolutionaries courted all European powers, but ended with Germany, which had its own imperialist, expansionist agenda. Whereas the Young Turks were focused on prestige and pride, the European powers were in pursuit of markets and resources. The European investor in the Baghdad Railway was less interested in modernizing the vast Arab hinterland than competing in the Great Game. Kaiser Wilhelm, who seduced the Sultan Hamid so openly and vainly, was the great opportunist. German capital, technology, and know-how, especially in military terms, were viewed by "the Istanbul elite" (Aksakal, 2008, 56) as the vital ingredient to develop the Ottoman army into a fighting force to regain Ottoman greatness. This elite failed to understand the technological forces behind European imperialism, specifically the rivalries over oil in the Sultan's domains. There were, of course, dissenting and contrary views to these unrealistic expectations. But they were marginal, simply ignored, and dismissed. In 1914, the Ottoman State was no more than an empty shell, a hotbed of intrigue, driven by German warmongers to utilize the willing pro-German camp in the Sultan's capital to deliver the British Empire a mortal blow. It was all bravado!

The Turkish Petroleum Company

Early in 1914, the British government purchased a controlling interest in the Anglo-Persian Oil Company (APOC) and, in return for London's consent to the Baghdad–Berlin Railway, the Germans recognized southern Mesopotamia, as well as central and southern Persia, as the exclusive field of operations of APOC. Moreover, regarding the Turkish oil fields in the vilayets of Mosul and Baghdad, an Anglo-German syndicate was formed earlier, and the Turkish Petroleum Company (TPC) established in 1912. Half of its stock was granted to Sir Ernest Cassel and the D'Arcy group, 25% to the Royal Dutch Company, and the remainder to the Deutsche Bank (Earle, 1966, 261). This budding Anglo-German cooperation did not last long as warmongering interests and events prevailed, including the assassination of the Austrian Archduke, putting a stop to such cooperation.

What is remarkable in these concessions is the fact that nothing was reserved for the host nation. Only imperial interests counted. It was fashionable at the time to use false labels for concessions. Thus, the Ottoman Bank, TPC, etc., were all foreign institutions, foreign owned, using national names simply to make them more palatable in the host nation. In the Ottoman world of foreign concessions, middlemen, called *dragomen*, were the key. In the case of the TPC, Calouste Gulbenkian, an Ottoman Armenian, was the vital player. He represented the British banking interests due to his knowledge and influence in the Ottoman government. For his services, he was granted 5% holdings in the TPC, a share which reputedly made him the richest individual in the world for many years. Gulbenkian acquired the nickname, "Mr. Five Percent." In 1928, Gulbenkian achieved fame, once again, keeping his 5% for drawing the red line in the notorious Red Line Agreement, which divided all the oil fields in the Middle East as a monopoly of the "Seven Sisters," the oil companies of the British, French, Dutch, and American, each getting 23.75% of TPC (Dept. of State, 2022). Just imagine what the Sultan's government could have achieved, if only rationality had prevailed to enable it to hang on to the TPC! What kind of Middle East would now exist?

In the Young Turk government, there was hardly any opposition to the TPC concession. Oil was as new a commodity as the automobile age. Cavit Bey, the Minister of Finance, alone in the Young Turk cabinet had a fairly accurate idea of the imperial games that were being played at the expense of the national interest of Turkey. But, as a *dönme* Jew, a convert, his loyalty, as indeed that of the Christian minority subjects, was questioned. With incredible courage Cavit Bey declared his opposition and spoke his mind. He denounced the "extension of German influence in Turkey" (Earl, 1966, 220), but his protests fell on deaf ears.

In fairness, however, it has to be admitted that in 1912–1913, against the humiliating defeat in the First Balkan War, when imperialist powers, including Germany, were openly discussing partition plans of the Ottoman Empire, the CUP leaders, at least its more nationalist members like Enver and Talat, were preoccupied with "saving" the Empire. In a collective note to the Sublime Porte in January 1913, these imperialists attempted to impose plans for direct involvement in the administration of Istanbul and the provinces. The serving *Sadrazam*, Kamil Pasha, seemed willing to negotiate these terms. Furious at this turn of events, Enver and Talat led a coup d'etat, rushing into the Grand Vezir's chambers with pistols, shooting and killing the War Minister Nazim Pasha. In the end, the Ottoman Empire got closer to Kaiser's Germany and modernizing the Ottoman military emerged as the top priority for the CUP. In June 1913 Kaiser Wilhelm II selected General Otto Liman von Sanders as head of the German military mission to Sublime Porte (Aksakal, 2008, 79). In this context, oil politics and the TPC were of little or no concern for the CUP, but not for the Entente Powers.

After the defeat of the Ottomans in the war, the British renegotiated the TPC stock ownership and rewarded the French with the German share (321). The San Remo Conference of 1920 provided for permanent British control of Iraq and all the Mesopotamian oil. The Italian and United States governments protested their exclusion. After prolonged and sharp diplomatic exchanges, American oil companies were permitted to buy into the TPC, but negotiations dragged on until 1928. We shall discuss these topics in detail in later parts of this study.

Turks, Arabs, and Jews

This study is about the three principal peoples of the Middle East, ancient peoples, each with its own historic past. Based on evidence, this study is not intended to favor any particular people. Our point of departure is WWI, which shaped the modern identities of these peoples. The Jews, with ample capital and technical know-how, were far ahead of the other two. The House of Ottomans lost, yet the modern Turkish identity was resurrected and reborn, phoenix-like, thanks to the military genius of one man who also turned out to be a brilliant nation-builder, Ataturk. The Arabs had no comparable leader; worse, they were unprepared and disunited: Neither the Arab goals were well defined, nor the means and resources essential for nation-building were at hand for nation-building. The Palestinian tragedy is only the most glaring example.

The Post-Ottoman world was all about identity, the essential prerequisite of nationhood. The Jewish identity was the clearest, based on language, culture, and scripture. But Who is an Arab? Who is a Turk? What do they have in common? It is easier to answer the second question, and an attempt was made in II&D (15–18) that is still valid after 32 years: someone who speaks Turkish, professes Islam, and is a Turkish citizen. This is by no means perfect, but it corresponds to a Turkish homeland, with clear boundaries set in international law, the Treaty of Lausanne. Turks in the Republic also share a common heritage and culture with other ethnic Turks not fortunate enough to live in Turkey.

Defining an Arab is much more challenging. Seeking guidance in a standard text such as the one by Choueiri's *Arab Nationalism* (2000), one is overwhelmed by the great multiplicity of paradigms: Arab nation, Arab unity, Arabism, Pan-Arabism, and ideologies such as Nasserism, and Ba'athism, not to say anything about country-specific variations. If, *watan* is homeland worthy of "local patriotism, focused on a particular Arab country" (24) how many Arab homelands can there be? One is hard pressed to attempt any reconciliation of these ideas. Certainly, an Arab speaks Arabic and is Muslim, but when it comes to citizenship, there are so many subdivisions, any sense of Pan-Arabism becomes difficult to conceive. In the end, there are Egyptian Arabs, Saudi Arabs, Syrian or Jordanian Arabs, etc. Indeed, these national identities extend to Islam as well, creating Egyptian Islam, Saudi or Lebanese Islam, and so on, each one manifesting its own (domestic) variation. Geographic or territorial factors, too, are vital, as in the case of Egyptians, whose love of Egypt as the land of Nile in Africa, or a Berber in the Sahel, are undeniable characteristics.

Oil, as much as Islam, has shaped modern identity and development in the Arab Middle East. Imagine an Arab from Kuwait, Saudi Arabia, or from the Emirates without oil. The lifestyle would be completely different than what it is. Undoubtedly, oil wealth has shaped what these Arabs are today, and destinies in future will shine or dim according to oil. Thus, currently oil-rich Arabs can look forward to a new identity beyond the inevitable phasing out of oil and climate change, but how exactly this new identity will evolve is difficult to forecast. In later parts of this study, we embrace the rising prospect of a new Silk Route Economy that may open new horizons not only for Central Asia, but the Islamic Core.

In contrast, the Turks have been blessed by relative lack of oil. By the end of the Ottoman Empire, one ideology prevailed: Turkism, which has guided modern Turkish nation-building. The Balkan Wars clearly demonstrated the emptiness of Ottomanism, while WWI similarly put an end to the idea of Pan-Turkism or Turanism. In the Treaty of Lausanne, even the reserves in Mosul were traded for national independence. The Turkish experience has been primarily a case of identity formation by self-reliance in a compact homeland. The Arab masses, however, have been cursed by an overabundance of oil, which, in the age imperialism, has brought invasion and virtually endless war. Consequently, imbedded in the Arab identity is a quintessential sense of rejecting the colonizer, the alien invader. Even when the colonizer has gone, however, the colonizer's language and culture, as in Algeria, and in the Magreb generally, weaken the authenticity of a purely Arab identity.

Although the Ottoman Empire was a Muslim state, it is surprising how few Arabs rose to the highest echelons of the government. By contrast, Albanians, Greeks, and numerous Christian minorities have excelled in the Ottoman administration and the military. After the penetration of the European imperialism into the Empire, and the rise of national consciousness (following the French Revolution), the Arab elite began to pull apart from the Empire, claiming the Ottomans had "usurped" the Caliphate. Turks and Arabs have differed even in their response to British imperialism driven by Jewish finance. British imperialism, which climaxed in WWI, was arguably the most dedicated diplomacy the world has ever seen. It was a teamwork, not just military, but a multifaceted enterprise using the talents of geologists, geographers, historians, novelists, and missionaries who all believed passionately in the White Man's Burden. Most recently, starting with the invasion of Afghanistan and Iraq, the White Man's Burden has been Americanized, ultimately turning into Trump's America First slogan.

The Turks, a warrior people, originating in Central Asia, and fiercely independent, resisted both imperialism and Jewish finance. The Arab elite collaborated with both. Jewish finance opened the floodgates for colonial penetration into the Arab Core. After the British acquired the Suez Canal, first Egypt, then Arab territories from the Mediterranean to the Gulf, lost their dignity. The Turks fought, in vain, in the deserts of Gaza and Beersheba for Islam, while the Arab dynasties competed with one another for the British gold that financed the Arab Revolt.

On the eve of the Balfour Declaration, it was again the Jewish bankers who prevailed. While Sykes and Picot were secretly plotting to carve up spheres of influence, the British and Ottoman armies had fought and exhausted themselves into a stalemate. At the crucial moment the British diplomacy geared up into action, appealed to highly placed American Jewry to entice a reluctant USA into the war. The Declaration was nothing else than a sweetener to procure American help to save British imperialism at the very moment when the Bolshevik Revolution had knocked out the Tsar from WWI and an entire British army had surrendered to the Ottomans in Kut.

WWI was a bloody contest of European imperialisms: The British versus the German. Behind both stood Jewish financiers. The Baghdad Railway threatened not only the British interests in the Suez and Arabia, but British India as well. Oil, newly discovered black gold in the Muslim Core, by then fueling the British navy, was in peril of falling into enemy hands. British diplomacy ensured that the oil remained in British and American hands, come what may. The Jewish Homeland was the creation of the British diplomacy, crafted on the way toward controlling Middle East oil. Poorly equipped for nation-building, Arab rulers were willing collaborators in the recolonization of the Muslim Core and eagerly jumped from the pan into the fire.

The Turks, on the contrary, fought to the bitter end. A further four years of fighting, 1919–1922, the Turkish War of Independence, followed. This time it was Lloyd George's folly. The short-sighted, Philhellenic Prime Minister, failed to heed Churchill's advice that London should "come to terms with Mustapha Kemal and arrive at a good peace with the Turks" (Fromkin, 1989, 494). Instead, he encouraged the Greek leader Venizelos to embark on an invasion of Anatolia to establish a new Byzantium Empire. Out of this disastrous four-year war, so courageously reported by Arnold Toynbee (1948), the Anatolian Greeks lost ancestral land, and Greece was so traumatized, it suffered a civil war, coming very close to going Communist.

Out of the ashes of the Ottoman Empire a new Turkish identity was forged and led by Gazi Mustafa Kemal, the future Ataturk. He won against the imperialists, first on the battlefield. The unequal Treaty of Sevres, partitioning Ottoman lands, was replaced with the Treaty of Lausanne. The greatest achievement of the Gazi, however, was his founding of a secular Republic, resting on the bedrock of Turkish nationalism. Without oil, the Turks had no choice but to rely on themselves to redefine their identity in the new world.

The Arabs never had their Ataturk. Betrayed by imperialists, ambitious dynasties fought one another to become puppets of imperial powers. Tribalism, too, must be acknowledged as a causal factor of disunity. In recent times, Islam was taken hostage by military dictators and terrorists. The Arab masses never had a chance, except briefly during the false start known as the Arab Spring that quickly turned into a new cycle of state repression.

Arabs and Turks differ also on the all-important issue of legitimacy. Whereas for the Arabs, legitimacy issues from the divine, confirmed as lineage to the Prophet, for the Turks it derives from popular consent codified in Constitution and man-made Laws, *Kanun*, an originally Greek word, reflecting the multicultural heritage of the Turks. The two greatest rulers in Turkish history, Sultan Suleyman (Lamb, 1951; Merriman, 1944) and Gazi Mustafa Kemal (Mango, 1999; Kinross, 1964) were known, first and foremost, for the laws they enacted, building on their subjects' understanding of justice and statehood. In Kemal's case of nation-building, there was no hesitation to borrow from the West to give content to his modernization project, but always adapted to Turkish requirements.

In the momentous years of 1916–1917, imperialism succeeded to divide the Turks and Arabs. Capitalism and Jewish finance had won, and Muslims had lost. Today, more and more Muslims in the Arab Core are living in refugee camps, under the care of Western charitable organizations. This is all to make room for a Homeland, to accommodate those who survived the Holocaust and other forms of persecution in the West, going all the way back to the destruction of Muslim Spain. It is unlikely that, any time soon, Muslim unity can be achieved. Only a glimmer of hope in the long run exists.

Nation-Building: Leadership and Resources

Building a nation, a homeland is a momentous task, especially if the land is under foreign occupation. Liberation or independence is first and foremost, an end that needs to be well articulated and grounded in the population upon whose aspirations the homeland is to be constructed once the foreigner is gone. This may require bloodshed and tears, a huge sacrifice. That is the role of national ideology, a task undertaken typically by academic and military elites. A national struggle for liberation without popular support is bound to fail. Wide popular support is both the justification as well as the nourishment for the national struggle.

The real challenge of nation-building begins with liberation. Having achieved independence, concrete benefits must be delivered quickly to the population in whose name the liberation struggle has been conducted. This is where accountability of the elite leading the national liberation struggle begins. Liberation requires teamwork, led by a leader, a person of vision, and ability to link goals with action on the ground. The leader must win and sustain legitimacy from grassroots, but, at the same time, a leader must enjoy the trust of the elite, the team with whom he must work. One of the most crucial characteristics of leadership is timing, knowing when to act and stop, and how far to push. Timing and limiting action depend on resources that can be mobilized to achieve ends.

A leader can legitimately demand sacrifices from followers. But sacrifice cannot become permanent, burdensome, or remain one-way. Persuasion rather than force is the tool of a true leader. Concrete benefits to the grassroots must be delivered in a timely fashion. Here, too, budgetary resources are required to translate means of development into actual reality. In confronting Western colonialism, three of the most successful leaders are Gandhi, Sukarno, and Atatürk, although many other names can be cited. Gandhi won against the British imperialism at its height with his iron-will commitment to independence through an uncompromising philosophy of nonviolence to overcome an unjust Raj (Ghosh, 2000). Sukarno's winning formula was *Pancasila* (Sarah, 2021), a program clearly defining the path to defeat the Dutch for *Merdeka* (Independence). Atatürk's supreme achievement was his unifying role in war and peace, getting results, but knowing the limit "to cut his country's losses" (Mango, 1999, 269).

If liberation is the end, the means of nation-building start with institution-building, be it irrigation works in agriculture, schools for the young, health and housing for the citizens. On all these criteria, the Jews and Zionists won because they were prepared, diplomatically, ideologically, and, above all, in investable resources. The Zionist elite worldwide worked behind the scenes in London, Washington, and elsewhere as a team committed to a single idea, to create a Jewish Homeland in Palestine.

Let's briefly look at the earliest institution-building of the Jewish Homeland in Palestine. The first kibbutz, a socialist experiment in pioneer lifestyle, an embryo of regional or frontier development began 40 years before the creation of Israel (Jewish Virtual Library, n.d.). Kibbutz and moshavim movements were designed to motivate especially the youth, to challenge them with participation in early settlement. For Jews, oppressed in Russia and elsewhere Europe, the movement became a visionary means of contributing to nation-building. Of course, one cannot forget the role of complementary resources: land acquisition and funding from wealthy Jewish organizations and technical skills going into the designing of communal housing, schools, and clinics. The result was the creation of social capital, investment in people to be the citizens of a new nation.

The Kibbutz Movement

As an example of institution-building in the Holy Land, it is instructive to look briefly at the Kibbutz and Moshavim movement in Israel. In 1910, a group of 12 young men launched the first Zionist farm in Israel. They called it Degania, near the Sea of Galilee. It was a revolutionary, socialist experiment driven by Zionist ideology (Jewish Virtual Library, n.d.). The Moshavim was another type. The movement aspired to the creation of Israel, relying on socialist utopian principles using collective farm methods. The founding group shared the cost of operations, supplies, and profits made. The founders first lived in a one communal house in Umm Juni, subsequently settling by the mouth of the Jordan river. In 1920, a new kibbutz, named Degania Beth, was formed nearby. By then, communal living enabled establishment of a children's school. The population of the kibbutz are not only farmers, but also soldiers, constantly on guard in defense of their settlement.

More than agricultural development, the kibbutz movement has been social capital formation. Members of the kibbutz bond together, work and share together, and trust is the core value of the community, ensuring solidarity, cohesion, and unity of purpose. Recently, their popularity has decreased, fewer than 150,000 people now live in 274 kibbutzim, 74 of which are communal. Although Kibbutz residents constitute less than 2% of the population, they remain economically significant, producing 40% of Israel's agricultural output (Regev, 2021).

Technical Knowledge in Nation-Building

The role of technology, more specifically technical knowledge, as a means of nation-building is of special importance and may, once again, be best illustrated by the case of Israel. Scientific agricultural research was brought to the Holy Land while it was still part of the Ottoman Empire.

Aaron Aaronsohn was an early Zionist, but more significantly he was an agronomist. He spent 37 years in Palestine conducting a wide range of agricultural experiments, on plants, trees, and soils, hoping to make the desert bloom as in ancient times. In a sense, he was a realist, a practical man: "All high-minded Zionist principles aside, he frequently pointed out, the first prerequisite for the Jews' return to Israel was to have something to eat: Aaronsohn knew how to feed them" (Anderson, 2013, 50). His roots were in Romania. The Russo-Turkish war of 1877–1878 displaced his family, causing them to emigrate to the USA. At 16, Aaronsohn was selected by Rothschilds' agents to study botany and agronomy in Paris before being sent to Palestine to work as agricultural advisor to a large absentee landlord. His big "breakthrough came in 1906 with his discovery of wild emer wheat, a progenitor of cultivated wheat long thought extinct, growing on Mount Hermon" (51), a new variety he later introduced in the American West. Aaronsohn paved the way for modern farming, with new seeds and technology ranging from new methods of irrigation to aquaculture, turning the Negev into a new "land of milk and honey."

By contrast when we look at Arab nationalism, it sadly lacks anything comparable on the means and resources as prerequisites of national development. Comparing Antonius' *Arab Awakening* (1939) with a more recent text such as Choueiri (2000) one is struck by the lack of any discussion on accountability, popular support, or consent for an ideology of nation-building. In Antonius, the Arab nationalism is in "infancy," but when does the infant become a mature, adult? Instead of clarity, ambiguity reigns. In Choueiri and others, there are long historical accounts of theories and paradigms on Arab unity, Nassirism and Ba'athism, and so on, but these are all high-minded declarations of leaders in power or visionary academics. There is overabundance of goals and objectives, but a dearth of means and resources essential for nation-building.

Ideology: Zionism, Turkism, Arabism

Nation-building begins with ideas. It evolves into an ideology, a national movement, partly romantic and visionary, partly realistic and organizational, driven by intellectuals, academics, clergy, or military leaders who articulate a definite cultural golden age in the past, and create a party or organization ready for collective action. Military leaders or militants in armed groups fight for a homeland with clear geographic boundaries for cultural revival around a language, religion, or common identity. Organizations and movements die without funding. There must be financiers as well, ready with ample funds, to invest in national movements and organizations, sometimes in secret, using terrorism as a means.

Not all ideologies are legitimate or authentic. If force or terror is used to sustain or spread ideology, it becomes a tool of oppression, almost certainly it will be short-lived. On the other hand, a national movement, which reflects popular aspirations and rests on consensus, is likely to succeed. For this reason, an authentic national movement needs social grounding, with grassroots support and social capital to nurture it. Leadership of a national movement must enjoy the trust of the people whose aspirations it reflects.

Historically and philosophically, nationalism is a European idea linked to a nation-state. It took its shape in the national struggles such as the Italian or German unification, first articulated in the writings of philosophers and poets (Goethe, Manzoni), and finally in the field by men of action (Garibaldi, Bismarck). When nationalism first penetrated the multinational Ottoman Empire in the 19th century, the Ottoman rulers and elites confused it with a reform movement, attempting a top-down modernization program (the *Gülhane Proclamation*, 1839) around the ill-defined idea of Ottomanism, that all subjects of the Osmanli dynasty are equal before the law. By then, the Greeks had fought and won their independence, and naturally other ethnic groups followed more the Greek example than the reform idea of Ottomanism. When Bulgars, Serbs, and other Balkan people achieved their national homelands, the Ottoman elite belatedly acknowledged the emptiness of Ottomanism. In the final 50 years of the Empire, Ottomanism was often redefined as Pan-Turkism, with Hungarian and French inputs (Kushner, 1977, 9–10), a mystical land of Turan, extending from Anatolia to the ancient Turkic lands in Central Asia. It took the WWI to reduce and refine Turanism into Turkism (II&D, 9–10).

Arabs and Jews in the Ottoman Empire were different from the people of the Balkans. The Jews, expelled from Spain, had been saved by the Ottomans, and the Jewish culture and business had flourished in the Empire, especially in Istanbul, Salonika, and Izmir. Jewish nationalism was not some anti-Ottoman movement; it had its roots and drivers in the European persecution of the Jews. Theodor Herzl, the spiritual father of Israel, was inspired by the Dreyfus case (Finer, 2009). For Herzl, this case was a defining example of the systemic racism the Jewry faced in Europe. Escaping from the Russian gulags and "emancipation of Jews" (Schechter, 1967, 38) from an anti-Semitic Europe required the creation of a national homeland in the land of Zion, the ancient Jerusalem. Those who stayed behind in Europe faced the Holocaust.

Arabism was the most ambiguous. Ottoman Arab elite, landowning, and professionals like doctors and lawyers or clerks in the civil service were generally satisfied living in an Islamic Empire, although dynastic elites claimed their own, more authentic, lineage to the Prophet and Caliphate. In its infancy (Antonius, 1939, 79–100), the Arab national movement, centered in Mount Lebanon and Syria, was led by Christian Arabs. In the final years of the Empire, during the Young Turks period, Arab representatives in the Ottoman parliament were more interested in opposing the centralizing reforms of the Ottoman reformists than seeking a separate Arab homeland. In the subsequent, more definitive years of the WWI, Arab nationalism was shaped by imperialism. When, at the end of WWI, imperialists won, Arab expectations had soared to the skies, until, very quickly, such high expectations were dashed by two reinforcing dynamics: betrayal by imperialists and disunity among the Arab leaders. Imperialists left for a time, only to return as Neo-imperialism; Arab disunity grew after 1918, spending years in search of a theory of Arabism, subsequently, in the early postwar period, turning to socialism and pan-Arabism (Choueiri, 2000), and most recently descending into religious terror.

The Dreyfus Case

Ideas shape nation-building, money finances it, and men of action implement the idea. An idea, a proposal, develops into an ideology and patriots and dedicated sponsors transform the ideology into the creation of nationhood. In the case of Israel, the definitive idea of a Jewish Homeland began with the Dreyfus case, in 1894.

Colonel Alfred Dreyfus, a Jew, was a French staff officer in the army, who in the fall of 1894 was accused of treason on behalf of the German government. France then was immersed in an anti-Semitic fervor, news media blaming the Jews for financial scandals and there was a general belief that "the French Jews were acting as agents for enemy powers" (Schechter, 1967, 10). In 1886, Edouard Drumont published a book in which he described the French Jews, as "infidel people," proposing that they should be "expelled from the country and their property confiscated" (22). "Jewish magic" was widely believed to be responsible for natural disasters like earthquakes, and epidemics, and the Jewish people were condemned as "Christ killers" (34). The government of the Third Republic, never secure since the defeat of 1870, and the army echelons, actively promoted a campaign of anti-Semitism. The war indemnity had been paid off within an incredibly short time of three years, and in 1894 a military alliance was forged with Russia. France was ready for the restoration of military greatness. The path to greatness lay through revenge on the Germans who had inflicted the humiliating defeat of 1870: The French extremists wanted: "Vengeance on the hated conquerors!" (6).

Colonel Dreyfus was the innocent victim, the scapegoat, to achieve French military grandeur. His pleas of innocence to the charge of treason fell on deaf ears, his distinguished career and his patriotism counting for nothing. Here was a solitary Jew who was innocent, yet all the power of the French government was mobilized to prove him guilty. Forged documents, false evidence, all tricks were used to secure a guilty verdict. Dreyfus was sent to exile in Devil's Island.

Fortunately for Dreyfus, the great French writer, Emile Zola, Georges Clemenceau, a renowned French statesman, and journalist Jean Juárez steadfastly championed his innocence. Zola wrote a passionate "J'accuse" article in the journal *L'Aurore*, which, with a normal daily circulation of 60,000, sold 300,000 copies the day of publication. A public hysteria erupted over the great injustice, yet it took nine years, five with Dreyfus on Devil's Island, to win him a pardon and amnesty.

The case was the sensation of its time. All the leading newspapers of Europe sent reporters to Paris to cover the case. Theodor Herzl, who in his late thirties came from Vienna to represent the *Neue Freie Presse*. Herzl saw the Dreyfus case for what it was: state discrimination against a people. It was here that he began contemplating a solution to the ancient 'Jewish problem' of finding a Jewish Homeland for the dispersed and persecuted Jews of Europe. From this point on, Herzl became obsessed with the Zionist cause. He became an incurable dreamer. He wrote his famous book, *The Jewish Homeland*, sought support in every possible direction, visiting the Pope, the Ottoman Sultan, the British Colonial Secretary, Chamberlain, and many other notables.

In 1897 Herzl summoned the first Zionist Congress, in Basle, and it was the first time that Jewish leaders met collectively to decide on a common political program called the Basle Program. It states that the object of Zionism is to establish for the Jewish people a home in Palestine secured by public law. Second and Third Congresses followed, and then, in 1902, the British Cabinet was willing to further Zionist goals by granting the Sinai Peninsula to the Jews. It was under Ottoman rule. Nothing came of this project. Then, the British government offered Uganda and Herzl gratefully accepted and submitted it for ratification at the 1903 Congress. The Russian Zionist delegates objected, and the Uganda offer was dropped, but only after a royal commission was sent to Africa to study and report. It was rejected formally in 1905.

Then the financial powerhouse of Edmond de Rothschild moved in, pouring funds initially on an individual basis to colonize Palestine. He sent his agents to acquire small pieces of territory and to set up an organization to train and select settlers. He financed the early development and thus enabled the implementation of Herzl's dream of a Homeland in Palestine. Herzl never saw the fruits of his tireless efforts. When he died in 1904, the dreamer who had started it all was heartbroken and disappointed that his dream would not be realized. It was more than a decade before the Balfour Declaration (Finer, 2009).

Christian Nationalism, the Eastern Question, and the Destruction of the Ottoman Empire

In the late 19th century, the Ottoman Empire was a contested land. The Sultanate was seriously weakened, corruption from within and imperialist designs from outside, all plotting for their opportunity. The Porte, atop a multinational Empire, was unable to adapt to the challenge of modernization reconciled with nationalism. The European powers called it: "The Eastern Question," how to expel the Ottomans from Europe?

Arnold Toynbee, always questioning (1970, 8–14), termed it the "Western Question" in the Near East. It was his way of exposing the Orientalism reflected in "the Eastern Question," a story of never-ending intrigues in the 19th century European diplomacy to purify Europe by kicking out the Ottoman Turks, "an army of occupation in a conquered land" (Marriott, 1969, 73). The Eastern Question was a perennial issue of how to get rid of Ottoman Turks out of Europe, and what to do with their legacy? While, generations of politicians, moved by Christian zeal, were agreed on throwing the Turks out of Europe, national interests conflicted over the distribution of the Ottoman legacy. It seemed every imperial power wanted to partition the Ottoman Empire, but no one wanted their European rival to become the dominant power by filling the vacuum created by the expulsion of the Turks. The Eastern Question, in short, was a racist project with undefined aims. Except in one respect: All the prominent European diplomats were united at fostering Christian nationalism in the Balkans, aiding, and abetting the independence of Christian minorities of the Empire (Yavuz and Blumi, 2013), particularly the Orthodox nations of the Balkans and Armenians. Nationalism entered the multinational Ottoman Empire through religious politics. Greed, however, in the end prevailed, and in its last phase, from the Treaty of Berlin in 1878 to the outbreak of the WWI in 1914, great rivalries emerged, pitching Germany on one side, and Britain, France, and Tsarist Russia on the other.

The emergence of Russia was the critical factor in the demise of Ottoman power and the 1774 Treaty of Küçük Kaynarca the turning point. When, under Empress Catherine the Great, Russia became strong and powerful, Crimean Tatars, descendants of the Golden Horde, split into two rival groups. Şahin Giray sought the protection of Catherine, while the traditional *ulema* and ruling families remained loyal to the Ottoman Sultan-Calif. Tatars, who had become prosperous from the Silk Road trade, and had built a magnificent Muslim civilization centered in Bahçesaray and Keffe, had by mid-18th century suffered not only a reversal in ancient trade links due to the rise of the Atlantic mercantilist system, but they were also constantly engaged in cross-border skirmishes with the Cossacks on the northern borders of Crimea. Russia took advantage and expanded its influence southward at the expense of the Ottomans. After disastrous wars, 1768–1774, they were obliged to sign a Treaty acknowledging Crimean independence (Fisher, 1970, 51–56). Within a decade, Tatar independence ended in the Russian annexation of Crimea and the Tatars lost their ancestral homeland.

The Treaty, however, empowered Russia by granting it the right to become the protector of all Orthodox millets in the Empire. Henceforth, Moscow had in its hands the powerful tool of the Greek Orthodox religion to destroy and dismember the Ottoman Empire. Russia took the lead, especially in the 19th century at the height of European imperialism, to create the "Sick Man of Europe" claiming the seat of the Ottomans, Istanbul, for itself. The Sultanate only managed to survive for the next two centuries, thanks to its ability to exploit rivalries among European powers, playing one against the other.

After the Treaty of Berlin, 1878, Gladstone, the British Prime Minister, driven by Christian zeal, took the lead to kick the Ottomans out of Europe, "bag and baggage" (Seton-Watson, 1971, 75). He found in Russia a ready and active supporter. First, the Slavic nations in the Balkans fell under Russian influence. Through the Orthodox Church, a bastion of Christian identity, and one nationalist rebellion after another, the Christian nations of the Balkans fought and gained their independence from the Ottomans, finally ending up as satellites in the Soviet era. Second, the Armenian *millet*, which traditionally had been the privileged one, designated as the *Sadık* (loyal) *millet*, suffered the most because, unlike the Balkan peoples, Armenians lived intermeshed with the Turks and Muslims in Anatolia. Still, in WWI, the Armenians had come very close to winning a national homeland in Eastern Anatolia. They failed primarily because of the sudden disintegration of the Tsarist armies in the Caucasus during the Bolshevik Revolution which allowed the Turkish nationalist movement its first victory on the road to creating the new Turkish Republic (Mango, 1999).

Arnold Toynbee was a witness to it all and was horrified. He saw firsthand, the bloody and tragic end of the Ottoman Empire and how the partition plans of the Imperial Powers had laid the foundation of the Greek–Turkish War of Independence. What really moved Toynbee was the scale of war atrocities perpetrated by the invading Greek armies in Anatolia. The Greek soldiers had come to recreate a New Hellenic Empire in Anatolia, but they put villages and town to fire, massacring the Turkish population en masse. Toynbee paid dearly for his courage and commitment to truth. The deep disgust he experienced influenced Toynbee for life, a disgust that has been manifested in several books condemning Western aggression in Muslim lands and making him a lone voice in support of internationalism (Toynbee, 1948, 90–91).

The Greek Independence

Heroism or valor had nothing to do with Greek independence: it was a gift of European diplomacy. For centuries after the Ottoman conquest, the Greeks preferred Ottoman rule to the alternative of domination by the West. The Orthodox-Latin/Catholic schism of the 11th century had not been forgotten. Always conservative, the Phanariot Greeks and the Patriarch of Constantinople, at the top of the *Rum millet*, (the descendants of the Eastern Romans, speaking Greek), were very much part of the Ottoman establishment. The Moldovian and Romanian principalities, for example, were traditionally governed by Hospodars, who were the wealthy Phanaroid Greeks, who invested huge sums of money for these offices, thus becoming, effectively, tax farmers of the Sultan. In the Greek mainland proper, the shepherds, farmers, and fishermen were very much on their own, living according to time-honored traditions and customs under the strict control of the local clergy, only superficially under the Patriarch.

At the start of the 19th century, revolutionary ideas from France penetrated the Ottoman Balkans. There was a general belief that the Ottoman Empire was about to collapse, and the time had come for the Christian subjects of the Sultan to rise and take matters into their own hands. The poet Rigas Pherres advanced the creation of a Hellenic republic of the Balkan and Asia Minor Christians. When he attempted to instigate a Serbian rebellion, he was arrested by the Austrian authorities and handed to the Ottoman government who executed him for treason in Belgrade. The Ypsilantis brothers, Alexandros and Costantinos, whose ancestors had been the Hospodars, appealed for the restoration of the Byzantine Empire were equally unsuccessful, Alexander failing to start a rebellion in Moldovia (Gerolymatos, 2001, 126). Greek merchants of Odessa took the lead and established the *Philiki Hetairia*, the Society of Friends. The dominant Orthodox Patriarchy and the privileged Phanariot were happy with the Ottoman status quo and wanted nothing to do with revolutionary proposals.

What followed next was a bizarre set of events, mixed with free love festivals in the court of the ambitious Ali of Yenena on the Greek–Albania border, interference by the ever-opportunistic Tsarist Russia and a strange combination of European diplomacy, all attempting to take advantage of the Ottoman weakness. Poets and romantics came from Europe to fight for the Greeks, mistakenly equating them with Ancient Greeks. Lord Byron not only jumped on the bandwagon, but he also came with a large loan. He was thoroughly disappointed at disunity he witnessed, Greek fighting Greek. Byron died a broken man in the swamps of Mesolonghi, but he became a martyr for the Greeks (Kinross, 1977, 447).

Strangely, Austria alone stood by the Ottomans. The Sultan, declaring Ali of Yenena a rebel for mishandling tax collections in his domain, suddenly faced a rebellion of Greek irregulars and *klepht* (bandit) chieftains in the Peloponnese, and appealed to another Ali, this one Mehmet Ali of Egypt for help. Ibrahim Pasha, Mehmet Ali's son and able commander, came and managed to put down the Greek rebellion. At this point, the European powers intervened, and, after prolonged nego-tiations, Greek independence was achieved. "The modern Greek state emerged not as a result of an organic process facilitated by domestic forces … it was a state created by Britain, France, and Russia to address their respective geopolitical concerns" (Gerolymatos, 2001, 183). Greece, a product of European diplomacy, has always depended on European aid and support.

A thoroughly disappointed Sultan Mahmut then turned on the Janissary corps and annihilated them in one bloody operation, and then started the *Tanzimat* reform era, which managed to keep the Ottoman Sultanate alive for almost another century. But it was all too little, too late, amounting to no more than centralization at the top, with half-baked ideas imported from Europe. In the final years of the Empire, at the hands of the inept Young Turks, these European ideas led to insolvency and paved the way to the demise of the Empire.

The Christian Heritage of Europe

European life and culture, that is, identity, has always been shaped by the Church, which remains today as a pillar of society. "Christian heritage" is a passionately guarded slogan for keeping Europe Christian. By necessity, this purist/racist worldview means keeping outsiders, Muslims out. In the Roman Empire, Popes legitimized monarchs and bestowed crowns. When the Ottomans burst into Europe, their biggest enemy was not the nations of Europe, it was the Pope. At first, Hungary was the Christian Kingdom facing the Ottomans, later it was the Habsburgs of Austria. When the French Bourbons were found to be less Catholic than Isabella and Ferdinand, Spain was awarded the Papal favors and the New World. The gold of the Aztecs and the Maya was cart-loaded to Iberia, while proselytizing the indigenous peoples emerged as the excuse for genocide and conquest. Shut out of the New World, Frances I forged an alliance with Süleyman the Magnificent. Queen Elizabeth of England followed suit (Brotton, 2017). Thus, at its zenith, the Porte welcomed European merchants; imperialism penetrated the Empire, the Sultans got embroiled in European intrigues and politics from which the Ottomans never recovered.

Nationalism emerged out of the religious wars of Europe. Luther who revolted against the corruption of the Papacy, cheating the congregation with promises of Heaven for money, he was being more of a Christian fundamentalist than a national hero. Garibaldi was strictly a 19th century hero, but in the centuries earlier, the European history of the Reformation is a bloody story of persecution and massacres in the name of Christianity. Intolerance and conformism in the Medieval Ages was the European way of life. Knights, as soldiers of Christ, went happily on Crusades, plundering and slaying, convinced they were doing God's work. Massacres of Huguenots and the extermination of Jews, Moslems, Bogomils, and heretics were regarded divine duty. Columbus, a passionate Christian, was well-known as a *Matamoros*, slayer of Moors and Muslims (Mikhail, 2020, 2); he had learnt his strategic "lessons" sailing the West African coast, searching for gold and passage to the land of the Grande Khan, bypassing the Ottomans. Most significantly, he discovered that in this region, "the Atlantic's predominant pattern of wind and current" went westward, "the exact opposite of the pattern in Portugal" (Mikhail, 2020, 109–110). His end, however, was far less than merited the discoverer of the New World. Columbus was accused of cruelty toward his crew and mismanagement of Hispaniola, and Francisco del Bobadilla was appointed as a special prosecutor by Ferdinand and Isabella. Bobadilla became Columbus' "nemesis" (Bergreen, 2011, 288), jailing, and humiliating Columbus. He was fortunate to be pensioned off by the grateful Ferdinand and Isabella (274–289).

A new Age of Enlightenment was now opened: The separation of politics and religion opened the doors to secular science and liberated the minds, but it did not end nonconformism. Men of science discovered wonderful new methods, paving the way for Industrial Revolution, but nowhere in Europe was there any case of disestablishment of Christianity. The reign of terror in Revolutionary France did not last long. When, in 1620, the Pilgrims set to sail from Plymouth to America, they had left behind a continent torn by religious wars. Ironically, when the Mayfair sailed into the New England colonies, the pilgrims passionately believed they had brought with them Liberty, but it only meant liberty to practice their own brand of Christianity; it did not extend to the native populations, nor to the slaves, which made the plantation system possible (Mayflower Myths, 2017).

Thus, in today's France, the land of Liberty, Fraternity, and Equality, these are ideals allowed only for the citizens who are Catholic and who speak French. Republican France claims to be secular, yet it feels no remorse at denying the religious freedom to French citizens of the Muslim faith. No French author or newspaper dare criticize, let alone indulge in hate literature against the Pope, but it is considered fair game to malign the Prophet. More popularly, it is considered justifiable act of defending the Republic to legislate how people should dress or practice their faith. Meanwhile anti-Muslim politicians are free to exploit Islamophobia in the name of freedom of speech.

A Hypothesis

A major working hypothesis of the study is that the Jews, led by rich Zionists won because they were well-prepared and ready for nation-building. First and foremost, they had all the financial resources. But more than money, the Zionists, recently introduced to the idea of a Jewish Homeland in Palestine, were experts in the game of diplomacy. The masses of Jews, persecuted in Russia and elsewhere, were hungry for a homeland. Their culture had been driven by a religious zeal: "Next year in Jerusalem." With dedication and investment of funds, above all, smart leadership, they were ready to create Israel.

Our hypothesis will be tested against the latest evidence available, statistical data as well as the most recent scholarship. This is not a history book, based on archival research. Rather it is political economy, utilizing theories of nation-building, identity formation, adopting a multidisciplinary approach. Economic and social development is a huge field of study, borrowing from political science, economics, and other disciplines with relevance to international and geopolitical affairs. The time frame used in the study is long-term, extending over centuries: we are concerned with the rise and fall of empires. Short-terms, like waves in the sea, come and go, but institution-building and, even more significantly, sustainable institutions, take time to grow and acquire stability and survival. Nation-building is not short-term. It requires sustained commitment on the part of key actors, from grassroots to the leaders at the top.

Neo-Ottomanism

This study utilizes Neo-Ottomanism as a methodological approach, that is, seeing today's problems as a continuity of the Ottoman world, wherein the root causes of problems lie. It is a rather unique approach as most scholarship on the making of the Middle East has tended to avoid the Ottoman past. Recently, however, as we shall see in Chapter 2, there has been a new trend to link the present in the Middle East to the Ottoman past. The present study is a small contribution in this fruitful line of research.

However, Neo-Ottomanism needs clarification. It does not mean restoration of the Ottoman Sultanate. That is dead and buried. Nor does it mean some sort of Turkish hegemony in the region. What it means is simply learning from the long Ottoman rule, especially from its best in the classical period when trade-based prosperity prevailed widely. What lessons can be learned from the Ottoman capability to govern a vast Muslim Empire, full of diverse cultures and religions, for as long as it did? At its best, the Circle of Equity governed not only administration of justice, but it was also the foundation of fair trade. Ottoman trade, centered in the Levant, but linked with caravans and sea routes, to the far distant parts of the known world, preceded Western mercantilism across the Atlantic. Tolerance prevailed in the *millet* system, which ensured freedom of faith and worship. Jews expelled by Isabella's Inquisition found a new home in the Ottoman lands. Ottoman architecture, arts, and sciences were truly Pan-Islamic, many sites surviving to this day, all over the Empire.

The Ottoman legacy is shared. The relative success of the Ottomans stands in sharp contrast to imported ideologies and virtually permanent state of conflict in failed states, civil wars, military takeovers. Majority of Arab people did not share equally in national wealth and have been deprived of freedom and liberty. State violence is the prime reason behind displaced populations and refugees threatening international peace and security.

Failed States in the Arab Core

In the following pages we shall explain why the Arabs lost, the Jews and Turks won. The explanation will be within a Neo-Ottomanist framework. Ottomanism is dead and buried. No one is interested in its revival or restoration. But much still can be learnt from its success over some six centuries in ruling over so vast a territory with so many different cultures and peoples. They did so because they practiced tolerance and respect for cultural diversity, values so badly lacking today.

Nation-building is a long-term process of sustained development. It requires investment in economic and social capital. Infrastructure and human capital are costly and need technical expertise. Oil-rich countries, theoretically, are well placed to launch such investment. However, when oil wealth is misallocated into war and terrorism, the result is "failed states" (Chomsky, 2006), the classic example being Iraq under Saddam Hussein (Ismael and Ismael, 2015). Failed Arab states, under authoritarian rulers, rely on foreign powers, principally the USA, for regime survival, rather than consent of their subjects.

Chomsky (2006, 202–204) rejects the notion that the United States is dedicated to a "messianic mission" to bring democracy and development to the Middle East. Indeed, the United States supports authoritarian regimes and their oppressive status quo so long as American interest in the Near East oil is sustained. This is especially true in the case of dynastic regimes, including the Saudi regime. Egypt receives US aid in exchange for following American policy, while the House of Saud relies on huge quantities of American military equipment for its repressive policies. In the case of the Palestinian conflict, no Palestinian leader could accept the Camp David accords that left 12% or 13% of the West Bank in Israeli hands (179). Settlers, many from the United States, who take over Palestinian lands are, in fact, subsidized in their illegal occupation, in gross violation of international law (197).

The Islamic Core is in chaos. How did this come about? We deal with this question in Chapter 2. What have the Arabs gained since the demise of the Ottomans? Muslim unity, symbolized by a titular Caliphate in Istanbul, has gone. In its place, there are many artificial or unsustainable countries in the Arab Core, where rivalries and disunity prevail. Worse, since the Ottomans, dynastic and military regimes have been engaged in a virtual state of permanent warfare, most recently enjoined by terror groups, each following a new brand of messianic Islam and using violence as an instrument of oppression. The ordinary people have suffered untold misery, as will be documented in Chapter 2.

References

Ahmad, Feroz, 1969, *The Young Turks, the Committee of Union and Progress in Turkish Politics, 1908–1914*, New York: Columbia University Press.

Aksakal, Mustafa, 2008, *The Ottoman Road to War in 1914, The Ottoman Empire and the First World War*, Cambridge: Cambridge University Press.

Anderson, Scott, 2013, *Lawrence in Arabia*, New York: Signal.

Antonius, George, 1939, *The Arab Awakening, The Story of the Arab National Movement*, Philadelphia: J.B. Lippincott.

Bergreen, Laurence, 2011, *Columbus, the Four Voyages*, London: Viking.

Brotton, Jerry, 2017, *The Sultan and the Queen, The Untold Story of Elizabeth and Islam*, New York: Penguin.

Chomsky, Noam, 2006, *Failed States, The Abuse of Power and the Assault on Democracy*, New York: Henry Holt.

Choueiri, Youssef M., 2000, *Arab Nationalism: A History*, Malden: Blackwell Publishing.

Country Studies, n.d., "The Turkish Petroleum Company", http://countrystudies.us/iraq/53.htm, accessed on 14 Nov. 2021.

Dana Regev, "Israeli Kibbutz: Communal Idealism or a Privileged Few?", Deutsche Welle, https://p.dw.com/p/1IojA, accessed on 17 Oct. 2021.

Dept. of State, 2022, The 1928 Red Line Agreement. Office of the Historian. https://history.state.gov/milestones/1921-1936/red-line, accessed on 11 Feb. 2022.

Earle, Edward Mead, 1966, *Turkey, The Great Powers and The Bagdad Railway, A Study in Imperialism*, New York: Russell and Russell.

Finer, Harry, 2009, "The Dreyfus Case and the Zionist Movement", *The Jewish Magazine*, May 2009, www.jewishmag.com/133mag/dreyfus_herzl/dreyfus_herzl.htm, accessed on 26 Sept. 2021.

Fisher, Allen, 1970, *The Russian Annexation of the Crimea 1772–1783*, Cambridge: Cambridge University Press.

Fromkin, David, 1989, *A Peace to End All Peace: The Fall of the Ottoman Empire and the Creation of the Modern Middle East*, New York: Avon Books.

Ghosh, B.N., 2007, *Gandhian Political Economy: Principles, Practice and Policy*, Aldershot: Ashgate.

Gerolymatos, Andre, 2001, *The Balkan Wars: Myth, Reality and the Eternal Conflict*, New York: Stoddart Publishing.

Inalcik, Halil, 1973, *The Ottoman Empire, The Classical Age 1300–1600*, London: Phoenix Press.

Ismael, Jacqueline S. and Ismael, Tareq, 2015, *Iraq in the Twenty-First Century, Regime Change and the Making of a Failed State*, London: Routledge.

Jewish Virtual Library, n.d., "The Kibbutz & Moshav: History & Overview", www.jewis hvirtuallibrary.org/history-and-overview-of-the-kibbutz-movement, accessed on 20 Sept. 2021.

Kinross, Lord, 1964, *Atatürk: The Rebirth of a Nation*, London: Weidenfeld and Nicolson.

Kinross, Lord, 1977, *The Ottoman Centuries, the Rise and Fall of the Turkish Empire*, New York: Morrow Quill Paperbacks.

Köprülü, Fuad M., 1992, *The Origins of the Ottoman Empire* (Translated and Edited by Gary Leiser), Albany: State University of New York.

Kushner, David, 1977, *The Rise of Turkish Nationalism, 1876–1908*, London: Frank Cass.

Lamb, Harold, 1951, *Suleiman the Magnificent, Sultan of the East*, New York: International Collectors Library.

Mango, Andrew, 1999, *Atatürk: The Biography of the Founder of Modern Turkey*, New York: Overlook Press.

Marriott, John A.R, 1969, *The Eastern Question, An Historical Study in European Diplomacy*, 4th ed., London: Oxford University Press.

Mayflower Myths, 2017, African Slavery and the Mayflower Story, https://mayflowermaveri cks.wordpress.com/2017/08/17/african-slavery-and-the-mayflower-story/, accessed on 29 Sept. 2021.

Merriman, Roger Bigelow, 1944, *Suleiman the Magnificent, 1520–1566*, Cambridge: Harvard University Press.

Mikhail, Alan, 2020, *God's Shadow: The Ottoman Sultan Who Shaped the Modern World*, London: Faber and Faber.

Said, Edward, 1993 *Culture and Imperialism*, New York: Knopf.

Sarah, 2021, "Definition of Pancasila: Meaning, Purpose, and Function of Pancasila for the Indonesian State", https://loveinshallah.com/understanding-pancasila/, accessed on 17 Oct. 2021.

Schechter, Betty, 1967, *The Dreyfus Affair, a National Scandal*, London: Victor Gollancz.

Seton-Watson, Robert William, 1971, *Disraeli, Gladstone and the Eastern Question*, London: Frank Cass.

Shaw, Stanford J. and Ezel K. Shaw, 1976, *History of the Ottoman Empire and Modern Turkey*, 2 vols., Cambridge.

Toynbee, Arnold J., 1948, *Civilization on Trial*, London: Oxford University Press.

Toynbee, Arnold J., 1970, *The Western Question in Greece and Turkey: A Study in the Contact of Civilisations*, New York: Howard Fertig.

Wikipedia, 2021, "List_of_Ottoman_Grand_Viziers", https://en.wikipedia.org/wiki/List_o f_Ottoman_Grand_Viziers, accessed on 21 Sept. 2021.

Wikipedia, n.d., "World War I", https://en.wikipedia.org/wiki/World_War_I_casualties, accessed on 6 October 2021.

Wittek, Paul, 2012. *The Rise of the Ottoman Empire: Studies in the History of Turkey, Thirteenth-Fifteenth Centuries* (Edited by Colin Heywood), London: Routledge.

Yavuz, M. Hakan and Isa Blumi, eds., 2013, *War and Nationalism, the Balkan Wars, 1912–1913 and Their Sociopolitical Implications*, Salt Lake City: University of Utah Press.

2
DAR'UL ISLAM AFTER THE OTTOMANS
The Modern Middle East

The dissolution of the Ottoman Empire after WWI has been bad for the Arabs and the Muslim unity. The Caliphate was abolished in 1924 (II&D, 1999, 117–119), destroying the universality of Islam derived from the Brotherhood of the Faithful, and *Ummah* in *Dar'ul Islam*, under One God without ethnic identity. In an Age of Nations, ethnic identity trumped religious affiliation, and nation-building, through economic, political, and social development, took the center stage. The Arab Core has been almost a total failure in nation-building, as we have seen in Chapter 1, unable to reconcile Islam with development.

A few Wahhabist dynasties, at most, gained because they collaborated with the imperialists to destroy the Empire, but that was gain through deceit and deception. Arab people at the grassroots have suffered civil war, oppressive dictatorship, dispossession, and displacement. Living under one failed state or another, the grassroots have been deprived of basic human freedoms. In most recent times, terrorism and civil conflict has created huge waves of migrants as victims desperately tried to seek peace and safety elsewhere.

One group of refugees, the Palestinians are unique. They lost a homeland, and now live as a nation of refugees, under the care of international charitable organizations. The origins of the Palestinian – indeed Arab – tragedy, go back to the historic betrayal of the Arabs at the end of the WWI. The sad reality is that the Palestinian model has been generalized as wars and conflicts have created waves upon waves of refugees and displaced persons. Unwanted in rich countries, these Muslim victims have been forced into camps, a modern phenomenon of our divided and mismanaged world, a tragedy that began at the end of WWI.

The contrast in 1918–1919 between the Arabs and Turks is most telling. At the darkest moment in Turkish history, the Turks mobilized behind a new leader, Mustafa Kemal, and fought for four years, 1919–1922, against imperialists and proxy

DOI: 10.4324/9781003268994-2

armies of Greeks and Armenians, on several fronts, winning in the end their brand-new Republic. The Arabs descended into disunity and conflict.

The Damascus Debacle

The pattern of Arab disunity and infighting began in Damascus, at the very moment when the Ottomans were defeated, and the Allied forces moved into the city. Chaos set in immediately. The imperialists had their own agenda, control of oil at all costs, and fought each other over the division of the territories of the Ottomans, drawing new maps to take possession of oil. The Arab dynasties were obsessed with power and ready to fight each other over who should rule after the Turks. The ordinary people were simply ignored.

The infighting began even on the day of "liberation" of Damascus. On 30 September 1918, Damascus fell to the Allies and the Arab tragedy began. The Ottoman administration was gone, and now a vacuum prevailed in the city. Local Arab notables, the Emir Abd el Kader and his brother Said, with Algerian connections, moved into some sort of control, hoisting his flag. The two brothers were considered personal enemy by Lawrence who had his own arrangement with Feisal, backed by Allenby-Clayton. But Allenby's forces were late in arriving. On the morning of 1 October, an Australian cavalry brigade entered the city, and a few hours later the French general Chauvel and the British Major-General George Barrow moved in, and an order was issued to get Nuri el-Said, a Feisal loyalist, to clear the Algerian brothers out. But the French general had his own agenda: He wanted Feisal, representing his father King Hussein, to be under the protection of the French, who controlled Lebanon as well. This was too much for Feisal and his idea of a kingship over a huge Arab confederation. Lawrence tried, in vain, to reconcile the impossible situation, in the end swallowing the bitter pill that Syria as well as Lebanon were promised by London, to the French, while the British acquired Palestine. Allenby's forces, meanwhile, arrived, but were afflicted by an outbreak of malaria. In the ensuing mayhem, clashes started between the Bedouin and city dwellers. Emir Abd el Kader was killed by pro-Feisal police. Thus the "liberation" of Damascus turned into a fiasco (Fromkin, 1989, 336–341).

The dynastic families in Arabia were duped into revolt by Lawrence, who was part of a team of spies and agents, some searching for oil while pretending to be archeologists, but in fact, gathering intelligence for the coming war. The Ottomans fought to the bitter end for empty ideals such as the Caliphate and Muslim unity. In the end, even the Turkish nation gave up on the House of Islam. The Turks, led by Mustafa Kemal, fought for four more years to achieve the Republic. The Arabs, never a unified nation, but a collection of tribes owing traditional allegiance to dynasties, some claiming lineage to the Prophet, had only recently been exposed to nationalism. Neither the dynasties nor the Arab masses knew much about nation-building. Arab awakening, a romantic idea, at the time was no more than in its "infancy" (Antonius, 1939, 79–100). Arabs were simply duped. No one has put it more aptly than Antonius, a contemporary scholar and diplomat.

Antonius on the Sykes-Picot Agreement

Written soon after the end of WWI, *The Arab Awakening, the Story of the Arab National Movement* (1939), by George Antonius is a remarkable, if not always reliable, book. A Lebanese-Egyptian scholar, Antonius wrote his story, "from an Arab angle" (x). It is, however, contradictory. In earlier parts of his book, he strongly condemns the Sykes-Picot Agreements, but later, he changes his mind and goes along with the partition plans, praising the British installed Faisal, the first King of Iraq (360).

In 1920, this is what he had to say on the partition plans:

> The Sykes-Picot Agreement was a shocking document. It is not only the product of greed at its worst, ... it also stands out as a startling piece of double-dealing. ... What ... the Agreement did was first, cut up the Arab Rectangle in such a way as to place artificial obstacles in the way of unity ... it provided for a topsy-turvy political structure ... The absurdity of the provisions is particularly evident in the case of regions destined to form the British sphere of influence ... But more serious even than those errors of judgement was the breach of faith.
>
> *248–249*

The final act of betrayal of Arabs took place at the San Remo Conference where the British and French confirmed their partition plans without any Arab consultation or input. The plans were initially kept secret.

> The whole of the Arab Rectangle lying between the Mediterranean and the Persian frontier was to be placed under mandatory rule of the imperialist powers. The decisions taken at San Remo were finally made public on the 5th of May, and their promulgation gave birth to a new sentiment in the Arab world – that of contempt for the Powers of the West.
>
> *305*

On news of the betrayal, the affected Arab regions erupted into rebellion.

The Syrian Rebellion: The Middle East was left to the end at the Peace Conference at Versailles, 1919. Intrigue and betrayal dominated the negotiations over the partition of the Ottoman lands. Earlier, on 27 April 1920, at the Conference of San Remo, British and French negotiators concluded "a secret oil bargain" (Fromkin, 1989, 534). The two Allies, ignored all their earlier promises to the Arabs before, and monopolized the "whole future output of Middle Eastern oil between them." When Americans saw the deal, they were furious (535), but the real storm over the San Remo broke out when it was made public in the summer and the Arabs found out that they had been betrayed. The French determined to spread French Catholic culture in a Greater Lebanon, including Syria, Latakia, and the Sanjak (Province) of Alexandretta, all three to be governed by a French governor (Antonius, 1939, 372). The French rule was, effectively, dictatorship, brutal in the extreme, aimed at forcing the local Arab population to adopt French culture. School children were taught to sing *la Marseillaise* (374).

The Arab dynasties were ignominiously abandoned, the national dreams were dashed. Public opinion makers started talking of rebellion. Yet, the rebellion did not start for a few years. The Syrian Rebellion erupted in July 1925. The Governor, General Sarrail, used tyrannical methods to enforce French rule, and his offensive treatment of some Druze leaders suddenly erupted into open rebellion. It quickly turned into a national insurgency, other tribes, and even exiles from abroad rushed in to join the rebellion. It spread beyond Damascus to Homs, Hama, and Tripoli (ibid., 377). The people had had enough of the French and now they demanded independence and a unified country. The response of the Governor was brutal. Using an armed force of Armenians and Circassians, houses were burnt, shops looted, and innocent persons killed (378). Order was restored with difficulty.

The Iraqi Rebellion: The San Remo decisions also sparked a rebellion in Iraq. For many months in 1920, diverse nationalist leaders across Iraq rose to fight the British military administration. The popular uprising united the Sunnis, Shi'a and the Kurds, elites and commoners, city dwellers and tribespeople. Armed resistance broke out in all parts of British Iraq, from Kurdistan in the north, in the fertile plains south of Baghdad, all down to Basra and the Gulf, as bands of tribespeople swept in from the desert to attack isolated British military outposts and destroy vital railway lines. Churchill, then the Secretary of War, launched "carpet bombing whole villages with explosives and teargas," justifying this inhuman action by an astonishing confession: "I am strongly in favor of using poison gas against uncivilized tribes." Such was the imperialist mind at its worst; a mindset which failed to understand "the impossibility of ruling Iraq by military might (at a time when) Britain nominally transferred sovereignty to a puppet regime ..." (Ismael and Ismael, 2015, 14).

The postwar pattern was clear: the imperialists prevailed. Ordinary people, oppressed under the various mandatory regimes, revolted against the injustice of it all. Rebellions and violent resistance against foreign rule followed not only in Syria and Iraq, but in Palestine, and elsewhere in the post-Ottoman lands. Imperialists had imposed their will on the Arabs through deceit and greed. But hard though it must have been to swallow the betrayal by Britain and France, a key fact must be noted: the Arabs were not ready for nation-building. Their inept and opportunistic leaders, the dynastic families that collaborated in the defeat of the Ottomans, were easy prey to the imperialists and the Arab masses were ignorant of the basic elements of nationhood. Lacking a central leader, these revolts did not last long; the Great Powers imposed their will, created artificial countries, and got the oil.

As for Antonius, in an amazing change of heart, he passionately endorsed the proclamation of Faisal as King of Iraq on 23 August 1921 and went on to hail his installation as a major achievement in stabilizing the country, praising him as a ruler of the multiethnic country. Antonius argued:

> The debt which the country owes to its first king can scarcely be overstated. His gifts and his experience fitted him to play a determining part in the

handling of some of its most difficult problems, and it is the unanimous verdict of all those who are in a position to judge that his influence was the decisive factor in the creation of the modern state of Iraq.

Antonius, 1939, 360

In fact, however, Faisal was no more than a British puppet, collaborating with the imperialists. His statue, along with that of General Maude, the British Commander who occupied Baghdad in 1917, representing the old regime, was destroyed in the revolution of 1958 that brought about the downfall of the monarchy and the proclamation of the Republic (Khadduri, 1969, 50).

The Ottoman Legacy

In their glory, the Ottomans were Lords of the Horizon (Goodwin, 1998), in command of virtually all the Mediterranean. This theme will be historically analyzed in Chapter 3. The Ottoman failure in Malta in 1565 (Bradford, 1968) against an all-European Crusade was the turning point. As ethnic cleansing raged in Phillip-Isabella's Spain, the Muslim people, first in the *Magreb* and subsequently in *Masreg*, fell victim to European penetration. Imperialism carved North Africa and all over the colonial world for the enrichment of Europe, a theme explored extensively elsewhere (Mehmet, 1995). The French occupied Algeria, importing one million settlers to run urban businesses and own the most fertile lands. During the Algerian liberation war, lasting from 1954 to 1962, half a million soldiers, waged a "savage war" during which an estimated "half a million lives" might have been lost (Hardy, 2017, 181–182). Italy, a late comer in the Scramble for Africa, the Italians seized Libya.

The Arab Core was sheltered by the Ottomans, until the Suez Canal was completed in 1869, after which Egypt and Cyprus fell to British imperialism. Sudan experienced a brutal occupation and gunboat diplomacy. Gordon Pasha and Lord Kitchener gained their field experience fighting the Mahdi, an early precursor of the Muslim messianic, false prophets of al Qaeda and ISIL. The destruction of the Ottoman Empire began in earnest when oil was discovered (Rogan, 2015, 79–87), and the conquest of Basra at the top of the Persian Gulf was launched, significantly as an Anglo-Indian Expeditionary force (124–127). London, awash with riches cumulated from the India trade, plantations, and slavery, used its cash to enlist Muslim soldiers from present-day Pakistan and Bangladesh to fight the Muslim Turks in Mesopotamia (McMeekin, 2016). By contrast, the Ottoman Sultan's call for Pan-Islamic *Jihad* and solidarity fell on deaf ears. What on earth, were the Ottoman Turks fighting for in the sands of Arabia? Only the future Ataturk had the foresight to ask that question. He hit back with a vengeance: at the first chance he had, he abolished the empty-shell Caliphate and disestablished Islam.

The Ottoman Decline

At the beginning of the 19th century signs of Ottoman decline were evident. The age of European imperialism was beginning in earnest. The Tsar was by then master of Crimea and increasingly active in the Balkans, ostensibly protecting the Christian subjects of the Sultan, but effectively expanding Russian influence at the expense of the Ottomans. The British were already in control of India, but maritime routes were vulnerable. In 1798 Napoléon Bonaparte decided to take advantage of this vulnerability by launching a strategic invasion of Ottoman Egypt, an invasion directed against London as much as the Porte. The French were finally forced out of Egypt in 1801 by combined British and Ottoman forces. In the meantime, Napoléon launched an expedition into the Levant, spreading French influence in Syria-Lebanon, and in 1799 returned to France as a hero; he carted back to France huge quantities of ancient monuments and treasures to enrich the Louvre Museum. While finally defeated by the British, Napoleon's Egyptian campaign revealed the Ottoman Sultan's inability to protect his Empire against the rising European imperialism. The British were now ruling the waves, gradually acquiring Egypt and thus buttressing her control of India.

Once the Ottoman inability to protect and defend its territorial integrity was obvious, European powers dismembered the Empire almost at will, sometimes acting in concert, as in the case of the Greek Independence in 1829, followed in quick succession with other Balkan states. Dismemberment was euphemistically referred to in European diplomacy as "the Eastern Question," how to manage the process of expelling the Ottomans out of Europe (see Chapter 1). When it came to the Arab territories of the Empire, Europeans adopted a twofold strategy. In the first instance, after nationalism had invaded the Sultan's lands and such *millets* as the Armenians, and Christian minorities in Syria and Lebanon, missionaries and schooling were utilized to promote ethnic "awakening" (Antonius, 1939). Then, around the turn of the 20th century, highly trained and educated cadre of discoverers and explorers, such as Hogarth, Lawrence, Bell, and others, were dispatched far and wide into the Arab Core to prepare the ground for Arab Revolt. In the decade prior to WWI, when the Scramble for Africa was put into full steam, there was also an intense imperialist competition for partitioning the Empire and simply taking over the Sultan's provinces. The end of the Ottomans in the Balkans was essentially achieved through the Balkan Wars. The Ottoman weakness encouraged Italy to invade Libya, where the Ottomans led a brave but futile defense; the Italian navy occupied the 12 Islands in the Aegean next door to the Turkish coast.

In the desperate days of the Young Turks, war was seen as the only way of regaining Ottoman pride. It was wishful thinking on the part of the naïve and inexperienced regime that could not even see the paradox in plotting to go to war against the very same powers whose shipbuilding yards were expected to rebuild the Ottoman navy. Only the opportunistic Kaiser came to the "aid" of the Ottomans. British-German imperialist rivalries in the Middle East were, essentially, fought on the backs of the Turks, Arabs, and Muslims.

In 1914, at the start of WWI, a confident German Kaiser, the Sultan's financier, believed a *fetva* from Istanbul by the Caliph-Sultan, proclaiming a *Jihad*, would cause a widespread revolt in *Dar-ul-Islam*. He had completely misunderstood that a bankrupt Sultanate was powerless, that only money talked. With the Baghdad Railway still incomplete in 1914, the Ottomans were hardly capable of defending the Arab Core. With the betrayal of the Sultan by the Wahhabist dynasty, it was an impossible task, and the Arab Core fell to the British and French. The Ottoman army performed well in Iraq, defeating the British at Kut-al-Amara, but it was no more than a stopgap. At the Suez and the Gaza, the Ottomans were no match against the British reinforced by the Arab Revolt. European imperial penetration in the Arab Core created new countries, often artificial because it was all about oil. Welfare of the ordinary people did not figure in the partition plans. So far as oil is concerned, it has been a bitter story of "the poisoned well" (Hardy, 2017).

Historically, there is mistrust between the Arabs and Turks, going back all the way to the early Muslim era when the Turkmen tribes, moving westward out of Turkistan and Central Asian steppe, first appeared in the Persian, Arab world (Brockelmann, 1948, 171–172). Eventually, these Turkmen expanded their power, and especially after Alp Arslan's defeat of the Byzantian Emperor in 1071 at Malazgirt in today's Mus in eastern Turkey, the Selcuk Turks emerged as the preeminent power in the region. The Muslim "Golden Age" centered in the Baghdad Caliphate was by then in decline, falling prey to Mongol invaders who also destroyed the Selcuk empire centered in Konya in central Anatolia (ibid., 240). The Ottomans succeeded the Selcuks, and over the next five centuries, they became the Sword of Islam against a Christian Europe.

Pan-Islam and Neo-Ottomanism

In the last stages of the Ottoman Empire, the Arab thinkers and elite were unsupportive of the Sultan. The Arab awakening (Antonius, 1939) was a passionate, idealistic dream, hoping that, with European help, a democratic transition could be achieved. The Ottoman intellectual elite, at the time, were still preaching the virtues of Ottomanism, professing interfaith allegiance to the Sultan Caliph (Lewis, 1968, 140–142). However, the Caliphate, in an age of nationalism, was reduced to an empty shell. Its advocates, such as Afghani (Mehmet, II&D, 1990, 65–66) pursued impractical Pan-Islamic ideals supported only a fringe element in the capital. The Ottoman state in late 19th century was bankrupt and its army and navy weak. It could defend neither the Islamic periphery, nor the Core. Imperial powers, like hungry wolves, helped themselves to the territories of the Sultan virtually unopposed.

The Ottoman Empire died a violent death. But it died because of old age, fatigue, and failure to keep up with the march of nationalism. Virtually everywhere in the Muslim world, identity was redefined in national terms. As a dynasty at the top of a multinational empire, the Ottoman Sultanate was doomed. It could not reinvent itself into a national state. Turks, finally, realized that, and they were ready to fight a national war of liberation for their nationhood based on modernity. The Arab awakening was, at best, a limited ideal: as a movement, it was led by a few idealistic Christian Arabs in places like Beirut and Damascus. Elsewhere dynasties and tribalism ruled. This pattern is still largely relevant today.

In this context, neo-Ottomanism, revival of the Ottoman dynasty, would be an absurd idea. It is like restoring the *Ancien Regime* in France. In this study, this kind of neo-Ottomanism is totally rejected. The Ottoman heritage, however, is something else. It is worth studying only to better understand the chaos into which the Islamic Core has descended. The Ottoman past was far from perfect, but historical continuity can neither be avoided nor broken. Learning from the past helps avoid mistakes and chart a meaningful path forward.

Nowadays, there is much resistance to Neo-Ottomanism, but it may be based on a misunderstanding as explained earlier. It is uncertain how genuine this resistance is, owing to the lack of freedom of expression in Arab lands. When Erdogan visited Tunisia and Egypt during the short-lived Arab Spring, when Mohammed Morsi was in power and Islamic Brotherhood was legitimate in Egypt, he was welcomed as a hero. In Saudi Arabia, anti-Turkish feeling is strong, especially in circles around the Saudi Crown Prince, the mastermind behind the Khashoggi murder in the Saudi embassy in Istanbul. Shortly before the outbreak of the civil war in Syria, at a period of the Arab Spring, the then Turkish Prime Minister Davutoglu, promoted his version of Neo-Ottoman policy, but totally failed to sell the al Assad regime the idea of democracy, causing ever-widening rift between Ankara and Damascus.

The Caliphate in the Ottoman Endgame

Old Europe of dynasties and political elites were long united in a Crusade-like mindset, called the Eastern Question, to expel the Ottoman Turks, "an alien substance" out of the land of the "European family" (Marriot, 1969, 3). The Allies, including the Tsarist Russia, finally got their opportunity in WWI. The Ottomans' end was a suicide, a self-inflicted death, more in the hands of the Turks themselves than the Europeans.

Going into the war in 1914, the Sultan-Calif declared a *Jihad* with *Sheik-ul Islam*, the titular head of the Sunni Muslims, issuing a *fetwa*, enjoining all the faithful to join the Sultan, Defender of the Faith in the holy war against the enemy. It fell on deaf ears virtually everywhere in *Dar'ul Islam*, save for a small-scale Singapore Mutiny in 1915 when Malay Muslims refused to be sent off to the Middle East to fight Muslim Turks (II&D, 1990, 27). The *Jihad* idea was endorsed by none other than the odd man of Europe, "Hajji" Wilhelm, the German Kaiser who believed that "the world's 300 million of Muslims" (McMeekin, 2016, 301) would heed the call to arms, especially in British India, causing havoc; the call went out, but it did nothing of the sort.

When Gazi Mustafa Kemal moved ahead with his plan to abolish the Caliphate, he knew well that it was a dead institution with no following in the Muslim world. No Arab voices were heard against the abolition. Only two prominent Indian Muslims, Agha Khan, leader of the Ismaili sect, and Ameer Ali, a jurist and activist against the British Raj, had addressed a plea to Ismet Pasha, Mustafa Kemal's trusted lieutenant and the serving Prime Minister, to save the Caliphate, arguing that the move would safeguard Turkey's honor (Mango, 1999, 400). It was too late and futile.

When the motion to abolish the Caliphate was submitted before the Turkish Grand National Assembly on 2 March 1924, it was passed quietly. The iron determination of the Gazi on the subject was well-known, all the opposition having been cleared beforehand. The institution was incompatible with the secular Republic that was being established. Moreover, the risk of splitting the nation was too great at the crucial moment when all energies were required for making the Republic a homeland for Turks. At 1 am on 4 March 1924, the last Caliph Abdülmecit left Dolmabahçe palace to go into exile. He left a note behind stating that in future he would devote himself to fine arts. But, after crossing the Bulgarian border, he issued a second statement stating that the decision to depose him was null and void. No one took notice (406).

In his six-day speech delivered in 1927, Mustafa Kemal defended the abolition with the counterargument that there can be only one head of state in the Turkish Republic. He warned those religious leaders who still supported the institution: "You understand that the Caliph would be Head of State ... Gentlemen, let me say this clearly: Those who wish to fool or mislead Muslims with an imaginary caliphate are nothing else than enemies of Turkey" (*Author's translation from the Turkish original*) (Gazi Mustafa Kemal Atatürk, 2010, 567). For Atatürk, whose views were shaped during WWI campaigns in Arab lands, the usefulness of the Caliphate had ceased to exist a long time ago. It had become no more than a political tool.

This was proven from the earliest reactions coming from the Arab world. When, in mid-1920s, some interest was raised to reinstate the Caliphate in Arab countries, in fact three countries had come forward: Iraq, Saudi Arabia, and Egypt. Each one had its own agenda, and merely wished to use the Caliphate for domestic politics. By 1930s, the issue of the Islamic Caliphate had faded "into the background" (Choueiri, 2000, 99). In all the discussions on Arab unity or nationalism, the subject has hardly merited any further discourse until, that is, the Arab Core descended into the inferno of Islamic terrorism. For a period, Pan-Arab Unity emerged as an idealistic project, but it proved futile due to intercountry rivalries.

Tribalism and Tribal warfare

Within most Arab countries, disunity and tribalism prevail. Tribalism is an essential ingredient both in Arab culture and, by extension, Islamic identity in the Muslim Core. Tribalism rests on a traditional nomadic lifestyle which requires extensive land, while it maximizes the number of children and livestock. Family members, especially children and women, help provide unpaid labor. Nomadic pastoralism is multitasking, with family members contributing to common interests without reciprocity or reward, over and above daily sustenance at the family table. Large families also enhance political status. A husband must produce children, and a wife achieves status when she becomes a mother. Sons are prized as they are stronger. The larger the family, the greater the social standing of the man in the tribe. A father with five or six adult sons plus a similar number of sons-in-law commands high social standing, enjoys self-esteem and independence of mind, mindful of having assured his progeny.

Livestock ownership is wealth. In tribal society, livestock is both income and savings. Livestock generates income, in addition to regular supply of consumption goods like milk and meat. In addition, animals provide a wide range of products and services. Camels, sheep, goats provide wool, and input for tent roofs. Camels enable long-distance travel. Sold in the traditional market, animals supply money to purchase goods not produced locally, such as firearms, household wares, durables, and fixed assets such land, even urban villas. In weddings, value exchange is between families, often in kind.

Livestock may also cause conflict. Nomads are constantly engaged in gaining access to grazing lands and watering holes. As populations expand, competitive pressures mount for more tribal resources through geographical expansion. Encroachment on neighboring lands, seizing pastures, and water resources through predatory raiding results in warfare. On the other hand, when members of a tribe fight, whether in defense or aggression, tribal structures are reinforced, enhancing group solidarity and antipathy against outsiders. In countries like Somalia (Mehmet, 1971) and Yemen, these lifestyles shape identity and conflict far removed from European idea of nationhood.

The Endless War in Yemen

Often considered, mistakenly, as a proxy war between the Shi'a Iran and a US-backed Wahhabist Saudi Arabia, the roots of the war in Yemen lie in British gunboat diplomacy. In the days of Marco Polo, it was a prosperous land, and under the Ottomans it was a significant trading port handling the Oriental spice trade. From Hadhramaut in Yemen, Muslim traders went out to the Indonesian archipelago, intermingled with the local people, spread Islam, and rose to prominence, finally, participating in the struggle for Malay independence (II&D, 1990, 28).

Table 2.1 provides a statistical summary of the human tragedy in Yemen, (additional tragic figures shown in Table 2.3), created by the author using the latest internet sources. Admittedly, these are not always reliable, subject to change, but they do reflect a general tragic picture. No less than 16.5 million people are facing starvation, 2.5 million children in a state of acute malnutrition. The fighting seems endless, while the major suppliers of weapons used in the conflict are the principal oil producer along with top Western powers. The tragic story of Yemen started with British penetration into the region.

★★★

In 1839, two British warships and 700 men captured it in the name of Queen Victoria, and for the next century it was administered by the Raj in Bombay (Hardy, 2017, 184). The British immediately encountered resistance from the Imam, ruler of the northern hinterland who had a claim to Aden and Southern Arabia. After the opening of the Suez Canal in 1869, Aden's importance grew, but the troubles

TABLE 2.1 Hunger and Weapons of War in Yemen

1 People facing starvation	16.5 million
2 Children in a state of malnutrition	2.5 million
3 Major suppliers of weapons used in the Yemen war:	
UK to Saudi Arabia★	15 billion pounds
Canada to Saudi Arabia★★	$14,8 billion
USA+	$80 billion sales globally. $3 billion sales to Middle East/North African countries

Author's creation from internet sources: For 1 & 2: www.intersos.org/en/hunger-in-yemen-the-coun try-of-the-ignored-war/. For 3★ www.globaldefensecorp.com/2020/04/16/bae-systems-sold-15bn-worth-of-weapons-to-saudi-arabia-during-yemen-assault/. For 3★★ https://theowp.org/reports/the-human-cost-of-the-yemeni-civil-war/ For 3+ www.al-monitor.com/originals/2018/03/yemen-us-weapons-saudi-arabia-uae.html, accessed on 22 Dec. 2021.

with the hinterland, home of the Houthi tribe along with many others, persisted. It was not until 1934 that some sort of peace treaty was achieved with the Imam. But the intertribal conflict over territory and clan feudalism has continued ever since, the latest phase pitching the Crown Prince of Saudi Arabia in a regional war with Shi'a–Sunni rivalries. If Afghanistan, has been described as a "graveyard of empires," Yemen is not far behind (Purple, 2022).

In 1937, with oil becoming an increasingly strategic commodity, Aden was made a Crown Colony, directly administered from the Colonial Office in London. After WWII Aden had become the second busiest port in the world after New York (Hardy, 2017, 185). In the mid-1950s, trade unionism and class struggle entered Yemen. In 1952, Nasser staged his successful coup in Egypt and revolutionary politics took hold in Yemen. Tribalism, however, confronted Marxist revolutionary ideology. In 1959, the British pushed for a Federation of the Arab Emirates of the South, dependent on British protection. It got nowhere. In 1962, the Imam was overthrown in a coup backed by Egypt, sparking civil war, with Nasser backing the revolutionaries and Saudi Arabia the monarchists. Not even Nasser's humiliation in the Six-Day War against Israel was enough to end Egypt's participation in the civil war in Yemen.

Britain, too, was bogged down in the sand. In a humiliating decision, London announced withdrawal in 1967, "The British had not simply retreated under fire. They handed power to the first Marxist Republic of Yemen in the Arab world, which established the People's Democratic Republic of Yemen and became an ally of the Soviet Union" (196).

With departure of the British, the vacuum was filled by the opportunistic Americans who were at the time busily abandoning the Shah and picking the House of Saud as the new partner in the game of oil politics. The US-backed Saudis fighting in Yemen is not a simple rivalry between Riyadh and Tehran, between

Sunni and Shi'a Islam; its roots are much deeper and longer. It has become one of the greatest humanitarian catastrophes in the Arab Core, with no end in sight, while the United States and the Western military-industrial complex is making huge profits from the sale of weapons to keep the war going (Bidder and Hoges, 2022). Yemen is a sad case of perverse social capital, as discussed earlier. Sadly, it is not the only case in the Arab Core.

Arab Unity and the Arab League

At the end of WWII, Egypt emerged as the leading Arab country. This was a time of global optimism, with discussions leading to the establishment of the United Nations. Arab leaders met in Alexandria and seven countries (Egypt, Saudi Arabia, Iraq, Syria, Lebanon, Yemen, and Jordan) agreed to create the Arab League. It is an umbrella organization to coordinate foreign policy, and to promote cooperation in economic, political, and cultural affairs. Its main impact has been to underscore Egypt's central role in the Arab world.

As regards the promotion of Arab unity, intercountry rivalries and political upheavals in the Arab world have predominated. A delicate challenge for the League was the dictatorship of Saddam Hussein: The League did not wish to call for regime change, yet it wanted Saddam to go, the dilemma which resulted in inaction. Later, the League's response to popular protests during the Arab Spring in 2010 was more principled, but equally ineffective. Libya's participation in the League was suspended amid Qaddafi's violent response to the street protests. It was reinstated after Qaddafi was overthrown. Less than two weeks later, amid reports that the Syrian forces had continued to kill demonstrators protesting the Assad regime, the Arab League voted to suspend Syria's participation. In the conflict between Saudi Arabia and Iran in Yemen, the League sided with Saudi Arabia. A move condemned by the Houthi authorities that the League "stands with the executioner against the victim" (Debriefer, 2022). Even on the Palestinian conflict, the League remains divided as several key members opt for normalizing relations with Israel (Ephron, 2022).

The League has not been a stellar performer in terms of Arab unity or in the promotion of democratic development of Arab countries. By necessity, it welcomes military dictators and autocratic dynastic rulers and, as such, it has little more than a ceremonial role. Military dictatorship in the Arab Core, however, is systemic, reflecting a path to the top through a military career, combined with a coup or revolution. In Chapter 5 we examine, in greater detail, six country cases of Islamic dictatorship of all types, religious, dynastic, military (Iran, Saudi Arabia, Iraq, Syria, Libya, and Egypt), with the latest statistics of human loss.

Post-Pandemic World

Now, at the end of 2021, in our Pandemic-ridden world, two notable trends are discernible in the Muslim world. First, there is a sad fact of Muslim crisis with much of the Muslim word bogged down in civil war, terrorism, masses living under repressive regimes, and millions are displaced; millions more seeking to become refugees and economic migrants in nearby countries and further afield. The second fact is the poor quality of life in the Arab Core as failed states are unable to meet the basic needs of the people. More and more displaced persons and refugees are pushed into camps. Palestinians have become a nation of refugees; many others face the same fate. A Muslim refugee crisis, a symptom of systemic failure, is an undeniable fact.

Human Loss, Quality of Life in the Arab Core

What are the indicators of the Muslim regression since the destruction of the Ottoman Empire?

The independent Freedom House has the data, summarized in Table 2.2. In the 18 Muslim majority countries listed in Table 2.2, there is only one country that is "free," the special case of North Cyprus, which is discussed at the concluding part of the book. Of the other 17 countries, three (Kuwait, Morocco, and Pakistan) are "Partly Free." The remaining 14 are "Not Free." These are "failed states," countries under military or dynastic dictatorship, as illustrated by the six cases reviewed in Chapter 5.

TABLE 2.2 Free Country Rankings by Freedom House, 2020*

Country	Total Score	Category	Political rights	Civil liberties
Afghanistan	27	Not Free	17	23
Egypt	18	Not Free	6	12
Gaza Strip	11	Not Free	3	8
Iran	16	Not Free	6	10
Iraq	29	Not Free	16	13
Jordan	34	Not Free	11	23
Kuwait	37	Partly Free	14	23
Libya	9	Not Free	1	8
Morocco	37	Partly Free	13	24
North Cyprus	78	Free	28	50
Pakistan	37	Partly Free	15	22
Qatar	25	Not Free	7	18
Saudi Arabia	7	Not Free	11	6
Somalia	7	Not Free	1	6
Sudan	17	Not Free	2	15
Turkey	32	Not Free	16	16
United Arab Emirates	17	Not Free	5	12
Yemen	11	Not Free	1	10
Average score	24.5		9.6	16

Source: Mehmet (2022, 309) with permission of the editor.

The average total score for the set of 18 countries is 24.5 out of 100, with political rights score averaging 9.6 and civil rights score 16. Major countries, including Saudi Arabia, Iran, and Egypt score below the average. Pakistan, Kuwait, Iraq, Jordan, and Turkey are above the average.

The UN Development Index (UNDP, 2020) is another international measure of development in the modern world. The Index is an average of physical indicators including life expectancy at birth and income per capita. This measure of income is simply an arithmetic number, showing national income divided by population, regardless of how the income is distributed. For example, every woman is granted the same average income per capita, but how true is that? There is also the question of reliability as the index is based on official figures.

As a measure of quality of life, gender equality index is far better. It captures the quality of life of Muslim women. The UNDP gender inequality groups range from 1 to 5, Group 1 being the most equal and Group 5 the lowest. The picture that emerges for the Muslim Core countries is highly negative: Almost all major Arab countries are in Group 5. Exceptions are Kuwait, Libya, Qatar, and the United Arab Emirates. These cases demonstrate that even the highest gender equality is feasible and achievable in the Muslim Core. In other cases, repression of gender equality reflects failed state.

Failed states in the post-Ottoman Arab Core have been bogged down in conflict. Civil and proxy wars, invasion and regime change have taken a huge toll in human lives. Ignoring property or material damage, Table 2.3 uses the latest available statistics, admittedly imperfect, giving estimates of the death toll, and persons who have been internally displaced or forced to become refugees in just five selected countries in the last two decades.

The human toll of war and conflict in just five countries listed in Table 2.3 add up to about 30 million, including deaths, displacement, and refugees. The figures in the table are rough estimates by sources cited and they are valid on dates accessed, subject to change. As such, the statistics may not be accurate, but there can be little doubt of the cruel picture they reflect.

Social Capital

What makes a nation is social bonding, coming together, trusting each other, and cooperating and sharing to face adversity and challenges to achieve common goals. This is social capital, embodied in networks and institutions, an invisible quality expressed in social life, customs, politics, and culture (Mehmet et al., 2002). Typically, social capital formation occurs in a wide range of organizations, from football and sport clubs to political parties, women and youth organizations, and other similar institutions. In vibrant neighborhoods neighbors help one another, share, and cooperate. War and conflict destroy not only physical capital, embodied typically in roads, buildings, and infrastructure, but social capital as well. Physical capital can be rebuilt after a conflict or war, social capital cannot be so quickly rebuilt. It takes time to regain trust, to share and come together in civil society organizations.

TABLE 2.3 Estimates of Civilian Casualties Due to Conflict In Selected Countries in Post-Ottoman (Recent) Times

Country	Civilians killed	Internally displaced	Refugees
Yemen	233,000	5 million	4 million
Syria	380,000	9 million	6.6 million
Iraq	189–208,000 (war with Iran)	3 million (since 2004 US invasion)	>4 million
	Other estimates as high as 1.2 million (Ismael & Ismael, 2015, 21)		
Iran	Iraqi war casualties: 100,000 plus 50,000 or more Kurds		
Libya	15,000–25,000 during 2011–2013	200,000 as of 2019	600,000–1 million Libyan refugees in Tunisia only
Total (crude est.)	>1 million	>17.2 million	>15 million

Notes: 1. Civilian numbers exclude combatants/soldiers. Includes indirect casualties due to side-effects of conflict such as starvation, disease as well as direct killing by civil war, massacre, terrorism, or genocide by state forces. "Internally displaced" are civilians forced by conflict to leave their homes and move elsewhere within their country. "Refugees" cross national boundaries to live in camps in neighboring countries or elsewhere. 2. Figures from sources cited are valid as of dates accessed; subsequent change/revision is possible.

Source: Mehmet (2022, 310) with permission of the editor.

Conversely, in war-torn societies, where in Hobbs' poignant phrase, life is solitary, poor, nasty, brutish, and short, there is no social capital. In much of the Arab world, tribalism reigns; intertribal networking or cooperation is rare. Durable institution-building is impossible, only temporary marriages of convenience are possible. As a result, there is no social capital accumulation. Instead, perverse social capital prevails due to mistrust and systemic violence. Disagreements erupt into violence. Religious or dynastic power struggles, utilizing Islam as a tool, erupt. This is how Osama bin Laden emerged and formed Al Qaeda. *Jihadism*, as perverse social capital, uses extortion and systematic violence, including arbitrary killings, to dominate a society. ISIL is only the most notorious example. Terrorist groups, drug-dealers, warlords or illegal arms trading, and human and weapon trafficking abound in the Muslim Core because there is no room for legitimate dissent; the use of brutal power is the only path to the top. Taliban's rise to power in Afghanistan is perhaps the best example, while the seemingly permanent war in Yemen illustrates inconclusive inter-dynastic and intertribal warfare. Both cases are examples of dire shortage of social capital in the Muslim Core.

The tragic case of Afghanistan is illustrative of how invasion, civil war, and terrorism destroy social capital. The country has witnessed one invasion after another, no one ever caring to build trust and sustainable institutions for people's welfare. Islam has shaped custom and beliefs in a highly diverse society where primal loyalties are to one's family and in-group. In modern times, first the Soviets invaded the country and set up a puppet regime, far removed from the highly conservative masses strongly attached to Islam. In the leadership vacuum, the *mujaheddin* fighters emerged victorious against the Soviets, but lacking skills to govern. Then the Americans, looking for revenge on Communist ideology from their defeat in Vietnam, moved in, initially partnering with Osama bin Laden. Bin Laden had his own ideological agenda, to purify Islam by violence. Any remnant of social capital was swept away by brutality. After 9/11, bin Laden became both the cause and target of US intervention in Afghanistan. Poppy cultivation and illegal arms trading created a false and illicit economy. The ordinary people of Afghanistan suffered at the hands of invaders as well as home-grown *Taliban* terror.

The US Invasion, Rise of Islamic Terrorism, and False Caliphates

Until the US invasion of Iraq, when the Bush–Blair duo came in a futile search of weapons of mass destruction, the Caliphate issue was dead. The invasion in March 2003 was launched without international legitimacy and it was brutal. The use of excessive American force was heavily criticized by Sergio de Mello, the UN Secretary General's independent-minded human rights representative in Baghdad, who was killed in a bombing incident, which has remained a mystery to this day, with no investigation to unearth the truth behind the bombing (Menta, 2022). Perhaps the most important consequence of the invasion was the rise of Islamic terrorism. Islam itself was taken hostage by Al Qaeda and Jihadist groups. The brutal Islamic State of Syria and the Levant (ISIL),[1] proclaiming a new Caliphate, was an American creation.

The roots of ISIL are in Sunni Wahhabism from Saudi Arabia, but it began in Jordan in 1999 (Hasan, 2022) as *Jama'at al-Tawhid wal-Jihad* aimed at toppling the Jordanian monarchy. It was a Jihadist movement also known as *Dae'ish*, brutal and militant group which has twisted Sharia law with brutal Islamic Darwinism in action. In Iraq, ISIL was one of the central actors in a larger Sunni insurgency against the Iraqi government and foreign occupying forces. At that time, it was led by Abu Musab al-Zarqawi, but after Zarqawi's death in 2006, the group combined with several smaller extremist groups and renamed itself the Islamic State of Iraq (ISI), a change that reflected the group's aim of using its territory as a base to achieve universal leadership of the Islamic community to establish a Caliphate.

Taking advantage of the withdrawal of US forces during the Obama administration in 2011, huge amounts of war equipment left behind, and weak governments in Baghdad, ISIL filled the vacuum, taking control oil-rich parts of Northern Iraq first, and then expanding into eastern Syria. In 2014, ISIL launched an offensive and drove the Iraqi government forces out of key western cities, while in Syria it fought both government forces and rebel factions in the Syrian civil war.

The Caliphate was declared in June 2014, following spectacular territorial gains in Iraq, led by Abu Bakr al-Baghdadi who had served a five-year sentence in a US-run prison in Southern Iraq. The Syrian civil war, which started in 2011 against the Assad regime, provided new opportunities for ISIL, including alliance with local Islamist rebel groups such as the Nusrah Front led by Ayman al-Zawahiri, linked to Al Qaeda. Soon afterward, rivalries emerged, and the two groups started open fighting. Al Raqqa in eastern Syria, oil-rich, became the group's headquarters, and oil funds attracted significant numbers of radicalized recruits from outside Iraq and Syria. It started developing international links in Africa and elsewhere in the Middle East, referring to itself simply as "the Islamic State." The group's claim to universal leadership of the Muslim community found no response.

In areas under its control, ISIL began to assume some governmental functions such as collecting taxes, and organizing basic services. Policing, education, and health care were carried out in accordance with its hardline interpretation of the *Sharia*. Extreme violence against civilians became routine to enforce its edicts: executions, beheadings, amputations, and lashings were carried out in public and the corpses of the executed were often displayed to the public as a warning against disobedience. Widespread reports circulated of sexual violence carried out by ISIL, including forced marriages and sex slavery.

Moreover, ISIL began a campaign of cultural cleansing, in demonstration of its own, extreme version of the *Sheri 'at* destroying Shi'a and Christian places of worship, as well as the Sunni shrines that it deemed idolatrous, including the ancient Mosque of the Prophet Jonah in Mosul. In early 2015 it began to destroy the region's ancient heritage, including Assyrian artifacts in the Mosul Museum and demolishing archeological ruins at Nimrud and Hatrain Iraq. In May 2015 ISIL took control of Palmyra, the site of one of the largest collections of Greco-Roman ruins in the Middle East. After becoming a party in the Syrian civil war, and awash with funding from oil fields under its control, ISIL went international, and began to develop terrorist networks in other lands, Nigeria, Libya, and connections to the Taliban in Afghanistan (Editors of Encyclopedia Britannica, 2021).

ISIL was defeated, finally, in 2018 by an unlikely coalition of a US-backed Syrian Kurds (PYD) and Arabs known as the Syrian Democratic Forces (SDF). PYD was an extension of PKK, the separatist Marxist–Leninist group engaged in a long and bitter fight with the Turkish armed forces. As such, it became a wedge between Ankara and Washington. During its reign, ISIL carried out atrocities against the Yazidis and ancient Christian communities in the areas under its control, its only mark of uniqueness being the living proof of how the post-Ottoman Arab Core has been taken hostage by terrorist organizations. If Jihadist terrorism is one extreme model in the Arab Core, military dictatorship is the other.

The Arabs, at least the dynastic leaders who were partners in the Arab Revolt, have continued in their path of dependency on the Western powers. Now, it is evident that the United States, however much it wants to be an international policeman, cannot depend on anyone to sort out the Arab chaos. No outsider can do it. As revealed painfully during the four years of the Trump administration, the United States is a biased, pro-Israel party looking after, first and foremost, its own interest, especially oil and selling weapons. Every outside power has its own agenda. Russia seems partially to have filled the American void, and the Iran of the Ayatollahs is keen on exporting its influence. Clearly, outsiders are unable to help; only Arabs themselves can. Failed states won't go away because no one in the Arab world will step up to the plate.

Note

1 Often the organization is referred to by its Arabic acronym, *Da'ish*, for *Dawla al-Islamiyaji Iraq wa al-Sham*, even though ISIL leadership has opposed this usage, going to the extreme of persecuting those using it in areas under ISIL control.

References

Anderson, Scott, 2013, *Lawrence in Arabia*, New York: Random House.

Antonius, George, 1939, *Arab Awakening: The Story of the Arab Movement*, New York: Hamilton.

Atatürk, Gazi Mustafa Kemal, 2010, *Gençler İçin Fotograflarla Nutuk* (The Speech with Photographs for Youth), Ankara: Cultural Publications of İşBank.

Bidder, Benjamin and Clemens Hoges, 2022, Weapons Sales to the Arab World Under Scrutiny, https://archive.globalpolicy.org/security-council/index-of-countries-on-the-security-council-agenda/small-arms-and-light-weapons/general-analysis-on-small-arms-and-light-weapons/50094-weapons-sales-to-the-arab-world-under-scrutiny.html, accessed on 27 Feb. 2022.

Bradford, Ernle, 1964, *The Great Siege, Malta 1565*, London: Penguin.

Brockelmann, Carl, 1948, *History of the Islamic People*, London: Routledge and Kegan Paul.

Choueiri, Youssef M., 2000, *Arab Nationalism, A History*, Blackwell Publishing, Carlton, Victoria, Australia.

Debriefer, 2022, Houthi Government Criticizes Arab League's Role in War in Yemen, https://debriefer.net/en/news-7640.html, accessed on 2 Oct. 2021.

Editors of Encyclopedia Britannica, 2021, accessed on 30 Sept. 2021.

Ephron, Dan, 2022, How Arab Ties With Israel Became the Middle East's New Normal. https://foreignpolicy.com/2020/12/21/arab-ties-israel-diplomacy-normalization-middle-east/, accessed on 27 Feb. 2022.

Fromkin, David, 1989, *A Peace to End All Peace, The Fall of the Ottoman Empire and the Creation of the Modern Middle East*, Avon Books, New York.

Goodwin, Jason, 1998, *Lords of the Horizons, A History of the Ottoman Empire*, London: Vintage.

Hardy, Roger, 2017, *The Poisoned Well, Empire and Its Legacy in the Middle East*, New York: Oxford University Press.

Hassan, Hassan, 2022, The True Origins of ISIS, www.theatlantic.com/ideas/archive/2018/11/isis-origins-anbari-zarqawi/577030/, accessed on 30 Jan. 2022.

Ismael, Tareq and Jacqueline Ismael, 2015, *Iraq in the Twenty-First Century, Regime Change and the Making of a Failed State*, London: Routledge.

Khadduri, Majid, 1969, *Republican Iraq, A Study in Iraqi Politics Since the Revolution of 1958*, London: Oxford University Press.

Lewis, B., 2008, *The Emergence of Modern Turkey*, London: Oxford University Press.

Lynch, Marc, 2016, *The New Arab Wars, Uprisings and Anarchy in the Middle East*, New York: Public Affairs.

Mango, Andrew, 1999, *Ataturk, The Biography of the Founder of Modern Turkey*, Overlook Press, New York.

Marriott, John A.R, 1969, *The Eastern Question, An Historical Study in European Diplomacy*, 4th ed., London: Oxford University Press.

McMeekin, Sean, 2016, *The Ottoman Endgame, War, Revolution, and the Making of the Modern Middle East, 1908–1923*, New York: Penguin Books.

Mehmet, Ozay, 1971, "Effectiveness of Foreign Aid – The Case of Somalia", *Journal of Modern African Studies*, Vol. 9, No. 1, pp. 31–47.

Mehmet, Ozay (II&D), 1990, *Islamic Identity and Development; Studies of the Islamic Periphery*, London: Routledge.

Mehmet, Ozay, 1995, *Westernizing the Third World, the Eurocentricity of Development Theories*, 2nd ed., London: Routledge.

Mehmet, Ozay, 2022, "Islamic Identity and Development after the Ottomans", *Journal of Contemporary Iraq and the Arab World*, Vol. 15, No. 3.

Mehmet, Ozay and Vedat Yorucu, 2020, *Modern Geopolitics of Eastern Mediterranean Hydrocarbons in an Age of Energy Transformation*, Switzerland: Springer.

Mehmet, Ozay, et al, 2002, "Social Capital Formation in Large-Scale Development Projects", *Canadian Journal of Development Studies*, Vol. XXIII, No. 2.

Menta, A., 2022, Is 'Sergio' on Netflix a True Story? Here's the Real Story of Sergio Vieira de Mello, https://decider.com/2020/04/17/sergio-netflix-true-story-sergio-de-mello-carolina-larriera/, accessed on 22 Jan. 2022.

Purple, Matt, 2022, Why Saudi Arabia is Hammering Yemen, https://nationalinterest.org/feature/why-saudi-arabia-hammering-yemen-15748, accessed on 27 Feb. 2022.

Rogan, Eugene, 2015, T*he Fall of the Ottomans, the Great War in the Middle East*, New York: Basic Books.

UNDP, 2020, http://hdr.undp.org/sites/default/files/hdr2020.pdf, accessed on 15 May 2021.

3

RECENT SCHOLARSHIP ON THE END OF OTTOMANS AND THE MAKING OF THE MODERN MIDDLE EAST

The ghost of the Ottomans still haunts us a century after its demise in the peaceful exiling of the last Sultan in 1922 (Mango, 1999, 369), at the creation of the modern Turkish Republic. But we are still far away from an objective account of why the House of Osman committed "suicide" at the hands of the inept Young Turks who gambled their way, "all-in," to the European imperialist war in 1914, at the very birth of the new Automobile Age. All the oil wealth of the Middle East, as we know it today, lay underground in the vast Arabian desert, all in Ottoman hands. The vast oil wealth could be used to rescue the Ottomans and Muslim unity, and an immeasurable amount of human suffering avoided, if the Ottomans had at least chosen neutrality in the senseless European war. Smart politicians rather than the juvenile dictatorship at the helm of the Sultan's government could have facilitated a way forward to prosperity; the fate of the Middle East, of Turks, Arabs, and Jews (as well as the Christian subjects of the Sultan) would have been far better, more peaceful and less suffering all around.

The end of the Ottomans, however, was determined not by the Turks, but foreign powers at the height of European imperialism. Secret deals were forged to partition the Sultan's vast territories, deceit, and greed motivated leading political leaders. Fromkin (1989) emphasized the role of Britain, opening his masterful early study with the Great Game (chapter 2), a metaphor borrowed from Rudyard Kipling. On 16 May 1916 Britain and France signed the secret Sykes-Picot Agreement to partition the Ottoman Empire. Syria and Lebanon went to France, and Mesopotamia and Palestine to Britain. These annexations subsequently were formalized under the Peace Treaty at Versailles, 1919, and legitimized as mandates by the newly formed League of Nations. In 1923 the French Mandate for Syria and the Lebanon was created along with the British Mandate for Palestine. The British also acquired control of Mesopotamia under the Anglo-Iraqi Treaty of 1922, which also established the Kingdom of Iraq. Under another secret deal, Tsarist Russia was to get Anatolia

DOI: 10.4324/9781003268994-3

as its zone of influence, and in Western Anatolia a new Hellenic Empire was to be created. Kemalist forces, motivated by Turkish nationalism, defeated these imperialist plans in the creation of modern Turkey, but in the case of the Arab territories imperialism won.

The books selected for critical review below shed new light on the current popularity of Neo-Ottomanism and the bloody endgame of the Empire in 1918. They will be utilized extensively throughout this study, but it is useful to highlight these contributions at the start in this chapter.

The Berlin–Baghdad Railway (BBR)

The BBR was a bitter German-British imperial rivalry, a contest for new markets and resources in the emerging new industrializing world. In *The Berlin-Baghdad Express*, McMeekin (2010) has produced a highly credible book. Despite its title, the book is inadequate as it is less about railroad geopolitics than about the general World War I (WWI) history. Specifically, the strategic and economic role of the German railway project is inadequate, in comparison to, for example, the saga of the warships *Goeben* and *Breslau*. All the standard topics, such as Enver Pasha's ill-fated adventure in Sarıkamış in the Caucuses, Cemal Pasha's misrule in Syria and his mismanaged campaign in Suez, as well as Mustafa Kemal's miraculous victory in Gallipoli, are all there, albeit sometimes unevenly.

There is a wonderful section about Max von Oppenheim, "the wayward son of the Oppenheim banking dynasty" (16–30), the German version of Lawrence, and the most dedicated supporter of the BBR. He was an idealist, a visionary, lover of the Middle East culture, especially the Arab women, and a personal ambassador at large for the Kaiser Wilhelm, submitting a huge volume of intelligence about the Arab world, often misleading, none more so than in his wildly exaggerated significance of the Caliphate. Like Lawrence, Oppenheim was an admirer of the Bedouins, but he totally missed out on their opposition to the building of the railway, which they (Bedouins) perceived as a threat to their traditional way of life, depended on the traditional annual pilgrimage caravans.

In his chapter 2, McMeekin (2010) gives interesting information about bare bones of the contract awarded to the Deutsche Bank. On 23 December 1899, the Ottoman Minister of Public Works, Zihni Pasha, signed an agreement with Georg Siemans, representing the Deutsch Bank and the Anatolian Railway Company, which obliged the German group to build a railway within a maximum of 8 years, the line running from Konya in central Anatolia via the Taurus mountains to Baghdad and then on to Basra (42). The Taurus range was a "logistical nightmare with impassable mountains as far as the eye could see" (44). Under a secret royal decree, the Berlin Museum was granted rights to cart away historic monuments (43). Surprisingly, however, the Germans did not always provide the requited finance. A new company, the Baghdad Railway Company was incorporated under Turkish law in 1903 with a capital stock of 15 million francs, but only 10% was subscribed by Turkish interests (Earle, 1923, 70). Effectively, the Sultan was mortgaging his Empire. In 1905, the construction was, once again, halted for financial reasons, only 200 km of the railways having been completed to Bulgurlu, an insignificant town in Anatolia. Already insolvent, the Ottoman government was obliged to borrow 54 million francs at 4% annual interest for a term of 98 years, to make the payment of the per kilometer subsidy.

In his chapter 5, McMeekin offers interesting material on the unfinished Hejaz railway, the difficulties of carting war material on mules through the difficult Anamos mountains, all contributing to the failure of the Suez Canal campaign. The decisive factor in the building of this section was that it sparked the Arab Revolt. For the Bedouin, the railway brought 20th century "steel horses" to a 15th-century caravan trade route. It was to replace the camel with the locomotive.

The rest of McMeekin's book is standard WWI writing. The Sultan entered the War financially and militarily dependent on the emperor. The Germans carry much "war guilt" (100) for pushing the Ottomans into the War. Seizing on the "gift from Mars," the assassination of the Austrian Archduke Franz Ferdinand (chapter 4), Pan-Islamic Jihad ideology was German war propaganda (chapter 6), imposed on an insecure Sultan and his weak Young Turk advisors. It is small wonder then, that the Sultan's call to arms failed so miserably, while the British and French successfully recruited tens of thousands of Muslim soldiers from India and North Africa to fight the Ottoman armies in the sands of the Middle East. McMeekin, unlike Rogan and other authors, underestimates oil politics in the Mesopotamian campaign and his treatment of the Sykes-Picot partition plans is inadequate.

Despite these limitations, McMeekin's study is a welcome contribution, particularly shedding much light on the German role in pushing the Ottomans into the War. The Germans used adventurist Enver Pasha, and a Sultan with a deep mistrust of the French and English, in a global war of imperialism. The Turkish nation paid dearly for the Young Turks "gamble." Had it not been for the foresight and military-diplomatic skills of Mustafa Kemal, the future Atatürk, the Turkish nation, almost certainly, would have vanished in the ruthless casino, which was the WWI in the Middle East.

Surprisingly for an academic teaching in Turkey, McMeekin's treatment of Turkish nationalism is thin and short, Kemalist ideology is underestimated, and the treatment of the War of Independence is minimal. While Mustafa Kemal's victory in winning the heights of Chanak Bair is there (187), the National War of Independence is inadequately covered. The reader looks, in vain, for a discussion of the rising modern Turkish nationalism, the role of the fiery patriots such as Halide Edip Adıvar. By contrast, he has a useful discussion on Zionist politics in his epilogue (340–366). Significantly, McMeekin notes that "Zionism was originally, if not a German Jewish idea, at any rate it was an Austrian Jewish idea ... (and as late as August 1914, the British) ... feared a German-Jewish connection" (342–343). He also raises the intriguing possibility that had the German war propaganda not "promoted anti-Christian, anti-Semitic prejudice" (351), Arab-Jewish relations might have evolved differently.

As for a more detailed economic and financial analysis of the BBR, Edward Mead Earle's classic study, *Turkey, the Great Powers and the Bagdad Railway* (1923), remains the indispensable source. According to statistics given by Earle, BBR was to cover an estimated 3,773 km or approximately 2,400 miles, making it one of the biggest railway networks in the world at the time (90). Only part of the railway remained in Turkish possession at the end of the WWI, and it was a hot topic at the peace negotiations at Lausanne. On 20 October 1921, the French and the Kemalist Turkey reached the Ankara Agreement, which not only ended the war between the two countries but established the Turkish-Syrian border (324–326). At Lausanne, Ismet Pasha and Lord Curzon finally concluded a deal. Under the deal, the British bankers became the majority stakeholders in the Baghdad Railway, the Nationalist government in Ankara managed the line from Haidar Pasha to the Cilician gate on the Syrian border, the line running all through the Turkish territory. The border was adjusted in Turkey's favor. The Iraqi segment passed into British-Iraqi hands. Subsequently, American interests got involved and no less than 2,800 miles of railways were built all over Anatolia (339). A Chester concession, an American investment, was negotiated for the development of Anatolian resources, thus America took over the German dreams of controlling the vast resources of the Ottoman Middle East. The BBR was not completed until 1940.

The War over Oil

Rogan's *The Fall of the Ottoman* (2015), much to the author's credit, explicitly links the British war efforts in the Muslim Core to oil. British India played a vital role in this campaign, not only with prewar intelligence concerning the oil wealth and trade opportunity, but crucially with the supply of raw manpower, Hindus, and Indian Muslims, to drive the Ottomans out of the oil fields.

Rogan's unique style is that he writes with a personal perspective. Starting in the Preface, he talks about Lance Corporal John McDonald who died at Gallipoli on 28 June 1915. McDonald was "my great uncle." This personal style adds flavor and richness to history writing, making history more human and events more touching. Thus, when he writes of the Ottoman campaigns on the Caucuses or in the Sinai, he starts with the key personalities involved, Enver Pasha, the war minister, who "took on himself to lead the attack on Russia." The Germans had pressed the Ottomans to send five Ottoman corps, 50,000 troops, to Odessa to relieve the Austrians in Galicia. But Enver had no interest in such plans; with his Turanist ideas, Enver went to Caucuses because he believed "a sizeable Muslim population would respond enthusiastically to an Ottoman offensive" (101). Similarly, Djemal, the marine minister who was assigned the governorship of Syria, and assumed responsibility for the campaign in Sinai, "was carried away with war enthusiasm." When the patriotic crowd (at Haidar Pasha railways station) hailed him "prematurely as the 'saviour of Egypt,'" Djemal responded with equally wild emotionalism declaring that he would not return "until I have conquered Egypt."

In Mesopotamia, after the Indian Expeditionary Forces had captured Basra, the Ottomans were faced with increasing number of desertions. Arab soldiers, deciding that the British would win, simply abandoned the Ottomans. Izzet Pasha, the commanding officer, first issued a voluntary return call encouraging the deserters to return to duty, with no consequences. When that approach failed, he sent out his troops to conduct house-to-house search. The local Arabs were outraged. Deserters had joined the Bedouin who turned on the Turkish soldiers in al-Kufa, al-Shamiyya, and Tuwayrij. "In the end, their futile efforts to force deserters to return to active service cost the Ottomans the Euphrates basin" (219).

In February 1916, well before the Arab Revolt, when the Sultan's government expected concrete support from his Arab chieftains in the Jihad against the British, Djemal and Enver travelled together by train to review the Hashemite forces and press Sharif Huseyin to contribute *Mujahidin* (soldiers of Jihad). Much gold had been paid to the Shariff for this mission. Huseyin, however, remained noncommittal because he was negotiating secretly with Lawrence. He responded not as a loyal subject of the Sultan, but instead he demanded from the Young Turk his own conditions, including "amnesty for all political prisoners currently on trial" (294). In April, the military tribunal completed its work, and dozens of defendants were found guilty of treason. Twenty-one men were hanged on 6 May 1916 (295). That was the last straw. The Arab revolt was now inevitable.

Rogan's strength is in his analysis of how the oil age started in the Middle East. It began with William Knox D'Arcy, a Devon-born millionaire who, in May 1901, secured a 60-year concession to explore oil in Persia (79), finally dying in poverty. His company had the backing of a British syndicate, the protection of the Royal Navy. He first struck oil in the south-western Persian city of Ahwaz, selecting the island of Abadan in the Shatt-al-Arab, not far from Basra, and 140 miles distant from the oil field. The owner of the island was Shaykh Khazaal, a British protégé. The area was Ottoman, but in 1914, the British prepositioned troops near Basra, ahead of the formal declaration of war. The Raj, in full control of India, considered Basra and the Persian Gulf, as strategically vital, and was ready to send a large expeditionary force to safeguard it.

Rogan also well documents the diplomacy of betrayal of Sharif Huseyin (402), his final (secret) meeting in Cairo in 1921 with Churchill, when the Arab national cause was traded for British-dependent dynasties in Saudi Arabia, Transjordan, and Iraq. Rogan's account of battles is especially unique and fascinating as he stresses the ordinary soldier and minor actors caught in a wider conflict, which few could decipher.

Likewise, Rogan is impressive in documenting the strategic significance of another Middle East asset, newly acquired by Britain, namely the Suez Canal and Egypt. This was vital for keeping India British. As early as September 1914, before the onset of hostilities, British India began flooding Egypt with troops from Britain, India, and the dominions. The Indian Expeditionary Force from Bombay reached the Suez Canal zone toward the end of October. A first wave of 30,000 Anzac arrived in Alexandria in early December (90) in readiness for the Gallipoli expedition, which proved nothing short of disaster for imperial powers, but a turning point for Turkish nationalism.

Regretfully, Rogan dismisses Turkish nationalism, and the creation of modern Turkish republic in barely two pages (393–394). He discusses, in greater details the partition plans under the Treaty of Sevres, but his treatment of the Lausanne Treaty is far too brief. He gives far more attention to the Armenian-Ottoman conflict, its history (9–14), and its tragic result (165–184).

Salvation through War?

Decision-makers in the Sultan's capital were in a totally different world, with a completely different agenda, (ethnonational and emotional), in which oil politics did not even appear.

Aksakal's brief study, *The Ottoman Road to War in 1914* (2008), is a superb contribution, providing perhaps the most persuasive motive for the Ottoman entry into WWI, an imperialist fight to the bitter end in which Ottomans had no business. But the warmongers in the Sultan's capital, humiliated recently by defeats at the hands of the Italians in Libya, and more recently the Balkan upstarts, financed and supported by European imperialists, were eager for revenge. As recently as 1897, Greece had been defeated in a war by the Ottoman army, and now on the eve of a European war, the Ottomans were engaged in a raging dispute with Athens over the Aegean islands (44–45). In August 1914, the Ottoman navy was on the verge of acquiring two modern dreadnoughts, built in Britain, and paid for in full. Churchill, the first lord of the admiralty, then seized the warships. It was a deliberate, hostile act against a nation not then at war, because "by the end of August the Foreign Office was pretty sure that the Porte's entry into the war [on the side of the Central Powers] was inevitable" (92).

The seizure bolstered the war party in Istanbul. Enver, hero in the recapture of Edirne in the second Balkan war, considered himself "… the ultimate leader of the movement opposing European imperialism" (15). The warmongers were ready to play their last card, in an emotional daring all-in mindset, supported by a nationalist press and public opinion, hoping that an insolvent and exhausted Empire could somehow defeat the imperialists at their own game and recover lost prestige and lands. It was an act of suicide. *Damat* Enver Pasha, the war minister, of lowly personal origin, but recently admitted into the royal family, despite misgivings on the declaration of a *jihad*, justified borrowing from Germany to finance the war, creating a German naval base in the Sea of Marmara (168–169), and issued authorization to the German admiral Souchon for a naval attack on Russia on 24 October 1914 (177).

Two days after the attack, Enver reported to the grand vizirate a "doctored description" of the event (180) claiming that the Russian officers taken as prisoners of war during the engagement were involved in a planned occupation of Istanbul and the Straits. Enver went over the heads of the Grand Vezir Said Halim Pasha and the finance minister, Cavid Bey, when he and Cemal Pasha sent notes of congratulation to Souchon (181). Enver bears a huge responsibility for his adventurous behavior that resulted in the bitter end of the Ottomans.

The Ottomans finally entered the War committing political suicide. Along with Enver, blame for the Ottoman folly must rest with the Committee of Union and Progress (CUP). This motley group contained Turks and non-Turks, each group pursuing their own hidden agenda, and, instead of promoting stability and progress, it aggravated disunity and hastened the dissolution of the Empire. Imperialists took advantage of the Young Turk weaknesses: Austria-Hungary annexed Bosnia-Herzegovina, the territory occupied by the Habsburgs since 1878. Bulgaria unilaterally declared its independence and patriots in Crete announced ENOSIS, union with Greece. Russia, for its part, gained the right of passage through the Straits, (58), and furthermore, demanded that "Russian officers must be part of reforms in eastern Anatolia" (60), effectively, establishing Russian control of the area.

Deceit and Imperial Folly

European failure in the Middle East is perhaps best demonstrated in Scott Anderson's *Lawrence in Arabia, War, Deceit, Imperial Folly and the Making of The Modern Middle East* (2013). Anderson's book is an impressive study showing that lies and deceit, as much as military power, were instruments of war at the height of Western imperialism. The story, built around the personality of Lawrence, is far more than about a misguided and pathetic hero who, to the bitter end, chased a mirage in the desert.

Lawrence's moment of glory and defeat came at the same point in time, the moment when imperialism triumphed. In December 1918 at the end of WWI, Lawrence marched into Damascus to install Faisal, Sharif Hussein's son, as the King of Syria. That would have fulfilled his promise of reward in return for the Arab Revolt that, in so small way, had paved the way for the Ottoman defeat at the Suez and Gaza. Imperial treachery and deceit negated this reward. Lawrence was rudely rebuffed by General Allenby, commander of the British forces, who categorically declared that Syria was to be delivered instead to the French. Sykes-Picot lines in the sand were drawn well before, carving the Great Ottoman Loot between Britain and France. Betrayed, Lawrence quietly went back to England to face his own hell and finally die a broken man, while Faisal first fought the French, but then took the consolation prize to become the British puppet ruler in Iraq. Palestine became Jewish. The French ruled Syria and Lebanon in their own interest.

Anderson has done a magnificent job, painting Lawrence as a lost soul in the age of imperialism, victim of his own vanity. Lawrence's Arab Cause was formulated early, when the young Oxford student was doing archaeological excavation in Jerablus, northern Syria. That is where he had spent "the happiest days of his life" (481). There, he formulated his "noble Arab," a purely abstract model, and its nemesis, the "cruel Turk." This ethnic stereotyping was the essential element of Lawrence's racist reality.

Throughout his life, Lawrence was his own man. Reconstructed "reality" was his guide. The abstract "noble Arab" ideal was both his greatest achievement and folly. In his manners, dress, and behavior Lawrence imitated the noble Arab. His military bosses, uncomfortable with his trade mark Bedouin garb, tolerated

Lawrence going "native." He became the super-spy, the willing facilitator of the Great Game, snatching the Arabs from the Sultan's *Jihad*, enlisting them to the cause of the colonial-industrial complex mentality, the neo-imperialism resurgent. It was all about oil. Churchill, in 1912, had converted the British Navy from coal to oil. Lawrence was an expert at using desert tribes for intelligence and for map-making. His style, that of "unconventional war," relying on Fifth Columns, revolts, and sabotage behind enemy lines, soon emerged as the necessary extension of imperial warfare; Lawrence wrote it all down: In his *Twenty-Seven Articles*, penned in Summer 1917, after his Aqaba triumph (Anderson, 2013, 346–347), he decoded for his military bosses, the Dos and Don'ts of winning Arab hearts and minds, in fact ennobling the desert Bedouin who made up less than 1% of Arabs!

Yet, Lawrence was always a private person, waging very much his own war within the War. He had a near-obsession, strongly favoring the Alexandretta landing, rather than Gallipoli. In 1915, he saw a grand opportunity to knock Turkey out quickly by splitting the Ottoman Empire down its middle by invading at Alexandretta where the Hejaz Railway was so perilously exposed on the Syrian coast. Not only the local Armenians (97–98), but the Arabs were ready to revolt against the Turks (140–141), in support of such a landing. Critically, a much smaller force would be adequate, against the half million dispatched to Gallipoli. "The French, not the Turks, are the enemy" (95) he fumed, because France regarded Syria as "theirs," under secret partition plans. The French-British rivalry was to prove fatal.

Anderson does an excellent job of detailing it all. About the time when in Jeddah, Lawrence was winning Sharif Huseyin for the imperial cause, Mark Sykes and Francois Georges-Picot were secretly carving up the Sultan's inheritance (352–354). Lawrence never liked Sykes, and how much he knew of the details of the secret agreement of 1916 is debatable. However, in retrospect, one must wonder whether it is possible to fairly allocate treachery and betrayal in the Arab-British-French-Zionist wheeling and dealing in dividing up Osmanli's Loot when imperialism won, and the Arabs lost.

One thing is certain: just about everyone, in some degree, lied, betrayed, and conspired in self-interest. The Sharif of Mecca betrayed the Sultan, taking huge amounts of gold to raise an army to fight the British at Suez, only to change sides at the last moment. The Sharif betrayed Arab independence for dynastic interest under British protection. According to Anderson, Sykes lied both to Lawrence and to the Sharif by deliberately misleading them with a "bastardized version" (309) of his agreement with Picot. How much Huseyin conveyed to his son, Faisal, is also moot. In the end, Syria and Lebanon went to the French, while the British got Iraq and Palestine. Faisal, the third of the four sons of Emir Hussein from the vast Hejaz region of Western Arabia, and his dynasty ultimately accepted the Sykes-Picot terms. The Zionists got their Balfour Declaration.

Arab unity was sacrificed on the altar of expediency. Ordinary Arab masses, as much as the Ottomans, were betrayed. The first to expose it all was surprisingly Djemal, the last Ottoman governor of Syria who revealed it all in Beirut in November 1917 denouncing the secret agreements publicly and warning that "the unfortunate Sharif Hussein fell into the trap laid for him by the British" (Antonius, 1939, 255). By then, it was too late. Imperial interest had won. As for Lawrence, in the end he got his bittersweet revenge on those cruel Turks he had spent a whole life hating. On the battlefield of Aqaba, leading his Arab warriors in the ultimate Lawrence-style daring attack in the most unforgiving desert country, only a heartless human could stand over the pile of fallen Turkish soldiers, massacred without exception in the surprise attack, and glorify mass killing: "The dead (Turkish) men looked wonderfully beautiful. The night was shining gently down, softening them into new ivory …" (336).

The bitter end arrived for the Ottomans and Lawrence at the same time. In Damascus, at the end of WWI, with a colossal human toll of 16 million dead, Lawrence was a defeated man as much as the Ottomans. Mustafa Kemal, not far to the north, was about to launch the War of Turkish Independence, thanks, in no small way, to the strategic pullback of Anatolian armies into the Turkish homeland to fight in another war. Betrayed and abandoned, Lawrence returned to England to become an occasional champion of the lost Arab cause. Lloyd George and Churchill made use of him for short-term assignments selling imperialism to Arabs. He died a broken man in 1934 of injuries sustained in a motorbike accident. Arab disunity and conflict have continued ever since.

The Ottoman Endgame

The Ottoman Endgame (2016) *by* Sean McMeekin is a rich and detailed summation of a complex story of imperial destruction. He analyzes, in 550 compressed pages, all the important historical facts and related dynamics of decision-makers, the unceasing stories of intrigue and scheming that finally brought about the destruction of the near-thousand-year-old House of Osman, The Great War, 1914–1918, started as a senseless European fight in which Ottomans had no business. The key figure was Wilhelm II, the ambitious Kaiser who felt cheated out of imperial plots, most recently in the "Scramble for Africa." In desperation, he looked East. In İstanbul Sultan Abdul Hamid and the adventurist Enver, the pro-German War Minister were all too willing to lead the warmongers. The Kaiser, "backed by a wide circle of German scholars and politicians, promoted pan-Islamist ideology to a much greater extent than Enver ever did" (Aksakal, 2008, 16). The linchpin of this German-Ottoman conspiracy was a global *Jihad* to shake up the British and French colonial rule in India, North Africa, and Central Asia. The Sultan-Caliph's *Jihad*, the German military believed, "… would fire up a global rebellion among the millions of Muslim subjects living under Entente colonial rule …" (Aksakal, 2008, 155) beating the anti-German imperialists at their game.

Alas, the poor Muslims of British India and French Africa massively enlisted against the Ottomans, save for some pious Malays who rioted in Singapore (II&D, 1990, 27). In India, the British encountered some difficulty as documented by Coles (2022), but by force or choice, Muslim troops took the enlistment cash and joined the imperial fight in the deserts of Iraq and Palestine against their coreligionists.

The bitter irony did not escape the attention of the keen Ottoman warrior, Mustafa Kemal. His plans for the salvation of what became the Turkish Republic were first crafted in the Middle East deserts with these hard realities etched in his mind. Witnessing in Palestine the inevitability of Ottoman defeat and the futility of Pan-Islamism, he dared to withdraw as many Turkish soldiers as he could back into Anatolia to fight later in the War of National Liberation. Betrayal and deceit determined Kemal's willingness to give up on the vast Arab territories in exchange for modern Turkish identity and homeland. That willingness was to pay dividends at Lausanne.

McMeekin gives us a more complete picture of Mustafa Kemal than Rogan. He tells a magnificent story of the rise of Modern Turkey and Atatürk's victory, not only on the battlefield but equally in diplomacy. Kemal's success in replacing the unequal Treaty of Sevres with the Peace of Lausanne is summarized masterfully, with a humane understanding of the massive population exchanges it legitimized. There is a whole chapter on Sevres, and Lausanne is covered in the epilogue along with a brief resume of the Ottoman legacy in Arab-speaking countries of the Empire. One might have wished McMeekin had delved more substantively beyond the creation of Modern Turkey and explored the failure of the Arab world to produce its own Atatürk or, at least, embrace Kemalist secularism in nation-building. Kemal's realism and sense of the limit, where to draw the line for the sake of the Turkish Republic, was only part of the Ottoman heritage. For Arab lands, as McMeekin states, "… we should not romanticize the Ottoman past" (p. 492). But the Ottoman past is an integral precursor of the imperial Divide and Rule that followed. To this day Western powers are ready to invade, overtly or covertly, to protect their interest. Neo-imperialism, now termed, globalization, continues.

Poisoned Wells

Roger Hardy's *Poisoned Well, Empire and Its Legacy in the Middle East* (2017), is a well-documented and highly readable account of nation-building following the end of the Ottomans. Appropriately, Hardy's first case is the Turkish Republic, created out of the "ashes of the Ottoman empire" (8). Chapter 1 begins poignantly with Halide Edib Adivar, the early Turkish feminist and nationalist. No such feminist voice exists in the Arab world. Reading her one gets a glimpse of the popular patriotic sentiment at the outset of the Great War in the Sultan's capital. In Halide, we see a strong awakening of Turkish nationalism, a passionate yearning for freedom and liberty in an independent Turkish homeland. Halide's passion was shared by her compatriots across the entire Anatolia. It provided the essential foundation, shared at the grassroots and the elite alike, the social grounding of the Kemalist Republic, mobilization of the masses as a first step in nation-building. By contrast, there was no Arab grassroots movement in the Arab world, only collaborating elite families at the top.

Imperial interests in collusion with self-serving Arab leaders prevented similar social grounding in the post-Ottoman Middle East. In chapters 2 to 9 devoted to case studies of specific Arab countries, Hardy provides an impressive, yet a pathetic story of failed states, betrayal of people by military or dynastic rulers. Imperialism created the Arab countries and Neo-imperialism dominates them still. Oil wealth has been a curse, the wells poisoned. Limited national attempts, from Mosaddeq to Saddam Huseyin and Qaddafi never had a chance because the CIA or other big power interests always intervened.

In chapter 4, entitled "Lovers of Zion," Hardy has documented the creation of Israel as "a Jewish triumph, an Arab tragedy, and a British failure" (86). European domination of the post-Ottoman Middle East may be coming to an end, though the future is far from certain. Hardy dates the demise of the European hegemony in the Middle East in 1967. That was the year of Nasser's defeat in the Six-Day War. It was also the last withdrawal of the British colonizers in Yemen, handing power to the first Marxist regime in the Arab world.

The British and the French replaced the Ottomans in direct rule, but they lasted not quite half a century. He aptly recognizes the depth of anti-Western sentiment in the Muslim Core. Often Western officials dismiss such sentiment as "artificial, whipped up by a few malcontents." Hardy, realistically, terms this view as "delusion" noting that from "Khomeini and Mosaddeq, Nasser and Bin Laden all believed that the big, burning issue was standing up to the West: it was on this issue they would sink or swim" (204). In the post-Ottoman world, the Arabs have had failure after failure. Hardy's conclusion is clear: "… the West is deeply implicated in the region's failure" (205).

Oil Kings

Oil has been the curse of the Arabs. It has invited imperialism into the Muslim Core, fragmenting Islamic unity, destroying identity, and distorting development at the hands of oppressive dynasties, military dictators, and terrorists who hijacked Islam. Cooper's (2011) is a fascinating record of the latest American phase of neo-Imperialism.

During 1969–1974, the Shah, Muhammed Reza Pahlavi, was the darling of the USA. Mired in the Vietnam, the USA depended on the Shah to protect the Persian Gulf. No less than 89% of the oil consumption of the US military in Southeast Asia originated in the Gulf. Next-door Iraq was under Soviet influence, and Kuwait and Saudi Arabia were at loggerheads. Nixon and his key advisor Kissinger were anxious to secure the Gulf (19–20). Britain, Iran's former colonial overlord had pulled out its troops and a nationalist leader Mohammed Mossadegh was the strongman and Prime Minister, threatening nationalization of Iran's oil to finance social and economic development. He also had some links to the Soviets.

Palace politics, heated debates in the *Maclis*, and most significantly in the bazaars of Tehran raged, the Shah confronting his Prime Minister. Unable to pacify the domestic politics, the Shah temporarily abdicated, but the Americans helped him return and reclaim his Throne. A young ayatollah Khomeini accused the Shah of being an American puppet. He had spoken for most of the Iranians. The CIA's chief of operations at the time was Richard Helms, and the Agency's lead field officer, Kim Roosevelt, was the grandson of President Theodor Roosevelt. In August 1953, acting together with the British intelligence, the CIA team planned and carried out a coup in Tehran, code-worded Operations Ajax (22–23). The day after the Shah's return, Mosaddeq was overthrown and arrested, ending an era in Iran. For most Iranians, the United States had now replaced Britain as the foreign power pulling the strings and controlling Iran's oil wealth.

The Shah lived in a fantasy world, vainglorious, believing that he was a rightful reincarnation of Darius. In 1969, he attended the funeral of President Eisenhower in Washington, possibly the highwater mark of his reign. In the US Congress, realists such as the Senator Church, openly admitting that "… it is going to be a miracle if we save the Shah of Iran" (23). Nixon, too, had a low opinion of the Shah who constantly demanded higher oil prices, fighting with the Saudi Arabian oil minister, and the strongman in OPEC, Yamani over pricing of oil. The Shah was less interested to finance national development than making deals with the Pentagon procuring American military jets and equipment (218–219). In 1972, he purchased warplanes, F-14 and F-15 equipped with laser-guided bombs, to be used against the Iraqi dictator Saddam Hussein. He armed the Kurds in the process, in collaboration with the Nixon administration (67–68).

The shattering October 1973 Six-Day War, and the OPEC oil embargo were decisive events. Kissinger travelled to several Arab capitals as well as Israel. On 13 October he was in Riyadh meeting King Faisal, asking for help to restore stable oil prices to avert perilous conditions in Europe. "If Italy goes Communist, France will follow, and the political map of the world will change," Kissinger argued (220). The King was more interested in containing the Shah and implored Kissinger to "make the Shah see reason." Thus began the strategic American shift, abandoning the Shah and embracing the House of Saud. In Iran, the economy nose-dived amid uncontrolled inflation; the ayatollahs led the people in increasingly hostile anti-Shah demonstrations. Students and youth carried signs: "Down with the Shah," "No more for the Fascist Shah," and "US Advisors out of Iran" (381).

On 15 November 1977, the Shah visited the USA one last time. The Pahlavis and the Carters walked together. His dynasty gone; the Shah died a broken man in exile in Egypt on 27 July 1980. Power in Iran had passed on to the Ayatollahs and the Saud dynasty had become the new oil King, thanks to the American oil politics.

Neo-Imperialism at Its Worst

Iraq in the Twenty-first Century; Regime Change and the Making of a Failed State (Ismael and Ismael, 2015) is a masterful study, a humane blending of political science and sociology. The criminality of the American-led "shock and awe" invasion is amply documented. The Bush Administration invaded Iraq for regime change; but tyranny replaced dictatorship. Iraq has been ruined, its people killed or displaced by the millions. Not only Iraq, but the entire region has been systematically destabilized to serve the interest of the industrial-military complex.

The tragedy of Iraq, indeed the entire region, started with the collapse of the Ottoman Empire in WWI. It underwent several brutal phases, each one worse than the former, ultimately resulting in the US-led brutal invasion in 2003. The illegal Anglo-American invasion was a war crime, with roots in the destruction of the Ottoman Empire in WWI.

There never was a country called Iraq in Ottoman times. What British imperialism created was an "artificial" state, juxtaposing three Ottoman provinces (Mosul, Baghdad, and Basra). Similarly, in the south, Kuwait was carved out, under British protection. Behind all these imperialist schemes was the British control of the oil in Iraqi Kurdistan, Kuwait, and the Gulf.

Imperialists, old and new, do not care about the people they dominate. The British-appointed King Faisal himself questioned the existence of an "Iraqi" nation (26). The alien British model was a failure from the start. In the Revolt of 1920, the then British Secretary of State for War, Winston Churchill, a forerunner of the Bush–Blair duo, carried out the first "shock and awe" military tactic of carpet-bombing whole villages, and declaring openly: "I am strongly in favor of using poison gas against uncivilized tribes" (14). Racist stereotyping did not end with Churchill.

The British occupation lasted until 1958. Military failed state replaced colonial failure. General Qasim abolished monarchy with a sham republic. Qasim himself was overthrown in 1963, ultimately paving the way to the Ba'ath party dictatorship, a "totalitarian regime" (15) finally producing, Saddam Hussein, the granddaddy of all dictators.

Iraq in the Twenty-first Century is particularly rich in the details of the Anglo-American "orchestration of war in Iraq," (50) and the ill-conceived "neoliberalization" (60) mandate of regime change. The Bush Administration declared "mission accomplished" on May 22 2003 and secured the UN Resolution 1483 granting some degree of legitimacy to American occupation. A decade-long period of military reconstruction followed in a mixture of tyranny and anarchy (115). No weapons of mass destruction were ever found. The US occupation, built on lies and deceit, simply mirrored a confluence of military-industrial complex with neo-conservatism: "the institution of militarism within the American social fabric" (43), was crafted by Pentagon and CIA to show the Bush administration as champions of a post-9/11 global "war on terror."

In the post-Saddam era, several failed models were imposed. First Ahmed Chalabi, a Chicago-trained secular Shi'ite was proposed to lead Iraq by the neo-con circles in Washington. He shared with his American masters "a common fascination with how Kemal Ataturk (had) created the modern, secular Turkish state – seeing it as a model for the new Iraq Chalabi would lead" (57–8). Then, under Paul Bremmer's Coalition Provisional Authority (CPA) the objective shifted "to build not just democracy but a free market" (63). In the process the business class of Iraq was decimated; CPA was ended in a wave of insurgency.

Then, the US military toyed with elections. Under conditions of martial law, a strange general election was held in 2005 based on a military-drafted constitution.

The "voting reflected not a nation-state, but segmented communities in an uneasy co-existence." (65). Sectarian politics were thus institutionalized. The inconclusive 2010 elections seemed to reward only Iran (100). When President Obama declared the Iraq war officially over on August 31 2010, *The Guardian* observed: "Two million (Iraqis) remain abroad as refugees from seven years of anarchy, with another 2 million internally displaced" (96). In haste, American troops left Iraq, leaving behind a country in chaos. The power vacuum and huge quantities of war material facilitated the rise of Islamic terror movements like the Al Qaeda and ISIL.

One of the strengths of the book is its emphasis on the status of Arab women. During the long British occupation, the status of women changed little, or even regressed because "Britain aligned itself with conservative tribal and feudal forces advocating maintenance of the status quo … which undercut the Ottoman modernization efforts of the *Tanzimat* policy …" (172–173). In March 1929, the first Arab Women's Congress was held in Cairo, and the Iraqi women's club was invited to send a delegation. The invitation had to be declined; the club was "unable to name even one Iraqi woman to attend the conference" for fear of being terrorized by reactionary forces (174–175). Women's rights had to wait the overthrow of the Old Guard in Qasim's revolution of 1958 (176–177). The US occupation was especially bad for the Iraqi women, pushing them into "neo-feudal bondage" (184).

On prospects ahead, Ismael and Ismael are realistic, acknowledging that the future is "grim indeed" (201). They acknowledge realistically that the consequences of the American-led destruction of Iraq, has been a total "human catastrophe," which will be "long-lasting" (203). The American occupation led not only to Al Qaeda and ISIL brand of terrorism, but also the "stench of corruption," which has poisoned all public institutions.

The New Arab Wars

The book by Marc Lynch (2016), *The new Arab Wars, Uprisings and Anarchy in the Middle East*, is not about oil politics, neither is it about the making of the Middle East from the demise of the Ottoman Empire. It is an American perspective, a narrative written in exasperation at the American failure to build on the Arab Spring uprisings to transform the Arab countries into functioning democracies. Lynch's hypothesis is that the "Arab autocrats" resisted democratic transition and would go to any length to "prevent positive change" (xv). Still, he is not pessimistic, believing that "it is too soon to conclude that the uprisings have failed" (xiv).

According to Lynch, four overlapping lines of conflict explain the Arab chaos and anarchy: first, the Sunni–Shi'a rivalry, reinforced by Israel's priorities; second, there is the "battle for leadership of the Sunni Arab world between Saudi Arabia, Qatar, the United Arab Emirates"; third, the challenge posed by "different Islamist networks, from mainstream Muslim Brotherhood and Salafi networks to the violent extremists of al Qaeda and the Islamic State"; and finally, "a broader struggle between autocratic regimes and mobilized societies … framed by three regional wars" (44). Except for the reference to "Israel's priorities" in the first case, Lynch fails to attribute any role to third parties, and invading powers in the Arab wars. It is simplistic to argue that Arab wars are purely internal, that there has been no desta-bilizing invasion or intervention by Western powers. Lynch was a policy advisor in Washington and had strong opinions on several issues (e.g., endorsing the NATO bombings in Libya to remove Qaddafi and his critical opinion on Obama's failure to intervene in Syria). He ignores the invasion of Iraq. Accordingly, he takes as given the existing borders and assumes that somehow an enlightened United States, given a chance, could have succeed to democratize Iraq, Libya, Yemen, and other countries.

Much of Lynch's analysis is about missed opportunity for democracy. From Tunisia to Egypt and Syria, as late as 2012, there were positive signs of democratic transition. In Egypt, the parliament had gone ahead, producing a freely elected body dominated by Islamists. Morocco's king allowed the appointment of a government led by the leading Islamist Justice and Development (PJD) party, following elections in November 2011. In Qaddafi's Libya federalism was on the agenda. Egypt was the turning point. Mohammed Morsi, the narrowly elected president, misplayed his hand and attempted to grab all power. An alarmed Saudi Arabia and the UAE cut off aid and Egypt's stability was threatened, even though Qatar stepped in to help (147). As a result of these intra-Arab politics, the tide began to turn, and Arab Spring was soon a lost cause. Sisi's military coup in 2013 reversed the democratic transition, with Egypt receiving financial aid from Saudi Arabia, UAE, and Kuwait. The old dynasties, continually resisting democracy, had won out. Lynch ignores the crucial support for Sisi from the USA, blaming America's closest regional allies for Egypt's prematurely truncated experiment with democracy (155).

In the end, Lynch acknowledges only a personal word of moral failure for America's missed opportunity. "The dreams unleashed by the Arab Spring of 2011 has left far too many friends … dead, imprisoned and in exile." hoping that his book will help "to get it right next time" (255). Will there be a next time, any time soon, or ever again? As for the USA, his sober advice is that "America would be better served to consolidate its retrenchment from the region and invest its support not in its brutal regimes but in those Arabs seeking a more democratic future" (254).

The major weakness of Lynch's book is its lack of historical context. The coun-tries of the Middle East were created at the end of WWI out of intrigue, broken promises, and betrayals. Imperial interests in controlling oil were then paramount. American involvement in recent times is no different; wishful thinking is unlikely to alter that fact.

A (Levantine) Paradise Lost

When the Ottomans blundered into the WWI, they had collectively committed "suicide," gambling the future of the Empire on the outcome of the War, and in the end, they lost it all.

The Ottomans had company among the losers of the War. One of the oddest case of people who lost was that of the Levantines of Izmir. Their story is the subject of the next book selected for review here, *Paradise Lost, Smyrna 1922*, by Giles Milton (2008), a journalist and not a historian. Milton's book is well written and highly readable, a typical orientalist storytelling full of pathos for a way of life lost. In this case, the loss is suffered by what Gertrude Bell aptly called a "tribe" (20), the Levantine tribe, so prosperous and privileged that it lived in the most exclusive part of Izmir called Paradise. To the Levantines, a mixture of Greek, Armenian, Jewish, and European, the city was Smyrna, a city of tolerance reflecting the Ottoman concessions granted to the Levantine families to become intermediaries, the comprador class in the Levant trade. To the Turkmen and Muslims, the city was *Gavur* Izmir, the infidel Izmir, reflecting the social chasm between the Levantine families and the Turkish/Muslim masses who lived in poverty.

The great socioeconomic disparity was the result of Levant trade, which emerged so rapidly in the 19th century that the earlier oriental, land-based caravan routes had, by the early 20th century all but disappeared. The Ottoman state, obliged to reform and grant trade privileges to non-Muslim minorities, including lower taxes and trade dispute settlement by European, instead of Ottoman, judges, facilitated the decline of Muslim oriental trade. In 1839, a secret trade agreement was signed by the Ottoman state with Britain, granting the latter virtually tax-free importation of textiles and manufactures into the Empire. By the rules of extraterritoriality, these concessions were extended to other European states. Greeks, Armenians, and Jews quickly opted out of Ottoman citizenship and took out European passports. More significantly, Muslim merchants had no knowledge of, or trade links to Western firms in Europe. The caravan routes in Anatolia, linked to cities like Damascus, Tabriz, and Baghdad, and further afield to ancient cities in Central Asia, suffered a mortal blow.

In the second half of the 19th century, Izmir, and its hinterland (cities like Aydin and Manisa), suffered a trade reversal. Up till 1850, the value of Ottoman exports via the port of Izmir exceeded the cost of imports (Kasaba, 1988, chapter 4). During the 1860s, there was an export boom in cotton, due to the American civil war. Then economic depression followed, and wages declined. Landowners, facing reduced revenue, began borrowing and indebtedness to Jewish and Armenian *sarrafs* (moneylenders) skyrocketed, further inflaming relations between Muslim and non-Muslim communities.

The rich Levantine families, the Whittalls, Girauds, La Fontaines, and many others (Milton, 2008, 19) continued in luxury in their palatial mansions, oblivious to rising Turkish nationalism. Edward Whittall's passion was gardening. In his many glass greenhouses, he propagated rare and exotic specimens. He even had a mountain garden on the slopes of Nymph Dagh where he grew tulips and orchids, sending thousands of specimens to Kew Gardens in London, a quaint sign of loyalty and attachment to things British. Such luxury on lavish scale was normal living for the Levantine tribe. Their wealth extended to municipal politics, where permits and papers were always obtainable on demand, thanks to the intermediation of Greeks and Armenian *dragomen* (middle men); it also procured privilege at the highest level.

Whenever the Ottoman Sultans visited Izmir, inevitably they were hosted by the Levantine families, much to the resentment of the Muslims of the city.

In the end, however, it all vanished. The world of the Levantine families suddenly ended on the 9 September 1922. Having taken for granted that the Greeks would defeat the Kemalist forces, the Levantines were utterly shocked and totally unprepared at the speed at which Kemalist forces overran the Greek invaders. The city was flooded with defeated and demoralized Greek soldiers trying to escape. The dream of a Hellenic Empire was no more. Levantine families were suddenly left in the cold, totally abandoned. Their world collapsed overnight. Their Paradise was lost forever.

Whether the Levantines of Izmir could have the foresight to see the end of the Ottomans may be a matter of speculation. The point did not even enter Milton's mind. No sane person in 1919, when the Greek army landed in Izmir, could have foreseen the outcome of the next four years of war between the invaders and the Kemalist forces of national independence. The comprador class of the Levantine "tribe" was too deeply entrenched in their privileged lifestyle to know much about the national struggle launched by Mustafa Kemal, let alone develop a sympathetic understanding of it or the Turkish nationalism. Therein lay the Levantine's own "suicide." The Levantines of Smyrna lived at the top of wealth and luxury in an Ottoman Paradise, but their Paradise vanished into oblivion with the end of the Empire. Many, such as the Greek shipping magnate Onassis, managed to rebuild new fortunes; but most Levantines ended in poverty, so sadly recorded at the end of Milton's book.

★★★

The books selected above capture well the emergence of the new Middle East in the age of oil and Western economic penetration into Ottoman lands. They are short, however, on local nationalism and nation-building. This is hardly surprising. The new Arab countries of the Muslim Core failed miserably in forging new national identity, shaping a new sense of nationhood. Of all the successor states of the Ottoman Empire, only one state, Turkey, managed to mold its own national identity. The significance of the book by Milton lies precisely in its brilliant articulation of the cultural divide that existed at the time between the Muslim and Western world. A fringe non-Muslim minority like Levantines of Izmir, much to their cultural shock, was completely unaware of the national sentiments of the Muslim majority surrounding them. In their failure to adjust to Turkish nationalism lay the foundations of their tragic end.

History is written by the last victor. The Ottomans were defeated and gone in 1918. Mustafa Kemal, the ultimate victor in 1922, was the victor. His victorious army entered Izmir on 9 September 1922, only to find a city put to torch by the departing Greeks and Armenians. After the total defeat of the invading Greek army, the future Ataturk was able to replace the unequal Treaty of Sevres with a brand new one negotiated at Lausanne. A modern Turkey was created, secular and equal under international law to all modern states. The defeat and demise of the

Ottomans has been costly for the Arabs. Left at the mercy of imperialists, the masses lost all dignity, deceived and betrayed by their own dynasties and tribal chiefs.

Oil has been a curse for the Arabs. The Kemalists, so eager to forge a sovereign, modern Turkey, were willing to give it all up. For the Arabs, oil invited foreign invasion and occupation of the Muslim Core. New countries and artificial boundaries were created to suit oil interests. A few collaborating dynasties gained, while the Arab masses became victims of one failed state after another. Initially, the Arab Core endured feudal dynastic rulers, then under military dictatorships, and most recently the Arab Islam fell hostage to terrorism.

What did the Middle East lose with the Ottomans gone? The briefest answer is one word: *Multiculturalism*. Some elaboration is needed because the region needs it still, as does the world. Ottoman multiculturalism was a deliberate policy of tolerance, allowing different religious and ethnic communities, *millets*, of Muslims, Jews, Christians, and a myriad of ethnic groups in the Empire to coexist with mutual respect in relative peace and security. The Sultan's government, to varying degrees, provided peace and security in return for taxes and other obligations. Mutual respect came from custom and tradition. The system, though far from perfect, fitted very well the multiethnic world of the Middle East.

When the Sick Man finally died, so did multiculturalism and tolerance in his empire. Intolerance took over. A millennium of good relations between Turks and Armenians [known in Ottoman Empire as the *Sadık Millet*, the loyal community] suddenly burst into an ethnoreligious inferno provoked by imperialist powers, the Tsarist Russia in particular. Similarly, colonial Divide and Rule fragmented the Ottoman Arab *millet* and opened the floodgates of the Arab-Jewish conflict. Gladstone's "Bag and Baggage" policy had earlier set ablaze the entire Ottoman Balkans in an unprecedented policy of ethnic cleansing, with its final genocidal finale delayed till the breakup of former Yugoslavia almost a century later.

In its last phase, when it was too late, the Ottoman intellectuals toyed with three alternative ideologies: Turkism, Pan-Islamism, and Ottomanism. These were made-at-home substitutes for the French Revolution ideals of Liberty, Equality, and Fraternity. Ottomanism was a feeble inspiration, intended to make official the idea of multiculturalism around the Sultanate in its deathbed. It died a most violent death in the holocaust of the Balkan wars for which Gladstone must bear heavy responsibility. Turkish refugees and survivors of this holocaust trekked into Asia Minor having bitterly learnt that nationalism is the foundation of a Homeland.

WWI ended Pan-Islamism. Arabs and non-Turkish Muslims who fought the Ottoman armies, rallying behind the calls of Lawrence, Kitchener, McMahon, and Churchill, killed more than their fellow Muslim Turks. They killed a defunct ideology. That, by the way, is why Mustafa Kemal, fighting imperialism in the deserts of Libya, Palestine, and in the steppes of Anatolia, had had enough of Islam, the Caliphate, and the Sultanate. Kemalist ideology replaced *millet* with *ulus*, ethnic nationalism, and Anatolia emerged as the Turkish homeland. Kemal redefined identity and put the Turkish nation on the road to modernity. "*Peace at home, peace abroad*" and "*What a privilege is to be able to call oneself Turk*" became the new slogans.

Turkish nationalism emerged late in the Empire. Halide's passion, so poignantly described at the beginning of Hardy (2017, 7) and Mustrafa Kemal's iron-clad vision and determination (Mango, 1999) represented a winning formula. It was sheer genius that Kemal went beyond the French Revolutionary ideals and embraced *Laicism* (secularism) as the cornerstone of the Republic. Mustafa Kemal created a political space, freed from the shackles of religion, that would allow national development based on basic freedoms, equality of all citizens, gender equity, and rule of law, to take root and flourish.

In the Arab Middle East, no such transformation occurred. Nation-building, a long-term process of economic, social, cultural, and political development, requires social grounding, mobilization of support from the grassroots up to the top. Even the oil-rich Arab countries are still at the early stages of such development, a century since WWI, dependent more on guest-workers than on their own human resources.

Nostalgia for an Empire Lost

Hakan Yavuz's book, *Nostalgia for the Empire: The Politics of Neo-Ottomanism* (2020), is about an Empire lost and its traumatic impact on Turkish consciousness. A sense of loss, nostalgia for past glory vanished, is very much ingrained in modern Turkish identity. "Bizler hüzünlü milletiz" (We are a nation of melancholy) (2). *Hüzün* is the key, a longing for a birthplace, rebellion against top-down modernity, or personal dissatisfaction with the human condition. Yavuz borrowed the idea of *Hüzün* from the great novelist Hamdi Tanpınar, the author of *The Time Regulation Institute*, the Turkish version of George Orwell, an attempt to reshape consciousness in some crazy Freudian experiment. Tanpınar's antihero, Ayarcı (Regulator), is a psychoanalyst gone mad in the new Kemalist Republic, dedicated to constructing a new citizen in total subservience to an authoritarian state.

Yavuz's Neo-Ottomanism is a personal account. He experienced tensions first in his childhood years in Bayburt in eastern Anatolia, attempting to reconcile Kemalist modernity with the Ottoman-Islamic heritage. During his university career in the United States, he observed the Bosnian genocide and the destruction of the last Ottoman community in Europe. Two specific elements have shaped Yavuz's view of Neo-Ottomanism. First, it represents "a pluralistic view of Turkishness, a weapon against Kemalist secularism (13)." Ottomanism was an inclusive, multinational identity. It did not fit into the modern world of nation-states. Second, the EU's nonaction of Turkey's membership, demonstrating the dead end of the top-down "Westernizing orientation" of the Kemalist Republic (2). The rejection was a wake-up call, forcing the Turks to turn to their endogenous roots of identity. For most Europeans, conditioned by their Christian heritage, the Turks were always before the "gates" in Europe, Vienna in 1683 or Brussels in 1987. Such internal and external forces and perceptions have shaped contemporary ideas of Neo-Ottomanism. One cannot remove the past from the present. Ottoman-Islamic heritage was suddenly taken out of the Kemalist closet and (re)embraced as an indispensable part of the Turkish soul today. Most Turks today feel a sense of national insecurity, remembering how close their homeland came to extinction at the end of WWI. Yavuz calls this insecurity the "Sevres Syndrome (ibid., 37)." With the end of Westernization, turning to one's roots, history and heritage is natural. For Turkey, delinking from Europe has been a gradual process. In 1960, after the Menderes years, Ankara still aimed at closer integration with Europe, signing a Protocol with Brussels, which identified as a target eventual Turkish membership of what became the EU. At the same time, a Turkish Islamic synthesis was underway, and an early attempt was made at "Turkification of Ottoman history" (ibid., 55).

Neo-Ottomanism as a contemporary political agenda goes back to Turgut Özal, the neoliberal reformer in Turkish politics, who surprised Turks and Europeans alike with his sudden application to Brussels back in 1987. In fact, Özal himself can be considered as an early proponent of Neo-Ottomanism. For Özal, "a Turk is someone who is Muslim by religion and an Ottoman by shared history and memories" (ibid., 110). His political success stemmed from coalitions with Anatolian entrepreneurs, who eventually became Erdoğan's supporters. These Anatolian bourgeois possessed their own culture and their own Kurdish, Alevi, and ethnic traditions, steeped in Ottoman-Islamic heritage, very alive still with Sufi sects such as the Nakshibendi, Nurcu, and others, which Atatürk had disbanded but could not eradicate. Yavuz's chapter 3 gives a rich account of these sects, including their impact not only on politics but on popular arts, literature, and media. The Gülen Movement, as it was called at the time, ingrained itself within this popular culture and, by the time of the 2016 coup attempt, FETÖ (Fetullahçı Terör Örgütü, Fetullah's Terror Organization) had become a real threat to the constitutional order.

Yavuz makes it quite clear that there are many versions of Neo-Ottomanism, discussing, besides Özal, variations introduced by Erbakan, and numerous others. In Ottoman times, each Sultan had his brand of ideology. Erdoğan may champion Abdulhamit, sharing his mistrust of Europe. Little wonder, too, that Neo-Ottomanism, as a Turkish foreign policy, has met with such firm resistance in former Ottoman lands in the Balkans and the Arab countries. Understandably, people's memories are short and, even then, only the worst is often remembered; for example, Cemal Paşha's brutal execution of Arab intellectuals when he served as the Sultan's Governor in Syria. However, for the present generation of Anatolian Turks, encouraged by Erdoğan, nostalgic search for Ottoman heritage is a widespread pastime. Yavuz's book is a beautiful illustration of this fact.

References

Aksakal, Mustafa, 2008, *The Ottoman Road to War in 1914, The Ottoman Empire and the First World War*, Cambridge: Cambridge University Press.

Anderson, Scott, 2013, *Lawrence in Arabia, War, Deceit, Imperial Folly and the Making of the Modern Middle East*, New York: Signal.

Coles, Juan, 2022, www.ingentaconnect.com/contentone/intellect/jciaw/2021/00000015/00000003/art0000 3, accessed on 7 Feb. 2022.

Cooper, Andrew Cooper, 2011, *Oil Kings, How the US, Iran and Saudi Arabia Changed the Balance of Power in the Middle East*, New York: Simon and Shuster.

Earle, Edward Mead, 1923, *Turkery, The Great Powers and The Baghdad Railway*, Russell & Russell, New York.

Fromkin, David, 1989, *A Peace to End All Peace: The Fall of the Ottoman Empire and the Creation of the Modern Middle East*, New York: Avon Books.

Hardy, Roger, 2017, *The Poisoned Well, Empire and Its Legacy in the Middle East*, New York: Oxford University Press.

Ismael, Tareq Y. and Jacqueline Ismail, 2015, *Iraq in the Twenty-first Century; Regime Change and the making of a Failed State*, London and New York: Routledge.

Kasaba, Resat, 1988, *The Ottoman Empire and the World Economy, The Nineteenth Century*, State University of New York, Albany.

Lynch, Marc, 2016, *The New Arab Wars: Uprisings and Anarchy in the Middle East*, New York: Public Affairs.

Mango, Andrew, 1999, *Atatürk, the Biography of the Founder of Modern Turkey*, New York, Overlook Press.

McMeekin, Sean. 2010, *The Berlin-Baghdad Express: The Ottoman Empire and Germany's Bid for World Power*, Boston: Belknap Press of Harvard University Press.

McMeekin, Sean, 2016, *The Ottoman Endgame, War, Revolution and the Making of the Modern Middle East, 1908–1923*, New York: Penguin Books.

Rogan, Eugene, 2015. *The Fall of the Ottomans, the Great War in the Middle East*, New York: Basic Books.

Yavuz, Hakan M., 2020, *Nostalgia for the Empire: The Politics of Neo-Ottomanism*, New York: Oxford University Press.

4

THE ROOTS OF ISLAMIC UNDERDEVELOPMENT

From Mercantilism to Imperialism

The rise of the West began when capitalism replaced mercantilism, the turning point being the publication of the Scot Adam Smith's *The Wealth of Nations* (1776). Ideas always led institutional development. Smith and other thinkers cumulatively shaped the Eurocentric system built on Western hegemony, an aggressive enterprise created to enrich the West and impoverish the Rest (Mehmet, 1999, Mahbubani, 1992). The Eurocentric economic system has gone through several phases, the latest being neo-imperialism, often called globalization. It is an unequal economic system in which the self-interest of the West is always uppermost, and all means, gunboat diplomacy or military invasion, are utilized to penetrate resource-rich lands globally in search of wealth, originally gold from the Aztecs and the Maya that flooded Europe via Spain and financed the Industrial Revolution.

Before Western capitalist system, the hub of the world trading system was in Muslim lands, centered in the Levant. Prosperity was in the East: Alexandria, Damascus on the Mediterranean: Yemen, Aden on the Red Sea, Zanzibar in East Africa, all participated in the Ottoman international trade. As the Circle of Equity, quoted at the outset of this book exemplifies, the Ottoman statecraft placed subjects' welfare at the heart of Islamic justice as the Ottomans understood it. Earlier, before the Ottomans, the Abbasid Caliphate in Baghdad was the center of high culture. Cultural hubs included Samarkand, Bukhara, and trade-based prosperity made it all possible. The Selcuk Turks were traders, Anatolia is still dotted with their *kervansarays* and caravan routes. Muslim trade reached as far as Timbuctoo in the western end of the Sahel, while sea trade linked Zanzibar on the African coast, Aceh in the Indonesian Archipelago, and Caffe in the Crimea Tataristan. The Balkans were, of course, the Ottoman heartland of *Rumeli*, the land of Romanized Christians, and *Türkeli*, the Turkish homeland stretched from Anatolia to Central Asia. Islamic civilization was supreme in the world, and European traders like Marco Polo trekked through Muslim lands to China in search of wealth and knowledge, the land of

DOI: 10.4324/9781003268994-4

innovation, where paper, gunpowder, and, most importantly, silk (to name only a few) were introduced. Europe was primitive and backward.

Yale historian Alan Mikhail's book, *God's Shadow: The Ottoman Sultan who Shaped the Modern World* (Mikhail, 2020) is a superb account of the global transformation launched by the Ottoman Sultan Selim, who, unintentionally, gave birth to Western mercantilism. Now, the USA is being overtaken by China. A new Silk Road Economy (SRE) is unfolding, the theme of another major book, by Oxford historian Peter Frankopan, *The Silk Roads, A New History of the World* (Frankopan, 2018), through Muslim lands of Central Asia, Caucuses, and the Middle East. Combined, these books signal the birth of a new, hopefully, a better world than the capitalist system built on inequality and injustice. Islamic social contract is potentially available to shape a more humane world order in future.

The world economy has always lacked an equitable foundation. Machiavellian power and Darwinian selection of the fittest have shaped the economy. This was always true, in the Ottoman period as well, right down to the contemporary multinational capitalist system. In the quarter century prior to WWI, social Darwinism was a major philosophical and political movement in England. Joseph Chamberlain expressed the prevailing general opinion in 1895:

> I believe in this race, the greatest governing race the world has ever seen: in this Anglo-Saxon race, so proud, tenacious, self-confident and determined, this race which neither climate nor change can degenerate, which will infallibly be the predominant force in future history and universal civilization.
>
> *Quoted in Evans (2017, 684)*

In the future, if ever a new SRE is realized, new ideas and institutions will have to be developed, going beyond racist world views and physical infrastructural investment, learning from the past to build a more humane world order.

The Modern Era, 1453

Our modern world emerged out of the age of medieval dark ages, in 1453 when Mehmet, the Conqueror triumphed in Istanbul. After a 54-day siege, lasting from 6 April to 29 May, the city became Turkish, and the world changed forever.

Why did Mehmet succeed? He had a superior army, equipped with the latest warfare technology, especially cannons larger than anything that had yet been seen. His army, maybe 50,000 against 8,500 defenders, was extremely well disciplined and well-motivated. Meticulous in detail, with an iron-clad determination, Mehmet had left nothing for chance. He first gained control of the Bosphorus by building the *Rumeli* Hisarı on the European side, opposite Anadolu Hisarı built by his grandfather Bayezid (Inalcik, 1973, 25). Henceforth all ships sailed only with his permission through the Bosphorus. But the city under attack was well fortified, the strongest fortifications of the Middle Ages, and the storming of the walls required a superhuman effort. It was Mehmet's genius and iron determination that prevailed.

Mehmet prevailed, not only because he had the best soldiers, but also because he was well prepared with diplomacy and, above all, in technology. In diplomacy, Mehmet's Sadrazam Çandarlı had already secured peace treaties with Hungary and Venice, two of the strongest Christian powers at the time. In warfare technology, Mehmet was an innovator, transporting his fleet overnight and overland into Haliç, a daring maneuver that demoralized a city population that realized the end was near.

There were also other contributing factors, uppermost, the ransacking of Constantinople by the Fourth Crusade. The fight between the Latin and Orthodox Churches had been costly. When the Crusaders descended on the city in 1204, they carried out the greatest genocide the world had witnessed. The city was looted as its most precious icons and monuments were carted away to embellish Rome and Venice. In the century before becoming Turkish, the Byzantium capital had been so depopulated, it was reduced to a skeleton. When the last and fateful attack was launched on 29 May, led by the elite *yenicheri* corps, the custom required three days of pillage for the victorious soldiers to cart away, as war booty, whatever they could. But Mehmet did not allow that. He marched into the ruined city, walked into the Hagia Sophia, prayed, and proclaimed: "Hereafter my capital is Istanbul" (Inalcik, 26).

Then, Mehmet did the most incredible, and unexpected: He did not build a Turkish city. No power could have stopped him from populating the ruined, virtually deserted city with the Turkmen tribes and start a purely Turkified nation-building. The idea of nation-building did not exist at the time. Mehmet was guided by *Şeriat*, the Muslim law that recognized Christians and Jews as people of the Book. He invited the Greeks who had fled the city earlier to come back and resume their lives unmolested. In fact, he went further: He executed the old Çandarlı who had opposed the conquest, and appointed Gennadius, who had earlier opposed the union between the Orthodox and Roman churches, as the Orthodox patriarch, and ordered him to compose a treatise summarizing the principles of Christianity (Inalcik, 29).

Mehmet had an unforgiving, ruthless understanding of power, a model for Machiavelli. Once he sat on the throne of the Caesars, he claimed all the territories of the Eastern Roman Empire. He remained a devout Muslim, but wanting no challenge to his power; he ordered the execution of his brother Orhan, and the death of his younger brother Ahmed by strangulation, setting the brutal precedent of fratricide for later Sultans. Mehmet the Conqueror started the Modern Era, but he also created several of the contradictions. He chose Islam over Turkish identity, preferring a multiethnic Empire governed by Islamic law, but his understanding of Law was more Turkish than Islamic, man-made rather than divine and canonical, and tolerant of minorities. He institutionalized a merit system based on master–slave relations, *Kul*, whereby all, including the life of the servant, belonged to the master.

The Ottoman System at Its Zenith

The last Muslim-majority empire ruling vast parts of Christian Europe, the Balkans, Crimea, the Caucuses, as well as Muslim lands in the Middle East and North Africa, was the Ottoman Empire. It was a multiethnic Empire, although the ruling elite was Turkish. At its zenith (Inalcik, 1973), it was a trade-based, guided by tolerance of "People of the Book," Jews and Christians. Under the Ottoman Merit system, non-Muslims could rise to the top in one centralized system once they converted to Islam. Raised under the *Devşirme* system, all were *Kuls*, literally slaves of the Sultan. Until the conquest of Istanbul, Turks had been the holders of the highest office, *Sadrazam* (prime minister). During the Conqueror's reign, Greeks and Albanians replaced the Turks as the *Devşirme* became institutionalized. Surprisingly, despite its Muslim character, very few Arabs emerged under the merit system, in fact not more than two or three, to become *Sadrazam* (Wikipedia, 2021).

Two of the most successful cases of the *Devşirme* system were Ibrahim and Sinan, the former Süleyman's Greek origin *Sadrazam*, and the latter of Albanian origin who became the Royal Architect. Süleyman, the law giver, became the first legally married Sultan, marrying Roxalena, originally a Russian slave, whose power exceeded that of Ibrahim's. *Devşirme* was essentially a Slave System under an all-powerful Sultan, pitting the converted elite in constant competition with the Turkmen aristocracy. The Sultan ruled, atop an Islamic social contract, articulated by the Circle of Equity (II&D, 64), answerable to God for ruling a harmonious society whose institutions rested on Justice. As always, the system worked superbly during times of prosperity, enriched by steady supply of revenue at the time of conquering sultans; it fell into disrepute when trade based prosperity was no longer an option.

An Ottoman Traveler: Evliya Çelebi

At the pinnacle of their power, the Ottoman world is best described in the ten-volume masterpiece, *Seyahatname* by Evliya Çelebi (1611–1684). It is nothing short of a magnificent door to a yet little-known, magical garden of knowledge. It is summarized in a recent book, expertly edited and translated by Dankoff and Kim, Selections from *The Book of Travels* by Evliya Çelebi (2011). In Dankoff and Kim's Çelebi, the reader will find exotic descriptions of Cairo and African animals like giraffes and crocodiles in Sudan. Rich diversity comes to life from the bazaars of Damascus, the Anatolian *kervansarays*, the gardens of Bahçesaray in the Khanate of Tatars, to the oil fields of Baku. The Siege of Malta, the conquest of Crete, and Safavid Persian borderlands in the Caucuses are recounted with a keen eye, all of which still make a fascinating reading, more than three centuries later.

Undoubtedly, the most amazing parts of Dankoff and Kim's volume are Çelebi's accounts of his portrayal of the late medieval Europe. It is written with an incredible degree of confidence, bordering on arrogance, of a devout Muslim. Europe is *Kafiristan*, the land of unbelieving Franks, Germans, and others. Normal is Islam, the land of Islam, *Dar-ul-Islam* expands in all directions, its domain extending in the West from Hungary to Persia and Central Asia in the East, from Sudan in Africa to Crimea and Ukraine in the North. With a haughty sense of superiority, Çelebi looks down upon the poor peasants of Hungary, Poland, and the petty Kings and

Princes of Germania and elsewhere. These are lands and resources weakly defended, ready for exploitation. The reader gets a fascinating insider story of the precarious relations between the Ottomans and the Hapsburgs. Çelebi describes his own adventures in these border regions when he joins the Ottoman *Gazi* warriors and *Yenicheri* troops, backed by Tatar regulars and irregulars on various campaigns. Every season, these border raiders, *akincilar*, go on campaigns for war booty, collecting slaves and valuables. In one case, Çelebi writes of an attack in a city in Holland, in obvious exaggeration or mythology, "10,000 infidels fell captive in this raid. God be praised, my share of the booty was one girl, one boy and seven horses" (190).

In 1665 Çelebi was in Vienna, the Golden Apple to the Ottomans. Churches, cathedrals, and two other things impressed Evliya: Watches and the free conduct of women. "All the infidel notables and sophisticates" of the city he wrote, "take their pleasure for weeks and months … their darling boys and lovely girls swim in the river that flows through the city" (231). He records:

> 5,500 shops … each worth an Egyptian treasure … And the shops are unequalled in the operation of wonderful objects and strange instruments. Alarm clocks, clocks marking prayer times, or the month and day, or the sign of the zodiac … all are functioning (232).

Çelebi had an audience with the young Habsburg Emperor Leopold I, whom he impressed easily with his knowledge of Christian holy places in Jerusalem. Two years later his audience was none other than Sultan Mehmed IV. In 1683 the Ottoman army was at the Gates of Vienna. They had come in response to request for aid by the French monarch, an archrival of the Habsburgs. When Evliya Çelebi died, the Ottoman expansion had reached its territorial limit. The rout in Vienna was followed by two and a half centuries of slow death when the Sultanate was finally abolished in 1922.

The Ottoman Trading System

The Ottoman state had become a world Empire under Mehmet the Conqueror, but it reached its zenith in the following century when Ottomans were the global superpower. Sultan Selim I conquered Egypt in 1517, for the first time the Ottoman Empire became a majority Muslim empire. Selim's victory made his vast Empire the center of the global economy. "Not since the days of the Roman Empire had the Black, Red, Caspian and Mediterranean seas been governed by a single polity" (Mikhail, 2020, 309–310). Trade and economic policy played a central role in Selim's conquest of Egypt and the Mameluke Empire. "When Piri Reis presented Selim with his world map in Cairo, the sultan, smartly had wagered on East over West" (327). Now the center of global trade was in Ottoman hands, and opportunities for trade expansion eastward had a magnetic effect on Selim. Yemen, at the entry of the Red Sea, was a strategic location and gave Selim several trade advantages. First, it allowed Selim to place an embargo on overland silk trade with Iran, thanks to his decisive victory over the Safavid dynasty in 1514 at Caldiran. Iranian silk merchants were now obliged to divert their trade to maritime routes, earning Selim's treasury handsome revenue from custom duties. No less significantly, Yemen opened the possibility of creating trade links with India and further east as far as Malacca. Already there were Muslim emissaries trekking to Selim's court in Edirne, seeking his protection against the Portuguese who were now making aggressive moves in the Indian Ocean. Lisbon's representatives in the Indian subcontinent started sending worrying messages to the headquarters: "The harbor of Diu is waiting for the Ottomans with open arms" (327–328). Similar demands came from the Muslim rulers in Malacca. Clearly, Selim's conquest of the Mameluke Empire had transformed the Ottoman Empire into the heart of the global trade system.

The Ottoman trading revenues financed imperial prosperity and led to good governance in accordance with the Circle of Equity, in which Sultan's authority and mercy reigned supreme. But the Sultan was also the springhead of Justice, and it was his divine duty to ensure that his governance was just. After Selim, his only son Süleyman carried on where his father had left off. Known as the Lawgiver to the Muslims, and Magnificent in the West, Süleyman was the ideal ruler, a man of the Renaissance, yet always guided by Islam. He was a dedicated disciplinarian, obsessed with the rule of law, as he saw it. In 1553, acting on dubious charges of treason, he ordered the death of his eldest son, Mustafa, and punished with death his childhood friend and devoted Prime Minister Ibrahim, otherwise another successful case of the *Devşirme*. Himself a poet, he employed a palace full of scribes, calligraphers, immortalized in the novel, *My Name Is Red* by the Nobel laurate, Orhan Pamuk and record-keepers to codify laws, promote Islamic arts, and update and enforce trade regulations. A man of Renaissance, he was fully aware of the works of Italian masters and Luther, and patronized masters in every field, paying especial interest in architecture, building magnificent mosques and monuments that, even today, glorify not only the skies of Istanbul, but many cities and towns all over the former lands of the Ottomans.

The Ottoman Sultanate personified Machiavellian power and Darwinian survival of the fittest. Selim and his son, Süleyman the Magnificent, represented role models for Machiavelli's masterpiece, *The Prince*, offering advice on how to win and keep power in politics. In its heyday, the Ottoman merit system made no distinction based on religion or ethnicity. All subjects of the multinational empire, Muslim, Jewish, or Christian, were equal, effectively slave subjects, all possessions, indeed the life of the subject, belonging to the Sultan.

When, under Süleyman the Magnificent, the Ottoman Empire reached its zenith, Spain was the rising Christian power. Isabella-Ferdinand launched their Catholic *crusade*, the Inquisition, their ruthless act of ethnic cleansing. The systematic expulsion of Muslims from Europe had begun. The homeless Moors moved to North Africa, many entering the Sultan's service in the Ottoman armies and navy. For the Jews, the Ottoman Empire became the New Jerusalem, "a paradise for the Jews" (Mikhail, 173). Jews, with gold and skills, flooded into Istanbul. Salonica quickly emerged as "the Jerusalem of the Balkan." In 1430, it had about 2,500 Jewish families; by 1533, the number had risen to 20,000 (Mikhail, 176–177).

For centuries before, technical knowledge had been in Muslim hands, but it began to weaken during the Abbasid Caliphate in Baghdad, well before it fell to the Ottomans in 1520. *The Gate of Ijtihad* (the closing of the gate of independent knowledge, critical thinking) was declared closed in the 10th century (II& D, 60–61); henceforth, no original thinking was allowed. Thereafter the Arab Core entered a new age of *Jahiliya* (ignorance), *taqlid* (rote-learning) became the new standard. In 1517, when Sultan Selim entered Cairo at the head of his victorious army, Spain had already emerged as the powerful state in the West. When Muslim Spain vanished, Moors scattered all over north Africa, the homeless became mercenaries, pirates, and some willingly became crew for Columbus. On his four ships sailing to the New World, Some Arab sailors in Columbus's crew were knowledgeable on the latest navigational maps and skills and Arab "teachers" taught Columbus what they knew (Mikhail, 125).

For the next century, the Mediterranean became a sea of contest between a Christian Europe, led by Spain, and the Ottomans. A great naval rivalry emerged between "Charles and Doria, and Süleyman and Barbarossa" (Crowley, 2008, 65). Tunis, Algeria, all North Africa became Ottoman, but the Ottomans did not look beyond Gibraltar toward the Atlantic; they focused their attention on the Orient. The conquest of Cyprus in 1571 was the last great Ottoman victory. Finally, at Lepanto, "Europe's Trafalgar" (288), a Christian armada, organized and funded by the Pope, overcame the Ottoman navy and all Europe celebrated. The Age of Mercantilism, centered on the Atlantic, had truly begun.

Selim's Conquest of Cairo

Selim II was not only a conquering Sultan, but a good administrator. He was the best example of the institutionalized system, which ensured that the sons of the reigning Sultan were first trained as provincial governors, learning the skills of city government, trade regulation, and delivering justice to the people of the region under his rule. Selim, in his youth had served at Trabzon and under his governorship the town, with its Pontus Greek heritage, prospered (Mikhail, 63–65). When he launched his Egyptian campaign, he defeated the Mameluke army at Marj Dabiq; the Sultan Al-Ghawri was killed in battle, but his successor Tuman bey continued to resist. Safavids, still smarting from Caldiran, could not come to the aid of Mamelukes. Selim marched triumphantly into the trading hub of Aleppo, where the townspeople welcomed him for delivering them from the oppression of the Mamelukes. He began with administrative and judicial reform, assuring traders of his protection, in exchange for their loyalty. It was the same when he led his army into Damascus; he immediately called "a meeting in which he assured Damascus's leaders that he would protect their authority as long as they recognized the sovereignty of their new Ottoman governor (292)." As an additional gesture, Selim took special action to venerate the town's saint, Ibn-Arabi, reputedly the spiritual advisor of Osman, the founder of the Ottoman dynasty (295).

While in Jerusalem, Selim met representatives of the Armenian, Coptic, and Abyssinian churches, as well as heads of the Rabbinate and assured them that their rituals and practices, including their properties, would be respected under the Ottoman rule. In fact, he increased the stipends of the Franciscan friars in the Church of the Holy Sepulchre and reduced the visa fees for Christian pilgrims.

When Cairo became Ottoman, a city of half a million, now swelled by flooding of refugees, was desperate, markets and trade stagnant. Selim celebrated his victory by announcing reforms and good governance: "he recognized longstanding property holdings, renewed the assignment of market inspectors and other vital officials, and kept tax rates essentially the same" (308). Similar administrative systems were introduced in the North African and Red Sea provinces. Cairo now became the second biggest city of Islam after Istanbul, and Selim became the mightiest Muslim ruler of his time, "servant of the two sacred cities, the victorious King Selim Shah" (309). At Cairo, Selim was only 46 at his prime of his youth and power. Mikhail explains a curious ceremony at which the Sultan was presented the new map of Piri Reis, which included *Vilayet Antilla* and parts of the American coast. Piri Reis advised the Sultan to conquer next the New World. But Selim looked East, leaving the New World to the Spanish and the Portuguese.

The Social Quality of Life under the Ottomans

Ottoman administration in Arab provinces was based on Islamic customs and jurisdiction. Islam as a common religion was a huge advantage, acting as a solid foundation on which to build durable institutions and codify Islamic law. The Ottomans, dedicated to man-made laws and obsessed with record-keeping, built on the Islamic foundation an elaborate system of provincial administration. Rich Ottoman archives of reports, *firmans*, and regulations are still largely unexplored. They have only been researched in recent times, thanks to the pioneering works of Halil Inalcik (1973, 1994, I & II) and his students. The brief documentation summarized in the following pages is primarily based on this research. Surprisingly, leading Arab historians have tended to ignore this wealth of scholarship (Issawi, 1995).

Following conquest, a new Ottoman *sanjak* was created under a military governor (*sanjak beyi*). The territory was a reward from the sovereign, and sometimes it was designated as "sovereign sanjak" (Inalcik, 1973, 104). In 1553, the *beylerbeyilik* of Algiers was created under Hayreddin Barbarossa, the highly successful grand admiral. Barbarossa was also successful in administration, creating no more than 13 sanjaks in Algiers known as *eyalets* or districts. In this he was following the model that applied throughout the Empire. Inalcik has provided a list of 33 such districts (1973, 106), almost half of which were in Arab territories.

Land was of special significance and the Ottomans provided extensive rules and regulations for ownership, inheritance, and transactions. Mehmet the Conqueror reviewed all land holdings in about 1470, and regulated the *vakif* system of endowments, ensuring that these trusts were guaranteed under the protection of the state. Any land not thus registered reverted to the state, becoming *miri* land, that is state-owned. This enabled the central government to expand the *timar* system, land grants especially useful in the cavalry-raising provinces. *Vakifs* were especially significant as religious endowments, sustaining orders, which often run Islamic charity and served as centers of mysticism. After each conquest, land registers were prepared, for taxing villages and households, and fiefdoms created, typically as *timar-holding sipahi* (cavalry) in exchange for land grants, a fiefdom would be obliged to raise a cavalry that constituted part of the Ottoman army (108).

The Ottoman Sultan was supreme and different sultans applied Islamic justice differently. But all conquering sultans were eager to build mosques and public buildings to ensure their legacy. Perhaps the greatest such sultan was Suleyman the Magnificent. There is no better example anywhere in the world of a ruler-architect partnership than of Suleyman with Sinan, the royal architect who built not only the glorious Süleymaniye in Istanbul, but as well the citadel and the Damascus Gate in Jerusalem (Stratton, 1972, 104), and countless monuments all over the Empire.

At its height, the state delivered high-quality Muslim justice through the *Kadi* system of courts that governed marriages, inheritance, and civil matters. *Kadi* was a jurist trained in *medrese*, Islamic college, an expert in law, the *Sharia*, subdivided into an intricate system of branches and disciplines. There were strict rules of procedure, evidence, and precedent and the quality of justice delivered was high, comparing highly favorably with equivalent institutions in Europe, where serfdom prevailed, and peasants lived at the mercy of lords, knights, and clergy, often subject to religious wars and conflicts, and intolerance was a way of life.

The Case of Nablus: This was a typical Arab town of 8,000 persons. An analysis of 107 marriage contracts recorded as late as 1750–1858 is revealing (Faroqhi et al., 1994, 785). Much depended on family wealth and status. Upper class and wealthier families often married cousins, typically minor females having no choice to keep land and wealth in the family. This social system ensured that upper-strata families sustained their privilege through generations. For lower-status women, marriage often was the only opportunity for upward social mobility and wealth accumulation through *mahr*, dowry. Custom and *Sharia* governed the determination of dowry, negotiated between contracting families. Interestingly, in Nablus the records indicate that little significance was attached to virginity and remarriage carried no stigma. On the other hand, polygamy was not the norm in the town, only 16% of men surveyed had more than one wife.

Trade was the key to Ottoman prosperity, and regulation of trade and markets constituted a major part of central and provincial administration. Tax revenue from duties levied on the movement of goods on trade routes was the lifeblood of the Empire. While the state built *kervansarays* (inns), and ensured safety of merchants on the trade routes, a steady inflow of custom receipts ensured the smooth running of the state.

The Damascus-Bursa Trade

A Florentine traveler, Bertrandon de la Brocquiere left a description of his journey along a land route from Damascus to Bursa in 1452 (124–125). In Damascus he was fortunate to join a group of pilgrims and merchants returning from Mecca with a caravan of 3,000 camels. The journey to Bursa took 55 days. When he reached Bursa, he found several Genoese and Florentine merchants engaged in the spice trade but primarily in silk products. Trade in Persian silk was the mainstay of the Bursa market, and at the time, a major international market for raw silk, as well as extremely fine silk textiles for Europe. The silk trade fetched huge profits. In Italy, one fardello (150 kilos) yielded a profit of 70 or 80 gold ducats. During the period, 1467–1494, the price of silk rose 40% in 1488. About 1,000 silk looms worked five fardello of silk a day.

The caravan trade to Damascus was wholly in the hands of Muslim merchants. Merchant shipping likewise was in Muslim hands managing the extensive networks from Gujerat to Atjeh. Highly prosperous Muslim merchant houses were not uncommon, and it was normal for these Muslim traders to extend lines of credit to Venetian and Western merchants. Trade disputes were settled in kadi courts in all Islamic lands, and the Oriental spice trade operated under a system of Islamic internationalism (Inalcik, 1994, 346).

In Damascus and Bursa, indeed in the Ottoman trading system, Italian and European merchants only handled merchandise destined for European markets. Damascus was a hub on land routes linked to other trading centers in cities like Baghdad, Cairo, and pilgrimage to Mecca was part of the Indian trade. Indian cloth and Indonesian spices were important merchandise. In 1562, custom revenue in Damascus amounted to 110,000 gold ducats (Inalcik, 1973, 127). The annual pilgrimage to Mecca was big business. Once over the Taurus Mountains, various land routes on which merchants and pilgrims travelled in caravans from Istanbul and points in Anatolia, converged on Damascus, and from there on to Mecca.

Although Muslim merchant families emerged and played a significant role in the zenith of Ottoman power, the Muslim trading system had one major deficiency: it could not sustain capital accumulation. Muslim law of inheritance required subdivision of family assets upon death. This did not apply in the case of the large and heterogeneous Orthodox community. Thus, after the peak of the Ottoman power, as European economic penetration into Ottoman lands became increasingly aggressive, Greeks, Armenians, and even Bulgarian and Albanians emerged as wealthy merchant families (Faroqhi et al., 1994, 705). Gradually, an internal shift of trade wealth and power passed out the hands of Muslims in such mercantile hubs as Damascus and Bursa, but generally throughout the multinational Empire.

The negative impact of the *Sheri 'at* in the case of Ottoman mercantile system also prevented the development of an Islamic banking institutions. The ban on interest rate effectively allowed credit and moneylending to become monopoly of Armenian and Jewish *sarrafs*. During the classical period of the Empire, this was not a problem, as all ethnic groups, Muslim, and non-Muslim, were treated fairly and reciprocated with equal loyalty to the Sultan. However, it hastened the demise of the Empire when indebtedness undermined Ottoman power and the non-Muslim subjects were obliged to shift their loyalties to Europeans.

The Ottoman Custom Zones, Taxes, and Slave Trade

At its height, the Ottoman trading system financed imperial prosperity as in the Circle of Equity, the Islamic ethical code for good governance, most succinctly summarized by Ibn Haldun (II&D, 1999, 64). With no income tax, indirect taxation was the core of the Imperial fiscal system, levied primarily on trade and land. Land taxes were nominal compared to taxation on trade, typically tax farming.

The Ottoman trading system was truly global (Inalcik, 1973, chapters 13 and 14). Spices came from the Orient; Chinese porcelain and merchandise moved along the Silk Route. The China trade was linked to the Black Sea trading ports like Kaffa, Azov, Taman, and Trabzon. Beyond the Caspian Sea, Samarkand, and Central Asia were trading hubs linking the Ottoman and Oriental worlds. Slaves came from Africa through the Red Sea and Alexandria. Italian traders, Venetians, Genoese, Florentines, Phanariot Greeks were at the forefront, with networks in the Ottoman trading cities like Aleppo, Damascus, and Alexandria. Muslim merchants and traders followed well-defined routes; caravans, inns, and kervansarays linked interregional flow of trade.

Revenue from taxation of international trade provided the lifeblood of the Ottoman civil and military establishment. At its zenith, trade taxation rested on organized custom zones. It was an elaborate fiscal system, regulating and collecting taxes from merchants and traders under the *mukataa*, or tax farming system. The eminent Ottoman historian İnalcık provides revealing detail about following four zones (Inalcik, 1994, 196–198): (1) Istanbul custom covering the region from Varna on western Black Sea, Gallipoli peninsula to the northern end of the province of Aydin on the Aegean coast. (2) Tokat customs, which regulated caravans from Tabriz in northern Iran, loaded with silk textiles going to Bursa, as well as spices and oriental goods destined to markets in Istanbul. (3) Crimean and Muscovy trade was in the Kaffa custom zone, and it included Trabzon and the Eastern Black Sea coast. (4) The Balkan and Danubian trade flows were taxed at Akkerman. Standard duty was at 4.2% *ad valorem*, uniformly applied for Muslim and non-Muslim traders. For peaceful trading, all traders had to follow designated routes and caravans stayed at *caravanserais* or inns under strict rules implemented by the Sultan's agents and tax collectors.

Ottoman slave trading was lucrative and extensive, but it never reached the huge mercantilist scale (see below). It consisted of two main sources: (1) Frontier provinces in the Balkans and (2) African sources. In the former case, along the Habsburg-Ottoman boundary, which changed constantly due to wars and skirmishes, slaving raids for booty became a pattern. The 17th-century Ottoman traveler Evliya Çelebi describes these cross-border *akıncı* raids in detail. In one case, in 1666, Çelebi himself acquired a number of slaves in the auction in a particular market involving 50 slaves, 10 of which were surrendered to the pasha in payment for the imperial one-fifth share (307).

In the 17th century, sub-Saharan African slave trade expanded. Massawa on the Red Sea and Zanzibar in East Africa emerged as key slaving centers, controlled by Arab traders, linked to African kingdoms as supply sources in the interior, and Alexandria and other intermediary cities in the Levant delivered slaves to the Sultan's capital, which was the biggest market. Significantly, Ottoman slave trading was not commodified because there was no plantation system as in the American Deep South or in tropical colonies of European powers, requiring steady supply of manual laborers. On *timars* (land grants) in the Ottoman Balkans and Danubian provinces, feudal serfdom prevailed along with *Devşirme* (see below). In Anatolia, traditionally, women helped or worked on land as unpaid laborers.

Perhaps the most famous slave going through the Istanbul slave market was Roxalena, the future wife of Sultan Süleyman. Originally from Ukraine, Hürrem, as she was named, was a concubine who, through skill and daring, managed to outmaneuver all competitors, including Ibrahim, the Sultan's first minister. The so-called Reign of Women in the Ottoman history began, marking the onset of the long centuries of decline.

Devşirme was a uniquely Ottoman system, part slavery, part taxation in kind, providing exemption for the non-Muslim subjects from military service. *Tithe*, land tax on the Christian *re'aya* was nominal, typically around 1% on agricultural output, a light burden for exemption from military service. Under the *Devşirme*, the *re'aya* was required to hand the first male child in the family to Sultan to be converted to Islam, educated, and raised as the Sultan's *Kul*. Notable *Kuls* managed to rise to the top of the Sultanate, becoming first ministers, like the original Greek Ibrahim and Croat Köprülü, many others distinguishing themselves in military or civil administration, but the system lacked basic human liberty.

Towns, Guilds, and Trade Regulation: The *Imaret* System

The Ottomans developed intricate and elaborate system for the regulation of trade, both domestic and international, as part of the *imaret* system (Inalcik, 1973, chapter XV). An *imaret* was a complex of public buildings and institutions suported by an endowment, *vaqf*, set up by a devout person as a Muslim trust for charity under strict public regulation. Under this system, each trade operated under the supervision of a self-regulating guild, elected democratically from its members, which ensured fair trade practice, defined in detailed regulations, including weights, quality, and prices. Markets and transactions were under the authority of officials who enforced rules and regulations. Any deviation was punishable by a local religious court, headed by a *Kadı*, a jurist in Islamic law trained in a *medrese*. It was normal for a successful trader to set a *vaqf* in performance of the Islamic duty of charity.

Ottoman trade was based on Islamic social contract, and traders were expected to be honorable and treat customers fairly. All trade disputes came before his court, rarely appeals were allowed to the headquarters. The Ottoman capitals, Bursa,

Edirne, and Istanbul occupied special place as the seat of Imperial Council, serving as supreme court. These imperial cities were trade hubs, where trade networks converged. Each town had its own provincial and civil administration. Trade moved on well-maintained highways and routes. Banditry, though not unknown, was severely punished, unlike centuries later when state authority had declined and highway robbers became organized terror on trade routes.

Traders and merchants stayed at *kervansarays*, inns where travellers and merchants rested. In 1555, the ambassador of the Holy Roman emperor, Busbecq, left the following description of the *kervansaray* in Nish: "There is nothing done in secret; there all are open, and everybody may see what another does." He appreciated the suites in the hostel, open to all traders, which contained "apartments for lodging ... either Christian or Jew, rich or poor, are equally open to all" (148). Trading was conducted in *bedestans* and *souks*, under the control of a market inspector, *muhtasib*, who had authority to enforced prices, fixed by custom, assisted by *kethüda* and *yiğitbaşı*, or guild masters, representing the guilds.

Balkans and Arab Provinces Compared

The Ottoman state was multinational, its ruling class consisting of three principal organs: civil, military, and religious. While the religious organ was Muslim, and the military backbone Anatolian, the civil organ was mostly Christian-born children, raised under the *Devşirme* system of levy, which produced most of the senior administrators, including majority of *Sadrzams*, prime ministers. An *imaret* was a complex of public buildings and institutions funded by a *vaqf*, an endowment set up for Muslim charity under Islamic rules governing trusts. Typically, senior administrators, as a sign of their success, would set up *imarets*, in their own province, build public institutions (e.g., *kervansarays*), public kitches for the poor, or bridges on major highways. The Balkans always represented the heart of the Empire. Thus, there were more *imarets* in the Balkans than in the Arab provinces. Of course, there were other reasons for the fact that *imaret* buildings were much more common in Anatolia and the Balkans than in the Arab provinces. There were public kitchens providing free food as a form of Ottoman welfare policy (Wikipedia, 2021a). The system was also linked to trade and more focused on inland cities and towns, rare in rural, less-settled or less-travelled regions. Within cities, *imarets* tended to be spread across the urban landscape and not clustered in one place, as were markets or manufacturers.

In addition to *imarets*, there were other Ottoman institutions at the popular level serving a variety of social and religious services: Sufi *zaviyes*, *kervansarays*, military barracks, imperial palaces, and the residences of wealthy and influential people. In the Arab provinces, which were incorporated into the Empire much later than the Balkans, the *imarets* system was found mostly in Damascus, Jerusalem, Mecca, and Medina. By then, the Ottoman state had reached its zenith, and trading in spices and slaves, rather than conquering more territory, had become the principal Ottoman concern. The Ottomans imposed their authority by redirecting the flow of cash taxes and payments in kind in the form of grain from Cairo to Istanbul.

In the Arab provinces, the Muslim subjects were generally submissive and peaceful. The Ottomans faced opposition to their conquest, mostly tribal in nature, but they did not have to win over the populace to the idea of a Muslim sovereign. Significantly, the Ottomans incorporated the judges and medreses into the official hierarchies of adjudication and learning, so that the appointments to them came from the imperial pool of trained jurists and scholars. Perhaps the underlying message in the Arab provinces focused on emphasizing that Ottomans were "good Muslims," in contrast to the one broadcast in the Balkans, where Muslim charity was viewed as a tool of public goodwill. The Ottomans did feel the need to demonstrate their standing as good Muslims. Accordingly, they put a physical Ottoman stamp on the holy cities of Mecca, Medina, and Jerusalem, and those with symbolic significance in Muslim history such as Damascus, Baghdad, and Cairo.

The Trade Regulation in Ottoman Cairo

At its height, the Ottoman trade regulation was both efficient and equitable. Let's take the case of Cairo as an example of the rise and fall of the Ottoman power in the operation of the markets. According to the Ottoman traveler/geographer Evliya Çelebi, who visited the city, Cairo's economically active profile around 1660 was as summarized in Panel A, Table 4.1. There were no less than 289 registered crafts, 25,884 workshops, and 147,366 individuals in the city.

Trade was highly organized, with an intricate system of self-administration. Each craft had its own guild, which set fair trade practices. At the top of the guild hierarchy there was a sheik, who enforced discipline, handled trade disputes, and ensured that customary taxes were duly paid to the Ottoman state. So long as these taxes were paid, the guild was free to conduct its trade without interference under the rule of its sheik. The sheik was assisted by an elected council of senior trade masters. Membership in the guild was hereditary, passing from father to son. Trade was carried according to customary and well-defined practices, including fair prices charged to customers, and quality protection. In Cairo, a multiethnic

TABLE 4.1 A Profile of the Ottoman Cairo Market

Panel A	*Panel B*	
No. of Crafts: 289	Price of pepper in Cairo (in gold ducats per *callo**)	
No. of Workshops: 25,884	1496	66–68
Individuals in the City: 147,366	1520	90
	1531	130
	*1 *callo* = 3 Egyptian *kantars* or (133 kilos)	

Author's creation with data from (Faroqhi et al., 1994, 191) for Panel A and (Inalcik, 1994, Vol. I, Table I-69, 344) for Panel B.

city, trade was typically on ethnic lines. Thus, goldsmiths and jewelers were Copts. However, some guilds were "mixed," in which case the principal guild officials were Muslim. Overall, these Ottoman city guilds compared favorably with their European counterparts at the time (Faroqhi, op. cit., 188).

The spice trade passing through Cairo was especially significant. There was a major expansion after the Ottoman conquest of Egypt in 1517, and the upward trend continued for the next decade at least (Panel B, Table 4.1). Ships loaded with spices journeyed through the perilous Indian Ocean, increasingly under the Portuguese threat, via the Red Sea, arriving in Jeddah before reaching Cairo. According to Ottoman historians, 20 ships from India with the precious cargo arrived every year. Custom revenues, which were estimated at 90,000 gold ducats in early 16th century, had risen to 150,000 by 1587. Half the custom revenue went to the Sharif of Mecca, the other half to the Ottoman treasury.

Venice played a key role in the spice trade. With Ottomans now masters of the India-Red Sea route, the Venetian Senate recognized the Ottoman control and quickly came to terms with the Sultan. Alexandria, Cairo, and Beirut were now the ports of choice for the Venetian merchants, who were obliged to make a strategic shift away from the Portuguese and adopted a "submissive" policy toward the Ottomans (Inalcik, 1994, 344).

Venetian power and opulence were intricately tied with the Ottoman. To give one example: "The Rialto, a distorted reflection of Aleppo, Damascus or medieval Baghdad, was the souk of the world" (Crowley, 2011, 270). When, ever so slowly, the Ottoman fortunes began their secular decline, the fate of Venice likewise took a downturn from which it never recovered. The English followed the Venetians in developing trade links with the Ottomans. The expansion of the English-Ottoman trade also significantly influenced English culture, as is evidenced in the works of Marlowe, Shakespeare, and English customs" (Brotton, 2017). The Ottoman-English alliance emerged out of Protestant–Catholic rivalry on the one hand, and commercial interest on the other. It began during Elizabeth's reign when Spain was the rising European power, and the Ottomans were ruled by conquering Sultans. Venice was then the preeminent trading republic in the Sultan's vast Empire. London merchants at first, led by Edward Osborne, collaborated with the Venetian traders, but in 1592 they established the Levant Company to handle the Ottoman trade. Osborne was appointed its governor. It was an immediate success. As the English-Ottoman alliance prospered, the Queen personally exchanging letters with Murat III, the Company exported cloth to the Ottoman Empire worth 150,000 pounds annually (Brotton, 2017, 204).

By the 18th century, the system began to manifest internal decay in Cairo markets as elsewhere. Military men, who earlier rarely participated in trade, began in increasing numbers to penetrate. Janissary officers, in charge of police duties, began to collect "fees" for service; worse, they demanded the right of *gedik* (the right to exercise a craft), abandoning their policing and overcrowding the craft. Moreover, increasingly they insisted on controlling the guild, which gradually lost its customary independence. By the turn of the 18th century, the process of military incorporation of Cairo guilds was so widespread that the only independent trading had passed into the hands of non-Muslims.

In 1804, Napoleon invaded Egypt, which from that point onward was de facto under European control. Napoleon carted off the treasures of the Pharaohs to fill the museums of Paris. However, more fundamental transformation was set afoot: The mercantilist system had penetrated Egypt. Within decades, Egypt became the cotton growing periphery for the British factory system, especially when the American Civil War had cut off the Deep South as the traditional supply source. In 1869, the Suez Canal finally opened and paved the way for full British control of the country. Mehmet Ali, the last Ottoman Governor, established a dynasty that ultimately brought down the financial ruin of the country and its British takeover in 1882.

The Arab Core in International Trade

The Arab Muslim lands occupied special place in the India and spice trade. There were two trade routes: over land and across the seas. One land-based trade route ran from Basra on the Persian Gulf to Baghdad and then to Aleppo in Syria. The most famous caravan route over land was the one carrying Chinese silk and merchandise through Central Asia and Tabriz in northern Iran, across Anatolia, terminating in Bursa. The spice trade was significant, linking Atjeh, on the tip of Sumatra, to the Ottoman world. By 1581, the annual income of the Atjehnese ruler from exports of pepper, ginger, benzoin, cinnamon, and precious stones and woods, amounted to three or four million gold ducats (Inalcik with Quataert, 1994, 396). The ports of call en route via the Indian and Red Seas, included Yemen, Hormuz, and other Arab ports, and Mombasa and Mogadishu on the Africa. After the Portuguese penetration in the East, the Indian Ocean become a contested sea, and Lisbon emerged as a significant outlet in spice trade, much to the resentment of Venice, which had hitherto held a near-monopoly in delivering spices to Europe. In 1500, Alexandria and Beirut each handled about 4 million pounds of spices; 13 years later in 1513, Lisbon trade volume in spices exceeded these Arab ports share (Table I, 48, 342).

Aleppo, An Ottoman Arab Trade Hub: To gain a deeper understanding of Arab prosperity at the zenith of Ottoman international trade, we now look at one typical trade hub, Aleppo. This is a major town on which caravan trade routes from Basra, Tabriz, and Hejaz converged. Up until the 17th century, Iranian silk continued to arrive in increasing quantity. Merchants obtained the silk from the Shah directly who was a monopoly trader in silk; his subject farmers could only sell to the Shah who, of course, fixed the buying price himself. Spices arrive from Atjeh and the Moluccas, and porcelain and myriad other oriental goods similarly came from China. As a sign of flourishing trade, five new *kervansarays* were built in the inner city during the 16th century, and four more were added in the following century (Faroqhi et al., 1994, 499–501). Prosperity was by no means limited to the inner city; Aleppo's hinterland shared in trade growth. Marat al-Numan produced

TABLE 4.2 Imports of Woolen Cloth into the Ottoman Empire (1820–1882) (Annual averages in tons)

Year	Total Imports into the Empire	Shares of Major Exporting Countries
1820–22	330	Austria 45% France 30%
1880–1882	2,800	UK 33% Austria 32% France 13%
1909–1911	8,000	Germany★ 30% UK 22 Austria 15%

Author's creation with data from Pamuk (1987, 196).

★Germany did not exist before 1870; its trade was "transited' through Austria.

silk and olive oil, Idlib had a flourish soap manufacture. The large village of Darit Issa was renowned for its cotton fabrics. Generally, the area was rich in olive groves.

Then adversity hit. Partly it was bad harvests caused by climatic factors. But primarily it was due to changing pattern of international trade. The Dutch occupation of the Moluccas cut the supply and hit the spice trade. In politics, the fall of the Safavid dynasty in Iran adversely affected the movement of silk caravans. Aleppo's decline was clearly discernable by the 18th century and continued throughout the 19th century. By far the greatest causal factor was the flooding of cheap, high-quality woolen cloth, and textiles from Europe, especially England then undergoing its Industrial Revolution. Winning concessions from the Sultan, English, and other western merchants started to replace Venice as the preeminent trading partner of the Ottomans.

Table 4.2 is illustrative of the woolen cloth trade. In 1820, total woolen cloth imports into the Empire were 330 tons, mostly originating from Austria and France. By 1880–1882, the volume had risen almost tenfold and UK had emerged as the leading source and the upward trend continued until the WWI. What happened in wool also occurred in cotton textiles, with an added irony. By the second half of the 19th century, and specifically during the American Civil War, the Ottoman Egypt had emerged as a significant source of raw cotton for the Lancashire and Midlands mills. At the eve of WWI, Germany had become the leading exporter, reflecting changed geopolitics.

The Western Shift of International Trade

Up to the 17th century, Venice had occupied the central role in Ottoman trade, largely through outsmarting other Italian trading cities like Genoa and Florence. They had trade privileges and their trade volume expanded commensurate with the Sultan's borders. They were always adept at winning privileged trade relations with Muslim rulers. They appealed to the Mamelukes and after 1517, when Egypt was conquered by Selim I, to the Ottoman Sultan who help in preserving their monopoly. But increasingly, the Ottomans, outgunned by the Portuguese, had to pull back from the Indian Ocean and concentrate on countering the rising Roman League power in the Mediterranean. By 1552, Hormuz had a Portuguese garrison, and in 1571, a year after the Ottoman conquest of Cyprus, the Ottomans suffered a huge naval defeat at Lepanto.

By mid-16th century, France, Holland, and then England followed the Italian states in seeking trade privileges in the Sultan's lands. Gradually, world trade shifted westwards. Profits from the Ottoman Euro-Asian trade system at first accumulated in Italy and then Europe. Banking began as family businesses by Medici's. The ascent of money was under way (Ferguson, 2008). Ottomans never developed banking and a solid currency. Interest was *haram* (banned) under Islam. In Europe, trade surplus first financed the Italian Renaissance, banking and finance spreading northward, enabling the rise of the Mercantilist economy.

By the turn of the 17th century, there were clear signs of Ottoman decline. The Portuguese had captured Goa on the Indian subcontinent and were rapidly growing in the Malay world. Sultan Süleyman had earlier developed highly profitable trade in spices and oriental goods beyond the Red Sea, as far east as Aceh, on the northern tip of Indonesia, but now the Ottoman navy was increasingly being outmaneuvered by the Portuguese. In 1511, they captured Malacca; the Sultan, despite pledges of support, could not come to the aid of the Muslims in the Malay Archipelago. In the next century, the Portuguese were followed by the Dutch who established themselves in Batavia in 1642. Suleyman the Magnificent granted the British merchants trading privileges in 1553.

The Levant Company was founded in London in 1581 (Wood, 1964, 11), and quickly became profitable. It opened trading agencies, called factories, in Aleppo, Damascus, Cyprus, Smyrna, and elsewhere. The British joined other European merchants in the penetration of traders into the Ottoman Middle East. Better quality and cheaper cloth and textiles from Europe began to flood the Mediterranean markets. The Levant Company was so successful, it was even paying the cost of the British embassy in Istanbul (chapter V). Trade became a major instrument of diplomatic relations, especially in Ottoman-Russian relations. Moreover, the European economic penetration into the Ottoman lands had a deep socioeconomic impact. Within the next century, the Oriental trade shifted out of the hands of the Arabs and Muslims and passed into the hands of non-Muslim subjects of the Sultan (Inalcik, 1973, 138) as European traders relied on non-Muslim intermediaries. Smyrna (modern Izmir) was typical of the rise of Levantine trading families as a comprador class. Gradually, the Muslim merchants and traders were either replaced by Christian traders in their own lands or became subordinate.

There was always intense competition among the Europeans for trading privileges granted by the Porte. Initially, the Venetians and Italians were dominant, but gradually English traders rose to prominence. Shifts in diplomacy influenced trade, as when England and the Porte combined against Spain. During the Napoleonic Wars, the French navy imposed a blockade in the Mediterranean, and the Levant trade suffered. Finally, the Levant Company folded in 1825. However, during its life, the company was "complimentary to that of its great rival, the East India Company" rendering significant "political" role (Wood, 1964, 204). "The Turkish Empire, as Napoleon saw, was the key to India, ... The work of the Levant Company ... was a sound preparation" (ibid.) for British penetration into the Middle East.

From a Muslim perspective, however, the picture could hardly be worse. The Levant Company was part of the European trading system, and it facilitated the emergence of Western mercantilism centered on the Atlantic. Especially after Napoleon's invasion of Egypt, and his defeat by Wellington, the British economic occupation of Egypt began, and the Middle East entered a period of secular decline (Issawi, 1981). The roots of decline, however, were planted much earlier.

Capitulations: The Road to Economic Ruin

At the height of their power, the Ottoman Sultans granted European merchants trade privileges known as *capitulations*. These would typically be exemption from import duties or monopoly trading available to merchants of one power exclusively. It was a discretionary use of commercial policy which worked in earlier periods of the conquering Sultans. In times of decline, especially in the 19th century, it resulted in deindustrialization of domestic manufacturing, effectively ruining the Ottoman economy. It was, as if, the top echelons of the government were "uninterested in the economic consequences" (Issawi, 1995, 9) of their commercial and tariff policies so damaging to domestic producers. There was little effort to protect domestic producers against foreign competition; indeed, imports were encouraged, and exports discouraged.

Inalcik has argued that the Ottomans "always tried to use these commercial privileges as a political weapon" (Inalcik, 1973, 137). For example, Genoese merchants might be preferred over Venetian in a period when Ottoman-Venetian relations were in crisis. Sultan Süleyman, keen to foster an Ottoman-French alliance, granted the first formal trade privileges to France (137), these becoming the model for later *capitulations*. In 1581, when the Ottomans and the British faced a common enemy in Spain, the English merchants of the Levant Company, were granted a preferential custom rate of 3%, while other nationalities paid 5%. In 1673, the 3% duty was extended to all foreign merchants.

The worst was in 1838, when the modernizing Sultan Mahmut, facing a crisis with Muhammed Ali's army marching on Istanbul, signed a secret free trade agreement with Britain in appreciation of its diplomatic help. Henceforth, imports of British manufactures into the Empire would be at a concessional 5%, a privilege soon extended to other European countries. Astonishingly, exports were subjected to a 12% tariff (Pamuk, 1987, 20). In addition, foreign merchants were exempt from an 8% internal customs duty, while domestic merchants were obliged to pay it. This was discrimination against domestic producers; any export capacity was prevented, while cheaper imports destroyed domestic production. Thus, while European countries were being protectionist, the Ottoman government was unconcerned about the damage it was doing to domestic production. With custom revenues falling, the Ottoman government began a ruinous policy of foreign borrowing to finance wars, such as the Crimean War in 1856. Financial bankruptcy inevitably followed such unwise trade policy.

The Creation of the Atlantic Mercantilist Economy

In 1492, two momentous events occurred: In January, Granada, the last Moorish state in Muslim Spain surrendered, and in August, Christopher Columbus sailed for the New World. Atlantic Mercantilism was thus launched. It was all driven by greed and unforgiving, naked power. The Aztec and Maya gold flooded Spain, then moved to such financial centers like Antwerp in Belgium, and finally flowing across the channel to finance the British Industrial Revolution.

The first revolutionary idea was not economic, it was religious. It was directed against Islam. In 1502, King Ferdinand and Queen Isabella officially made Islam illegal throughout Spain. The Muslims of Spain rose in revolt, but they had no clear plan nor a clear leader. They simply believed that Islam would save them. In Granada, which was still all Muslim, the rebellion took a defensive form. Christian soldiers were well equipped and better trained and the town finally fell. Massacres and forced conversions of villages continued, but it was futile. Finally, the rebellion petered out and Queen Isabella officially declared an end to toleration for any Muslim in Spain. Many fled to North Africa or fought to the death. Most, however, officially converted to Christianity, while keeping their true beliefs hidden.

Ferdinand and Isabella's Crusade did not go unanswered. On the eve of the total collapse of Muslim Spain, the Ottoman dynasty emerged as a new Islamic power in southeastern Europe (Ali, 2002, chapter 5). Under a series of incredibly able conquering Sultans, from 1300 on, the Ottomans took Bulgaria, Greece, Serbia, Hungary, and then in 1453 conquered Constantinople, now named Istanbul. For the next three centuries, the Ottomans became the Sword of Islam, ruling over much of eastern Europe. A new age of Crusades and Jihad began, with the House of Osman acting as the Caliph of Islam against a Christian Europe led by the Pope.

But it was not merely a *Clash of Fundamentalisms* as Tariq Ali has labelled it. Ottoman centuries were as much about trade routes, state revenues, and prosperity. It was a clash of Machiavellian power, one looking east to the Orient, beyond the Red Sea and the Indian Ocean, the other toward the New World across the Atlantic. Inadvertently, it was the Ottoman Sultan Selim who shaped the modern world (Mikhail, 2020). Thus began the modern world of mercantilism.

The Origins of Mercantilism: Ideas First, Institutions after

In building a Christian Europe, prosperous and powerful, ideas led the way. First, it was Nicolo Machiavelli (1469–1527) of the trading Republic of Florence, who, in a brief book, *The Prince*, put forward an original, and brutally realistic theory of power and political survival: A successful prince must pursue power ruthlessly, eliminating all competitors. Machiavelli's ideal prince was Süleyman the Magnificent who, in 1553 had his ablest son, Mustafa, beheaded, to preserve his reign. Machiavelli's central idea was that a powerful prince must be ruthless; in the pursuit of power nothing could stand in the way. Ferdinand and Isabella in Spain were no less ruthless; they were unmatched in their zeal in clearing Islam from Iberia. When she died, her last testament was the conquest of Muslim Africa and a Crusade against Islam (Mikhail, 2020, 337).

The other epoch-making idea for mercantilism was pure economic; it came from the Scot, Adam Smith, another realist. After the decisive English victory over Scottish clans in 1749 at Culloden, the Scots turned their attention to ideas and moneymaking. Pursuit of wealth was deemed to be rational human behavior and markets emerged as arenas of rational choice (Herman, 2002). The economics of Adam Smith emerged out of this intellectual environment.

In 1776, Smith wrote his *Wealth of Nations*, putting forward the idea that man is self-interest driven. National interest resides in the hands of a strong state. The foundations of such a state are its army, navy, rule of law, and institutions. Currency and banking reforms were pioneered in the European central banks (Ferguson, 2008). Bank of England was established by the Royal Charter in 1694, shortly after the Glorious Revolution, to function as the government's banker. Napoleon created Banque de France in 1804.

Amsterdam became the world's first financial center by the 1690s. Financial innovation led the way: The Dutch improved the Italian banking and lending system, by introducing the first central bank to stabilize currency and even experimented with the public lottery to mobilize public savings. But the most popular innovation was legislation to enable joint-stock companies. This enabled the Dutch shareholders to invest, with tolerable risk, equivalent to the amount of one's investment, in new ventures, especially in the Asian spice trade. At this time, European diets craved spices like cinnamon, cloves, nutmeg, and pepper. The famed VOC, the Dutch East India Company, established in 1602, acquired monopoly control of Indonesia (Ferguson, 2008, 128–129).

The English East India Company was perhaps the model. Granted a royal charter in 1600, it was the first global trading company. From its headquarters in London, it controlled trade in India for the next three and a half centuries, cultivating tea and opium under monopoly production. Tea was exported to England, while opium was forced upon China, backed by the British navy. When China banned opium imports, Britain sent its navy, getting its way in the Opium Wars that effectively extended British imperialism over China till Mao's Communist victory in 1949. In 1786 the East India Company acquired Penang Island and penetrated British Malaya. During the next century and a half, Britain followed a "cheap labor policy." Millions of Chinese "coolies" were shipped from China to work as virtual slaves in tin mines. Fortunes from tin were made by British investors in Perak and Larut. Then, in the late 19th century, rubber plantations were introduced; the rubber trees were stolen from Guyana and introduced to Ceylon and Southeast Asia by way of Kew Gardens.

By the end of the 19th century, the Age of Imperialism was global, as Europe expanded in search of new markets for its industrial products and raw materials for its factories. The idea of national prosperity was recast in the Darwinian theory of survival of the fittest. Geographers and explorers "discovered" the Nile, while geologists went after gold mines, and capitalists like Cecil Rhodes exploited them. Literature, newspapers, novelists, and journalists emerged in the service of imperial expansion, writing, and informing the public of exotic, mysterious but rich Orient. In this way, a whole new genre, Orientalism emerged as mainstream literature. D.G. Hogarth, author of *The Penetration of Arabia*, published in 1904, paved the way for his appointment as head of the Arab Bureau in Cairo during the WWI. Subsequently, "a band" was formed, as Lawrence termed it, consisting of Gertrude Bell, St. John Philby, Lawrence himself, and quasi-scholars, working as agents of imperialism. H.G. Wells summarized this Eurocentric system in racist terms: "*In the closing years of the 19th century it was assumed ... to be a natural and inevitable thing that all the world should fall under European domination*" (Wells, 1971, 851). Mercantilism was built on slavery and plantations in the tropics, reaching its climax in the age in 19th-century imperialism and colonization.

The Plantation System, Slavery as Pillars of Colonialism

Plantations are large-scale, labor-intensive production systems in the tropics taking advantage of ample rainfall and sunshine. A long list of tropical commodities and primary products were produced: spices, sugar, coffee, cocoa, bananas, cotton, and minerals, shipped to Europe for consumption or further processing.

Colonial mercantilism's chief bottleneck was labor. First, the slave trade and then "cheap labor policy" were implemented. Massive profits from slaving enriched Europe. According to the Trans-Atlantic Slave Trade Database (National Endowment for the Humanities, 2021), between 1525 and 1866, the total number of African slaves shipped to the New World was 12.5 million. Of this, 10.7 million survived the dreadful passage, landing in North America, the Caribbean, and Latin America for work as slaves on plantations. Additionally, the British transported some 2 million "indentured" Indian workers to various British colonies, including Fiji, Mauritius, Ceylon, Trinidad, Guyana, Malaya, East and South Africa, from 1834 to 1914. How the British colonialism penetrated Malaya, in the Islamic periphery, has been told in the author's *Development in Malaysia, Poverty, Wealth and Trusteeship* (Mehmet, 1986). The British East India company led the way, colonizing first Penang, then taking over the tin mines of Perak in what was to become the Federated States of Malaya. The Residency system was an indirect rule, controlling the Sultans, while extracting all the natural wealth of the country for the benefit of "mother" country, Britain. Under the Cheap Labor Policy, millions of Chinese "coolies" were imported from China. During the rubber plantation development, millions of indentured Tamils from South India were imported. The demographics of the country completely changed, while the British ruled the waves. By the end of WWII, the British corporate interests owned 70% of the economy, the Chinese 20%, and the Bumiputera merely 5%. Worse, the country was about to go Chinese communist. Islam was very much in the background.

The Dutch in Indonesia were worse than the British in Malaya. They subordinated Muslim population to a monopoly cultivation and spice trading system for the great benefit of "motherland" Holland. The Dutch cultural system was brutal, exploiting both the land and the Muslim population in the most inhumane way. Dutch imperialism first was developed in the Dutch East Indies, centuries later spreading into South Africa, where the racist Apartheid system was introduced. It all reflected the arrogance and superiority of the Eurocentric mentality.

At the beginning, in the 16th century, European mercantilism was driven by Christian passion, but the search for gold was no less passionate. The pursuit of gold exterminated Aztecs and Maya. In Europe, gold and mercantilist revenues created banking, originally controlled by families such as the Medici and Rothschilds. Gradually chartered companies, like the Levant Company, the Hudson Bay, and the Dutch VOC, emerged as chartered or joint-venture companies. In the age of imperialism, it evolved into a Eurocentric system, enriching European nations who controlled shipping, insurance, banking, and financial services, the prototypes of the contemporary Multinational Corporations, when the American hegemon assumed leadership of modern capitalism after the WWII.

Globalization and MNCs

The Eurocentric spirit of mercantilism still drives globalization, now dominated by multinational corporations (MNCs). The MNCs are the modern-day versions of the chartered companies in the age of mercantilism, such as the Levant or the East India Company. As in earlier times, the capitalist system always enriched the West, where the system was born, because the system requires inequality to generate profits that flow to the West. Impoverishment of the periphery is the converse of prosperity at the center. The system is never static; it has gone through several cycles of growth, but always standing on Eurocentric roots.

In the 19th century, the steam engine pioneered railways and shipping. At the turn of the 20th century, the Automobile Age was launched, and fossil fuel energy emerged as the biggest single-trade fueling industries, homes, and cars. In the postwar period, import-substituting consumer goods manufacturing, highly capital-intensive, was transferred into labor-surplus developing countries. These new industries, urban-based with limited jobs, suddenly became magnets for jobseekers. Rural exodus led to urban poverty in shantytowns with no end to the poverty of developing nations. Now, new information technology is the new frontier and new trade wars are all about digital technology, smartphones, and robotics and ownership of intellectual property.

Self-interest still drives the system, but in its latest manifestation, capitalism is increasingly searching for new opportunities of exploitation to generate rising "rewards." The French economist Thomas Piketty has shown that profit is no longer the system's driver; it is capital gains. Greed in stock exchanges has shaped casino-like gambling institutions. Huge volumes of speculative capital movements do not search for net profits, but rather short-term capital gains realized in shorting, hedging, and currency manipulations by financial elites (Piketty, 2014). MNCs engaged in manufacturing are increasingly foot-loose, locating in cheap labor regimes, but ready to pull up stakes and move to new places once wages rise under trade union pressure, or high-cost labor standards emerge in the domestic political arena, or from international consumer movements demanding fair trade practices (Mehmet, et al., 1999, 46–54). Global sourcing and production assembly lines are creating a new form of slavery, a "race to the bottom" in labor-surplus countries. Often, these host countries compete with one another offering MNCs tax holidays, free land on export processing zones, and other incentives at the expense of workers. Informalization and casualization of employment are the necessary consequences, with rampant violation of the rights of workers, especially female and underage workers.

Techniques of creating functional inequality in the globalization process are endless. Too often, capital movements and transfer pricing by MNCs are practiced avoiding taxation in host countries, shifting profits to home countries where sophisticated corporate rewards beckon. The industrial military complex and hegemonic politics, such as "America First" variety are notable examples, resulting in trade wars between superpowers. Nowadays, MNCs are increasingly taking advantage of modern information technology and ease of global mobility, increasingly hiding in tax havens avoiding national tax. Trade-based money laundering is now big business (Egmont Group, 2021), often linked to illegal arms trading. Drug trade and human trafficking are expanding exponentially (Exeter, 2021). Failure to take progressive measures to tax capital movements for an equitable world would mean that our postmodern, pandemic-ravaged world is doomed to deepening inequality and injustice. Equitable international development, financed and paid for by international corporations, is long overdue. This is a moral obligation, in lieu of reparations, for injustice and exploitation done to the colonial people under the mercantilist system. MNCs, the contemporary descendants of the chartered and joint-venture companies of the age of imperialism, must be taxed and revenue channeled into global sustainable development. That would be equitable and efficient to contain the refugee influx into rich countries.

The Pandemic has exposed the fragility of the Eurocentric mercantilist economy. The First World economies have been shattered, and world trade checked. The Pandemic has accelerated the rise of China, at the expense of the American hegemony. It is unclear yet as to how the post-Pandemic trading system will evolve, as many economies are in recession and how speedy any recovery will shape, at what rate? Such questions are for the future. A new trading system will be devised, no doubt transition will be long-term, although with much pent-up demand, supply bottlenecks and inflationary pressures may be encountered. In the meantime, vaccine nationalism has emerged. Rich countries are first in the global line while the WHO is attempting to help low-income countries with programs such as COVAX. Poverty, war, and conflict have devastated many Third World countries already suffering from poverty, injustice, and now the virus. In war and conflict zones, waves of refugees in camps and economic migrants on desperate journeys, crashing against the gates of the First World, Europe, and the USA, severely hit by the Pandemic, also torn by systemic racism, and xenophobia. It is ironic and sad that the First World, which got rich in the age of imperialism, invading and exploiting Third World people and resources, are now shutting their borders. Economic migrants and refugees are unwelcome.

The contemporary multinational capitalist system is still very much neo-mercantilist. Machiavellian power and Darwinian survival of the fittest still rule the world, creating inequality, exploitation, and injustice. To cite one example: Children are especially at risk due to their specific vulnerabilities and the threat of traffickers exploiting children online is growing: for example, the National Center for Missing and Exploited Children in the United States "reported an 846% increase from 2010 to 2015 in reports of suspected child sex trafficking – an increase the organization has found to be directly correlated to the increased use of the Internet to sell children for sex" (UN, 2021).

References

Ali, Tareq, 2003, *The Clash of Fundamentalisms: Crusades, Jihads and Modernity*, London: Verso.

Brotton, Jerry, 2017, *The Sultan and the Queen, the Untold Story of Elizabeth and Islam*, New York: Penguin.

Crowley, Roger, 2008, *Empires of the Sea: The Final Battle for the Mediterranean, 1521–1580*, London: Faber & Faber.

Crowley, Roger, 2011, *City of Fortune: How Venice Won and Lost a Naval Empire*, London: Faber & Faber.

Dankoff, Robert and Sooyoong Kim, 2011, *Selections from the Book of Travels* (Edited and Translated by Evliya Çelebi), London: Eland.

Egmont Group, 2021, www.egmontgroup.org/sites/default/files/filedepot/external/Trade-Based-Money-Laundering-Trends-and-Developments%5B1%5D.pdf, accessed on 25 Jan. 2021.

Evans, Richard. J., 2017, *The Pursuit of Power, Europe 1815–1914*, London: Penguin Books.

Exeter, 2021, Trends in Drug Trafficking. Drug Trafficking on an International Scale; a growing problem. http://people.exeter.ac.uk/watupman/undergrad/Kirsty/ws2%20trends%20in%20international.htm, accessed on 25 Jan. 2021.

Faroqhi, et al., 1994, *An Economic and Social History of the Ottoman Empire*, Vol. 2 (Edited by Inalcik and Quataert), Cambridge: Cambridge University Press.

Ferguson, Niall, 2008, *The Ascent of Money, A Financial History of the World*, New York: Penguin.

Frankopan, Peter, 2018, *The New Silk Roads*, New York: Vintage Books.

Herman, Arthur, 2002, *How the Scots Invented the Modern World*, New York: Random House.

Inalcik, Halil, 1973, *The Ottoman Empire, the Classical Age 1300–1600*, London: Phoenix Press.

Inalcik, Halil (with Donald Quataert), 1994, *An Economic and Social History of the Ottoman Empire, Vol. 1: 1300–1600*, Cambridge: Cambridge University Press.

Issawi, Charles, 1981, *The Arab World's Legacy: Essays by Charles Issawi*, Princeton: Darwin Press.

Issawi, Charles, 1995, *The Middle East Economy, Decline and Recovery: Selected Essays*, Princeton: Marcus Weiner.

Mahbubani, K., 1992, "The West and the Rest", *The National Interest*, Summer.

Mahbubani, K., 2022, *The Asian 21st Century*, Singapore: Springer Verlag.

Mehmet, Ozay, 1986, *Development in Malaysia, Poverty, Wealth and Trusteeship*, London: Croom Helm.

Mehmet, Ozay (II&D), 1990, *Islamic Identity and Development, Studies of the Islamic Periphery*, London: Routledge.

Mehmet, Ozay, 1999, *Westernizing the Third World*, 2nd ed., London: Routledge.

Mehmet, Ozay, Errol Mendes, and Robert Sinding, 1999, *Towards a Fair Global Labour Market, Avoiding a New Slave Trade*, London: Routledge.

Mikhail, Alan, 2020, *God's Shadow: The Ottoman Sultan Who Shaped the Modern World*, New York: Norton.

National Endowment for the Humanities, 2021, Voyages: The Transatlantic Slave Trade Database, www.neh.gov/news/voyages-the-transatlantic-slave-trade-database, accessed on 21 May 2021.

Pamuk, Şevket, 1972, *The Ottoman Empire and European Capitalism, 1820–1913*, Cambridge: Cambridge University Press.

Piketty, Thomas, 2014, *Capital in the Twenty-First Century*, Cambridge: Belkap Press.

Stratton, Arthur, 1972, *Sinan: The Biography of One of the World's Greatest Architects and a Portrait of the Golden Age of the Ottoman Empire*, New York: Charles Scribner's Sons.

UN, 2021, Sexual Violence in Conflict. www.un.org/sexualviolenceinconflict/wp-content/uploads/2019/07/report/human-trafficking-and-technology-trends-challenges-and-opportunities/Human-trafficking and technology-trends-challenges-and-opportunit ies-WEB-1.pdf, accessed on 25 Jan. 2021.

Wells, H.G., 1971. *The Outline of History*, Vol. 2, New York: Doubleday.

Wikipedia, 2021, https://en.wikipedia.org/wiki/List_of_Ottoman_Grand_Viziers, accessed on 21 August 2021.

Wikipedia, 2021a, https://en.wikipedia.org/wiki/Haseki_Sultan_Imaret, accessed on 27 Oct. 2021.

Wood, Alfred C., 1964, *A History of the Levant Company*, London: Frank Cass & Company.

5

THE ELUSIVE QUEST FOR THE ISLAMIC SOCIAL CONTRACT

The Contest between Nationalism and Imperialism

Post-Ottoman Arab world is a tragic story of failed states, torn by coups, assassinations, military dictatorship, and foreign invasion in search of oil. The pursuit of Islamic social justice, the theme of II&D (1990),[1] has always been the driving force of domestic politics. But typically, it has been an exercise in futility, the achievement of social justice has always fallen far short of promises and expectations. In recent times, these failures opened the doors to neo-imperialist invasion exploding finally into Islamic terrorism.

This chapter will examine six case illustrative studies in the Islamic Core, Iran, Saudi Arabia, Iraq, Syria, Libya, and Egypt to document the contest between nationalism and imperialism. What is presented is no more than a short summary of each case. History is complex and every summary is bound to leave out certain facts. No claim for completeness is made; the attempt is simply to highlight the nature of "failed states" from the perspective of ordinary citizens.

A Synopsis of Arab Culture

Arab nationalism rests not only Islam, but cultural heritage. Like every other great civilization, the Arab culture is rich and glorious. It has great scholars in every major field. When Europe lived in its Dark Ages, Arab culture and learning was at its zenith. In philosophy, Ibn Sina, known as Avicenna in the West, was an Aristotelian, and was a teacher of St. Thomas Aquinas. Ibn Sina was born in a village near Bukhara. At the famous Samanid library, he acquired an encyclopedic knowledge of all fields of science, including medicine, mathematics, astronomy, and philosophy. His masterpiece was *Al-Kanun*, in which he showed the contagious nature of tuberculosis, recognized pleurisy, diagnosed bilharziasis, and described hundreds of drugs. This work was the authoritative medical reference in Europe from the 11th century to the 17th century, and it was translated from Arabic into Latin at the end of the 15th

DOI: 10.4324/9781003268994-5

century. He was widely respected as a master who made major contributions to the advancement of philosophy in medieval Europe.

Ibn Rushdie, another major Muslim scholar, lived in Cordoba, Seville, and Marrakesh. He built on the medical theories of al-Farabi and Ibn Sina. In philosophy he was a precursor of Kant, believing that human reason is one, a unified whole. He translated the works of classical Greek philosophers, Plato, Aristotle, and others, into Arabic, but he was more popular and well-known in the West than in Muslim lands.

The great center of medical knowledge emerged in the Abbasid dynasty in Baghdad. Islamic architecture, fine arts in mosaics, and calligraphy embellished royal palaces and religious sites, and many glorious examples survived to this day as testimony of a rich civilizational heritage in the Arab world. In sciences, the great works of ancient Greek masters like Galen, Hippocrates, and Dioscorides were translated into Arabic. Seven of Galen's books, lost in the original Greek, survived in the Arabic. In mathematics, Muslim scholars extended the Indian and Greek knowledge. A 9th-century scholar, Khwarizmi, gave his name to "algorism," he wrote on the solution of quadratic equations, and was the pioneer of algebra (*al-jabr* – integration). Through Muslim Spain and Sicily, these great ideas passed to Medieval Europe and greatly contributed to the emergence of the Enlightenment (Fisher, 1979, 102–109).

In Geography, too, Arab scholars preserved and transmitted ancient knowledge to the West. Ptolemy's *Geography* was translated into Arabic. Al-Khwarizmi followed Ptolemy and drew a map for his master the Caliph al-Mamun, a protector of scholars, which showed the Sea of Rum (Mediterranean) and the Sea of Fars (Indian Ocean) enveloping the known world (Middle East).

In poetry, literature, and all other fields of knowledge Arab contributions in the zenith of the Muslim civilization was glorious, and superior to the West in that era. Regretfully, from the 10th century on, this intellectual achievement was not sustained, critical thinking was discouraged, and the slow cultural decline began. Other factors contributed as well, notably the end of Muslim Spain in 1492, when the Age of Discovery was launched in the West, mercantilism emerged, and the economic center of gravity shifted from the Middle East to the Atlantic economy (see chapter IV). In the age of colonization, the Muslim Core was already so weak that it could not resist imperialist penetration.

★★★

Turning to the contemporary Islamic world, we start our case studies in Iran, not because it is the center of *Shi'a* Islam, but because oil politics emerged first there. Our concern is not the fundamentals of Islam, but oil politics, how the modern Middle East has been shaped by oil in modern times.

Oil hastened the end of the Ottoman Empire and opened the doors to foreign invasion of the Middle East. In 1901, William Knox D'Arcy (1849–1917), a successful British entrepreneur, who made a fortune in Australian mining, managed to obtain from the government of Iran a 60-year concession for oil exploration and production. The concession was huge, covering 480 square miles in central and southern Iran. The Iranian government received 20,000 British pounds in cash, paid-up shares of an equal value, and a promise of 16% of the annual net profits. In 1905, D'Arcy struck oil, but a wheeler and dealer, he immediately assigned his concession rights to Burma Oil, in return for 170,000 barrels of petroleum. Burma Oil is the oldest British oil enterprise, going back to 1886 (Corley, 1983).

In 1908, more oil was discovered in commercial quantity at Masjed-e Soleyman, and Burma Oil was reincorporated in the following year as the Anglo-Persian Oil Company (APOC, later, the Anglo-Iranian Oil Company, then British Petroleum, BP). BP emerged to become Britain's leading corporation.

In 1912, Churchill, the First Lord of the Admiralty decided to convert the British navy ships from coal to oil as fuel. The British government became the majority shareholder in APOC. Churchill's move proved highly profitable for Britain. Up to Iran's nationalization of the concession in 1951, APOC paid nearly $600 million in profits and $700 million in corporate taxes to the British government. By contrast, the Iranian government received a total of $310 million, or less than 25% in royalties. The distribution of revenue has been at the crux of oil politics, driving the relations between producing country and investing interests.

The Rise and Fall of Mohammed Mosaddeq

In Iran,[2] the national identity search in the modernization era, in the 1920's, Shah Reza has been shaped by passionate nationalists such as Mosaddeq and reforming Shahs, such as the Pahlavi dynasty. Party politics and debates in the Maclis, no less than in the Bazaar, pitted the progressives against the Shah who depended on the foreign powers, at the cost, ultimately, of the dynasty. When both dynasty and nationalists failed, the clergy emerged to claim power and Iran sank into theocratic dictatorship.

At the start of the modernization era, in the 1920, Shah Reza was very much an Atatürk-style modernizer, dropped Persia for Iran, and deeply resented the fact that the country's oil was in the hands of the British. Yet, the Shah fell victim to imperialist interests, abandoning nation-building; steady revenue for investment in social and economic development could not be sustained. In 1920, Iran's oil revenues amounted to a tiny half a million British pounds. Even by 1940s it stood at 4 million pounds (Hardy, 2017, 105). With constant fiscal constraint, the Shah relied on imperialist interests. This struggle between the monarchy and the progressives centered on the accusation of the Shah as a tool of imperialists.

Mossadegh was a progressive leader driven by modern ideas. Islamic customs and institutions, such as Islamic Social Contract, had no place in his agenda. He wished to channel Iran's oil wealth for social and economic development. A passionate nationalist, a revolutionary, he was born in 1882 in Ahmadabad, lost his father at an early age, and remained under his mother's influence. In early 20th century, Persia was a contested territory between the Tsarist and British Empires. Winston Churchill, the First Lord of the Admiralty, took two radical steps, both to advance British imperialism. Almost single-handedly, he acquired controlling interest in APOC, investing 2.2 million British pounds for 51% of its shares. In a secret deal, the Admiralty secured Persian oil for 20 years at heavily discounted prices.

Churchill had already taken another decisive step in converting the Royal Navy from coal to oil.

Iran survived the Second War as neutral, but in effect the country's north was under Russian domination, the south with its oil fields was British. When the USA joined the War, from 1943 the American forces arrived and the leaders of the Big Three, Churchill, Stalin, and Roosevelt, chose Tehran for their famous summit. By then, the pro-Moscow Tudeh (Masses) Party was the largest organized political movement, but Communism clashed with Islam. In 1946, Stalin withdrew his troops and Persia was left as the playground of the British and the Americans.

It was in this environment that Muhammed Mossadegh, now almost 70, emerged to embody Iranian national independence. He hated the British but loved the British constitutional system. His plan for nation-building set him up against first the British and subsequently American oil interests. Mossadegh first demanded 50:50 oil revenue sharing, already in force in the Latin American US dependency, Venezuela. This formula was also operational in ARAMCO in nearby Saudi Arabia. Finally, the crisis of 1951–1953 exploded, shortly after Mosaddeq became the Prime Minister in 1951. His target was nationalization of Anglo-Iranian Oil Company. The British regarded this as an act of theft; for Americans it was a Communist plot. Mosaddeq created the National Iranian Oil Company (NIOC). He did not have the technical capacity to manage NOIC, hoping to persuade the British staff to stay. The British technicians left, and soon operational obstacles emerged reducing oil production and revenues. Worker and popular discontent followed.

The crisis deepened both at home and in relation with the British and Americans. The Maclis politicians suspected sabotage. At home, Mosaddegh's crisis management opened the floodgates for the clergy to take advantage: Political Islam thus emerged as opportunistic, seeking and since 1979 taking power. Externally, relations deteriorated further with the West. The British appealed to the International Court of Justice. Negotiating with Mosaddeq was judged futile. The British navy was sent to the Gulf; Mosaddeq visited the USA seeking American help. Many Iranians expected American aid, but it did not materialize. For Americans, Mosaddeq was a Communist, while the British viewed him as a thief. His relations with the West worsened and the crises deepened, forcing the Shah to dismiss Mossadegh in mid-1952. Civil war looked immanent; the Shah then reinstalled Mosaddegh. For a year, political instability reigned as the army, opposition parties, and religious forces competed with one another. The climax was reached in the Spring of 1953, when the Americans "pulled the rug from under Mosaddeq" (Fisher, 1979, 557). A joint American-British plot, Operation Ajax, was launched to remove Mosaddeq. On 13 August, Mosaddeq dissolved parliament and usurped the Shah's power, but he lacked the courage or support to become a dictator. The Shah abdicated his throne, fleeing the country on 16 August, but a few days later, popular demonstrations took place in Tehran with shouts of "Long live the Shah." On 22 August, the Shah returned to claim his throne. The next day, Mosaddeq was arrested, tried, and sentenced to death for inciting rebellion.

The new US president Eisenhower, in September, provided $45 million aid to Iran, empowering the Shah with the understanding that the oil crisis would be settled. As the Shah fell increasingly under American influence, anti–Western circles became more aggressive. Protracted oil negotiations continued until 5 August 1954, when Iran signed an agreement with the Western oil consortium on a 50-50 revenue sharing basis. In 1960, in Baghdad, OPEC was established by the representatives of Iran, Iraq, Kuwait, Saudi Arabia, and Venezuela (Fisher, 1979, 551–560).

For the next 15 years, till his downfall, the Shah was increasingly alienated from his people. He was perceived as a puppet of the USA, "your masters" Khomeini labelled it (Cooper, 2011, 49). He began relying on his brutal secret police service SAVAK, wasting more and more of national wealth on military spending, all the time expecting US help for higher OPEC prices, so he could pass the cost of his costly fiscal policies to consuming countries. He expected Nixon, Johnson, and Kissinger to prevail over the Saudis and Gulf States to cut their production in support of his untenable policies. Kissinger never took him seriously, viewing him as a "showboat and lightweight" (Cooper, 2011, 171). When things turned worse, he blamed the Saudi oil minister Yamani and his own people, accusing them of being soft and spoilt.

Well before his demise, and ahead of the regime of the Ayatollahs, the USA had begun the strategic shift, dumping the Shah in favor of the more strategic partner, the House of Saud. It has proved equally unequal, Americans always enjoying the upper hand. The arrangement was a mere replacement of one brutal dynastic monarchy by another. Oil remained King. ARAMCO was now in the driver seat in production and refining. Pricing, however, rested with politicians like Yamani and Kissinger serving Kings and Presidents.

Cooper (2011) has done a superb job, untangling the politics of oil prices in the last years of the Shah as the White House gradually replaced the Saudi King as its key partner in place of the Shah. In 1970, the USA imported just $13.5 million worth of Saudi oil, increased to $76.8 million in 1971 or, sixfold increase in just one year. In three years, with American shift across the Gulf, Saudi Arabia had acquired 21% share of global oil production. King Faisal had replaced the Shah; Saudi Arabia became the "swing producer" of oil, USA calling the shots (Cooper, 2011, 79–80). US military sales to Riyadh skyrocketed.

Meanwhile, Khomeini launched his theocracy in Iran, a repressive Islamic regime, antidemocratic, and so intolerant of dissent, it ordered the death in London of writers like Salman Rushdie for his daring *Satanic Verses*. Inside Iran, America became the new Satan, all democratic voices ceased.

Saudi Arabia: Wahhabism, Deceit, Oil, and Imperialism

In Iran, oil shaped nationalism. In Saudi Arabia, where oil was discovered comparatively late, Wahhabism has shaped oil politics. Wahhabism is an old, puritanical version of Islam, targeted against foreigners operating, or even being present, in the sacred land of Arabia. Differences in interpretation of Islamic purity is what ultimately led to al-Qaeda *Jihadist* terrorism. The House of Saud grew out of Wahhabism, and it is sustained by a ruthless conformity imposed from the top.

Nation-building remains a challenge. The Saudi dynasty, like the Ottomans, is a family dynasty, not national or ethnic. Much of Arabia, a desert, is little different than pre-Islamic era when nomadic Bedouin tribes dominated the Arabian Peninsula and clans formed larger tribal units (Anonymous, 2022). In nomadic economies, pastoralists relied on herds of goats, sheep, and camels for meat, milk, cheese, blood, fur/wool, and other sustenance. Caravan trading was a major activity as was warfare to gain animals, women, gold, fabric, and other luxury items. Islam brought a huge sense of common religious identity, but many traditional values remained strong, including the feudal organization of society.

In the Gulf, modernization is entirely oil driven. The Saudi dynasty's fortune is not the result of some invention or technical achievement; it is the ultimate example of opportunism in full accord with foreign imperialists. Wahhabism grew out of the Arabian desert, originally as a tribal rebellion against the foreign Turkish-Ottoman rule in the mid-18th century. The brainchild of the Muslim cleric, Muhammad ibn Abd al-Wahabbi, Wahhabism grew rapidly when Muhammed ibn Saud was converted to the teachings of al-Wahabbi, a native of Nejd, who had studied in Baghdad and Damascus. He preached a simple form of Islam, a return to the model pronounced by the Prophet, set out in the Hanbali law, one of the four Sunni doctrines (Fisher, 1979, 574–575). It sought to purify Islam of foreign impurities, but under the Saud dynasty it rose to power collaborating with imperialism; it is now sustained by American protection.

Several oil-related dynamics contributed to the cozy relationship between the USA and the Saud dynasty. A vital one occurred in August 1971, when the Nixon administration, faced with huge current account deficits and debts from the Vietnam war, decided to end the convertibility of the US dollar into gold. To protect a sinking dollar, a renewed deal was struck with Saudi Arabia, updating the earlier 1945 deal to write oil contracts in dollar denomination. In the process, the petrodollar system was born, whereby the US dollar became the world's international currency, despite persistent US trade deficit. The arrangement ensures the American global economic hegemony, while protecting Saudi interests as the leading producer in OPEC (Kimberley, 2022). The cozy relationship has remained as the bedrock of American Middle East policy, climaxing in the Trump-Kushner deal brokering diplomatic relations with Israel. Earlier, when the Khashoggi murder in Istanbul on 2 October 2018 threatened the Crown Prince, Trump immediately came to the rescue, covering the crime to preserve the US-Saudi alliance.

The roots of the Saud family are buried deep in the Arabian revolt against the Ottomans. Ibn Saud was born in 1880 in Riyadh in the Nejd. His ancestors had acquired fame, battling Muhammed Ali and his son Ibrahim. After a period of exile in Kuwait, he rose to power when his father abdicated. In 1913, he captured the province of al-Hasa on the Persian Gulf, literally a territory floating on oil. The age of oil was yet decades ahead and revenues from pilgrimage still constituted the major income. Revenues being inadequate, ibn Saud depended increasingly on British subsidy.

The ambitious ibn Saud aspired to be King of Arabs. In 1920 and 1921 the British, implementing the Sykes-Picot partition plan, installed Abdallah in Transjordan and Faisal in Iraq. Ibn Saud felt he was surrounded by the Hashemite clan. But he was by then under British control, having decided in the World War I (WWI) to throw his lot in with the British, negotiating with Lawrence of Arabia to defeat the Ottomans, unaware of the intrigue ongoing at the time.

The imperialists did not have a monopoly of intrigue. They found a willing partner in the Saud dynasty. The interests of two parties coincided at this juncture in 1917: (1) imperialists chasing oil, and (2) an ambitious dynasty seeking power. The key in British imperialist penetration of the Middle East was, as has been pointed out, Lawrence. He marched into Damascus at the end of WWII as kingmaker to fulfill promises and install Faisal, Sharif Hussein's son, as the King of Syria. But imperial treachery and deceit prevailed. Lawrence was rudely rebuffed by General Allenby, commander of the British forces, who categorically declared that Syria was to be delivered instead to the French. Sykes-Picot lines in the sand were drawn well before, carving the Great Ottoman Loot between Britain and France. Betrayed, Lawrence quietly went back to England to face his own hell and finally die a broken man, while Faisal first fought the French, but then took the consolation prize to become the British puppet ruler in Iraq. Palestine became Jewish. The French ruled Syria and Lebanon in their own interest.

One thing is certain: In the Allied camp, just about everyone, in some measure, lied, betrayed, and conspired in self-interest. The Sharif of Mecca betrayed the Sultan, taking huge amounts of gold to raise an army to fight the British at Suez, only to change sides at the last moment. The Sharif betrayed Arab independence for dynastic interest under British protection. According to Anderson, Sykes lied both to Lawrence and to the Sharif by deliberately misleading them with a "bastardized version" (Anderson, 2013, 309) of his agreement with Picot. How much Huseyin conveyed to his son, Faisal, is also moot. In the end, Syria and Lebanon went to the French, while the British got Iraq and Palestine. The Sharif, Faisal, and the family dynasty begrudgingly accepted the Sykes-Picot terms. The Zionists got their Balfour Declaration.

The oil age in Saudi Arabia began in early 1930s, first discovered in the al-Hassa in 1932 and then in Dhahran in 1938. With a worldwide depression expanding after the 1929 Wall Street Crush, revenue from pilgrimage declined. In 1920, over 100,000 pilgrims came, by 1932, the number was 40,000. Ibn Saud could not pay his bills and depended on the British for advice and subsidy. On the recommendation of the British, in 1933, King Saud granted the American mining engineer Karl Twitchell a 60-year concession for exploring oil in the country. The Standard Oil Company of California (CASOC) gave the King 30,000 gold sovereigns.

During WWII demand for oil exploded. Pilgrimage trade plummeted and ibn Saud was in desperate financial straits. Britain seized the opportunity and provided rescue: by 1944, Saud's debt to London exceeded $50 million. Then the USA replaced a near-bankrupt London, which started depending on American Lend-Lease support as early as 1941 (Heritage, 2022). Saud received several million dollars from CASOC against future royalties. ARAMCO was born, the Arabian American

Oil Company. Saudi government revenue jumped from $7 million in 1939 to over $200 million by 1953. Oil thus emerged as the lifeblood of Saudi Arabia (Fisher, 1979, 578–810).

Oil wealth has empowered the Saud dynastic rule under Wahhabism. Personal freedoms have not been advanced. Aristocracy has been created, strictly under the control of the Saud family, with manual workers imported from the Philippines, Bangladesh, and the rest of the Arab world. It is a system reminiscent of slavery, as these imported workers lack basic human rights and are exploited at the whims of unscrupulous employers. Saudi Arabia has ratified a few core labor standards, but restrictions are widespread on the trade union rights, especially of foreign workers. Child labor and forced labor are legally prohibited but exist widely. There is systemic discrimination of foreign workers, especially female domestics are systematically abused (Peebles, 2022)

Technical and professional manpower has also been imported from Europe and the USA to build ultramodern towns and cities with luxury hotels, malls, golf courses, and other amenities, all elite controlled. These physical investments are primarily for a high rate of return on a massive scale. Ordinary people, while provided extensive welfare on discretionary basis, are strictly controlled, with an extensive system of internal security system including control of public morality and ethics. Gender equality is absent, and the social status of women was subordinate; patriarchy rules in a manner that compares negatively with the Prophet's own times and example (Walther, 1999).

In the political sphere, there is no accountability between the ruling elite and the people; no political parties exist; arbitrary justice prevails; no basic human rights are tolerated. Dissent is virtually absent. Wahhabism, along with a helping USA intelligence, produced Osama bin Laden, a member of the ruling Saud family, and the export of Islamic terrorism, first Al Qaeda in Afghanistan and the Islamic State of Iraq and the Levant (ISI), among others. In regional politics, the Saudi regime has squandered huge sums in fights in the Yemen and is pursuing a bitter rivalry across the Gulf with neighbors, especially Iran.

Recently, ambitious plans, such as the Crown Prince's Vision 2030, have made headlines. Announced in 2015, against falling oil prices, this plan is aimed at reducing the Kingdom's dependency on oil revenues through major diversification projects. Currently, up to 90% of the country's budget revenue is from oil. It soon run into obstacles. One leading advisor on the Kingdom's tourism development, the British business magnate Nicholas Branson, suspended his role following the Jamal Khashoggi murder in Istanbul. The Vision maintains the Saudi traditional preference for relying on imported advisors and technical personnel, even though job creation for the country's youth remains a huge challenge (Kingdom of Saudi Arabia, 2022).

Iraq: Military Dictatorship and Squandered Oil Wealth

Iraq has a glorious Islamic past. Home of some of the most sacred religious sites and events, including Karbala, where Shi'a-ism was born. In the heydays of Muslim culture and learning, the Baghdad Caliphate became the world's leading center of civilization. Sadly, from the 10th century, independent thinking was discouraged, and the Muslim science and culture entered a long period of decline (II&D, 1995, 60–62).

Iraq was born out of an imperialist betrayal. When, at San Remo in 1920, Britain divided Arab lands, as mandates to be administered by themselves on the basis of oil, primarily, there was a violent reaction at the denial of independence. Spontaneous violence turned into a full-fledged rebellion, lasting from spring to the fall and cost some 10,000 Iraqi and 400 British lives (Antonius, 1938, 312–316). What is ironic is that leaders of the rebellion were former leaders of the Arab Revolt who now felt cheated. A *jihad* was called in Karbala and in Baghdad, Basra and Mosul rebels took control. Anarchy ruled. Early in October, Sir Percy Cox arrived as civilian commissioner and a provisional Arab government, with British advisors, was set up. An Arabian prince called Faisal of the Hashemite dynasty, leader of the Arab Revolt, was installed as King of Iraq, in effect a British puppet. Even Gertrude Bell saw the futility of it all. At the installation ceremony, she confessed: "I'll never engage in creating kings again" (Hardy, 2017,149).

The mandate system was thus established, and British rule re-articulated traditional authority to suit its imperial interests ... seeking "to reinforce and strengthen tribal feudal organization as 'a method of control,' ... over Iraq through the tribal sheiks by recognizing their suzerainty over land" (Ismael and Ismael, 2015, 172). Iraq began as a British colony in everything except name. At the beginning, in 1920, the British masters chose the urban Sunni minority, remnants of the Ottoman ruling elite, as partner, dismissing the rural majority and especially the Shia in the south. When the Ottomans were gone, so was the Islamic heritage and institutions; the British rulers had no idea of an Islamic Social Contract. The country and its vast oil resources became a protectorate, governed indirectly to serve the British treasury.

For the next 37 years, until the military coup d'état in 1958, the British controlled Iraq through the Hashemite monarchy, the favorite British system of governance, used in Jordan, Saudi Arabia, and the Gulf. The coup, led by General Abd al-Karim Qasim, leader of the Free Officers group, was inspired by Pan-Arab nationalism, then widespread in the Arab world. It was modelled after Gamal Abdel Nasser of Egypt's 1952 overthrow of the Egyptian monarchy. For the British government, Nasser was an archenemy, the embodiment of Pan-Arab nationalist thought. "Nasserism" was a revolutionary ideology with the twin objective of driving Britain out of the Arab lands and unifying the Arabs. Qasim, an admirer of Nasser, was determined to join Egypt and Syria in the United Arab Republic (Khadduri, 1969, 59), but he was too weak to pull it off.

Under the British, the Old Guard system of indirect control reigned supreme; Iraq could not make any progress toward nation-building. Oil occupied the key concern of the government. In agriculture and rural areas, feudal land ownership by tribal sheiks dominated. In health, malaria, dysentery, bilharzia, and numerous other diseases, and frequent epidemics of smallpox, typhus, etc., occurred unchecked. In education, by 1950, there were only about 1,000 schools in the country (Bullard, 1958, 253). It was not until 1950 that a Development Board was set up for economic planning utilizing a fraction of the country's oil (256). It "reflected the insecurity of the regime" (291).

Qasim ruled Iraq till the Ramadan Revolution of 1963 when he himself was overthrown and killed in another military takeover. This signaled the advent of the Ba'ath Party and party dictatorship in Iraq. Although it was viewed as a "movement" with a revolutionary ideology, it was military dictatorship. General Ahmed Hassan al-Bakr became the new Prime Minister and Colonel Abdul Salam Arif became the President. The Ba'ath leaders accused Qasim of reneging on Pan-Arabism, denounced Syrian secession from the United Arab Republic, and pledged to bring Syria back into UAR. At home, the Ba'ath leaders were "young and inexperienced" (Khadduri, 1969, 207). They were divided on a socialist agenda, empowering workers and peasants. Most significantly, the nationalization of oil under Law 80 remained a dead letter. Oil nationalization had to wait for the advent of another, even more brutal, dictator in Saddam Hussain. Oil-rich Kurdistan remained at loggerheads with the central government on the questions of autonomy and control of oil to the limit of staging a brutal war. When on 5 June 1967, Israel attacked Egypt, Syria, and Jordan, Iraq joined the war totally unprepared. Iraq's was no more than a "token" participation.

Qasim pioneered in the system of ruthless dictatorship in Iraq, paving the way for Saddam Hussein. He began as a former protégé of General Nuri of the Old Guard; Qasim felt Iraq was "weak" and he cultivated regional alliances, such as the Baghdad Pact with Turkey and Iran, a British-American project that conflicted with Pan-Arab ideology, Arab Socialism, and the Non-Aligned Movement, which were closer to Qasim's heart (181–182). He was indecisive and inconsistent, even threatened the invasion of Kuwait. In the end, he achieved little: "Qasim was no less isolated from the outside world than from his own people" (185).

The Brutal al-Assad Regime

Ba'athism is also responsible for the al-Assad Syrian military dictatorship. The son has followed the father and the dictatorship has evolved into the typical Arab dynastic regime, brutal and ruthless, relying on state violence to stay in power. It is Alawite, a small Shi'a sect, and it has been supported by the major Shi'a power, the Ayatollah regime of Iran.

Damascus was the final setting in the fall of the Ottomans. It immediately became a scene of chaos. Conflicts followed ever since, first in the form of rebellion against the French imperialism. In 1946, the last French soldier left the Levant, and Lebanon and Syria became politically independent, but, weak facing an uncertain future. From then on, Syria was the scene of ideological battles, aimed at creating Greater Syria. The trauma of Palestine followed from Arab disunity and unpreparedness. Ideological battles took the centerstage: Nasserism, Socialism, and Pan-Arabism "turned into stillborn endeavor" (Choueiri 2000, 167). A series of coup d'états, staged by groups of military officers, finally resulted in the emergence of the Assad regime in 1970.

The Assad regime was brutal from the start. Originating from the relatively small Alawite tribe, Assad dynasty ruled Syria as a police state. When, finally during the Arab Spring, all the tensions of a multiethnic country were suddenly exposed, and people rebelled against a tyrannical leadership, the civil war began. Turkey and NATO countries, led by the USA, were initially demanding democratic transition. Oil politics, as always, complicated the Syrian conflict. It was quickly internationalized. Iran and Russia joined supporting Assad. Major power interest clashed Assad, like a seasoned chess player, played one against another, all the while using his forces to divide and conquer. Syria is a very diverse country, Kurds, Yazidis, various sects among its Sunni, Shi'a, Christian, and Jewish minorities. The death toll in Syria of innocent civilians skyrocketed. Citizens became refugees in their own land, as towns and cities were bombed, repeatedly, by regime forces and its Russian ally, in the vain hope of pacifying the country by brute force. Before the civil war, the Syrian population was 22 million; now it has been reduced to half.

The Syrian civil war led to Islamic terrorism funded by outsiders pursing hidden agendas. The Syrian civil war began in 2011, now in its 11th year. Eastern Syria quickly fell into the hands of terrorism, notably ISIL, the Islamic State of Iraq, and the Levant. ISIL is the direct by-product of American invasion of Iraq apparently to topple Saddam Hussein and democratize Iraq. Instead, it led to a long occupation. Popular resentment of the American forces, and the demand of the Pentagon that its forces should be above and outside Iraqi laws, led the Obama Administration to pull out Iraq at the end of 2011, but only after securing control of oil fields. The security vacuum attracted Al Qaeda and other terrorist groups. Out of Hell, a new terror group emerged, equipped with abandoned military hardware. ISIL suddenly appeared waving flags atop tanks and armored SUVs, declaring the dawn of a messianic Islam. Its leader Abu Bakr al-Baghdadi was a brutal murderer, beheading one and all who dared to oppose. He set up a Caliphate in Mosul in Iraqi Kurdistan, carrying out war crimes against the Kurds, Yazidis, and others to enforce its crazy ideology.

ISIL took over the oil fields in the region, and a new geopolitical challenge emerged. Its origin goes back to the Sykes–Picot partition plans in WWI. Under the defunct Treaty of Sevres, the Kurds were promised a homeland. Likewise, the Armenians were to be awarded Eastern Anatolia. Greece got Western Anatolia. Turkish national aspirations were ignored and resulted in the Turkish War of National Independence, 1919–1922, which created the modern Turkish Republic under Ataturk. Turks and Kurds had fought together in these wars, and at the armistice concluding WWI; oil-rich Mosul was in Turkish hands. The British, however, wanted the oil fields and threatened war against the Turkish Republic. As for the Mosul oil, Mustafa Kemal was a realist, opting for full national independence over economics. In 1926, under the terms of an out-court settlement with the British, he gave up Mosul's territory and oil in return for 10% of royalties which later was sold "for a lump sum of a mere 500,000 Sterling Pounds." (Kinross, 1964, 410 footnote). The Kurds' aspirations were ignored.

Now, with Americans rewarding the Kurdish PYD, it looked to Ankara that Washington was resurrecting the Sykes-Picot partition plans, attempting to redraw lines in the sand. NATO alliance was split. President Obama chose to partner, not with NATO ally Turkey, but with the Kobani Kurdish, the PYD, an extension of PKK (Ustun, 2021). Ankara was dismayed. It took US-led coalition way too long to defeat ISIL; some would argue that it was deliberate as it provided "justification" for American invasion and continued occupation. American support of Kobani Kurds upsets Ankara, which has its own war of terrorism against the separatist, Marxist–Leninist PKK, the Kurdish Workers Party that has claimed an estimated 40,000 killings in Turkey. PYD, the Syrian Kurdish Patriotic Front, is an extension of the PKK recognized by the Americans and Europeans as a terrorist organization. Paradoxically, the USA has chosen PYD as a partner in its fight against ISIL, upsetting its NATO ally. What alarmed Turkey was unconfirmed reports that the USA would reward Kobani Kurds with an independent state. It was a project supported by France and Israel. For Ankara it would mean changing the map, and worse, create a terrorist state on its border widening the PKK-PYD cross-border attacks. Under Trump, better relations between Washington and Ankara emerged, resulting in Turkish armed forces' incursion into Syria, which effectively eliminated that danger, while also preserving Syrian territorial integrity.

The human torn by civil war is horrendous, by all accounts. Data in Table 2.3 show 380,000 killed, 9 million displaced persons, and 6.6 million refugees escaping into neighboring countries of Jordan, Lebanon, and Turkey. In Turkey alone, there are now more 4 million Syrian refugees, costing some $40 billion in resettlement. As well, the Syrian refugee crisis has generated exodus into Europe creating unplanned and massive waves of migrants trying to enter EU countries, using Turkey as transit country. In 2016, a Refugee Agreement was signed, but that has not solved the problem of Syrian refugees. Ideally a political solution would do that, but more likely a regime change, or military compromise may be realized to permit a significant number of refugees from returning home.

The Qaddafi Dictatorship

Libya has the largest proven oil reserves in Africa. It was the last Ottoman province to be wrested out of the Ottoman Empire during European imperialism. It remained an unimportant desert Kingdom until oil was discovered in 1959. On 1 September 1969, Qaddafi staged a coup, abolished the monarchy, and became the dictator of Libya. In 1973, he nationalized the oil industry and henceforth oil revenues were all at Qaddafi's disposal, used at his discretion to create his own brand of Islamic welfare state (Cooper, 2011, 109), tackling the country's serious poverty challenge. His Green Book was inspired by Mao's Red Book and was regime's gospel, obligatory to be read by "all people" (Gaddafi, 2021). Qaddafi was a megalomaniac, saw himself as leader of oppressed African and Third World countries and, according to American sources, gave financial support and sanctuary for various Al Qaeda terrorist activities, fighting the French and Western forces in Niger, Chad,

Mauritania, and Burkina Faso. In fact, he claimed Al Qaeda was involved in a coup to oust him (Al Jazeera, 2022). For a revolutionary, he was surprisingly "reluctant" to lend support to Pan-Arabism (Choueiri, 2000, 206).

His dictatorship was mild by Arab standards. In return for submission to his rule, the state provided public housing, education, health care, and he believed in his own cult of personality. His last words were cynical, begging for mercy: "What have I done to you" (Sam, 2021). Max Forte, an anthropologist from Universite de Quebec, in a well-researched study, has argued the real motive behind the bombing was Pentagon's interest in stopping the Pan-Africanist ambitions of Muammar Qaddafi (Forte, 2022).

After Qaddafi, Libya became yet another case of Muslim country torn civil war, foreign intervention backing one competing tribes, and warlords backed terrorist groups and mercenaries. In Libya, the UN recognized GNA based in Tripoli, the Government of National Accord. However, a former Gaddafi-era military officer, Khalifah Haftar, quickly emerged to establish the self-proclaimed "Libyan National Army." He is ambitious, an American citizen whose commitment to Libya is dubious, using Libya for personal gain, while his sons are addicted to luxury, fast cars, and drugs. In May 2014, Haftar launched Operation Dignity in Benghazi, ostensibly to eject Ansar al Sharia, a Salafist militia that arose during the 2011 uprising. Egypt, United Arab Emirate, Russia, and France soon joined the conflict on either side with mercenaries and aid.

Then, the GNA appealed for help to Turkey and the balance has shifted to a delicate draw ever since. In return for its support of the GNA, Turkey signed a maritime delimitation agreement in defense of the Turkish continental shelf in the hydrocarbon dispute with Greek Cyprus and Greece (Mehmet and Yorucu, 2020, chapters 7,8,9).

After considerable international mediation and negotiation, finally, the UN managed in 2021 to broker an agreement between Haftar and the GNA with promised elections in December 2021 but have been postponed due to political differences. A delicate cease-fire prevails with rival groups and personalities attempting to take power. The UN-recognized interim president Abul Hamid Dbeibali has stated he will only hand over power to a duly elected president. He is opposed by the Haftar-backed Fathi Bashaga, a wheeler and dealer, so the future is far from certain (Middle East Eye, 2022).

The Libyan civil war, lasting a decade, has been relatively less costly in human lives with an estimated death toll of a few thousand at the time of his bloody downfall. According to the data in Table 2.3, as of 2019, up to 25,000 were killed, 200,000 internally displaced, and at least 1 million became refugees. As well, there are unknown numbers of migrants and refugees drowning in the Mediterranean tiring to escape to Europe.

The Syrian and Libyan civil wars have deep Ottoman roots. Ankara is involved in both conflicts that are reminiscent of imperial designs on the Ottoman Empire. Now, it is oil politics, local people being used as pawns in pursuit of oil wealth by Western powers. France is seeking to carve Libyan oil for French oil company Total.

In Iraq and Syria, the Americans have secured heir control of oil in the region. The Kurds, once again, may feel abandoned, but they need to learn that imperialists' "divide and rule" strategy has no future. The Kurds are but one ethnic group in the region. They must learn to live in peace with other ethnic groups of the region, Arabs, Turks, Shi'a and Sunni, and others. This is what has happened in the case of the autonomous Kurdish administration in northern Iraq, which has good relations with Ankara. Kobani Kurds need to do the same. After all, at the end of the day, foreign invaders will go; local people will stay, although their proxies may take over.

The Egyptian Case of Nation-Building

Egypt is the preeminent Arab country. It was the first case of modernization in the Arab Core and its history is illuminating in explaining why the Arab leaders fail in modern nation-building.

It goes back to Muhammad Ali, the ambitious Ottoman governor who charted his own course.

Muhammad Ali was a pioneer modernizer, a nation-builder. During his rule, 1805–1849, which was marked by many wars, he was a pioneer in economic development. He built irrigation systems and canals and brought additional land under production. He carried out land reform, redistributing idle Mameluke lands to the villagers. He expanded cotton cultivation. Beyond agriculture, he was also a successful reformer in public administration and taxation. He himself was quite frugal and expected fair accountability in tax collection from the tax farmers. He set up village councils, and an elaborate dispute settlement machinery. He had a high regard for the peasant, the *fellaheen*. "There are two sovereigns" he would say, "Sultan Mahmut (the Ottoman ruler in Istanbul) and the *fellah* … and the *fellah* must not be regarded with an evil eye" (Quoted in Dodwell, 1931, 216). In Cairo and Alexandria, he established new courts to modernize the archaic ecclesiastical law relating to marriage, divorce, and, above all, inheritance. He also carried out reforms in education, health, and sanitation. Cholera and bubonic plague, constant source of terror, were largely brought under control. He applied strict quarantine in the Great Plague that fell upon lower Egypt in 1835. In the higher education system, he introduced Western knowledge, and new schools were opened (Dodwell, op. cit., Chapter VII). Today these reforms would be described under the heading of grassroots democracy. When he died in 1849, Egypt's population had almost doubled, the acreage of cultivated land increased by 25%, exports rose by tenfold, especially the new crop of cotton (Pudney, 1969, 22). Yet, Muhammed Ali's reforms failed to lead to sustained, long-term development. Bankruptcy and British takeover followed within a decade of the completion of the Suez Canal in 1869.

During his life, Muhammed Ali's most passionate desire was to establish a dynasty, which he succeeded to do in 1839. That dynasty turned out to be Egypt's ruin. A crucial missing element in Muhammed Ali's reforms was a solid accountability system to prevent abuse of power, especially in public expenditure. His son, Muhammed Said's big achievement was the start of the construction of the Suez

Canal. But Said was "putty" (ibid., 239) in the hands of Ferdinand de Lesseps, the French engineer who was the mastermind behind the construction of the Canal. De Lesseps was always in financial difficulty and never managed to convince a reluctant British government of the economic viability of the Canal. He depended on the British to secure the official permission from the Ottoman Sultan in Istanbul, but there was always delay owing to other pressing issues.

Said died in 1863 and was succeeded by his French-educated grandson Ismail. Unfortunately, the grandson turned out to be a spendthrift. He lived a life of luxury, spending extravagantly without accountability. Unlike his grandfather, he exploited the fellaheen, overtaxing them, and he used slave labor to build the canal. He himself lived in the Abidin Palace, a 500-room Italian-style building of extravagance, set in 24 acres, where Ismail lived in delusions of grandeur. On opening ceremony, in 1869, he spared no expense to impress his star-studded list of guests that included the Empress Eugenie of France: He hosted his guests on a lavish scale: "The Viceroy had brought over 500 cooks and 1,000 servants from Trieste, Genoa, Leghorn and Marseilles" (ibid., 143). Shortly after the opening of the Canal, Ismail was obliged to sell his shares in the company.

Conclusion: A promising start is no guarantee of long-term success in nation-building. Dynastic rule, in the hands of poor successors, or without a free parliament to provide checks and balances on public expenditure, can negate all the development accomplishments of one modernizing leader. In the end, his grandson undid all the good works Muhammed Ali had spent a lifetime to achieve. Within years, in 1882, Egypt, while still nominally an Ottoman territory, fell under British occupation. Egypt was incorporated into the Eurocentric mercantilist system, first with the development of cotton plantations in the Delta, and subsequently due to the Suez Canal, a project of European imperialism. We now discuss, in great, these two events.

The Egyptian Cotton Plantations: In the 1860s, Egypt experienced an unprecedented growth of cotton cultivation in the fertile Delta region. Large plantations were developed using African slaves and Greek immigrants, but the unique feature of this system was the manner in which it was brought about. It was the direct consequence of the American Civil War. The Deep South and its slave society, immortalized in Margaret Mitchell's *Gone with the Wind*, was the traditional source of raw cotton for Lancashire and Yorkshire textile factories. The war made this impossible and the British entrepreneurs turned to Egypt as an alternate source of supply. The cotton plantations expanded rapidly because the major problem of large quantities of cheap labor was solved partly by using African slaves, and increasingly Greek migrant workers. In just six months, February to August 1864, no less than 12,000 foreign workers, mostly Greek, had arrived. Alexandria soon became home to Greek migrants, and Greek merchants and traders quickly emerged as the comprador class. Cotton exports boomed, doubling in quantity between 1861 and 1853, rising to 1.3 million *cantars* (1 *cantar* = 100 pounds). Export earnings from cotton represented 90% of government revenue (Schwartztstein, 2016).

The political elite and the comprador class benefitted greatly from this new source of wealth, not the Egyptian grassroots, because the khedives, the son and grandson of Muhammad Ali, were unlike the modernizing founder. The state's share of revenues was not channeled into public health, education, and urban development for the benefit of the public. Muhammed Ali's son, Said, ruled for a relatively short period of time, but his grandson Ismail was in power longer. He was the ultimate squanderer of public funds, indulging in luxury and waste on an unbelievable scale, until the country went bankrupt. The Suez Canal, the second major Western project, which solidified Egyptian incorporation into the Western capitalist system, was the linchpin in the imperialist penetration into the Middle East.

The Suez Canal: The Canal Company was, as the British expected, unprofitable for several years. With unrestrained spending, Khedive Ismail was obliged to sell his shares, representing 44% stake in the canal, for a "paltry" (Hardy, 2017, 125), 4 million British Pounds. That was Disraeli's opportunity. He dramatically loaned the funds from the Rothschilds, without Cabinet approval, bought the Egyptian stake, beating the French interests out. The Suez Canal became British overnight and Queen Victoria, Empress of India, was one happy monarch (Pudney, ibid., 183).

Disraeli's opportunistic takeover of the Canal was all connected to British India. After the suppression of the Indian Mutiny in 1857, the East India Company emerged as the monopoly trader, sitting atop an economic empire built on tea, coffee, but most of all opium. All were highly profitable, the rising revenue enriching the upper classes in England. The opening of the Suez Canal greatly reduced the shipping costs, which, in turn, increased the profits accruing to British stakeholders. Even though unprofitable at the time of the British takeover, the Canal, in British hands soon became highly profitable. Disraeli was shrewd enough to know the misrule in Egypt and realize the potential. With his move, Egypt was now solidly ensnared in the mercantilist system.

At the start, the funds to finance the Canal was international, to be subscribed as follows (Pudney, 1969, 76–77): France 207,111, Ottoman Empire, exclusive of Viceroy's personal investment, 96,517, Spain 4,046, Holland 2,615, Tunis 1,714, Piedmont 1,353, Switzerland 460, Belgium 324, Tuscany 176, Naples 97, Rome 54, Prussia 15, Denmark 7, Portugal 5, Sums held in reserve for Austria, Great Britain, Russia, and the USA 85,506 (ibid., 76). When subscriptions were called, it was not a success. Of the 400,000 shares only 286 were taken up due to general opinion that the project was not financially viable. This did not deter Lesseps from persisting in the venture. Of note is the relatively large number of shares earmarked for the Sultan, nominally owner of the territory through which the Canal was built. By that time, the Ottoman Sultan in power was Abdulmecit, another grand spendthrift who borrowed hugely in the European capital markets, only to squander the funds in his huge harem and futile wars against the Tsar, paving the way to bankruptcy. The Ottoman Empire became the first official defaulting country in the world, leading to the financial control of the Empire through a creative European institution called the Ottoman Public Debt Administration (Pamuk, 1987, 61–62). The Ottoman default preceded the British takeover of Egypt by only a few years.

Debt, Imperialism, and the Urabi Revolt, 1882: In the age of European imperialism, European debt creation was as powerful as an instrument for taking over countries in the Muslim world as armies. By lending huge sums to spendthrift rulers, imperialist powers caused claims against states and dynasties. This was most clear in the creation of a Jewish homeland by Zionism. When Rothschilds provided the funds to Disraeli to acquire the Suez Canal, the first step was taken in the British occupation of Egypt.

The imperial control of the Suez Canal sparked the first popular revolt against the British, what is known as the Urabi Revolt, in 1882. By then, not only the khedive, but his master the Sultan was broke. In Egypt, when Egyptians resented European domination of their country, the first nationalist revolt led by Colonel Urabi took place. Some 50 Europeans were killed in the rioting. Britain and France responded with gunboat diplomacy; a joint naval fleet was sent to Alexandria.

The tragedy then moved to Istanbul. Europeans attempted to use the bankrupt Sultan to depose the khedive and replace him with a European puppet. When the gambit did not work, the British acted. On 11–12 July 1882, the British navy burned Alexandria and installed their own khedive, Mohamed Tewfik Pasha in the Ras El Tin Palace. The khedive then declared Urabi a rebel, who then obtained a religious ruling, a *fatwa*, signed by three al-Azhar sheikhs, declaring Tewfik Pasha a traitor. The British controlled Alexandria, while Urabi was in full control of Cairo and the provinces.

Then the final act in the British gunboat diplomacy unfolded. In August, General Garnet Wolseley and an army of 20,000 came ashore at Ismailia in the Suez Canal Zone. In the decisive battle at Tell el Kebir on 13 September, the Urabi forces were routed after two hours of battle with a loss estimated at 2,500. On 15 September 1882, Cairo was occupied. The British-controlled khedive was restored, and the British occupation of Egypt began, lasting until 1956 when all British troops were finally withdrawn from the country in the closing chapter of gunboat diplomacy at the hand of another military leader, Abdul Nasser, a topic discussed elsewhere.

Notes

1 As Islamic social justice is extensively discussed in II&D, from the Constitution of Medina on, it will only be summarized here.
2 Again, it is stated that Iran is not an Arab country. It is in the Islamic Core, the home of Shi'a Islam. In this study Islamic Core and Arab Core have been used as appropriate.

References

Aljazeera, 2022, Gaddafi blames al-Qaeda for revolt, www.aljazeera.com/news/2011/2/25/gaddafi-blames-al-qaeda-for-revolt, accessed on 9 Feb. 2022.
Anderson, Scott, 2013, *Lawrence in Arabia: War, Deceit, Imperial Folly and the Making of the Modern Middle East*, New York: Signal.

Anonymous, 2022, Pre-Islamic Arabia. https://resources.saylor.org/wwwresources/archi ved/site/wp-content/uploads/2011/08/HIST351-1.1-Pre-Islamic-Arabia.pdf, accessed on 14 Oct. 2021.

Antonius, G., 1938, *Arab Awakening: The Story of the Arab Movement*, New York: Hamilton.

Bradford, Ernle, 1964, *The Great Seige, Malta 1565*, London: Penguin.

Brockelman, Carl, 1948, *History of the Islamic People*, London: Routledge & Kegan Paul.

Bullard, Sir Reader, ed., 1958, *The Middle East, A Political and Economic Survey, 3rd ed., under the auspices of the Royal Institute of International Affairs*, London: Oxford University Press.

Cooper, Andrew Scott, 2011, *The Oil Kings: How the US, Iran and Saudi Arabia Changed the Balance of Power in the Middle East*, New York: Simon & Shuster.

Corley, Thomas, A.B., 1983, A History of the Burmah Oil Company, 1886–1924, www. goodreads.com/book/show/3468497-a-history-of-the-burmah-oil-company-1886-1924, accessed on 1 March 2022.

Dodwell, Henry, 1931, *The Founder of Modern Egypt: A Study of Muhammad Ali*, Cambridge: Cambridge University Press.

Esposito, John L., 1988, *Islam, the Straight Path*, New York: Oxford University Press.

Fisher, Sidney Nettleton, 1979, *The Middle East: A History*, 3rd ed., New York: Knopf.

Forte, 2022, Slouching Towards Sirte. Nato's War on Libya And Africa. http://openanthropol ogy.org/libya/, accessed on 9 Feb. 2022.

Frankopan, Peter, 2018, *The Silk Roads: A New History of the World*, New York: Vintage Books.

Frankopan, Peter, 2020, *The New Silk Roads, The New Asia and the Remaking of the World Order*, New York: Vintage Books.

Gaddafi, Muammar, 2021, Gaddafi's "The Green Book". www.amazon.ca/Gaddafis-Green-Book-Muammar-al-Gaddafi/dp/1541241312, accessed on 20 May 2021.

Goodwin, Jason, 1998, *Lords of the Horizons, A History of the Ottoman Empire*, New York: Henry Holt & Co.

Hardy, Roger, 2017, *The Poisoned Well, Empire and Its Legacy in the Middle East*, New York: Oxford University Press.

Heritage, 2022, The 1941 Lend-Lease Agreement. www.heritage.nf.ca/articles/society/lend-lease-agreement.php, accessed on 1 March 2022.

Ismael, Tareq and Jacqueline Ismael, 2015. *Iraq in the Twenty-First Century, Regime Change and the Making of a Failed State*, London: Routledge.

Khadduri, Majid, 1969, *Republican Iraq: A Study in Iraqi Politics since the Revolution of 1958*, London: Oxford University Press.

Kimberley, Amadeo, 2022, What Is the Petrodollar? www.thebalance.com/what-is-a-petr odollar-3306358,. accessed on 1 March 2022.

Kingdom of Saudi Arabia, 2022, Vision Saudi 2030. www.vision2030.gov.sa/media/rc0b5 oy1/saudi_vision203.pdf, accessed on 1 March 2022.

McMeekin, Sean, 2016, *The Ottoman Endgame, War, Revolution, and the Making of the Modern Middle East, 1908–1923*, New York: Penguin Books.

Mehmet, Ozay, (II&D), 1990, *Islamic Identity and Development; Studies of the Islamic Periphery*, London: Routledge.

Mehmet, Ozay, 1995, *Westernizing the Third World, the Eurocentricity of Development Theories*, 2nd ed., London: Routledge.

Mehmet, Ozay and V. Yorucu, 2020, *Modern Geopolitics of Eastern Mediterranean Hydrocarbons in an Age of Energy Transformation*, Switzerland: Springer.

Middle East Eye, 2022, Fathi Bashagha: Libyan tyre trader wheeling and dealing for power, www.middleeasteye.net/news/libya-fathi-bashaga-tyre-trader-wheeling-dealing-power, accessed on 17 Feb. 2022.

Mikhail, Alan, 2020, *God's Shadow: The Ottoman Sultan Who Shaped the Modern World*, London: Faber.

Pamuk, Sevket, 1987, *The Ottoman Empire and European Capitalism, 1820–1913: Trade, Investment and Production*, Cambridge: Cambridge University Press.

Peebles, Graham, 2022, Fathi Bashagha: Libyan tyre trader wheeling and dealing for power. www.redressonline.com/2013/12/the-abuse-of-migrant-workers-in-saudi-arabia/, accessed on 1 March 2022.

Pudney, John, 1969, *Suez, De Lesseps' Canal*, New York: Praeger.

Rogan, Eugene, 2015, *The Fall of the Ottomans, the Great War in the Middle East*, New York: Basic Books.

Sam, Christopher, 2021, https://hypercitigh.com/featured/gaddafis-last-words-as-he-begged-for-mercy-what-did-i-do-to-you/, accessed on 20 May 2021.

Schwartztstein, Peter, 2016, How the American Civil War Built Egypt's Vaunted Cotton Industry and Changed the Country Forever, www.smithsonianmag.com/history/how-american-civil-war-built-egypts-vaunted-cotton-industry-and-changed-country-forever-180959967/, accessed on 8 Sept. 2021.

Ustun, K., 2021, US Alliance with Syrian PYD Alienates Turkey, www.aljazeera.com/opinions/2016/6/2/us-alliance-with-syrian-pyd-alienates-turkey/, accessed 19 May 2021.

Walther, Wiebke, 1999, *Women in Islam: From Medieval to Modern Times*, Princeton: Markus Wiener.

Wheatcroft, Andrew, 2008, *The Enemy at the Gate, Habsburgs, Ottomans and the Battle for Europe*, New York: Basic Books.

6

THE MAKING OF THE MODERN MIDDLE EAST

Western Invasion, the Sykes-Picot Legacy, Failed States, and Terrorism

Invasion of the Middle East from WWI era led to occupation of Arab lands. Lines drawn in the sand, from the Sykes-Picot partition created several artificial countries in the post-Ottoman, multinational Middle East. The division of the Ottoman lands divided Arabs, setting one *millet* against another. Imperialists imposed their will with a map, based on lies and deceit. It was a recipe, on a grand scale, to create chaos, civil war, and almost permanent warfare. The map was drawn to enable the imperialists to control oil and ensure that it went to fuel industries and homes in the West. The share of revenue to oil producers themselves, was secondary, worse still, that share did not finance sustainable development to benefit the ordinary people. In the case of dynastic regimes, it has gone into physical development, infrastructure owned by privileged families or arms purchases for regime survival and to wage wars in neighboring countries. In the case of military dictatorships, oil wealth has gone into military buildup, either to build police states to oppress people, create one-man rule, or wage wars. The result for ordinary citizens has been a tremendous human loss and suffering on a huge scale.

Chapter 5 briefly reviewed six country cases. Here we will examine the expenditure priorities in the Arab world, to document state failure to achieve economic and social development. We compare health and education, with military expenditures based on the latest statistics compiled by the most reliable international sources. First, however, we discuss what "Socio-economic development" means and what constitutes state responsibility in delivering development benefits to ordinary citizens.

What Is Socio-Economic Development?

Standard definitions of socioeconomic development recognize that it is a dynamic process led by the state to bring the benefits of progress to citizens, to improve

DOI: 10.4324/9781003268994-6

human well-being (UNDP, 2021). The development process is multidimensional: it has investment, technical, legal, and institutional dimensions. All must be coordinated in harmony to result in improvement in the human well-being. Coordination is the task of a development-oriented state. Sustainable development evolves from a successful state governance and management.

Progress in human well-being is through investment in socioeconomic development, which is largely measurable. The UN, the World Bank, and numerous other international agencies have development statistical indicators for this purpose. They include income growth, life expectancy at birth, health, literacy, and employment levels. Income is typically gross domestic product (GDP), the value of all goods and services produced by a country within a given year. GDP growth is critical, but it is only one indicator.

Less tangible or nonmeasurable determinants of development are personal security of life, human dignity, freedom of association, freedom from fear of physical harm, and the extent of participation in civil society organizations. Free press is essential for informing citizens and ensuring transparency in public policy. Laws and legal institutions enable socioeconomic development when they guarantee and enhance these nonmeasurable determinants, otherwise they become oppressive as in a police state or dictatorship.

Socioeconomic progress is achieved by state investment in human well-being. Investments are included in a development budget that reflects state priorities for education, health, housing, food, and all the essential human needs. These are all productive investments; there are also unproductive, but essential investments for legitimate defense, such as for security forces, military, and weapons of war, but these should not be used to oppress citizens. Finally, development depends on new technologies, technical know-how, and the protection of the physical environment and ecology.

Statistics on development indicators in the Arab world are difficult to obtain. Often concepts and methods are inconsistent and incomplete. Some, admittedly sketchy figures in Table 6.1 show that overall military expenditures in the Arab world surpassed health and education expenditures. Elsewhere in this study, we have used several indicators of socioeconomic development, measurable and nonmeasurable (see Chapter 2). Below we compare military expenditures against those in education and health as a proportion of the GDP.

Military expenditure averaged 5.4% for the Arab world in 2019, slightly higher than Israel (5.3%). The country with the highest military spending was Libya, Egypt being the lowest. In the case of education, over the period 2004–2008, on average there was a 7.14% decline, the education share of GDP representing 4.34 in 2008, and 4.67 four years earlier. Expenditure on health averaged 5.23% for the Arab world, Jordan's share being the highest (7.79%) and Djibouti's lowest (2.32).

There are further World Bank data summarized in Table 6.2 on literacy rates for total adult population aged 15 and over, infant mortality rates per 1,000 of live births, number of physicians and hospital beds per 1,000 of population. These are the latest statistics available, for the year 2019, except indicated otherwise. They

TABLE 6.1 Government Expenditures on Health, Education, and Military In The Arab World (latest figures as % of GDP)

Latest government expenditure (as % of GDP) on	Arab world, average	Arab Country with the highest %	Arab Country with the lowest %
Health, 2018	5.23	Jordan (7.79)	Djibouti (2.32)
Education, 2008	4.34		
2004	4.67		
Military, 2019	5.4	Egypt (1.2)	Libya (15.5)
2014			

Sources:
Health expenditure: https://data.worldbank.org/indicator/SH.XPD.CHEX.GD.ZS?locations=1A, accessed on 27 August 2021.
Education expenditure: https://knoema.com/WBGS2019/gender-statistics?tsId=1644770, accessed on 27 August 2021.
Military expenditure: https://data.worldbank.org/indicator/MS.MIL.XPND.GD.ZS?locations=IL-1A, accessed on 27 August 2021.

TABLE 6.2 Comparative Development Indicators, Arab World Versus World, 2019

Indicator	Arab World	World
Literacy rates, total adult population 15 years +	73	86
Infant mortality rate/1,000 live birth#	26	28
Physician per 1,000 population★	1.0	1.57
Hospital beds per 1,000 population. 2017★	1.4	2.9

Sources: (All accessed on 9 Oct. 2021): +https://data.worldbank.org/indicator/SE.ADT.LITR.ZS
#https://data.worldbank.org/indicator/SP.DYN.IMRT.IN
★https://data.worldbank.org/indicator/SH.MED.PHYS.ZS

are averages, reflecting the fact that conditions in war-torn Arab countries are, to some extent, offset by conditions in oil-rich countries. With this caveat, it will be observed that the Arab world is significantly behind in literacy rates (73% versus 86%), slightly ahead in infant mortality rates, (26 versus 28 per 1,000 live births), and significantly behind in terms of physician per 1,000 population. These statistics are before the COVID-19 epidemic, and generally against a global trend of advances in education and health care.

Labor Market and Youth Unemployment

Youth unemployment in Arab countries is high, much higher than in other regions of the world. It is the major reason behind civil unrest and popular uprisings. Frustration among young people, more prevalent among university graduates, spills over into extremism, and push the youth into *Jihadist* terrorist groups. This is what happened during Arab Spring in 2011 (USIP, 2011), leading to rebellion against regimes in Egypt, Syria, Tunisia, Yemen, and elsewhere. Jobless youth anywhere, but especially in the Arab world where freedoms are restricted, is always explosive.

What are the causes of high unemployment? The primary cause is lack of a labor-friendly labor market policy. There is insufficient investment in human capital formation, skill development, to increase the technical and skilled supply. No less significantly, firms in the private sector generate relatively few job opportunities, due to low investment in economic development and industrialization. Gulf countries have recruited high-level skilled workers globally, preferably from the West, and relied on cheap inflow of manual workers from labor-surplus Asian and Far Eastern sources. Finding new job opportunities in the Middle East and North Africa (MENA) region has become more critical in the Pandemic period than at any other time in the past. This adds to the poverty challenge of households and jobseekers themselves.

The labor force participation rate (LFPR)for females in the Arab world is another useful indicator of social and economic development. LFPR shows the percentage of females of working age who are economically active. Data in Table 6.3 summarize the most recent data, 1990–2019.

The first remarkable fact about the data in Table 6.3 is the stationary trend of LFRP during the period 1990–2019 when otherwise rapid growth occurred, especially in oil producers. Yet, over this 30-year period, only one in five Arab women participated in the labor market. There are, of course, many factors behind this low LFPR, but the dominance of patriarchy and general acceptance of feudal values are some of principal factors.

When the labor market prospects in future are considered, the population in MENA is forecast to double by 2050 despite slowing demographic growth (UNICEF, 2019). Additionally, the labor force is getting younger, with those under the age of 14 constituting more than 40% of the total. Moreover, the trends indicate that the women's labor force participation rate is increasing, which means the jobs crisis will worsen, and take a gender dimension as well. Informal sector and the underground economies may be expected to grow rapidly. Unless a radical shift is adopted in the immediate future by formulating and implementing an active labor market policy, especially in non-oil MENA countries. The status of women must

TABLE 6.3 Female Labor Force Participation Rate (Lfpr) in the Arab World, 1990–2019

Year	LFPR
1990	20.34
2000	20.72
2010	21.38
2019	21.93

Source: www.indexmundi.com/facts/arab-world/indicator/SL.TLF.ACTI.FE.ZS, accessed on 11 Oct. 2021.

be enhanced with enabling legislation. This is the strategy recommended by the International Labor Organization (ILO, 2021).

Energy Transformation: Can Saudi Arabia Do It?

The age of the automobile using fossil fuel is ending. Climate change and consumption patterns are rapidly shifting to renewable energy (Mehmet and Yorucu, 2020). As global transformation accelerates, and the hydrocarbon age gives way to renewable energy, oil producers need to diversify their economies. Saudi Arabia has announced an ambitious Vision 2030 led by the Crown Prince. In 2018 two renewable energy projects were launched in the northern region of Al-Jouf: Sakaka, a 300-MW solar PV powerplant, and the Dumat Al-Jandal 400-MW onshore wind project. Since then, seven more solar power stations have been announced (Utilities, 2021). To change the desert into green ecology is a huge challenge requiring reforestation and ample water supply. Vision 2030 makes the necessary promises: A mega reforestation to plant 10 billion trees (Middle East Eye, 2021) and water desalination projects using solar energy (Saudi Arabia, 2021). These are essential schemes to diversify the Kingdom's economy and ecology in the age of energy transformation.

Will the Kingdom be able to do it? Only time will tell whether Vision 2030 investments are on a sufficient scale or whether they will achieve the expected transformation. A major constraint will be the human resource availability, whether the Kingdom will have its own skilled manpower to manage these and other energy transformation projects. The key requirement will be how to push these ambitious projects under an authoritarian regime with little concern for basic human freedoms and rights. The Vision 2030 is a top-down plan with little, if any, input from civil society groups that function best under freedom. Saudi Arabia has, at best, weak civil society organizations. In much of the developed world, energy transformation is led by popular demands as reflected by changing consumer habits.

As for the Bedouins in the vast Arabian desert, they remain fiercely independent, although their numbers have declined rapidly due to the decline of nomadism, they are by no means reconciled with modern nation-building. The war in the Yemen is a clear indication of the inability of the House of Saud to impose its authority at will, especially in other countries. Traditional loyalties, especially Sunni–Shi'a divisions remain very much alive, indeed rivalry between Iran and the House of Saud is a threat to peace in the region, with as always, significant American role (Meyssan, 2022).

Oil as a Curse

Oil wealth brings huge windfall gains, enabling sustainable development and energy transformation, but it can also have distorting influence on development. While windfall oil revenues remove the saving constraint, they encourage the ruling elites to adopt and implement strategies incompatible with sustained development. Instead of investing in social and economic development, putting top priority on labor market policies, as outlined above, elites pursue different, antidevelopmental objectives.

Historically, states created in a manner to be dependent on imperial powers feel vulnerable to threats for takeover, assassination, or civil wars. It all adds up to the fact that, typically, Arab state creation has been a story of "failed states" (Chomsky, 2006), a highly apt paradigm expertly applied in the case of Iraq (Ismael and Ismael, 2015). The paradigm has wider relevance in explaining the chaos in the Arab Core. Now, we shall briefly review the cases of Jordan and Algeria later, the former case being the creation of British imperialism, the latter of French, for a deeper understanding of the impact of imperialism on state failure.

In the immediate period leading to the WWI, 1914–19118, imperialist powers perceived oil as a key military asset. Armies, navies, and the new air forces were in the process of a big technological transformation. Navies were being redesigned with oil-powered ships, armies were reformed with new horseless army vehicles such as tanks and trucks, and most novel of all, aircraft. Already civilian use of the automobile was already a new fashionable way of life. The quest for oil was on; the West was experiencing a shortage of the strategic commodity. Oil politics shaped military strategy, which, in turn, led to foreign invasion (Yergin, 2008).

The oil business, on both sides of the Atlantic was adjusting to the new market reality of oil demand exceeding supply. Early exploration work indicated that the Ottoman Sultan's desert territories in the Middle East was rich in oil. The imperial contest for the control of Mesopotamia had begun. The Germans, ahead of all others in courting the Sultan, were busy with the Baghdad Railway (Earle, 1966). When the Kaiser visited the Sultan a second time in 1898, German capitalists, including French interests, were well advanced in drafting a concession for the railway to run from Haidar Pasha in Istanbul to Baghdad. The principal financier of this mega project was the Deutsch Bank, which had received the original railway concession in 1888. Although it took more than a decade to realize the project, in the following years, German exports to Ottoman Turkey rose almost fourfold, while Turkish exports to Germany jumped almost eightfold (36). German capitalists, led by the

> Hamburg entrepreneurs established the Deutsche Levante Linie, a direct steamship service between Hamburg, Bremen, Antwerp, and Constantinople … Promoters, bankers, traders, engineers, munitions manufacturers, ship-owners, and railway builders, all were playing their parts in laying a substantial foundation for a further expansion of German economic interests in the Ottoman Empire.
>
> *36–37*

Shipping lines and railways facilitated an aggressive German penetration into the Ottoman Empire and threatened the British hegemony in the region and set the stage for the bloody war that followed. The French, who controlled the Ottoman Bank, endorsed the railway project, a senior Bank officer becoming the vice president of the Baghdad line (165). The British, who earlier had supported the project, by 1913 had become quite hostile, feeling that the railway threatened British interests in Egypt and India (204).

The German capitalists persisted. Sultan Abdul Hamid II finally signed an imperial *irade* (royal order) on 18 March 1902, enabling implementation of the Baghdad Railway by the Anatolian Railway Company (68). Westminster, ruling over the largest colonial empire, already controlled the newly discovered oil in Persia through the Anglo-Persian Oil Company. British geologists had already discovered huge reserves in Mosul in northern Mesopotamia, an area of the Ottoman Empire with Kurdish population (Hardy, 2017, 146). Mosul immediately became a hotly contested area. At the onset of the WWI, strangely enough, a British and German partnership was in the works, providing for joint participation in the newly founded Turkish Petroleum Company that held prospecting rights in Mesopotamia. The Baghdad Railway and the German concessions surrounding it were significant elements of German imperial penetration into the oil-rich region. But WWI changed all that; the USA imperialism took the place of German imperialism after the War through, for example, the Chester Concession, over a huge territory in Eastern Anatolia and northern Mesopotamia, with a tax holiday for 99 years (Earle, 1966, 342–343).

The defining British act, which changed everything on the eve of WWI, was a tragedy played out in Newcastle, England. At the end of July 1914, the Ottoman navy expected to be significantly bolstered by the addition of two dreadnoughts, *Sultan Osman I* and *Reshadie*, built by British shipping companies. These boats were already paid for, the funds raised through voluntary contribution by patriotic Ottoman Turks. The Turkish crews were already in Newcastle to take possession. At the last minute, with pressure from the Tsar urging Westminster not to permit these dreadnoughts to join the Ottoman navy, the First Lord of the Admiralty Churchill ordered the seizure of the ships in a "flagrantly illegal act" (McMeekin, 2016, 98). The Kaiser rose to the occasion and offered two German warships: *Goeben* and *Breslau* to the Ottomans (99). The pro-German War Minister Enver was delighted. In September, the German boats, still manned by German crew, but now flying the Ottoman flag, sailed through the Bosphorus into the Black Sea, ready to launch an attack on Russia. For several tense weeks, neutral party played a futile tug of war with the stronger warmonger's camp: in the end, on 29 October the German admiral Souchon, on orders from the Ottoman War Minister Enver, attacked the Russian warships in Sevastopol and Odessa, and the Ottomans were suddenly in War on the German side (130).

The war ended not only the nascent Anglo-German oil partnership; it dealt a mortal blow to what appeared as a reenergized Ottoman Empire under German imperialism. That prospect was simply too much for British imperialists in London as well as the Raj in India, which considered Mesopotamia a strategic area as its own zone of interest. Churchill, the First Lord of the Admiralty, took the lead, but he was actively encouraged by the Raj who "envisaged Iraq one day coming under Government of India's control" (Rogan, 2015: 224). The viceroy did not wish to compromise India's security. But the British planners prevailed in their quest for a direct British attack on Basra and Mesopotamia. The Indian Expeditionary Force easily took control of Basra, but then at Kut al Amara they suffered defeat. General Townshend's' 23,000 strong army surrendered to the Ottomans (247–252), and the British invasion of Iraq was temporarily halted. At Armistice, the British did not control the oil fields of Mosul.

Earlier, as WWI continued, oil acquired an increasing strategic value. The top military planners in Westminster recognized that control of oil fields had become a major war objective. Sir Maurice Hankey, the powerful Secretary of the British War Cabinet, wrote to Foreign Secretary Arthur Balfour pointing out that oil had become indispensable to Britain and that oil resources in Mesopotamia should remain in British hands. Hankey summarized: "… everyone in the cabinet had come completely round to Lloyd George's view … that it is necessary to devote our main efforts against Turkey" (McMeekin, 2016, 353). Expelling Turkey out of Mesopotamia was necessary for Britain to gain control of the oil fields.

Hankey's view, however, was in direct contradiction to secret negotiations with the French. Already the British had ceded much of the oil-producing area in northern Iraq to their French ally in the notorious Sykes-Picot Accord of early 1916. Subsequently, the British diplomacy and military plans changed course and promises were broken. Not only Arabs, the French ally, too felt betrayed. Days after the armistice was signed, the British forces raced to capture Mosul. The Turks were furious, but they could do nothing as a feud was raging between the Sultan's government in Istanbul under Allied occupation and the Kemalist nationalists in Ankara. Once the Turkish Republic was established, Turkey went for arbitration, as part of the peace treaty at Lausanne, 1923. In October 1927, oil was discovered in Kirkuk near Mosul. On 31 July 1928, the Allies finally reached a famous accord, known as the "Red Line Agreement," which brought the US oil companies into the picture with just under a quarter of the shares, equal to the British, French, and Dutch shares. The dragoman Gulbenkian, who drew the red lines, retained his 5% share (Historian, 2022).

The restoration of peace had greatly increased the global demand for oil. Now, it was even more valuable as the driver of industries, factories, and homes as well as cars. The French-British competition over the control of Mesopotamia intensified. In October 1921, the French went ahead and signed an accord with the Kemalists in securing the borders of the Turkish Republic and the French-mandated Syria. The accorded also included an exchange of prisoners and a promise that French schools and companies in the Turkey would not be harassed (Mango, 1999, 327). Earlier, at the Versailles Peace Conference, British Prime Minister Lloyd George and his French counterpart Georges Clemenceau disputed bitterly the control Mesopotamian oil; US President Woodrow Wilson apparently barely managing to restrain them. In the end, a face-saving compromise was achieved whereby France received almost the German quarter share in the old Turkish Petroleum Company. The irony was that the British-French feud happened before a drop of oil had been discovered in northern Iraq, but once it was discovered in 1927, the US government got into the Mesopotamian oil feuding as well. Feeling aggrieved at the hands of ungrateful European allies, and the prospect of an "Anglo-French monopoly" over the Middle East oil, the USA demanded a fair share, which it finally managed to obtain under the Red Line Agreement, as discussed in the previous paragraph.

Meanwhile, at Lausanne, the Turkish and British negotiations over Mosul reached a compromise, whereby the matter was referred, by mutual consent, for arbitration by the newly established League of Nations to which the Turkish Republic was not yet a member. In 1926, a friendly deal was reached between Ankara and London. Turkey gave up its claim on Mosul in return for a 10% stake in oil royalties, a share that was sold for a mere half a million English pounds early in 1930s to finance Ankara's water supply.

The Mosul Question (Musul Meselesi)

Oil in northern Iraq was in the territory of Kurds and Turkmen of northern Iraq. Under the terms of the peace deals among the Allies, these unfortunate people benefitted almost nothing from it while suffering so much. The Treaty of Sevres, an unequal treaty imposed on the Ottomans, partitioning the Turkish homeland, included provision for creating independent Armenia and Kurdistan in Eastern Anatolia. At the conclusion of WWI, Ottoman armies were in control of the *Vilayet of Musul* (Mosul). The province also contained a sizeable Turkmen population, especially in Kirkuk, another major oil zone.

According to the terms of the armistice agreement ending WWI, the Ottomans would retain control of Mosul, a condition that commanded wide popular support among the Turkish nationalist movement. It was incorporated in the National Pact (*Milli Misak*), the guiding platform for fixing the boundaries of the new Turkish Republic. Mustafa Kemal, the future Atatürk, embraced it, but, in the bitter reality of the negotiations leading to the Lausanne Treaty, 1923, he took a more realistic position, and sacrificed Mosul to achieve a truly sovereign Turkey, freed of financial strangulation under the hated system of foreign control, known as *capitulations* (Demirci, 2011, 101–102). In the National Assembly in 1922–1923, heated debates raged on over the declaration of the Republic and dissolution of the Caliphate. *Milli Misak* (National Pact) had to be revised because the peace negotiations in Lausanne dragged on. Ataturk, the realist, and his trusted lieutenant Ismet İnönü, recognized that they must secure British support, first and foremost, to win peace at the Lausanne negotiations and guarantee Turkish independence. Ankara's relations with France were improving, but İnönü needed the British agreement to overcome differing positions among Allies, especially over the status of the Turkish Straits and Thrace. To insist on Mosul at all costs was judged to be futile (ibid., 105–107).

The Treaty of Lausanne was finally signed on 24 July 1922 and İnönü returned, in triumph, to Ankara, the new capital of the Turkish republic, hailed as a hero (Mango, 1999, 386–387). The humiliating Treaty of Sevres was thrown into the dustbin. Atatürk, the realist, knew that giving up Mosul would divide the Kurds, causing "perpetual trouble" for the Turkish government (Mango, 1999, 367). In his long six-day grand speech, Atatürk acknowledged that unlike Sevres, Lausanne was "silent" on Kurdistan (Atatürk, 2010, 505). Independent Armenia and Kurdistan were dropped altogether. It was a necessary price to be paid for Turkish sovereignty.

Sykes-Picot Agreement: A Story of Deceit

The secret negotiations for the partitioning of the Ottoman lands, known as the Sykes-Picot accords, were contradicted even by its architects, almost before the ink was dry, as we have seen in the case of the feuding over the oil fields of Mosul. Likewise, there were many broken promises made to Arabs and dynasties who had helped in the Allies' victory in the Middle East, the Balfour Declaration of 1917 being perhaps the most notorious. The partition plans created several countries and spheres of influence, always the imperialists' interest prevailing. The Wilsonian principles of "the consent of the governed" (McMeekin, 2016, 419) were deliberately ignored in the hard bargaining over Middle East oil, as discussed earlier. The one exceptional case was the creation of Israel (even though no Jewish majority existed at the time), which had its origins in the Sykes-Picot secret negotiations. From Sykes-Picot to Truman, the Zionist project of a homeland for the Jewish people remained as a solid "divide and rule" objective of imperialism, at the cost of the Arab population of Palestine.

On 2 November 1917, the Foreign Secretary Arthur James Balfour wrote his famous letter:

> *Dear Lord Rothschild,*
>
> *I have much pleasure in conveying to you, on behalf of His Majesty's Government, the following declaration of sympathy with Jewish Zionist aspirations which has been submitted to, and approved by, the Cabinet.*
>
> *"His Majesty's Government view with favour the establishment in Palestine of a national home for the Jewish people and will use their best endeavours to facilitate the achievement of this object, it being clearly understood that nothing shall be done which may prejudice the civil and religious rights of existing non-Jewish communities in Palestine, or the rights and political status enjoyed by Jews in any other country."*
>
> *I should be grateful if you would bring this declaration to the knowledge of the Zionist Federation.*
>
> *Yours sincerely,*
>
> *Arthur James Balfour*

The Letter was the culmination of a long struggle by the Zionist movement for a Jewish homeland in Palestine. The struggle had been multidimensional: financial, political, and military. In financial terms it represented a kind of payback time going back to the acquisition of the Suez Canal by the Jewish Prime Minister Disraeli using Jewish credit in an overnight deal without Cabinet approval. In political terms, it was fruition of dedicated action by Jewish activists over the preceding decades, in the final stages led by the former MP, Baron Nathan Rothchild. In military terms, in a later period, while the British forces were in a stalemate in their fight with the Ottomans, dug in near Beersheba in the fall of 1917, an all-Jewish battalion was training with the British army, ready to contribute its part in the British victory and deliver Eretz Yisrael. Zionism had been gaining ground in British politics and high society for a long time, especially among the evangelical Christian organizations. The Zionist movement itself was an elite-managed movement: As late as 1914, merely 2% of the Anglo-Jewish community was part of the Zionist organization, and a good portion of the Jewry were hostile to the idea of fighting for a homeland in Ottoman Palestine.

The declaration in the Letter was the result of close personal links between the banking family Rothschild and Chaim Weizmann, head of the British Zionist organization. In January 1914, Edmond de Rothschild, the banker, had introduced his cousin Walter to Weizmann. The two immediately forged a close friendship that became the central pillar in political action that followed. Walter Rothschild was a former parliamentarian, and his collaboration with Weizmann led directly to the Letter four years later.

The war between Britain and the Ottomans was a huge opportunity for the Zionists. The prospect of defeating the Ottomans represented the fulfillment of "ultimate destiny" and the actual realization of a homeland in the Holy Land. The vital causal factor, however, was the presence of Zionists, and supporters of Zionism, in the war cabinet. Herbert Samuel was a Jewish nationalist, while David Lloyd George had been a pro-Zionist for over a decade. The two worked with Weizmann on a memorandum circulated as early as January 1915, which, for the first time, envisaged a British-supported Eretz Yisrael, pointing out that such a project would consolidate British control of the Suez Canal while providing a Jewish homeland. At time, the war cabinet was seized with the Arab Revolt and the memorandum got nowhere.

In 1916, the Arab Revolt was launched. A Hashemite Arab army moved into action, acting on the grandiose British promise of a single, sovereign Arab state stretching from Syria to the Yemen. It was undeliverable: simply put, the Arabs were duped. Already, in secret Sir Mark Sykes and François Georges-Picot were meeting to negotiate a mandate system, producing their document known as the Sykes-Picot Agreement. It aspired to dismemberment and partition of the Ottoman Empire. Modern Syria and Lebanon were allocated to France, and Palestine and Iraq similarly given to Britain. The Agreement guided the Allied war efforts. Sykes, now in cabinet, was in contact with the British Zionists even before his negotiations with Picot and was likely aware of Herbert Samuel's memorandum. When he concluded his deal with the French, he later wrote that "to my mind, the Zionists are now the key of the situation" (Israel Alliance International, 2020).

The turning point came in December 1916 when there was a new government in Westminster. Lloyd George became the Prime Minister. Pro-Zionists were now in control. Expecting a quick victory, the British army moved into action early in 1917, securing the Suez Canal, but then the military campaign was halted at the edges of the Gaza City. The Letter did not go out for almost a year. Balfour met

Weizmann in the summer seeking Jewish support while the Letter went through several drafts. Sykes met Weizmann and several members of the World Zionist Congress in Britain. Bogged down at Gaza, Balfour travelled to the USA looking for American intervention in the war, and during this time met the leaders of the American Zionist movement.

Finally, the die was cast. On 31 October 1917, Sykes left the Cabinet meeting to come out to Weizmann, eagerly waiting in the hall to make the historic announcement: "Dr. Weizmann, it's a boy!" (Rogan, 2015, 349). This was the time of suffragettes, when sexism was rampant, and women shut out of politics. Rogan has provided strategic evidence for the Declaration at the time it was delivered: "In supporting Zionism, the British government believed they would gain the support of influential Jews in the United States and Russia. America was a late entry into the war, its traditional isolationism making it a reluctant ally, and Russia's commitment to the war had been in doubt ever since the February Revolution and the Tsar's abdication in March 1917." In short, it all boiled down to the supremacy of the British interest: Israel was created because, in the making of the modern Middle East, it was seen as imperative for British imperialism; all else, including promises to the Arabs, even to the French, were secondary. In 1919, even the Americans, after long debates over mandates, went along with the British supremacy (McMeekin, 2016, 418–422).

The deception of the Arabs in 1919 was no accident. It was the result of naked imperialist bargaining. The feeling of betrayal hit all segments of the Arab community, even before the Arab Revolt was completed in Damascus where rebellion, assassination, and dynastic feuding immediately erupted. The creation of Jordan exemplified how the British, after getting their prize, were able to offer the Arab dynasties a consolation prize, even then, under their own control.

Creating an Artificial Country, A Consolation Prize

Jordan, "the oddest of all new states of the Middle East" (Hardy, 2017, 87) was created by the British at the end of WWI when Britain assumed a mandate over the Transjordan territories of the defeated Ottomans, while the French acquired Syria and Lebanon. Caught between inter-dynasty feuds, London was desperately looking for a credible family amenable to British rule through a resident advisory system. In March 1921, Winston Churchill, the Colonial Secretary, met an Arabian prince, Abdullah, of the Hashemite family of the Hejaz, claiming descent from the Prophet and thus enjoying popular legitimacy, and Transjordan was born at the discretion of one of top architects of British imperialism. The Colonial Secretary at the time, Churchill, would later boast that "he had created Transjordan with the stroke of a pen one Sunday afternoon" (Hardy, 2017, 87).

Abdullah, displaced from his own homeland, happily accepted British Mandate, becoming the King of the Hashemite Kingdom of Jordan, the country of Jordan today. Unlike Iraq, and other neighbors, Jordan had no oil. Its ruling dynasty was first financially supported by London, after the creation of Israel in 1948, by the

USA (Bullard, 1958, 349). The British Mandate was comprehensive, covering not only civil administration, but the army as well. Churchill's motivation in the 1921 deal was "the creation of a British-controlled territory from the Mediterranean to the Gulf ... to keep the French out" (Hardy, 2017, 87).

The British mandate over Palestine was never easy, always facing crisis, as London attempted to navigate between the Zionist plans for mass inflow of Jews to create Israel, and the Arab hostility to it. The Balfour Declaration was ambiguous, a perfect imperialist plan to divide and rule. Several times during the mandate, bloody massacres took place. In 1939, the British White Paper fixed total immigration for the next five years at 75,000 and froze discussions over the future of Palestine for the duration of the War. The Zionists rejected the plan, and the new leader of the Jewish Agency, Ben Gurion, was impatient to increase immigration in the face of Nazi atrocities and tragedies like the old cattle boat, *S.S. Struma*, carrying 799 visa-less Jewish refugees were lost in the Black Sea sinking in a storm. The British interned thousands of immigrants in Cyprus and Mauritius in a futile effort to contain the exodus. Illegal immigration into Palestine continued. In Palestine Zionist guerrilla tactics and terrorism accelerated under the leadership of the future Prime Minister Menachem Begin and Zvai Leumi (Fisher, 1979, 671–2). Against a background of continued terrorist acts and increased Arab-Israeli fighting, the UN Special Committee on Palestine called for the partition of Palestine and the establishment of Jewish and Arab states. On 1 October 1947, London declared that its mandate would be terminated on the following 15 May, and all British troops evacuated before 1 August. At the UN, President Truman, supporting Zionism, pressed several countries to secure a pro-Israel vote. On 29 November 1947, the UN adopted Resolution 181 calling for the partition of Palestine, and mass expulsion of Palestinians immediately begun. More than 1 million Palestinian refugees flooded into Jordan, whose population overnight jumped from 400,000 to 1.3 million. Amid the Palestinian exodus, on 14 May 1948, Ben Gurion in Tel Aviv proclaimed the establishment of the Zionist state in Palestine and, President Truman "minutes after" announced the *de facto* recognition of Israel. The next day, the Palestine war begun (ibid., 678).

The American interest in Israel predates the creation of the Jewish state, driven by adventurers and explorers, some searching for oil, others, like the famed Lawrence, collecting intelligence among the tribal Bedouins of the desert. In the case of Israel, two American university graduates, William Yale and Rudolf McGovern, came as agents of the Standard Oil Company, in search of oil (Anderson, 2013, 11). From oil exploration they moved into agricultural development. Lured by the vast prospect of modern agriculture in the Holy Land, they quickly became pioneers in the development of scientific land development, experimenting with new crops and working in collaboration with the American Zionist movement to realize the idealist project of a Jewish homeland in accordance with Herzl's 1896 book, *The Jewish State*. In the Peace Treaty, 1919, the Zionists had won the great prize; the Arabs lost their dream of "greater Arab nation" (Anderson, ibid., 490). Along with the Arabs, Lawrence felt betrayed as well; his own death, at the age of 46, in a motorcycle accident was violent and premature.

The case of Lawrence is tragic as is the case of Jordan, which was Lawrence's playground. He crisscrossed the Jordanian desert, in his Bedouin garb, always shrouded on secret missions: He was in towns like Maan, Kerak, Salt, Yarmouk in the north, Aqaba in the south, carrying secret meetings, intelligence gathering, negotiating with Faisal, and filing reports and inputs for war planning for, or aiding the British forces.

Along with imperialists, Arab elites conspired at the expense of ordinary people. The Sharif of Mecca betrayed the Sultan, taking huge amounts of gold to raise an army to fight the British at Suez, only to change sides at the last moment. The Sharif betrayed Arab independence for dynastic interest under British protection. According to Anderson, Sykes lied both to Lawrence and to the Sharif by deliberately misleading them with a "bastardized version" (Anderson, 2013, 309) of his agreement with Picot. How much Huseyin conveyed to his son, Faisal, is also moot. In the end, Syria and Lebanon went to the French, while the British got Iraq and Palestine. The Sharif, Faisal, and the family dynasty begrudgingly accepted the Sykes-Picot terms. The Zionists got their Balfour Declaration.

Arab unity was sacrificed on the altar of expediency. Djemal, the last Ottoman governor of Syria exposed it all in Beirut in 1918. It was too late; imperial interest had won. As for Lawrence, in the end he got his bittersweet revenge on those cruel Turks he had spent a whole life hating. The bitter end arrived for the Ottomans and Lawrence at the same time. In Damascus, at the end of WWI, with a colossal human toll of 16 million dead, Lawrence was a defeated man as much as the Ottomans. Mustafa Kemal, not far to the north, was about to launch the War of Turkish Independence, thanks, in no small way, to the strategic pullback of Anatolian armies into the Turkish homeland to fight in another war. Betrayed and abandoned, Lawrence returned to England to become a part-time champion of the lost Arab cause. Lloyd George and Churchill used him on short-term assignments selling imperialism to Arabs. In 1934, he killed himself in a motorbike accident. The Arab disunity and conflict have continued ever since.

Jordan is a country hopelessly embroiled in the Palestinian conflict, made worse by Arab disunity, always subject to shifting political winds from Egypt, Syria, and Iraq. In 1950, King Abdullah was killed by a Palestinian gunman with Egyptian sympathies, as he was entering the al-Aqsa Mosque, and was succeeded by his eldest son Tallal who was mentally sick, but nevertheless ruled the country for two years, democratizing the constitution, before he was declared unfit to rule. His son Hussein, only 17 and in school in England, became King. Its small army, the Arab Legion under the British general Glubb Pasha, had performed comparatively well in the Palestinian War, defending the West Bank and Eastern Jerusalem, losing it in the 1967 Six-Day War. The economy depended on British loans and subsidies, supplemented by occasional contributions from other Arab states friendly to London. After the British, the Americans became the source of occasional Arab funding for Amman. The strategic American aim has always been the security and growth of Israel, culminating in President Donald Trump's recognition of Jerusalem as the Jewish capital.

From the beginning of the Palestinian exodus, through the Six-Day War, Jordan has carried the heaviest burden of Palestinian loss and dispossession. It has been obliged to give up the West Bank for a possible future Palestinian state, but the prospects are anything but hopeful. Hamas in Gaza, Hezbollah in Lebanon, in defense of Palestinian rights, are engaged in a permanent state of war with Israel, with Jordan obliged to carry the consequences. Similarly, the Syrian civil war has hugely added to the refugee burden of Jordan.

Jordan's vulnerability persists, made worse by its refugee burden. Its economy is fragile, highly dependent on remittances from Jordanians working in the Gulf. Indeed, the Jordanian education system is a peculiar system producing graduates more than the country's limited labor market requirements. Excess manpower is deliberately for exports to fetch foreign exchange. At the same time, in agriculture and construction, the country relies on cheap imports of workers from neighboring Arab countries. The country hosts a huge refugee population, some living in official camps (operated by UNRWA, discussed in Chapter 9) or unofficially, but all under the care of NGOs and aid organizations.

Algeria: The Bloody Case of French Imperialism

The French took over Algeria in 1830, ousting the Ottoman Governor, in a desperate act of imperialism to prop up a struggling Bourbon monarchy in Paris. The Ottoman Sultan could not come to the rescue of the Algerian Muslims owing to his own preoccupation with the War of Greek Independence and the problems of Mehmet Ali in Egypt (Shaw and Shaw, 1977, 31–32).

Algeria is a vast country, four times the size of France. It had 3 million population at the time of French invasion, virtually all living in the narrow coastal strip. During its 132 years of occupation, the French faced resistance from the beginning, especially the indigenous Berbers who, centuries earlier, had been Arabized and converted to Islam, but still retained their own languages and customs. The French came as colonizers intent on a civilizing mission to impose French language and culture, wiping out Muslim religion and custom. In 1848 Algeria was formally annexed, making it an integral part of France. The Christianizing process was begun by importing large numbers of Catholic settlers from Spain, Italy, and Malta, who took over the most fertile lands, and transforming the wheat growing agriculture into vine cultivation, producing wine for export to France. French language and customs were quickly and widely imposed through education and in arts and sciences. Assimilation of ruling elites in civil and military service quickly followed; impoverished, dispossessed peasants, the non-French-speaking *fellahin*, were left with two choices: either migrate into *bidonvilles* (shantytowns) in rapidly growing cities and towns or stay in rural areas working as virtual serfs on *colon* estates. Newspapers and literature evolved in French as novelists and poets, even those writing in protest, like Mouloud Mammeri, the author of *Le Sommeil du Juste* (The Sleep of the Just), expressing loss of identity and culture, in French. Young nationalists, and idealists, too, wrote and disseminated their ideas in French.

In the first four decades the country was under continuous military rule, as tensions often erupted into violence between the local population and settlers. The first significant resistance to French rule was led by a Sufi scholar, Emir Abdul-Qader. It was just two years into the French rule, in 1832, and the tribes of western Algeria, in the Berber heartland of Kabylia, rushed to join him. Abdul-Qader created a state, which, at its height, extended over two-thirds of the country. The French military, with unrestrained brutality, put down the rebellion, but did not succeed until 1840, using an army of over 100,000. Abdul-Qader was not arrested until 1847, by which time Algeria had a settler population of 100,000 (Hardy, op. cit., 164). During a 50-year period, 1871–1919, the settler population in Algeria had risen to 833,000, 75% of whom lived in cities and owned no less than 215 million acres of land (Hardy, ibid., 166).

WWI had a terrible impact on Algeria, settlers, and Muslims alike. No less than 25,000 Algerian Muslims were conscripted into the French army, while another 100,000 worked in munition factories and digging trenches. Nationalism emerged out of the sacrifices on the battlefield. Two parallel movements began, one was Islamic reformism of *ulemas*, scholars of Islam, influenced by the ideas of the Egyptian scholar and reformist Mohammad Abduh (II&D, 66). Their motto was simple and clear: "Islam is our religion, Algeria is our country, Arabic is our language."

The other movement was controlled by French-educated Muslims, a small cadre of teachers and junior state officials, some with Communist links. They fought for equal rights within a French Algeria, comfortable with the policy of assimilation. When Independence finally came in 1962, it was late in comparison with several other colonial areas in the region: Libya became independent in 1951, Tunisia and Morocco in 1956, and Mauritania in 1960. More significantly, it was achieved in bloodshed, with a colossal loss of life. The Algerian War of Independence between the *Front de Liberation Nationale* (FLN) and the French army, lasting eight years from 1952 to 1962, "may well have cost half a million lives" (Hardy, ibid., 182). Some estimates put the figure as high as 1.5 million and no less than President Macron admitted "war crimes" (Aljazeera, 2018).

The Algerian War of Independence itself was extremely brutal but was more like guerrilla warfare. During the "Battle of Algiers," marking the launching of the Algerian War of Independence, FLN operated more as an urban-based terrorist organization bombing and attacking prominent French-owned cafes and shops. In the end, Ben Bella, with close links to the Algerian national army (ALN) emerged as the winner, caught in a vicious scramble for power in the summer of 1962, against Ferhat Abbas, the leader of the Provisional Government of the Algerian Revolution (GPRA).

In 1962, when Independence came, the French President de Gaulle transferred the power to GPRA, picking Ben Bella over Abbas to lead Algeria, primarily because Ben Bella had served in the French army and had ALN support. Ben Bella was a contradictory leader, who earlier had enjoyed the support of Nassir, but he also believed Islam was an advanced form of Socialism. He tried, in vain, to introduce socialist reforms. Lack of a clear nationalistic vision, especially an unclear boundary between politics and the military on the one hand, and Islam on the other, has bedeviled Algerian politics ever since. Under the Avian Accord settling the Algerian independence in 1962, Algerians were granted relative freedom of movement between Algeria and France, and many colons and assimilated Algerians took advantage of the opportunity. By 1965, there were over 500,000 Algerian nationals in France, but later, successive French governments have restricted access to France for economic migrants.

The Algerian Revolution had impact beyond Algeria influencing the ideology of Black consciousness and decolonization. It inspired Frantz Fanon's masterpiece, *The Wretched of the Earth*, which, contrary to some opinions, did not glamorize violence, but instead articulated how state oppression damages both the colonized and the colonist. Violence might be a necessary response by the colonized to state oppression, which may explain why Fanon himself became a member of the FLN and participated in the resistance against the French. However, for Fanon, a psychiatrist, violence is no more than the tool of an oppressor who lacks the humanity to understand the humanity in the oppressed. Fanon's work so greatly influenced Mandela that when released from prison, the first country he visited was Algeria to express his solidarity for the struggle for decolonization (Conversation, 2022).

The Sykes-Picot Legacy

In their secret partition negotiations, Sykes and Picot created the new countries of the Middle East, according to imperial interests in railway lines, mining and oil concessions, ports, and trading hubs (Sachar, 1969, 158–175), not for the welfare of the people of these lands. In the making of the post-Ottoman Middle East, imperial Britain and French interests paralleled other European powers' interests. Wherever imperial interests required, language and Christian "civilization" were imposed, and local history and culture were repressed, often brutally. The army, missionaries, teachers, novelists, and all worked as a colonial team, as articulated in Edward Said's *Orientalism*. Whenever local people resisted, massacres, genocide, and every possible means were used to pacify rebels. The paramount objective was wealth accumulation in European capitals.

The struggle for national independence, or decolonization, was bloody and very costly in human lives. In Africa, in the Palestinian Wars, loss of life and displaced persons as refugees amounted to millions. In the First Indochina War (1945–1955), 1.2 million native population was killed, hundreds of thousands wounded. The human toll of the Algerian Liberation War was huge. The irony is that in WWI, Muslim soldiers from British India and French North Africa fought the Ottoman armies. The liberation of France itself in WWII was made possible, thanks to African colonial soldiers. De Gaulle emerged as the strongman he was, out of the agony of Algeria. The root of chaos in Muslim lands even today, including homegrown terrorism, is a direct result of imperialism and forced assimilation.

Who Is a Terrorist? What Exactly Is Terrorism?

The roots of Middle East terrorism lie in Sykes-Picot Agreements. As our survey of the latest scholarship on the making of the Middle East shows, there is considerable Western guilt for the tragic condition of the Muslim Core. This fact, however, is not recognized in the scholarly study of conflict and security studies, except for solidarity voices like Chomsky. Generally, there is a lack of clear and objective key terms, in particular, key terms like "terrorist" or "terrorism." Widespread loose usage of these terms abounds not only in news and social media, but even in scholarly studies. As Said has emphasized, *Orientalism* is a long-embedded tradition in Western culture.

Looking at some studies on conflict and security studies, one is struck by a voice of anguish. Hoffman (2017), begins his study with a lament, aptly critical of the Western media, rejecting "... *the promiscuous labelling of a range of violent acts as 'terrorism'*" (ibid., 1). Hoffman points out that the origin of this term goes back to State Terror, as in the French Revolution, of 1793–1794.

Contemporary Muslim terrorism is driven by deep devotion to divine justice. Of course, Western imperialism has been brutal and bloody. But playing God is utter distortion. A suicide bomber is a pathetic soul, misled and misguided into a belief that he or she is doing a God-sanctioned duty, that the personal sacrifice will yield not only temporal justice, but eternal rewards to the bomber. The bomber is simply a victim of some demented master killer. A typical example is the case of *Jemaah Islamiyah* bombing of the British, Israeli, Australian, Singaporean tourists in Bali, "... *an all-consuming hatred of the predominantly secular country in which they lived*" (Hoffman, ibid., 307). This is the language of hatred, not divine justice.

Berger (2018) provides a useful guideline when he draws an essential link between terrorism and extremism: "*Terrorism is a tactic, whereas extremism is a belief system*" (ibid., 2018, 30). He argues that terrorist groups, which are by necessity small and therefore rely on asymmetric violence, tend to create ideological justifications to attack Western secular lifestyle in support of an ethnic, national, or religious agenda. The West is seen as the archenemy. This study has shown ample proof of the atrocities of Western imperialism. The chaos in the Muslim Core is, indeed, the direct result of Western imperialism at the end of WWI and its more recent manifestations. Radicalization of terrorists is far from simplistic; some causal factors are endogenous, such as poverty, deprivation, and oppressive states (e.g., Wahhabism in Saudi Arabia, Westoxication in Iran – see II&D, 1990, 72, 93), not forgetting personality or psychological factors.

Terror networks employ a variety of techniques for their terrible acts of violence. The recruitment of mercenaries and child soldiers is significant because it reveals a complex set of motives on the part of terrorists. Mercenaries may be soldiers of fortune or unemployed or psychopaths. Child soldiers are more likely to be cases of forced labor. Jones (2017), based on a study of 179 cases of insurgencies, (ibid., Appendix A) has highlighted "*external support*" for insurgency as critical in the group's chances of victory (ibid., 245). On the other hand, the state actor may win and defeat non-state actors in insurgency for a variety of reasons ranging from poor leadership of adversary, organizational hierarchy, strategic or operational factors, including resource availability.

References

Aljazeera, 2018, France Admits Torture During Algeria's War of Independence, www.aljaze era.com/news/2018/9/13/france-admits-torture-during-algerias-war-of-independence, accessed on 12 Feb. 2022.

Anderson, S., 2013, *Lawrence in Arabia*, New York: Signal.

Atatürk, Mustafa Kemal, 2010, Gençler için Fotoğraflarla NUTUK (The Speech, for Youth with Photographs), Ankara.

Berger, J.M., 2018, *Extremism*, Cambridge: MIT Press.

Bullard, Sir Reader, ed., 1958, *The Middle East, A Political and Economic Survey*, 3rd ed., Royal Institute of International Affairs, London: Oxford University Press.

Chomsky, Noam, 2006, *Failed States, The Abuse of Power and the Assault on Democracy*, New York: Metropolitan Books.

Conversation, 2022, What Mandela and Fanon learned from Algeria's revolution in the 1950s, https://theconversation.com/what-mandela-and-fanon-learned-from-algerias-revolut ion-in-the-1950s-107736, accessed on 12 Feb. 2022.

Demirci, Sevtap, 2011, *Belgelerle Lozan (Lausanne, with Documents)*, 3rd ed., Istanbul: Alfa.

Earle, Edward Mead, 1966, *Turkey, the Great Powers and the Bagdad Railway: A Study in Imperialism*, New York: Russel & Russel.

Fisher, S.N., 1979, *The Middle East: A History*, 3rd ed., New York: Knopf.

Hardy, R., 2017, *The Poisoned Well, Empire and Its Legacy in the Middle East*, New York: Oxford University Press.

Historian, 2022, The 1928 Red Line Agreement, https://history.state.gov/milestones/1921- 1936/red-line, accessed on 11 Feb. 2022.

Hoffman, Bruce, 2017, *Inside Terrorism*, 3rd ed., New York: Columbia University Press.

ILO, 2021, What Works: Active Labour Market Policies and Their Joint Provision with Income Support in Emerging and Developing Economies, www.ilo.org/global/research/ projects/active-labour-market-policies/lang--en/index.htm, accessed on 9 Oct. 2021.

Ismael, Tareq and Jacqueline Ismael, 2015, *Iraq in the Twenty-first Century, Regime Change and the Making of a Failed State*, London, and New York: Routledge.

Israel Alliance International, 2020, The Balfour Declaration and Sykes-Picot Agreement, https://israelallianceinternational.com/legacy-publishing/balfour-declaration-sykes- picot, accessed on 12 Sept. 2021.

Jones, Seth G., 2017, *Waging Insurgent Warfare: Lessons from the Vietcong to the Islamic State*, New York: Oxford University Press.

McMeekin, Sean, 2016, *The Ottoman Endgame, War, Revolution and the Making of the Modern Middle East, 1908–1923*, New York: Penguin Books.

Mehmet, Ozay, (II&D), 1990, *Islamic Identity and Development, Studies of the Islamic Periphery*, London: Routledge.

Meyssan, T., 2022, "Fanaticisms at the Service of the United States", *Voltaire Network*, 25 January, www.voltairenet.org/article215416.html, accessed on 11 Feb. 2022.

Middle East Eye, 2021, Saudi Arabia to Plant 10 Billion Trees, as MBS Launches Ambitious Climate Plan, www.middleeasteye.net/news/saudi-arabia-billion-trees-climate-change, accessed on 2 Nov. 2030.

Sachar, H.M. 1969, *The Emergence of the Middle East: 1914–1924*, New York: Knopf.

Saudi Arabia, 2021, Water Desalination Project Using Solar Power, www.vision2030.gov.sa/v2030/v2030-projects/water-desalination-project-using-solar-power/, accessed on 2 Nov. 2021.

Shaw, S.J. and Ezel Kural Shaw, 1977, *The History of the Ottoman Empire and Modern Turkey*, Vol. 2, 31–32, Cambridge: Cambridge University Press.

Shaw, Stanford J. and Ezel Kural Shaw, 1977, *History of the Ottoman Empire and Modern Turkey*, Vol. 2, Reform, Revolution and Republic: The Rise of Modern Turkey, 1808–1975, New York: Cambridge University Press.

UNDP, 2021, 2021/22 Human Development Report, http://hdr.undp.org/, accessed on 25 Oct. 2021.

UNICEF, 2019, MENA Generation 2030, https://data.unicef.org/resources/middle-east-north-africa-generation-2030/, accessed on 10 Oct. 2021.

USIP, 2011, Youth and the "Arab Spring", www.usip.org/publications/2011/04/youth-and-arab-spring, accessed on 2 March 2022.

Utilities, 2021, Saudi Arabia Launches 300MW Sakaka PV Solar Power Plant as it Unveils Plans for 7 More Solar Projects, www.utilities-me.com/news/17095-saudi-arabia-launches-300mw-sakaka-pv-solar-power-plant-as-it-unveils-plans-for-7-more-solar-projects, accessed on 2 Nov. 2021.

Yergin, Daniel, 2008, *The Prize: The Epic Quest for Oil, Money, and Power*, Canada: Schuster & Schuster.

Mehmet, Ozay and Vedat Yorucu, 2020, *Modern Geopolitics of Eastern Mediterranean Hydrocarbons in an Age of Energy Transformation*, Springer, Switzerland.

7

THE NEW SILK ROUTE

Long-Term Revival of the Muslim World?

The Muslim Core, shaped by imperial deceit, is so deeply trapped in conflict that in the short run there is no realistic opportunity for recovery to get onto a progressive path. Indeed, conditions may worsen further before they get better. However, in the longer run there is hope for a new frontier in our post-Pandemic world: a new Silk Route Economy (SRE) is emerging, with railroads and highways stretching out in all directions, reenergizing Central Asia and the Muslim world, recalling the days of Marco Polo (Frankopan, 2017, 2018).

At the other end, in the Caucasus, driven by Turkey-Azerbaijan, a new energy network, the Southern Energy Corridor (SEC), is being created to secure European energy sources. The SEC is expected to deliver not only Caspian, but also hydrocarbons from the Middle East and Central Asian fields through pipelines passing through Turkey to Europe. Linked together, the SRE and SEC herald, a new economic opportunity for the revival of the Muslim world. This chapter will document and discuss this new prospect.

The Spectacular Rise of China

The OPEC cartel in October 1973, suddenly tripled the price of oil to consuming countries of the West. Further price increases followed. This was the first time that primary producing countries were able to influence the terms of trade, specifically the prices of primary products. OPEC's model later was followed by other producer cartels aimed at better prices for Third World countries and observers began to talk of a new world economic order (Mehmet, 1995, chapter 5). It did not last. But there was a new phenomenon: The emergence of Four Dragons and autonomous development. A small group of Far East countries, Hong Kong, Singapore, Taiwan, and South Korea suddenly emerged as successful cases of rapid and equitable development. Within a period of two decades, 1970–1990, these countries managed

DOI: 10.4324/9781003268994-7

to achieve sustained development, achieving full employment and fairly equitable income distribution. Western observers were surprised: How could non-Western countries do it? They did it by redefining the rules of capitalism: They adopted export-led growth, investing in efficient industries, producing cars and other consumer products that competed in world markets. These were all authoritarian governments, led by development-oriented leaders, and they followed Japan, not the West, in their development strategy. They invested heavily in human resource development, skill training, and rural development. Leader like Lee Quan Yew of Singapore was a great believer in "Asian Values," a blend of Confucianism and pragmatism. The success of the Four Dragons represented a new "Growth with Equity" Model, which became an envy of even the World Bank.

Even more spectacular has been the rise of the People's Republic of China. Initially, much capital and entrepreneurial inputs were imported from Overseas Chinese in countries like Singapore and Taiwan. But soon, the Chinese authorities acquired endogenous capacity for homegrown technologies to build new cities, build modern highways and communications systems in major Chinese cities like Beijing, Shanghai, and Canton. The Age of China had arrived. China's economic performance is staggering. Its GDP was $14.3 trillion in 2019, representing almost 20% of the world's economy. The Chinese banking is the world's largest banking sector, with assets estimated at around $40 trillion. And it has the world's largest foreign exchange reserves, worth $3.1 trillion. Within the next decade, it is expected China will overtake the USA as the world's leading economy.

As in the case of the Four Dragons, endogenous values stand behind impressive economic performance. The Confucian principles of self-discipline, hard work, and patience in the face of adversity have been deeply ingrained in the minds and character of the Chinese people. PRC has put priority on infrastructural development, but it has not ignored the poverty challenge. The World Bank estimates that more than 850 million Chinese people have been lifted out of extreme poverty. No less than the UN Secretary General has stated:

> Every time I visit China, I am stunned by the speed of change and progress. You have created one of the most dynamic economies in the world, while helping more than 800 million people to lift themselves out of poverty – the greatest anti-poverty achievement in history.
>
> *Tricontinental Institute for Social Research, 2021*

COVID-19 has affected all countries, hitting different economies and regions differently. Overall, according to the forecasts by the Center for Economics and Business, Asia has performed the best while Europe worst and the USA moderately. China has joined the ASEAN and other Asia-Pacific countries in creating the Regional Comprehensive Economic Partnership (RCEP), the world's largest free trade bloc (ASEAN, 2021). The RCEP represents almost a third of total global trade volume with $10.4T, surpassing NAFTA and the EU. With these trends, the

Chinese economy is now forecast to overtake the US economy in 2028, five years earlier forecasts (CNCB, 2021).

China Expands in All Directions, SRE

At first, rapid economic growth was concentrated in Coastal China. But that phase is now past, as China is expanding westward toward Central Asia. This is the new and incredible Age of the new SRE. Central Asia is rich in natural resources, and it is quite logical that, increasingly, Chinese development fueled by resources, will turn to exploit these resources. According to the World Atlas (2021), Kazakhstan has the worlds 11th largest oil reserves and has more than 80 trillion cubic feet of natural gas; it also is a world leader in Chromite, wolfram, lead, zinc, manganese, silver, and uranium. Similarly, Turkmenistan has the world's seventh largest natural gas reserves and is also a major producer of cotton and wheat. Kyrgyzstan has 27 billion tons of coal, several mineral deposits, including gold, and is a major supplier of hydroelectric power. Uzbekistan has also coal reserves along with other mineral reserves. Tajikistan is the world's second largest silver producer and has significant reserves of gold and aluminum.

Kazakhstan's role in Central Asia is especially significant. It is a huge country, now rapidly reintegrating with the world. Freed from Russian domination, Kazaks have encouraged friendly relations with the West, especially the USA. Thus, they have welcomed American involvement in Afghanistan, and have gone so far as inviting the Americans to use two ports in the Caspian Sea, incurring the wrought of Moscow in so doing (Frankopan, 2018, 198–199). To balance itself against Moscow and Peking, Astana has developed close relations with Turkey, hosting conferences on Syria with Iran and Turkey. Both Ankara and Astana have steadfastly rejected the Russian annexation of Crimea, the historic homeland of the Tatars.

Kazakhstan is the nerve center of major infrastructural projects in the SRE. These include the Baku-Tbilisi-Kars railroad, which went into operation in 2017, and now there are new tracks connecting Yiwu with Tehran. The freight trade to Europe is now fetching billions of dollars in transit fees. New initiatives include the "Ashgabat Agreement," a free trade signed between Kazakhstan, Iran, India, Turkmenistan, Uzbekistan, and Oman, providing for greater freedom of movement for goods and people, and there are promises of a "Silk Visa" to enable visa-free travel not only within the Central Asian republics, but in Azerbaijan and Turkey (ibid., 41). From aid recipient, Kazakhstan has emerged as aid provider (Insebayeva, 2022). However, as the riots in early 2022 demonstrate, the road to modernity is never easy or a straight path.

Rapid economic growth requires investment and Kazakhstan is actively promoting itself as a land of opportunity for foreign investment. One crucial reform in this direction is the establishment of a reliable, independent legal system for the settlement of disputes. In the summer of 2018, Kazakhstan opened an innovative International Financial Centre, headed by Lord Woolf, former Lord Supreme Court judge in England and Wales (Ibid., 44). The court uses British legal principles to assist foreign investors who might otherwise get trapped by local and unfamiliar laws and customs.

None of these reforms and institution-building efforts are likely to lead to major results in the short term. With sustained development, however, there is a good chance that the Turkic republics, will, once again, regain their glorious days as in the original Silk Route period. However, as the riots in early 2022 showed, there is a long way before the Kazaks successfully emerge from a post-Russian world.

The vast potential of Central Asia covers not only mineral and hydrocarbon resources, but agricultural products as well. Rapid urbanization in China and Central Asia has generated an ever-rising demand for food, which, in turn, is resulting in agricultural transformation. Land is being reclaimed for agricultural production because of huge investments in irrigation works, water conservation technology, and farming techniques. The Kazakh Ministry of Agriculture has adopted a long-term strategy giving priority to raising yield rates in wheat production rather expanding area of cultivation. Elsewhere in Central Asia, there are moves to expand regional cooperation with agreements over border dispute settlement, cooperation in irrigation and water management issues (Frankopan, 2018, 35).

Water Management Challenges

The issue of water management is of especial importance, given the terrible experience with the drying up of Aral Sea since 1960s due to misguided Soviet agricultural schemes. Saltification and desertification have created water shortages and crop failures. Central Asia is vast, consisting of five countries, Kazakhstan, Kyrgyzstan, Tajikistan, Turkmenistan, and Uzbekistan. It is mostly arid, steppe, and desert, lying between the Ural Mountains to the north and the Hindu Kush to the south, and between the Caspian Sea to the west and the Tien Shan Mountain system (near the border with China) to the east. The area is 4 million km² (10% of the Asian continent and twice the combined areas of France, Germany, Great Britain, Italy, and Spain). It stretches 2,400 km from west to east and 1,280 km from north to south. If northern Afghanistan is included as part of the Aral Sea basin, the combined population will reach about 74 million.

Excluding steppe and desert areas and mountain ranges along the southern, eastern, and north-eastern borders, the region is suitable for farming. More than 6,000 rivers (over 10 km long) originate in the mountains, including the great Amu Darya River and the Syr Darya River. The vast Turan lowlands stretch out between these rivers, creating upstream and downstream countries with differing water management challenges. There are densely populated oases located mainly along the upper and middle reaches and the irrigated areas in the lower reaches and deltas, suitable for farming.

Central Asian water resources are typically transboundary in nature as most of the region's surface water resources are generated in the mountains in Kyrgyzstan, Tajikistan, and Afghanistan, waters flowing into the Aral Sea Basin. All countries of the region face common major water problems. Water resources are limited, and water scarcity is increasing as populations, industrialization, and urbanization grow, and competition over water increases among the different water users, especially in the case of transboundary rivers.

A huge advantage is a shared cultural Muslim heritage. This is of importance in that it may lead to a more humane blending of economic development with Islamic cultural values. The traditional Muslim and ethical rules of sharing water use prompted the desire of many people to initiate and implement this approach and particularly to involve water users in the management process. Experience so far in Central Asia, particularly in the Fergana Valley, suggests that an integrated, cross-country approach can provide the foundation for increasing water security. When people and organizations are willing to integrate ethics and development, it is far easier to achieve sustainable development. The outcome is not only supply of water to all sectors of the economy, but at the same time social development, and meeting the requirements of the environment (Academia, 2021). Water security links the dynamics of economic growth with social and environmental stability. In the case of upstream countries of Kyrgyzstan and Tajikistan, hydropower generation fuels serious political disputes in the region, putting water at the heart of regional security and stability.

The Muslim Cultural Heritage

The five Turkic countries of Central Asia have a common cultural heritage. It is this heritage that the Soviets were unable to eradicate. It is the shared bond that now is working to reenergize this part of the world. It is worth detailing the basic elements of the Turkic cultural heritage that is currently at work to shape and renew identities in Central Asia.

At the start of the 11th century, Qarakhanid Turks established a new empire centered in Ghazna, now in eastern Afghanistan, extending over much of Transoxiana (Frankopan, 2017, 127). The great river Oxus, Amu Derya marked the border between the Qarakhanids and Ghaznavids. The territory the Qarakhanids occupied was fertile, water-fed lowlands suitable for agriculture, producing a surplus, which enabled trading along ancient routes stretching out to China in the east and Baghdad, Tabriz, and Anatolian towns in the west. Bursa, for example, became the terminal destination for the silk trade, earning a reputation as the manufacturing center of the highest-quality silk textiles. Trade-based prosperity, in turn, enabled high culture. Qarakhanids championed a flourishing school of scholars. Perhaps the most famous surviving text is the *Diwan lughat al-Turk (The Collection of Turkish Dialects)* by Mahmud al-Kashgari. Another text is the *Kutadgu Bilig (The Book of Wisdom that Brings Eternal Happiness*, written in Qarakhanid Turkish by Yusuf Hajib) (128).

Transoxiana was a prosperous and a fortunate land, which, whoever was the ruler, equally championed the arts and architecture. Through trade, Muslim silver flooded into Europe. Bukhara, for example, under the Samanid dynasty was a trading center linked to Constantinople, Alexandria, or Cairo. Muslim merchants, Christian, or Jew carried on trade on equal basis. What mattered for merchants was not religion, but "how to pay for luxury objects that could be sold for a healthy profit" (126). The Samanid dynasty, based in Bukhara, was a passionate champion of Islam, introduced a system of madrasas (schools) for correct teaching of the Quran and hadith tradition. The madrasa model was borrowed from Buddhist monasteries. (102). In the late Middle Ages, Timur, whose empire stretched from Asia minor to the Himalayas, "embarked on an ambitious program to construct mosques and royal buildings in such cities as Samarkand, Herat and Mashad." "Carpenters, painters, weavers, tailors, gem cutters" were imported from Damascus, which was ransacked to embellish cities in Central Asia (191–192). Central Asian madrassas and Muslim learning rivalled or excelled other Muslim centers of knowledge such as Baghdad, Damascus, or Qum. One notable book is *Shahname* (*The Book of Kings*) by Firdawsi of Tus, and dedicated to Sultan Mahmud, praised as "the mightiest and most kindly of rulers" (Brockelmann, 1948, 170). Firdawsi also wrote the epic *Yusuf and Zulaykha*, which approximated Homer's *Iliad*. Numerous other great works were produced. Beautiful mosques, royal palaces, and public gardens have survived the Soviets to embellish today's cities of Central Asia.

In Persia, the home of the concept of the Silk Road, high culture reached its peak in Isfahan, the capital city of Shah Abbas (1588–1629), a contemporary of Sultan Süleymen, who oversaw an amazing urban reconstruction program. As transit trade flourished, indirect taxes and import duties filled Abbas's treasury. Old markets and gloomy streets were torn down and a modern city was built with shops, baths, and mosques. Public gardens watered by irrigation works beautified the city. *Bağ-i Naqsh-i Cihan* (world admiring garden) was a masterpiece of horticultural design, built at the heart of the city. Abbas built Masjid-I Shah, intended to rival Süleymaniye in Istanbul, or Selimiye in Edirne (Frankopan, 2017, 226–227).

Isfahan became the center of Islamic learning. Calligraphy, especially miniature painting, flourished, as did disciplines from astronomy to mathematics. As major transit point on the silk Road, Isfahan was the meeting point of Christian, Jewish, and Muslim merchants. It was a city of tolerance where copies of the Torah and a translation of the Book of Psalm circulated freely. Not only Islam, but variations of it emerged as well. *Sufism*, a form of Muslim missionary-cum-mystics flourished on the Central Asian steppes. It was a blend of influences from Christianity, Judaism, Zoroastrianism, and paganism. Mystics, known as *Sufis*, roamed the steppes, tending to the sick and attracting attention with their eccentric behavior, "winning converts, fusing the shaman and animist beliefs that were widespread in Central Asia with the tenets of Islam" (Frankopan, 2017, 102). To give one example, the *Bektashi Order* is a Sufi dervish order (*tariqat*) named after the 13th century Alevi *saint*, Haji Bektash Veli from Khorasan, but with headquarters in Tirana, Albania. It was influential throughout Anatolia and the Balkans, and was particularly strong in Albania, Bulgaria, and even among Ottoman Greek Muslims from the regions of Crete and Macedonia (Spiritual Life, 2021).

The rich Muslim cultural heritage in central Asia was constantly targeted by the Soviets. They totally failed to eradicate and replace it with an artificial culture of the socialist proletariat. Now there is a major restoration work underway and the cultural heritage is a source of inspiration and pride. Since the end of Soviet oppression, the Turkic republics are regaining their heritage and progressing forward to a new SRE with confidence.

The Aral Sea Disaster … and Rehabilitation

The Aral Sea was once the fourth-largest freshwater lake in the world. In the 1950s water from two rivers, the Amu Darya and the Syr Darya, were diverted away from the sea to irrigate Soviet collective farms in the steppes of Central Asia for cotton production for army and industry. As water levels dropped, the once abundant bream, carp, and other freshwater fish disappeared with the sea. By the turn of the 20th century, fishing villages lost their livelihood and desertification created an ecological catastrophe. The sea is now one-tenth of its original size, and it is split into two, the top half of the body of water lies in Kazakhstan. The smaller, South Aral Sea, sits in Uzbekistan. Both bodies of water looked set for extinction.

The World Bank then stepped with a rescue plan, providing Kazakhstan with a credit of $87 million to rehabilitate the Aral Sea. The funds financed construction of a 12-km-long dam across the narrow channel that connects the North Aral Sea to Uzbekistan in the south to prevent water loss. Improvements of existing channels on the Syr Darya river, which meanders northward from Kazakhstan's Tian Shan Mountains, also helped to boost the flow of water into the North Aral Sea. There was an increase in water levels of 3.3 m, achieved within 7 months. The World Bank scientists did not expect such results for 10 years.

By 2006, there was a revival of the fishing industry in Uralsk. By 2016, the Uralsk Fish Inspection Unit recorded 7,106 tons of fish as freshwater species returned, including pike, perch, breams, asp, and catfish. Fishing once more returned to the area and taxi drivers now became fishermen.

In the rehabilitation of the Aral Sea, much credit belongs to the Kazakh government that played a key role in this recovery process. Typically, bureaucracy moves slowly. That was not the case in this project. The restoration of the lake has allowed improved irrigation and water management. Crop production rose and, most significantly, ecological gains improved living standards of the people. Less successful in Uzbekistan, the success of the project in Kazakhstan is a story of sustainable development, demonstrating that ecological disasters can be turned into success. Justifiably, it has earned the World Bank an award (World Bank, 2021).

Financial Institutions

The dam construction at the Aral Sea was, comparatively, a small investment, one which nevertheless paid big dividends. Typically, sustainable development projects are large-scale projects, requiring huge amounts of finance. Mega infrastructural projects, water resource management, and socioeconomic development are costly, long-term projects. The World Bank is a major source of multilateral lending, and its regional equivalents, such as the Asian Development Bank, are important sources of finance for development projects.

China is the world's leading creditor country with $3.25 trillion amount of foreign exchange reserves (Trading Economics, 2021). With so much financial clout, the People's Republic of China can fund mega projects at will. And to be sure, it has invested hugely in the last few decades transforming the face of Chinese cities and economy. It is also spending huge amounts in the development of the SRE. But, as we have seen, China is regarded with suspicion because of its human rights record against the Uyghur Turkish minority, in Tibet and elsewhere. On the other hand, China has expressed willingness to work with Saudi Arabia, even becoming a stakeholder in Aramco (Frankopan, 2018, 180).

Still, multilateral financial organizations are, quite often, far more appropriate for financing SRE projects. The Asian Development Bank, as noted above, is already an active stakeholder in many SRE projects. There are several financial institutions as well as potential sources of finance. The new Asian Infrastructure Investment Bank is one, and there are groups like the Shanghai Cooperation Organization, the Euroasian Economic Union, and the Trans-Pacific Partnership. Members of these organizations, collectively, represent up to 30% of the global GDP, a funding capacity of up to $30 trillion (Frankopan, 2018, 31).

A Peaceful Future: TAPI Mega Project

As resource-rich Central Asian countries meet the challenges of sustainable development, exporting resources, they join the global market. Already mega highway and railroad projects are operational or underway. If they can also manage such common problems as water management and transboundary issues, the future can only be considered with some degree of optimism. Even war-torn Afghanistan may participate in the SRE once it achieves peace and stability.

Take for example, the case of the Turkmenistan-Afghanistan-Pakistan-India (TAPI) pipeline project. In September 2021, the Biden administration withdrew the US troops from Afghanistan and the Taliban took over the country. While the political stability of the country is increasingly in question, the country remains a vital link in the ambitious TAPI pipeline project. First proposed in 1995, its construction has been repeatedly delayed due to political factors and instability in Afghanistan. In 1998, a major US-based corporation supporting the project withdrew, following deteriorating US relations with the Taliban regarding Al Qaeda bombings of USA embassies in Kenya and Tanzania. Major impediment was caused by the US invasion of Afghanistan in 2001. However, in the following years, leaders from Turkmenistan, Pakistan, and Afghanistan signed agreements to cooperate on the project, and India joined in 2010. Survey work on TAPI began in 2018, when further delays were encountered due to geopolitical factors and regional rivalries.

Iran, for example, has been against TAPI, preferring instead a gas deal between Iran and Turkmenistan (Frankopan, 2018, 44–45).

The project, however, has its backers as well. One of the major shareholders of TAPI is the Asian Development Bank. When completed, the TAPI pipeline will be 1,600 km long, from the Turkmenistan-Afghanistan border to the Pakistan-India border. At its full capacity it will transport 33 billion cubic meters (bcm) of natural gas each year from Turkmenistan to Afghanistan, Pakistan, and India. The Turkmen gas will provide Afghanistan access to 5% and 47.5% to Pakistan and another 47.5% to India for 30 years. There will be additional benefits as well. Afghanistan may receive in transit fees, no less than USD $400 million and as high as US $1 billion.

The state company of Turkmenistan, Turkmengaz, is the main contributor to the project, providing USD $8.5 billion of the $10 billion investment costs as well as managing the TAPI pipeline. This would represent the company's first time managing an international project of this size. Afghanistan, Pakistan, and India have only committed to 5% of the project cost.

Turkmenistan politics are also often uncertain. Since its independence in 1991, the country has adopted "positive neutrality," a policy of cooperation, and actively working with different parties without taking a side while developing its infrastructure for exporting natural gas. In the past Turkmenistan has depended on the Soviet Union and Russia, and more recently China. Now, export diversification is an emerging goal (Parwani, 2021). Turkmenistan holds one of world's largest natural gas reserves, some observers putting it as the fourth. In the past, it has exported most of its product to China. In 2019, about 30 bcm (or around 90% of Turkmenistan's natural gas exports) were sent to China via the Central Asia-China pipeline network.

The TAPI pipeline is a critical economic project. If successful, TAPI would also bypass other major powers in the region, bring Central Asian gas to world and regional markets, lowering the global reliance on the oil from the Middle East. For this reason, the United States has supported the TAPI pipeline for the past three decades but is not directly involved in its construction, since the successful completion of the TAPI would lessen Russia and China's influence in the region.

China's Belt and Road Initiative have led many energy-rich countries in Central Asia, however, may carry excessive Chinese debt. For this reason, TAPI will remain a key geopolitical project, its future dependent on how east–west relations evolve in the aftermath of the US withdrawal from Afghanistan and how the Taliban in Kabul formulates its regional relations.

Iran-China Relations

On 27 March 2021, Beijing and Tehran signed a 25-year comprehensive cooperation agreement. This is not only a signal for strategic partnership in the building of the SRE, but also Beijing's support to Iran in its struggle to free itself from sanctions imposed by the USA. Both countries are at loggerheads with Washington, and both are key actors in efforts to resist American hegemonic plans in the Pacific Ocean, Middle East, or elsewhere.

The deal, five years in the making, is an ambitious framework, a roadmap, confirming Iran's important role in the Belt and Road Initiative (BRI), linking West Asia and East Asia to move closer to one another. From a Chinese perspective, Iran is a valuable partner to Beijing as that country is an important player, countering the USA in the Mediterranean, the Red Sea, the Hindu Kush, Central Asia, and the Persian Gulf (Saker, 2021).

Sustainable Development

Alongside infrastructural investments and projects, there must be a human development component. Sustainable social and economic development must also be undertaken, starting with human resource development in skills training and technical/vocational schools, all requiring huge amounts of investment. Already a World Bank style new bank has been set up for infrastructural projects (Asian Infrastructure Investment bank, 2022). However, infrastructural investment is not enough. It must be supplemented by massive lending for social development, including education, and skill training. Where are funds for this purpose to come from? While major funding will come from multilateral finance organizations, it is hoped that future growth will increasingly attract corporate investors, bringing in modern technology, know-how, and innovation. One creative funding option is to tax international corporations and capital movements, to create viable jobs and livelihoods in the Third World, including the SRE. These international tax revenues could then be invested in building a humane world, sustainable development, and stopping climate warming and degradation of our fragile ecology. Significantly, world leaders at the Rome G20 Summit in October 2021 agreed on a proposal to levy a minimum of 15% tax on MNCs (CBC, 2021). This was an USA proposal to harmonize corporate tax around the globe, but it may lead to international taxation essential for a more just order. Details remain to be worked out. Who will tax MNCs? Where will the tax revenue go? The European Union has discussed the topic, and there are proposals on how to do it from economists such as Tobin and Feldstein. An autonomous international tax, if it is to finance a more equitable world order, must be linked to a world development fund (Mendes and Mehmet, 2003, 199–201) to promote sustainable development and progressive climate change. Significantly, the Rome Summit was followed by a UN Conference in Glasgow on Climate Change.

In future development of the SRE, innovative fiscal reforms would be essential. A Silk Road Bank for Human Development would be critical because if humanity has learnt any lesson from the Pandemic, it is the necessity of investing in health, sanitation to build safe communities. Likewise, education and skill development are essential to meet basic needs. These are costly public investments. Only an international bank, funded by international taxation, tailor-made for the SRE can provide the financial resources needed. To its credit, China has uplifted more than half a billion people out of poverty, a huge leap forward in global equity. Can this success be replicated in the SRE economy, now being constructed westward from China, in Central Asia to the Caucuses, southward into the Indian subcontinent, and southeast into Malaysia?

Controversies abound and there is much propaganda in USA-China relations. From a Western perspective, the People's Republic of China is a party dictatorship with a terrible human rights record, including suppression of the Uygur Turks, Tibet, and elsewhere. Muslim countries might be able to play a moderating role. Turkey, as well, has a historic tie with Central Asian Turkic republics and may be able to mediate. It is evident that in a post-Pandemic world, a new world order may emerge in which equality, rather than liberty, may become the guiding principle. If China can replicate its poverty success achievement in assisting poorer countries to eliminate poverty, the world would certainly become more equal. That would surely outperform the Western efforts in the post-WWII to develop and democratize the Third World.

A Long-Term Revival: Silk Road Economy

While a great deal has already been achieved in the realization of the SRE, the greater part of this new economy is still in the future. What is quite clear is that the economic center of gravity is slowly but surely moving back to Central Asia, just like it used to be in the days of Marco Polo.

Look at megaprojects already completed and operational. A rail system linking Istanbul to Beijing has been completed. The first freight train from Turkey to China has completed its 12-day journey. The first freight train left Istanbul on 4 December 2020 passing through the Marmaray Tunnel under the Bosphorus, then travelling a total 8,693 km via Anatolia, Georgia, Azerbaijan, across the Caspian Sea and Kazakhstan, reaching in 12 days the Chinese city of Xi, the capital of Shanxi Province. This railway link is one of six components of the Chinese Belt & Road Initiative (BRI) megaproject. Under this massive BRI, China will open new trade links to the rest of Asia, Africa, and Europe. In the longer term, it may even be possible to link BRI eastward via an undersea tunnel from South Korea to Japan (MLTM/MLIT, 2018).

A global transformation is unfolding. China's energy requirement will triple by 2030 and already oil and gas companies are making strategic choices (Frankopan, 2018, 68). If trade expansion, as expected, is realized, then Tashkent, Samarkand in Uzbekistan, and other centers of Turkic culture may regain their glorious past. Turkmenistan already views itself as the "heart of the 'Great Silk Road.'" China, in possession of the largest reserves of dollars and hard currency, is already changing its economic growth strategy. No less than the International Monetary Fund (IMF) has noted the fact that there is now a decisive shift from sheer quantitative, "high-speed growth to high-quality growth" (Frankopan, 2018, 73). This is a promising shift, demonstrating that investing huge amounts in infrastructure alone is not enough; there must be improvement in human development, in such areas as public health, education, skill training to produce a productive labor force manning and managing infrastructural development. This is the way forward to a new world, hopefully more humane than the Western Mercantilist one, which the Pandemic has wounded so grievously.

From the Caspian Basin, via Iran and Turkey, it is very likely that the SRE will expand southward and penetrate the Islamic Core. Chinese capital may, in fact, join the oil-rich Gulf states, creating a huge global Look East frontier. Within a decade, China may overtake the USA as the leading economy in the world; in terms of purchasing-power parity, it already has. Post-Trump America is a country torn asunder by urban violence and police brutality, and the Biden Administration will have its hands full healing a divided nation. A new Euroasian hub is slowly, but surely rising once again, with new markets through Central Asia. Central Asia and Siberia are incredibly rich in natural resources. After the demise of the Soviet Union, these Turkic republics are, once more, emerging as rapidly growing countries. Their vast natural resources, together with those of Siberia, can be expected to fuel the next Kondratieff Cycle of economic growth in the new SRE Kondratieff was a Russian economist who discovered long business cycles, those lasting for half a century or more (Cycles Research Institute, 2022).

The Siberian Hinterland

The hinterland of Central Asia is Siberia with its vast, still untouched resources. Once the Central Asian countries emerge as dynamos in the SRE, it is certain they will become magnet for the development of Siberian resources, including forestry product, gold, copper, nickel, coal, potash, as well as large reserves petroleum (Mining IR, 2018). The Siberian ecology is fragile, and any development needs to be carefully designed not to damage the environment. While improved technology may promote sustainable natural resource practice, China is currently the leading environmental polluter in the world. Climate change, as dramatically illustrated at the UN Conference of Parties (COP26) in Glasgow in November 2021, has become a leading global concern, with several major countries announcing zero emission targets in the next half century (UN Climate Change, 2022). In the meantime, energy transformation, a demand-driven process of replacing fossil fuels with cleaner alternative sources of energy such as solar, wind, and hydroelectricity, is becoming global, and it is changing lifestyles especially in Europe and rich countries (Mehmet and Yorucu, 2020, 11–12).

The Islamic Core is a major producer of fossil fuels. In an age of energy transformation, these producers must change their dependence on fossil fuels rapidly. Producers like Saudi Arabia have announced Vision 2030. A defining prospect is the energy cooperation emerging between Turkey and Azerbaijan on the SRE. This cooperation will have to adjust to energy transformation, hopefully with the participation of existing and new producers over the next half century.

Turkey-Azerbaijan Energy Cooperation on a New Dimension of the SRE

Turkey is the gateway to Europe in the SRE, especially in energy security. In cooperation with Azerbaijan, a new SEC is emerging for European energy security (Yorucu and Mehmet, 2018). In October 2011, Turkey and Azerbaijan have signed an agreement on gas prices and delivery from the Shah Deniz sources, thereby opening a new chapter in energy cooperation on the SRE. The deal was made between Turkish State Gas Importing Company BOTAS and its Azerbaijan counterpart, SOCAR. The president of Azerbaijan Ilham Aliyev and the president of Turkey Recep Tayyip Erdogan have signed this bilateral agreement. Shah Deniz 2 has now been approved by both presidents, and the deal to build Trans Anatolian Pipeline (TANAP) pipeline has been ratified in June 2014. The share of Turkish Petroleum Public Company has increased from 9% to 19% and this project will include an additional offshore gas platform, subsea wells, and expansion of the gas plant at Sangachal Terminal. This project will add 16 bcm per year to the current gas production, to be exported mainly to Turkey (10 bcm per year) and to the EU (6 bcm per year). It is however expandable up to 32 bcm per year, in which Turkey has guaranteed to buy 16 bcm of gas annually and the remaining 16 bcm can be exported to Europe with Trans Adriatic Pipeline (TAP) via Greece to Italy. There is a further pipeline infrastructure project to connect TANAP into IONIC pipeline via Albania to up north of Adriatic coast of Montenegro and Croatia. (See the map in Yorucu and Mehmet, 2018, 57).

The Turkey-Azerbaijan energy cooperation is a unique opportunity on the SEC as it offers a feasible diversification option for European gas security. At peak capacity, SEC may deliver at least 12% of EU-27's annual gas consumption, thus reducing its dependence on Russia via the Northern Gas Corridor, which suddenly became unreliable as much of Europe froze in winter owing to interruption of Russian gas delivery. In 2008, the first Russian-Ukrainian-European natural gas crisis emerged forcing the EU to launch a new diversification policy. Under this policy, LNG receiving terminals are being constructed in Central and South-East Europe, while pursuing the Southern Gas Corridor, to bring natural gas from Caspian, Middle Eastern, and Central Asian sources without crossing Russia. Relations between Russia and Ukraine have not been resolved. Indeed, with the Russian takeover of Crimea, the EU-Moscow relations have worsened and, in 2022 invasion of Ukraine is a distinct possibility with serious consequences to follow. Energy pipelines delivering Russian gas to Europe may, once again, run dry.

Looking ahead, in the longer term, it has the potential to become a major player in international gas markets, selling all its gas to China, regardless of how its relations with the West evolve over nuclear energy. In the shorter term, considering geo-political factors, the location of its gas reserves, and the unpredictable nature of Iranian domestic politics, it seems less likely that Iran would fit into the Southern Gas Corridor framework. More likely, its gas exports will first target the global

LNG market and Asian markets via pipeline to the east, than west via Turkey. In the longer term, as SRE evolves, greater Iranian participation should not be ignored.

The Eastern Mediterranean region is another potential source of gas for the SEC. Recent discoveries of natural gas off the shores of Israel and Cyprus could soon become commercialized. The Israeli gas field at Leviathan has 622 bcm gas reserves and is expected, once it become operational, to deliver in the first instance to the domestic Israeli market. Beyond this, private companies, Zorlu Group of Turkey and Delek Drilling and Avner of Israel, are making plans for a $3.75 billion investment in an underwater pipeline from Leviathan to Ceyhan, Turkey. Such a pipeline would supply not only the Turkish market, but as well link up with TANAP-TAP delivering East Mediterranean gas to Europe.

Azerbaijan as a New Energy Actor

Azerbaijan has become a significant player in European geopolitics, and its role in future will increase along with the growth of the SRE. Now that TANAP is operational (at an increasing delivery capacity of 10–20 bcm), Azerbaijan has effectively emerged as a key partner with Turkey in the SEC. With the Russian-Ukraine war, the importance of SEC can only increase. Indeed, Azerbaijan has gone beyond and increased its presence in the Balkans, buying an interest in TAP, specifically in Greece and Albania. TANAP-TAP is now a major component in the SEC, delivering Caucasian gas to markets in Southern Europe and then through Italy to Western Europe.

The State Oil Company of Azerbaijan (SOCAR) has now adopted an aggressive role, which can only be expected to expand in future. Taking advantage of the weak Greek financial situation, it purchased a controlling stake in DESFA, the company that operates Greece's gas network. By doing so, Azerbaijan will have a geopolitical influence and may even lead to changes in Greek foreign policy. In 2020, the successful war against Armenia may now be expected to change regional geopolitics. For example, Greece may review its unquestioned support for Armenia, while also moderating its Cyprus policy and rethink its dispute with Turkey in the Aegean and North Cyprus.

Geopolitics of the Greater Caspian Basin Gas Reserves

The Caspian Sea has an enormous amount of proven gas reserves to turn the Azerbaijan-Turkey component into a new energy hub. As discussed earlier, the Caspian gas fields are potentially available to enhance European energy security via the development of the SEC. Great challenges, however, remain before this potential can become a reality. The existing gas pipeline infrastructure in the Caucuses is old as it was created under the Soviet period to supply gas mainly to Russia. Major investment is required to diversify and develop SEC so Azerbaijan and Caspian countries can export gas to Europe through non-Russian routes. As the two biggest suppliers of natural gas from the Southern Energy Corridor, the EU has started regular meetings with Turkmenistan and Azerbaijan to build a Trans Caspian Pipeline System adjacent to TANAP, which could play a pivotal role in natural gas delivery to Europe. Dialogue between the EU and these two Turkic republics was a new and important move to strengthen relations with the EU and hence to underpin the notion of SEC.

The Caspian Sea energy cooperation is an evolving process. On 12 August 2018, a breakthrough treaty on the Caspian Sea was signed between Russia, Kazakhstan, Iran, Turkmenistan, and Azerbaijan. These countries, bordering on the Caspian Sea, have reached this agreement peacefully, after many years of negotiations. The agreement involves maritime boundaries and equitable division of the energy resources of this inland sea (Yorucu and Mehmet, 2022, in press).

The energy linking of Azerbaijan and the wider Caspian Basin to Europe is smart. It will safeguard the supply security of natural gas to Europe via the SEC, connecting deliveries from the Shah Deniz Phase II, which is endowed with more than 1 bcm of proven gas. Hafner and Tagliapietra (2014) have emphasized that Turkmenistan could well become the key player to supply natural gas to Turkey and to the EU, but two major barriers will likely make such a development unfeasible, at least in the medium term. Turkmenistan's lack of knowledge of the European gas market is a handicap. However, this is a temporary handicap, given the peaceful agreement on boundary determination mentioned above (Toktassynov, 2022). It may now be expected to facilitate the construction of the Trans Caspian Pipeline linked to Europe. However, given the geopolitics of the SRE, it is no less likely that the Chinese market is more feasible for Turkmenistan gas exports. In brief, while the SEC is a potentially attractive prospect, it is by no means a done deal. The European politicians, especially with their ongoing problems with Ankara, will have to adopt a creative posture, and develop a more cooperative strategy with Turkey, if they truly wish to make SEC a reality.

Iran-Turkey Energy Relations on the SRE

Turkey is also expanding its energy relationship with Iran, another significant gas producer that will play an increasing role on the SRE. Since 1996 Turkey has moved closer to Iran, notwithstanding the former's NATO membership and the trade embargo on Tehran by USA. Unlike these Western powers, Turkey sits next door to energy-rich Iran and needs to import natural gas at affordable prices, from diverse sources. Its own energy consumption, both for household needs as well as to power industry, obliges Turkey to maintain good relations with Iran. Accordingly, Ankara has signed an agreement with Iran to buy a minimum 8 bcm of gas each year.

The Iran-Turkey gas deal did not please the USA, but Ankara needs to develop its own energy plans. The United States continuously puts pressure on Ankara to avoid dealing gas with Iran, as they believe it will undermine the diplomatic efforts to halt Iran's nuclear program. The most rational choice would be an agreement on Iran's nuclear capability and removal of trade embargoes. Former President Trump's unilateral decision to cancel out of the initial deal was unwise, but the

Biden administration is taking far too long to undo the damage. Turkish relations with Iran are subject to other problems, including terrorist attacks on pipelines by the Kurdish PKK on the Turkish border.

From an Iranian perspective, Hafner and Tagliapietra (2014) highlighted that the first international pipeline that Iran will likely develop will not target the European market, but the Asian market. In fact, Iran is already working on a pipeline to Pakistan, to export its natural gas not only to Pakistan, but also to India. Moreover, the Chinese interest on the country's natural gas reserves is also very strong and Iranian natural gas exports to China will likely take place in the future as well. For these reasons, Iran may not fit into Southern Gas Corridor concept, as it will first target the global LNG market and Asian markets via pipeline.

Turkish-Russian Pipelines

Turkey is a key NATO member and an ally of the West, and now it is emerging as an actor in European energy security. Like Europe, Turkey has high dependency on Russian energy supply. Over half of Turkish gas imports come from Russia (compared with over a third in EU's case). This high dependency is clearly a source of worry in Ankara and in NATO; however, Turkish-Russian energy cooperation is not only unavoidable but also essential in diversifying energy routes. There are solid geopolitical reasons in support of Turkish-Russian energy cooperation, including the fact of Turkish-Russian cooperation in the Caucuses, Syria, and elsewhere. The Turkish Stream Pipeline, in place of the abandoned pipeline to Bulgaria is now a reality (Yorucu and Mehmet, 2018, 58).

However, diversification of gas supply also raises important geopolitical challenges for Europe and Turkey. Europe faces a double-edged sword: On the one hand, it aspires to accelerate shift toward clean, alternative energy sources; on the other, it seeks to reduce its Russian energy dependency by means of diversification of energy sources and deliveries. As for the good relations between Moscow and Ankara, at least for the time being, it is feasible to develop the SEC, including Russian supplies, using the Turkish maritime and land routes. The Blue Stream, connecting Russia to Turkey under the Black Sea is already in use carrying Russian Gas to Samsun. Blue Stream 2, also running under the Black Sea, became operational early in 2020. However, longer-term geopolitics are uncertain. Russia has its own energy strategy, and the Turkish energy market is one component of it. It is likely that Gazprom may be seeking to "cordon off" Turkey to prevent any future competition from the Caspian Basin, especially from Turkmenistan.

Ceyhan, the New Energy Hub

In the meantime, Turkey is rapidly developing its own energy infrastructure. The Port of Ceyhan in the Bay of Iskenderun, southern Turkey, is fast emerging as the regional energy hub. The Baku-Tbilisi-Ceyhan (BTC) pipeline has been operational since 2006 (Yorucu and Mehmet, 2018, 123).

The BTC, 1,768 km long, is the result of a successful public–private consortium, which includes the British Petroleum (holding 30.1% of equity), State Oil Company of Azerbaijan (25%), Chevron of the USA (8.9%), Statoil of Norway (8.1%), Turk Petrolleri Anonim Ortakligi (6.53%), and other shareholders from France, Japan, the USA, and India. Its construction cost was $3.9 billion, and it was financed by the International Finance Corporation of the World Bank and the European Bank for Reconstruction and Development.

In addition to the BCT, Ceyhan is also the export terminal for the Kirkuk-Ceyhan pipeline, which delivers Iraq oil from the Kurdish Regional Government (KRG) in Northern Iraq. This 600-mile-long pipeline is the economic lifeline of the KRG. It is often a source of conflict between the KRG and the Baghdad government over revenue sharing, and it is often the target of terrorist attacks, but despite these difficulties, it is a functioning reality.

Other pipelines are also projected to connect to the Ceyhan export terminal. Russian deliveries from Samsun and Israeli gas fields in Eastern Mediterranean are the most likely projects to be realized in the near future. Longer-term prospects include pipelines from as far away as Qatar in the Persian Gulf.

Turkey Finds Gas in the Black Sea

A new game-changing development: On 21 August 2021, Turkey announced a major gas discovery, 320 bcm – over 11 trillion cubic feet (tcf) – lean natural gas find in the country's Black Sea EEZ, close to the Romanian border (Ellinas, 2020). Turkey's national oil company, Turk Petrol Anonim Ortakligi (TPAO), using the drilling-rig Fatih, hit success at Tuna-1 at a location named Sakarya. The area of about 7,000 km^2 may have more upside potential. The TPAO intends to carry out further seismic surveys and drilling.

Engineering reports indicate that, Tuna-1 was drilled in 2,115 m of water, reaching a total depth of over 3,500 m. The gas field is located about 150 km offshore, north of Eregli. While the exact size of the find and how much of the gas is recoverable will not be known until after more appraisal and drilling is carried out. Nevertheless, it is quite sizeable and when brought onstream, it could have the potential to produce 10–15 bcm/year over the next 15-20 years. With Turkey's consumption averaging about 50 bcm/year over the last three years, Tuna-1 could be providing as much as 20%–30% of the country's annual gas demand, easing import dependence and improving energy security. Construction of the required processing and production infrastructure and the pipeline to bring the gas onshore could cost over $6 billion and will more likely take over five years.

Changing Geopolitics in the Caucuses

The Azerbaijan-Armenian War 2020 has altered the geopolitics of the Caucuses in favor of Azerbaijan and Turkey. With military help from Turkey, Azerbaijan was able to recover its territories under Armenian occupation since early 1990s. This fact has further brought the two countries closer, while opening the doors for wider and friendlier relations in the region. Even Armenia may now embrace peaceful relations with its neighbors and benefit from the emerging SRE. There are signs, early in 2022, of Yerevan attempting to normalize relations with Ankara.

Energy-rich Azerbaijan is a key actor on the SRE. Baku, the capital city, is rapidly becoming a modern metropolis, an important meeting point of energy politics. Turkey and Azerbaijan are now so close; they are implementing a "two countries, one culture" policy. Georgia, a neighbor is already a partner in the Baku-Tbilisi-Ceyhan pipeline delivering gas to world markets through the Ceyhan terminal in southern Turkey. Northern Iraqi oil is also flowing to this terminal, which is rapidly emerging as a regional energy hub. Energy geopolitics are rapidly changing, but one certainty is that SRE is rapidly emerging. Over the next decade or two, the vast region from China to Turkey will be a scene of major investments as more megaprojects are realized.

Toward a New World Order

In addition to Turkey, the Muslim Core, rich in oil, needs to join the SRE as investor and economic actor in its future development. As the SRE expands, a new world order will emerge. The full consequences of the war in Ukraine, launched by Putin in February 2022, are now uncertain. But it will likely hasten the transition to a new world order.

The Muslim countries can help contribute to this new world order. Thus, leaders from the Muslim Core, countries like Qatar, may play a mediating role to put a human face and avert Islamic terror in Taliban-led Afghanistan. Turkey has historical and cultural ties with Central Asian Turkic republics and may also be able to mediate. Situated at the strategic point where the East meets West, Turkey sees itself as a Cultural Bridge, an actor in interfaith dialogue, but it takes two to tango: geopolitically, it may be too late for Ankara for accession to the Union, for reasons explained in Chapter 8. However, better relations should still be possible in a new world order that is slowly emerging, in which the liberal democracy is likely to give way to greater equality, as argued by Kishore Mahbubani (2022) and others.

References

Academia, 2021, Sustainable Development Strategy in Central Asia, www.academia.edu/29638640/Sustainable_Development_Strategy_in_Central_Asia, accessed on 22 Sept. 2021.

ASEAN 2021, China and 14 Other Countries Agree to Set Up World's Largest Trading Bloc, www.nbcnews.com/news/world/china-14-other-countries-set-world-s-largest-trading-bloc-n1247855, accessed on 2 March 2022.

Asian Infrastructure Investment Bank, 2022, 2022 Annual AIIB Meeting, www.aiib.org/en/index.html, accessed on 2 March 2022.

Brockelmann, Carl, ed., 1948, *History of the Islamic Peoples*, London: Routledge & Kegan Paul.

CBC, 2021, G20 Leaders Endorse 15% Minimum Global Corporate Tax, www.cbc.ca/news/world/g20-global-minimum-corporate-tax-15-per-cent-1.6231592, accessed on 2 March 2022.

CNCB, 2021, China Set to Surpass U.S. as World's Biggest Economy by 2028, Says Report, www.cnbc.com/2020/12/26/china-set-to-surpass-us-as-worlds-biggest-economy-by-2028-says-report.html, accessed on 2 March 2022.

Cycles Research Institute, 2022, Cycles Research Institute: For the Interdisciplinary Study of Cycles, https://cyclesresearchinstitute.org/cycles-research/economy/kondratieff/, accessed on 3 March 2022.

Ellinas, Charles, 2020, Turkey Finds Gas in the Black Sea, www.neweurope.eu/article/turkey-finds-gas-in-the-black-sea/, accessed on 18 Oct. 2021.

Frankopan, Peter, 2017, *The Silk Roads: A New History of the World*, New York: Vintage Books.

Frankopan, Peter, 2018, *The New Silk Routes*, New York: Vintage Books.

Hafner, M. and Tagliapietra, 2014, "Turkey as a Regional Natural Gas Hub: Myth and Reality", *European Energy Journal*, Vol. 4, No. 1, 60–66.

Insebayeva, N., 2022, *Modernity, Development, and Decolonization of Knowledge in Central Asia*, Singapore: Palgrave-Macmillan.

Mahbubani, Kishore, 2022, *The Asian Century*, Singapore: Springer.

Mehmet, Ozay, 1995, *Westernizing the Third World: The Eurocentricity of Economic Development Theories*, 2nd ed., London: Routledge.

Mehmet, Ozay and Vedat Yorucu, 2020, *Modern Geopolitics of Eastern Mediterranean Hydrocarbons in an Age of Energy Transformation*, Springer. Switzerland.

Mendes, Errol and Ozay Mehmet, 2003, *Global Governance, Economy and Law, Waiting for Justice*, Routledge, London.

Mining IR, 2018, New Horizons: Siberia, the Last Frontier for Mineral Exploration? https://miningir.com/new-horizons-siberia-the-last-frontier-for-mineral-exploration/, accessed on 18 Oct. 2021.

MLTM/MLIT, 2018, MLTM/MLIT – South Korea-Japan Undersea Tunnel – South Korea, www.globaldata.com/store/report/mltm-mlit-south-korea-japan-undersea-tunnel-south-korea/, accessed on 19 July 2022.

Parwani, S., 2021, The TAPI Pipeline in Post-U.S. Withdrawal Afghanistan, https://southasianvoices.org/the-tapi-pipeline-in-post-u-s-withdrawal-afghanistan/, accessed on 21 Sept. 2021.

Saker, 2021, Iran-China: the 21st Century Silk Road Connection, https://thesaker.is/iran-china-the-21st-century-silk-road-connection/, accessed on 28 Sept. 2021.

Spiritual Life, 2021, Bektashi Order, https://slife.org/bektashi-order/, accessed on 23 Sept. 2021.

Toktassynov, T., 2022, Caspian Sea Convention: The Reasons Behind Iran's Landmark Agreement, www.sryahwapublications.com/journal-of-international-politics/pdf/v1-i1/1.pdf, accessed on 12 Feb. 2022.

Trading Economics, 2021, China Foreign Exchange Reserves, https://tradingeconomics.com/china/foreign-exchange-reserves, accessed on 22 Sept. 2021.

Tricontinental Institute for Social Research, 2021, The Eradication of Extreme Poverty in China, https://popularresistance.org/the-eradication-of-extreme-poverty-in-china/ accessed on 12 Feb. 2022.

UN Climate Change, 2022, The Glasgow Climate Pact – Key Outcomes from COP26, https://unfccc.int/process-and-meetings/the-paris-agreement/the-glasgow-climate-pact-key-outcomes-from-cop26, accessed on 3 March 2022.

World Atlas, 2021, What Are The Major Natural Resources Of Kazakhstan? www.worldat las.com/articles/what-are-the-major-natural-resources-of-kazakhstan.html [and other countries cited], accessed on 4 Sept. 2021.

World Bank, 2021, Innovative Restoration Plans for Aral Sea Region Announced at Global Disruptive Tech Challenge 2021, www.worldbank.org/en/news/press-release/2021/04/ 09/innovative-restoration-plans-for-aral-sea-region-announced-at-global-disruptive- tech-challenge-2021, accessed on 2 March 2022.

Yorucu, Vedat and Ozay Mehmet, 2018, *The Southern Energy Corridor: Turkey's Role in European Energy Security*, Switzerland: Springer.

Yorucu, Vedat and Ozay Mehmet, 2022, *Small Islands in Maritime Disputes: Greek-Turkish Energy Geopolitics*, Switzerland: Springer (in press).

8

EUROPE, TURKEY, AND ISLAM

From Crusades to Interfaith Cooperation

Since the rise of Islam, relations between Europe and the Muslim world have been anything but friendly. In the last half a millennium, from the conquest of Istanbul by Sultan Mehmet in 1453, or the "Fall of Constantinople" (Runciman, 1965), European views of the Muslims have been primarily shaped by their relations with the Ottomans. The great historian of Rome set the precedent: Demonizing "Mahomet the Second (sic),""the great destroyer" (Gibbon, 1980, 833), was cast as the "Terror of Europe." The much-revered historian was, in this case, all passion, as if ignorant of facts. But, of course, Gibbon himself wrote at length of the enmity of Greeks and Latins, and of the "pillage of Constantinople" (ibid., 776–783). The seat of Byzantium was, by the advent of Mehmet the Conqueror, so depopulated from divisive Byzantian politics, that the Conqueror's first task was to re-populate his new capital by encouraging immigration, restoring property rights and freedom of worship to all, and granting tax exemption to the Greek families of the Fener district (Inalcik, 1973, 141), on the way to establishing a global Empire. The All-European defense against the Ottoman Turks in Malta in 1565 (Bradford, 1961) and at the Gates of Vienna in 1683 (Stoye, 1964) still run deep in European memory. In contrast, the Crusades (Hindley, 2003), those centuries-old messianic wars launched by Europeans into Muslim lands, or the expulsion of Muslims from Moorish Spain in 1492, are pushed to the background.

For the last 40 years, the EU-Turkey relations have been at the foreground in terms of European relations with the Muslim Middle East. As in the "Fall of Constantinople," today, taking advantage of Islamophobia, the Greeks are very much at the center stage in EU-Turkey relations. In this chapter we shall review these relations in detail, highlighting Greek-Turkish conflicts and the role of the EU in those conflicts, concluding with a hope that future relations will be more cooperative and peaceful than in the past.

DOI: 10.4324/9781003268994-8

Centuries of Crusades

Islam arose in the Arabian desert when Muhammad was born in 570 CE and he received "divine revelations over a period of 22 years, 610–632" (Esposito, 1988, 9). At first quite overwhelmed by his "call", Muhammad heard the voice say: "O Mohammad! You are the messenger of God, and I am Gabriel." Prophet Mohammed proclaimed his divine mission to correct the Christian misbeliefs, such as the Trinity, the deification of a human being, and the worship of idols. The Muslim message acknowledges the Sermon on the Mount, recognized the saintliness of Jesus, but rejected such key claims that Christ died for the sins of generations of humanity. In Islam, man is born without sin, but needs divine guidance to stay on the *Siret al Mustakim*, the True Path (II&D, 1990, 10–11).

These claims challenged Christianity's fundamental principles, and the power of the Church at a time when Europe was undergoing its own identity formation, struggling to liberate itself from the domination of the clergy, and on the road to nationhood. No less significantly, Islam expanded like a prairie fire into what used to be the lands of Byzantium and Rome. The Holy Land became the center of religious conflict, which, in a sense, has continued to this day as a contested land.

The origins of the Crusades lie in the contest between the papacy and the Germanic emperors, successors to Charlemagne, for "the undisputed supremacy ... of Western Christendom ..." The Roman Catholic Church, itself entangled with a power struggle against the Patriarch of Constantinople, took the lead. Although religious, Crusading was politically conceived to promote "the prestige of the papacy" (Hindley, 2003, 9). They were messianic campaigns, armies of God, sponsored by the serving Pope against Muslim forces in southern Spain, southern Italy, and Sicily, but primarily to capture Jerusalem, recapture Christian territory, or defend Christians in non-Christian lands. Some crusades were organized as a means of conflict resolution among Roman Catholics for political or territorial advantage and to combat paganism and heresy.

The First Crusade (1095–1099), called for by Pope Urban II, aspired to win the Holy Lands, ultimately resulting in the recapture of Jerusalem in 1099. Knights, peasants, and serfs from many regions of western Europe travelled over land and by sea, first to Constantinople and then on toward Jerusalem. The crusaders captured Jerusalem in July 1099, massacring many of the city's Muslim and Jewish inhabitants. They also established the crusader states of the Kingdom of Jerusalem, the County of Tripoli, the Principality of Antioch, and the County of Edessa.

The response from the Muslim world was a call for Jihad. It culminated in the fall of Jerusalem to Saladin on 2 October 1187. Saladin, of Kurdish/Turkish origin, the Sultan of Egypt, became the glorious hero in the Muslim world, whose mystique remains still relevant today among those Arabs and Palestinians who believe or dream of deliverance at some future date.

The news of the fall of Jerusalem so shocked the Christendom that it killed the elderly Pope Urban III (ibid., 121). On 29 October, his successor Pope Gregory VIII

TABLE 8.1 A Listing of Crusades and Jihads, 1095–1565

Date	Event
1095–1099	First Crusade proclaimed by Pope Urban II. On 15 July 1099 Jerusalem captured
1147–1149	Second Crusade led by Conrad III of Germany and Louis VII of France
1189–1192	Third Crusade led by Emperor Frederick I, Phillip II of France, and Richard I of England
1202–1204	Fourth Crusade. The Sack of Constantinople
1208	Albigensian Crusade proclaimed by Pope Innocent III
1217–1229	Fifth Crusade proclaimed by Pope Innocent III and Pope Honorius III
1307	Crusade against Constantinople proclaimed by Pope Clement V who who suppressed the Order the Order of Knights Templar in 1312
1329	Jerusalem restored to Christian rule. Frederick crowns himself as king of Jerusalem. The event once called Sixth Crusade
1248–1254	First Crusade of Louis IX of France to Egypt, once called Seventh Crusade
1444	Crusade of Varna crushed by the Ottoman Sultan Murad II
1565	The Great Siege of Malta. Knights Hospitaller under Grand Master Valette repel the forces of Sultan Suleyman I

Source: Table created by the author from data in Hindley (2003, xvi–xx)

issued a formal pronouncement initiating what is known as the Fourth Crusade. Altogether about a dozen campaigns amounting to crusades have been launched, the last being on the Great Siege of Malta in 1565 against Sultan Suleyman's armada to establish a base in the battle for the Mediterranean (Table 8.1).

For much of the faithful in western Europe today, the Jihad-Crusade mentality represents the crux of the European "Christian heritage." Muslims are seen generally from a crusading mindset, a threat to Christian civilization built on Christian foundations.

The Cartoons versus Liberty

The notorious Cartoons Affair must be seen in the context of the Christian European heritage. The Affair, deliberately insulting the Prophet, started in 2005, in one of the most liberal democracies of Europe, Denmark. On 30 September 2005, the Danish newspaper *Jyllands-Posten* published 12 cartoons demonizing the Prophet. Violent protests erupted outside Danish embassies in some Muslim countries, but after a delay of four months. Perhaps the delay was due to the slow transmission of the cartoons in repressive Muslim regimes, or maybe it was an orchestrated delay. It was after Muslim extremism had become a widespread, global threat, years after the 9/11 bombing (Larsen, 2010).

Just when it seemed the Cartoon crisis seemed to die out, it exploded even with more fury, years later, this time in France as the Charlie Hebdo controversy. In 2011, the satirical magazine republished offensive cartoons in an issue "guest-edited" by the Prophet Mohammed ("100 lashes if you don't die of laughter"). The magazine's website was hacked, and Paris offices firebombed. The worst came years later when it republished the controversial cartoons. Twelve people, including some of France's most celebrated cartoonists, were killed on 7 January 2015, when brothers Said and Cherif Kouachi went on a gun rampage at the paper's offices in Paris (Straits Times, 2020).

Was this all casual? An attack on the sacred principles of European liberty and freedom of expression? Certainly no one can argue with the centrality of these European values. But is there no limit to bad taste? Surely some good sense or self-censorship is justified. If anti-Zionism may be declared illegal and judged to be consistent with liberty, why not Islamophobia?

Muslims in Europe Today

In 2016, Europe had 25.8 million Muslims, the second largest religious commu-nity, but tiny considering that Europe is surrounded by a Muslim crescent from Gibraltar through the Magreb, Egypt, Palestine to Istanbul. The small Muslim presence, representing only 7.68% of the total European population, is growing rapidly due to high birthrate. Coupled with influx of refugees and asylum-seekers from war-torn Muslim countries in recent years, this phenomenon has contributed to Islamophobia. Like other immigrant communities, European Muslims refuse assimilation, holding on to their own (Muslim) customs, including dress; this, in turn, makes them target in religious politics. Racial/religious politics is driven by populist domestic politics, but its roots are deep in European society where pres-ervation of a "Christian heritage" is widespread, some parties calling themselves "Christian Democrats," unconcerned about secularism.

Table 8.2 gives statistics of the Muslim population in Europe by top ten coun-tries. The presence of Muslims in these countries is primarily due to European colonialization. This is clearly the case for most countries presented in in Table 8.2: France, UK, Italy, Netherlands, Spain, and Belgium. Ottoman conquest of the Balkans and central Europe is clearly the significant factor in Bulgaria and

TABLE 8.2 Muslim Population in Europe, Top Ten Countries, 2016

Country	Pop. (ml.)	Country	Pop. (ml.)
France	5.72	Spain	1.18
Germany	4.95	Belgium	0.87
UK	4.13	Sweden	0.81
Italy	2.87	Bulgaria	0.79
Netherlands	1.21	Greece	0.62

Source: www.statista.com/statistics/868409/muslim-populations-in-european-countries/, accessed on 19 August 2021

Greece. However, the Ottoman legacy looms much larger in European minds. It may be recalled that the French colonization of North Africa was preceded by long Ottoman rule in those countries. Constant threat from the Ottoman East still shapes public opinion in Europe; it is especially strong in countries like Austria, Poland, and Germany. In Sweden's case, humanitarian motivation is likely the dominant explanation.

Treatment of Muslims in Europe: The French Case

In January 2015, a French satirist magazine published 12 cartoons under the heading "Muhammad overwhelmed by fundamentalists." This event proved to be an explosive boiling point, highlighting the tense relations of French Muslims in a highly traditional Catholic country. The Charlie Hebdo cartoons caused an uproar, not only in the French Muslim community, but in much of the Muslim world. In the name of liberty and freedom of expression, these cartoons maligned Prophet Mohammed. In France, most Muslims live in overcrowded urban quarters, with substandard living conditions, as an unwelcome minority. Public services, including housing, education, and policing, are generally inadequate. In this chronic poverty environment, policing, as in American slums, may be less a law-and-order instrument than an instrument of discrimination, even causing arson, violence, and acts of terror.

There is a general opinion that Muslims resist assimilation and most French fear that their high birthrate is putting France in peril. A leading demographer has argued:

> Migration trends are to intensify over the coming thirty years ...All developed countries will be affected, including East Asia and the former communist countries. There will be an overall mingling of cultures and civilizations that may lead, as far as France is concerned, to the emergence of a predominantly African population and to rapid Islamization.
>
> *Gurfinkel, 1997*

Lack of steady employment job opportunities have pushed Muslim youth into criminal or illegal activities, where vulnerable youth easily fall prey to Islamic terrorism. In response, the French authorities have had recourse to legal ways of restricting Muslim personal freedoms, unaware, or unconcerned, about restricting freedom in general. Macron, the French President, is the latest politician who, while defending republican values, appears to believe that liberty, equality, and fraternity are not applicable to Muslim minority. Some Christian extremists go further, advocating expelling Muslims from Europe. Islamophobia, like all other antireligious extremism, is a social disease. Religious xenophobia represents fear of the foreigner. Sadly, such has been the fate of Turkish-EU relations, which will be detailed in the rest of this chapter.

EU-Turkey Relations as a *Clash of Civilizations* (Huntington, 1996)

President Turgut Özal on 14 April 1987 applied for Turkey's membership in the European Economic Community, precursor of the EU. He even authored a book (Özal, 1991), likely penned for him by a historian consultant, extolling the European heritage of Turkey. The application was rushed and ill-advised. A devout Muslim himself, Özal seemed to contradict himself as leader of a Muslim-majority country applying to join a Christian "club." Insufficient political preparation was undertaken. Even though it was well before Islamophobia, and well-intended, Özal seemed to forget six centuries of conflict between the Ottomans and Europe. Since 1987, anti-Turkish sentiment in Europe has worsened due to Islamophobia, for which, of course, Özal bears no responsibility.

Özal, a dynamic reformer, was following Atatürk's westernization policy. However, while Atatürk had succeeded in creating a Republic on Western ideas and had embarked on a modernization program borrowing Western norms, he never would have compromised Turkish sovereignty, accepting terms from Brussels in return for membership (see the case of Poland later). Özal's application surprised both the Europeans and the Turks. Out of politeness, the application was not rejected out of hand, but a worse outcome evolved instead. Turkey was simply kept waiting in the hall.

Successive Turkish governments, nevertheless, persisted and faced an uphill battle rather than throw in the towel. Many countries with weaker credentials have been able to join, while Turkish accession has been frustratingly slow (Yesilada, 2017). After Recep T. Erdogan's election, his personal style emerged as a problem; the Brussels politicians were not prepared, with the Hungarian and Polish examples in the background, to accommodate a tough Turkish leader with questionable democratic credentials. In the latest environment of Islamophobia, briefly discussed earlier, EU membership for Turkey is all but dead-end.

Ideally, Turkey as a full member of the EU would open the door for meaningful interfaith dialogue to avoid clash of civilizations. But here, too, European colonization stands as a major historical legacy. The French rule in Algeria, Syria, and the Sahel and the Dutch in Indonesia are not subjects that can easily be overcome. Much goodwill is required first to overcome deep-seated feelings of mistrust. In the meantime, the EU has its own internal problems with illiberal leaders in central and eastern Europe.

The Case of Poland

The constitutional tug of war between Poland and the EU is over sovereignty. As a member country, Poland receives significant amount of subsidy and payments and other benefits from the EU. In return, it is expected to follow the rules and regulations formulated in Brussels by nonelected officials and bureaucrats, which may undermine Poland's sovereignty. The Polish Constitutional Court, unsurprisingly, has ruled that in any conflict, Polish legislation must prevail. Hungary, with its own authoritarian system, is very supportive of Poland in this constitutional crisis, and there are fears the dispute may escalate. This is a fundamental crisis for the

EU, for its fundamental values and what the Union stands for. On one side, there are those, including many Poles, who uphold the view of the Union as a single European voice, and that EU rules are equally applied and respected everywhere in the 27 EU members. The Dutch, for one, are solidly behind the view of a strong Union. On the other hand, there are those who defend the supremacy of national legislation as a sovereign act. The Polish government has gone so far as to accuse Brussels politicians of "blackmail," withholding funds to force Warsaw to capitulate to an increasingly dictatorial Commission.

At the center of this controversy is the very soul and mission of the EU. Some hold the view that the EU is no more than a federation of equal, sovereign states with common objectives. Unlike national governments, the EU officials in Brussels, making EU standards and laws, are not elected; they have no democratic account-ability (Anderson, 2020). That is why Brexit took place; if Poland were to follow, it would be far more damaging, as it is in continental Europe, a key country in East–West relations. Poland's exit would possibly inflict a mortal wound on the EU, from which it may not recover. Meanwhile, in November 2011, the Polish-Belarus border emerged as a scene of yet another refugee crisis when thousands of migrants attempted to force their way across the frontier into the EU territory and Belarus retaliated with a threat to cut the transit gas supplies to Europe. The Ukraine war has overtaken all these issues, pushing relations between Russia, the EU, and NATO into a new Cold War framework with uncertain consequences.

European Imperialism

Unplanned economic migration into Europe is the direct result of European imperialism, a subject that is still an emotional topic. Perhaps it requires a Truth and Reconciliation process, although no such process is on anyone's agenda. A brief examination of European colonization is necessary not only to highlight the historic chasm that still exists between the rich and poor nations but also to understand the factors behind Islamophobia and immigrants risking their lives to get into Europe. Modern Muslim influx into Europe began at the demise of the French colonialism in North Africa. In 1961–1962, at the end of the bloody Algerian war, at least 1.5 million refugees escaped to France (Secret Army, 2022), overcrowding cities like Marseilles. Since 2015, at least another 1.3 million Muslim asylum-seekers flooded into Europe from Syria and other war-torn Muslim countries. About the same time, migrants began arriving in England from former colonies in Africa, the Caribbean, and the British India. Likewise, Indonesians emigrated to Holland.

European nations became rich through slavery and forced labor on plantations and mines. This is how railways, ports, and infrastructure were built to ship resources and raw materials to France. Cultural genocide was used extensively. French language and "civilization" were imposed, suppressing local history and culture. The army, missionaries, teachers, traders, and all worked for Motherland France. War, massacres, genocide, every possible means were used to pacify local people, while wealth accumulated in France.

National independence in former colonies after WWI was bloody. A few examples in the case of French decolonization: In the First Indochina War (1945–1955), 1.2 million of the native population were killed, and hundreds of thousands wounded. The Algerian Liberation War cost, as noted earlier, 1.5 million Algerian lives. Hundreds of thousands died in such French colonies as Madagascar, Congo, Cameroon, and the Sahel, where today Macron is still engaged in a neo-imperial war.

Ironically, the liberation of France itself in WWII was made possible, thanks to African colonial soldiers. That did not stop French racism against Asians, Africans, and other colonial people. Right after 1945, racist policies found expression in the French Union, a colonial policy of forced assimilation and French domination worldwide. It was doomed to fail in the age of the UN Charter of Human Rights.

France is a land of contradictions. The home of Voltaire, Liberty, Equality, & Fraternity was also home of the bloodiest religious wars, the Reign of Terror. Napoleon sacrificed a million lives in his Moscow campaign in 1812, and earlier had stolen all the Egyptian treasures he could loot to fill the museums of Paris. The Macron government, outdoing extremist opponents, has applied a dreadful assimilation policy in France. Settlers and assimilated North Africans flooded into France during decolonization, only to find they were unwelcomed. Now, in the name of secularism, the French leader intends to create a new religion called French Islam. Ironically, in the April 2022 runoff election, Macron defeated Marianne Le Pan with the support of the French Muslims because Le Pan embodied Islamophobia and her anti-Muslim policies were regarded as worse than Macron's. The fact, however, is that homegrown terrorism is a direct result of forced assimilation just as was resistance in the days of imperialism. France may have a lot to answer for its bloody imperial legacy, but it was neither the first nor the last in the ignoble history of European imperialism to exploit the rest of the world for Europe's gain. We will briefly review the Spanish and the Dutch cases later.

How the Inca/Aztec Gold Made Europe Rich

After Columbus came the conquistadors, all going for the gold and silver. Aztec and Incas were massacred for gold. The roots of poverty, inequality, and conflict today in Latin America are buried in a brutal history of colonization. In 1520, Cortez defeated the Aztec in today's Mexico City, carried out a massacre of the Aztec nobility (Adams, 2012, 67–68), acquiring Montezuma's treasure, estimated at 8,000 pounds of gold.

On an even larger scale, Pizarro, in 1532, killed the last Inca emperor Atahualpa in Peru. Pizarro took the ransom of gold filling a room, measuring 6.2 by 4.8 by 2.5 feet, and twice again with silver, and beheaded the King (ibid., 69). The conquistadors never found the golden city of El Dorado, but they carted huge quantities of gold and silver shipped to Spain.

What happened to the treasure shipped to Spain? It was first used to finance the Spanish state. Its debt was paid off, its armies and navies financed. A good part of the gold was stolen by the English pirates (e.g., Drake). A significant percentage went to the British Crown, a direct investor in the business of piracy and privateering. Piracy was, at that time, common among mercantilist nations of Europe.

A lot of Muslim sailors, expelled from Spain under Inquisition, joined the Ottoman Navy. Many turned to piracy, raiding far away Cornwall and even Iceland, capturing slaves, and looting churches. Flooding of gold and silver into Iberia caused inflation, a price revolution across Europe. Inflation wrecked the Ottoman Empire. In Europe, gold influx led to mercantilism. Innovation and institution-building followed. Banking and the emergence of international economy, as we know it today, was launched. It started first in Amsterdam (Ferguson, 2009, 128), but the innovation spread quickly to London and other European cities. Amsterdam became the world's first financial center by 1690s. Financial innovation led the way: The Dutch improved the Italian banking and lending system, by introducing the first central bank to stabilize currency. The most popular innovation was legislation to enable joint-stock companies. Shareholders thus invested in companies, assuming risk equivalent to the amount of one's investment. A new Asian spice trade began. At this time, European diets craved for spices like cinnamon, cloves, nutmeg, and pepper. The famed VOC, (United East India Dutch Company), chartered in 1602 (129), thus acquired monopoly control of Indonesia. South African colonization came later.

Later, England took the lead in mercantilism. Industrial Revolution was financed from Amsterdam. English chartered companies, the East India, Hudson Bay, Levant Company. Colonialism and imperialism were globalized to enrich Europe, impoverishing the rest of humanity. This is how our international economy today was founded. Today's multinational corporations emerged out of these early chartered and joint-venture companies.

The Dutch Colonialism

The Dutch prosperity was created from 350 years of Indonesian colonization. It lasted 350 years, from 1600 to 1950. While the Dutch got rich, Indonesian people suffered oppression, violence, and poverty. Indonesian Islam, with some Buddhism and Hindu influences, survived the Dutch occupation The Dutch colonization, like all European imperialism, was mercantilist, all for profit and prosperity of the Mother Country. In the Indonesian case, it was all about Spice Trade, especially pepper.

The VOC grew rich from its Indonesian monopoly. Spice cultivation was a brutal system depending on slavery and forced labor. The Company controlled production, marketing, pricing, and shipping. During its existence, the value of trade handled by VOC has been estimated at $7.5 trillion in today's worth. That amounts to ten times the worth of Apple or Google (Solomon, 2021).

The Muslim population of Indonesia suffered incredible horrors. Their rulers were used as pawns, their culture systematically suppressed. Dutch laws and language were forced on the people. Schooling was an instrument of assimilation. VOC finally went bankrupt in 1799 owing to corruption within its management and the high cost of maintaining its monopoly using force and oppression. Wars against local people never ceased. The Northern Sumatra kingdom of Aceh was finally subdued at the turn of the 20th century (II&D, 1990, 25–26), just 50 years before Indonesian *Merdeka*, (Independence).

The Japanese invasion of Indonesia in WWII was a turning point. When the Japanese imperial army so easily overrun Hong Kong, South East Asia, the British colonies of Malaya and Singapore, and then the Dutch Indonesia, the Asian people were shocked.

Finally, Merdeka came in 1948, led by Sukarno ably supported by Muslim intellectuals like Mohammad Hatta. Sukarno, however, was secular, an admirer of Mustafa Kemal Ataturk. He formulated Pancasila, a secular ideology, which led to Independence Proclamation, uniting the diverse peoples and cultures spread in the Indonesian archipelago. The Dutch made a last, futile stand after WWII, trying to regain their colony after the Japanese surrender. The Indonesians resisted and defeated the Dutch army. Merdeka was confirmed by the newly established UN. Today a leading "prophet" of Islamophobia in Europe is the Dutch politician Geertz Wilders who has pronounced Islam as a "fascist ideology" (Ray, 2021).

The Muslim Refugee Crisis

Today's Muslim refugee crisis in the West is the direct result of impoverishment of the former colonial areas in the age of imperialism. In the post-WWII period, in the name of globalization, a new system of neo-imperialism emerged, transferring capital-intensive technology from the capital-rich countries of the West to the labor-abundant countries of the Third World. A Eurocentric economic system was erected, not much different from the days of imperialism. The Third World was "Westernized" (Mehmet, 1995); the West continued to drain resources from the former colonies under a new dependency system of unequal trade (Mehmet, 1995, 96). A distorted economic system was created: The surplus labor in the poor countries became the economic migrants. The struggle for jobs and incomes exploded into civil wars and ideological battlegrounds. Warlords and mafia-like illegal networks emerged to control drugs, human, and weapon trafficking. Waves of refugees flooded to rich countries. The European response, exemplified by the EU leadership, is remarkably like the classical (Greco-Roman) times; then, it was barbarians; now it is Muslims. In the days of a Constantinople fearing conquest by the Muslim Ottoman forces, the Greeks are at the forefront, the frontline defending the gates of Europe against the Turks and Muslims. Wheatcroft (2008), *The Enemy at the Gate: Habsburgs, Ottomans, and the Battle for Europe*, captures the mood well.

The Crusading Mentality Today

No country can stand idle in the case of irregular influx of refugees and economic migrants. At the same time, the racist platforms of populist politicians and major public figures can hardly be justified. But xenophobia is no rational response.

When history is misused to create hatred, the result is even more chaos. Andrew Wheatcroft's (2008) *The Enemy at the Gate*, written before the Syrian civil war, and the refugee crisis, is a timely warning. Wheatcroft recounts well the history of the disastrous Ottoman Siege in 1683, detailing with amazing maps, battle plans, and sketches of personalities of the key figures in this tragic event. Missing, however, is a solid analysis of the motives behind this Ottoman adventure in Austria. Habsburgs versus Ottomans, an inter-dynasty conflict, is simply inadequate, and, in all fairness, Wheatcroft is aware of the complexity of why the Ottomans came to the gates of Vienna. However, the reader is left in the dark on the intricacies of the *Divan* politics at the time, especially how the Ottoman politics of the day had become an integral part of the French, Hungarian, Polish, and indeed European conflicts of the day. The Sultan and his Grand Vizier were at the gates of Vienna to help the Bourbon France that was passed over by a Pope who supported Spain as the preeminent power of the Holy Roman Empire. Spain had Aztec and Maya gold from the new world. The Pope, ever ready to seize a pecuniary advantage, had previously excommunicated Luther for exposing the Church as a den of corruption, complicit in selling indulgences to the rich.

It is noteworthy that in his concluding chapter Wheatcroft warns against bigotry with quotes from a former EU Commissioner and Pope Benedict XVI. These quotes are worth noting especially with reference to the Islamophobia and Xenophobia, which have engulfed Europe since 2008. Fear dominates European politics, breeding Le Pan and Geert Wilders, to say nothing of neo-Nazis and Skin Heads. The EU Commissioner Frits Bolkestein rejected Turkey's entry into EU with the argument that "the liberation of Vienna in 1683 would have been in vain." Cardinal Joseph Ratzinger, later Pope Benedict XVI, proclaimed more ominously: "The roots that have formed Europe, that have permitted the formation of this continent, are those of Christianity. Turkey has always represented another continent, in permanent contrast with Europe" (Wheatcroft, 2008, 267).

Turkey as a Cultural Bridge: The Idealist Scenario

But it does not have to be a clash of civilizations. Ideally, an optimist yearns for interfaith cooperation, an era of peace and tolerance between Islam and Christianity, indeed, wider peace embracing all three Abrahamic religions. They all have the same origin and, with goodwill to all men, it should be feasible to work out acceptable terms for peaceful coexistence built on interfaith cooperation.

Modern Turkey, by geography and Republican ideology, is a cultural bridge between the Middle East and Europe. Sadly, Brussels politicians have drawn an invisible line regarding Greek border as the eastern limit of the EU. More than that, these European politicians have gone to extremes in exploiting Greek-Turkish relations especially since the end of the Cold War.

In 1952, both Greece and Turkey joined NATO. Greece, just out of a terrible civil war between fascists and communists, was in a precarious way, politically and economically. Turkey was comparatively better placed, thanks to its neutrality in the WWII, but now it was threatened by an aggressive Soviet Union under Stalin. NATO membership stabilized and put both Greece and Turkey within the Western alliance. Turkish forces fought in Korea, and Turkey became a frontline state protecting European security in the Balkans and the Caucuses. Relations between Greece and Turkey were cordial, a legacy of Kemalist foreign policy tradition: Look West and "peace at home, peace abroad."

Turkey's relations with the EU (or its precursors) opened on an optimistic note with the 1960 Ankara Protocol. Recognizing the significant role in European security during the Cold War era, the Protocol envisaged Turkish membership of the Union within a 30-year time frame, that is, by 1990. A road map was devised and implemented to prepare for eventual Turkish membership. Turmoil in Turkish domestic politics, especially the rise of political Islam, upset the roadmap, causing delays and setbacks. Doubts emerged in Europe about the wisdom of admitting a large Muslim country. Relations further deteriorated when, in 1974, Ankara used its Treaty right for intervention in Cyprus to prevent ENOSIS (annexation to Greece), and the USA imposed sanctions on Turkey. Under the pressure of the Greek lobby in Washington the US President Ford signed, in December 1975, a sanctions bill to cut off military aid to Turkey, a ban not lifted until September 1978.

Cyprus Joins the EU and Turkey's Accession Is Put in Deep Freeze

When Greece joined the EU in 1981, the delicate equilibrium between Ankara and Athens was severely damaged. Greece attempted to use its membership as a tool for winning concessions from Turkey in its bilateral disputes, notably maritime entitlements in the Aegean. However, EU-Turkey relations limped along on an uneven road. In 1992, a Custom Union (CU) Agreement was signed while "Cyprus" (meaning the Republic of Cyprus with its 1960 international personality, but in effect Greek Cyprus, representing the whole island) was put on the path of membership. It appears that this was a strategic error on Ankara's part, in a large part owing to complexity of the then PM Çiller's coalition politics and the weakening of the Turkish economy. The Turkish negotiator at Brussels, Karayalçın, at the time signed the documents allowing Greek Cyprus admission in return for CU, and then, once outside facing the press, he disowned his signature, claiming Ankara objected to Greek Cypriot admission. This caused several years of conflict over the EU's demand for extension of the Ankara Protocol, requiring equal treatment of all members, to include Greek Cyprus, in effect Turkish recognition of a Hellenic Republic in Cyprus, something no Turkish government could do.

Çiller represented the last gasp of secular politicians in Ankara. She warned Brussels that Turkey would turn Islamist unless she was helped to contain it. It was a warning that fell on deaf ears. Within a few years, political Islam in Turkey led by the then mayor of Istanbul Recep Tayyib Erdogan and his AK Party (Justice and Development Party) promising clean politics emerged, at first promising improved Greek-Turkish relations. Some journalists began to talk of "moderate Islam"

(Akyol, 2011), an approach favored by Fetullah Gülen, then an ally of Erdogan. The youthful and energetic Socialist, Andreas Papandreou of Greece and Turkish President Abdullah Gül, took the lead, helped by the "earthquate diplomacy" in 1999, when Greece responded with aid in the wake of a devastating earthqake in Izmit and the Turkish government responded positively. Greece announced its support of Turkey's application for EU membership. Acadmic colloboration hailed Greek-Turkish relations (Aydin and Ifantis, 2004; Keridis and Triantaphyllou, 2001).

In April 2004, the UN Secretary General came up with his initiative to solve the Cyprus problem. The Annan Plan, a comprehensive, bizonal, bicommunal settlement Plan, was proposed and submitted to separate referenda. The EU, the USA, and the permanent members of the UNSC strongly supported the Plan. The ethnic Turks in the North approved it with a 65% majority. In the South, the Greek Cypriots rejected it with 76% OXI. The UN mediation efforts of 30 years to reunite the island in a biethnic federation came to nothing; a divided Cyprus was now an EU member.

On 1 May 2004, Cyprus, represented by the All-Greek regime in the South, joined the EU. Astonishingly, the EU accepted the divided island as full EU member in 2004 but suspended the *Acquis Communautaire* in the North. From then on, Cyprus emerged as the key determinant of EU-Turkey relations. Once a member, the Greek Cypriot leadership took control of EU-Turkey agenda; the Greek-Turkish equilibrium, already shuttered in 1984 when Greece was admitted as a member, was totally wrecked. The turning point was 2006. In the preceding two years, following Turkey's candidacy announcement, relations were moving in a positive direction. In June 2006, under pressure from Greeks, the EU demanded that Turkey sign a new Additional Ankara Protocol, allowing Greek Cypriot shipping and airlines to use Turkish ports, in effect recognizing the All-Greek regime as "legitimate." No Turkish government in Ankara could do that without a satisfactory settlement of the Cyprus Problem. As a result, the Greeks prevailed over the EU to permanently suspend eight chapters in Turkish accession. The double Greek veto took effect. Turkish-EU relations gradually worsened: European investment in Turkey, which has been rising impressively, was reversed and the Turkish economy, which had escaped the global recession due to sub-prime lending crisis originating in the USA, experienced foreign exchange shortage. As part of the Arab Spring, the Syrian civil war erupted, and millions of refugees began to flood into Turkey, many hoping to move into Europe. Turkey once more was in the limelight.

The Syrian conflict worsened, and the exodus of refugees into Europe escalated. Hurriedly, the German Chancellor flew to Istanbul and crafted a Turkey-EU Refugee Agreement with the Turkish government. In return for a pledge of $6 billion aid package to be released in stages, Turkey agreed to host these refugees, in effect becoming a "holding camp" to help Europe control the exodus. Upon Ankara's insistence on further incentives, the EU, for its part, agreed to move forward on the Visa Liberalization scheme and open new chapters in the accession negotiations. A few steps were then taken in this direction. Then, developments in Turkish domestic politics took the center stage: The Prime Minister Davutoglu, who appeared to increasingly challenge Erdogan (he had negotiated the Refugee Agreement almost single-handedly), was replaced. The fight against PKK, as well, intensified as did disagreement with Europe over Kurdish rights, now made worse due to Western support for Kurdish militants in Syria who were affiliated with the PKK. On 15 July 2016, an unsuccessful military coup took place against Erdogan (Yavuz and Balci, 2018). Erdogan accused Gülen, in exile in the USA, as its architect, declared his movement a terrorist organization, and emerged as an "executive" president, following a narrow constitutional referandum. The EU put Turkish accession negotiations on hold. They were officially suspended at the end of 2016 when the European Parliament took the lead, citing concerns over human rights and rule of law violations in Turkey, while virtually ignoring the coup on 15 July.

On the other hand, quite apart from the EU, the UNSG pushed on with its mediation role in divided Cyprus. In futile rounds of negotiations, without any time limits, Turkish and Greek Cypriot leaders negotiated the biethnic federation. In 2017, the talks continued under UN auspices, in Mont Pellerin between two Cypriot leaders, Mr Akinci and Mr Anastasiadis, but ended without success. Finally, at Crans-Montana the UN Secretary General declared a "failed conference" and the Turkish side decided to pursue a new, two-state agenda. The obstacle, all along, had been the fact that the EU had given Greeks all the incentives: Armed with EU support, the Greeks had no interest in sharing power with the Turkish side, and wished only to wrest concessions from Ankara giving nothing in return. This maximalist demand has continued ever since.

The EU and the Greek-Turkish Maritime Dispute

Meanwhile, the Turkish maritime dispute with Greece escalated, not only in Cyprus waters, but in the Aegean as well. The EU had endorsed the UNCLOS, every member being a signatory to this Convention, while Turkey was the odd man out. Accordingly, the EU acted out of solidarity with its member state, adopting a position on the Aegean dispute between Turkey and Greece that was identical to that of the Greeks. In terms of clash of civilizations, Greece and the All-Greek Cyprus regime emerged as a "front-line state" defending, as in the Crusading era, the Greek-Turkish border in western Thrace, the Aegean and Eastern Mediterranean. This EU border assumed additional significance after 2015, with barbed wire and walls erected to keep waves of refugees and economic migrants out of EU territory and in Turkey, keeping Europe safe and preserving its Christian heritage. Greeks have accepted this frontline role willingly, as it is highly lucrative. Indeed, Athens has exploited it as a means of wresting concessions in its disputes with Ankara.

In terms of maritime boundaries in the Aegean, the EU backs Athens unreservedly. In the Ionian Sea, two EU member states, Italy and Greece, have delimited boundaries peacefully and amicably, using the median line. No such amicable sharing has been adopted or implemented in the Aegean between Athens and Ankara. Only unilateral and maximalist demands have emerged from Athens, centered on the

UNCLOS provision that Greek Islands in the Aegean possess equivalent rights as Turkey.

Regional Issues in Greek-Turkish-EU Relations

Other regional and bilateral issues have also impacted on Greek-Turkish-EU relations. Regionally, Greeks have followed an "enemy of my enemy is my friend." This has resulted in support for a diversity of issues such as the PKK, Armenian-Ottoman question, and more recently Arab-Israeli conflict. Greece and Greek Cyprus have harbored PKK terrorists, expressed recognition to Armenian "Genocide," both nationally as well as in the European Parliament and other the EU organs. Regionally, the Greeks have courted Israeli, Egyptian, and Lebanese, even UAE alliance in its maritime dispute with the Turkish side. Two clear principles guided Greek regional efforts: keep Turkey out and maximize Hellenic aspirations. Excluding Turkey from the EU has paralleled search for regional alliances, especially in hydrocarbon and maritime disputes. A Seville Map has been drawn as an arbitrary attempt at transforming Greece into an archipelagic power from northern Aegean to Eastern Mediterranean (Seville Map, 2022). As Ankara see it, the map is an ambitious violation of the principles of international law (Pazarci, 2020, 274–275). The Aegean is a "closed sea," and Greece, unlike Indonesia and the Philippines in the Indian and Pacific Oceans, is not an archipelagic country. Article 46 of UNCLOS 46 entitles archipelagic states to a continental shelf only if they do not own any mainland. Greece is a state with its own mainland and the islands in the Aegean Sea cannot, therefore, lead to archipelagic entitlement.

European Factor in Arab-Israeli relations

The Holocaust was a European catastrophe, planned and carried out by Nazi Germany to exterminate the Jews of Europe. To its credit, the West German government accepted responsibility, paying in 1952 a sum of $845 million to Israel, representing $3000 per capita, as reparations in acknowledgement of loss and suffering from the heinous crime inflicted by the Nazi regime on the Jewish people (Jewish Virtual Library, 2021). Whether or not this extinguishes German responsibility for the loss and suffering of Jewish people is debatable. In no way does it extinguish the European moral responsibility inflicted on Palestinians' loss, displacement, and dispossession. We have documented, elsewhere in this study, European imperialist schemes to partition the Ottoman Empire at the end of WWI, leading, among other partition plans, to the creation of Israel in 1948.

The EU, originally an economic organization, expanded its role in global affairs, adopting a more political character in developing relations with ASEAN countries: China, Japan, and Latin America. These are primarily trade-driven relations such as the EU-Yaoundé Convention preserving commodity trade from former African colonies. Closer to home, Brussels has also taken steps opening relations with the Arab-League, and Arab countries, as in the Malta Communique in 2008, a political gathering, to review Middle East developments and calling for peace efforts in the Arab-Israeli conflict. More recently, Greeks have attempted to seek Arab support in their hydrocarbon dispute with Turkey, especially after Ankara signed a Maritime Delimitation Agreement with the Libya (Mehmet and Yorucu, 2020, 65–66). Significant European relations with Arab countries have been bilateral, driven by historical, imperial interests. French interest in Lebanon and Italy's interest in Libya are examples of this. In the energy field, Algeria is the second major source of natural gas supply to Europe, the Magreb Gas Pipeline being a major and strategic supply route (Mehmet and Yorucu, 2020, 135–136). In gas pipeline politics, the Greeks have also attempted to seek large amounts of EU funding for their favorite Eastern Mediterranean Pipeline (EMP) project, a 2,000 km undersea pipeline from Israeli gas fields via Cyprus, Crete, and Greece to Europe. Even though such a megaproject is uneconomic (far more costly than the Russian and Algerian alternatives), and increasingly unsustainable in the face of global transition to Green Energy (Mehmet and Yorucu, 2020, 113–114), Brussel politicians have not ruled it out, but the Americans have, advising Greeks' support of regional energy cooperation with neighboring countries, including Turkey.

In the Syrian refugee crisis, the European powers have not lived up to its moral responsibility, most clearly in the treatment of Syrian refugees. It may not be acceptable to allow millions of these refugees into European nations. However, there is no excuse for the meagre supply of funds to accommodate Syrian refugees in neighboring countries. The Turkish-EU Refugee Agreement is an example of broken promises from Brussels politicians. The amount provided from EU sources to house and care Syrian refugees in Turkey pales in comparison with the amount of aid provided by Turkish government sources. The humane manner in which Europeans have responded to the Ukrainian refugees stands in sharp contrast to the inhumane treatment accorded to the Syrian ones.

War or Peace?

In WWI, at the height of European imperialism, the Europeans succeeded in creating a wedge between the Turks and Arabs. The Sultan's call for a *Jihad* fell on deaf ears. Britain recruited thousands of troops from British India to fight the Ottoman Turks in Mesopotamia and Palestine. France likewise recruited thousands of soldiers from its North African colonies for the same objective. In 1919, at the end of WWI, the Greeks were encouraged to invade the Turkish homeland in pursuit of a Hellenic Empire. It ended in disaster for the invaders. The modern Turkish republic was created, replacing the Ottoman Empire. The Kemalist motto has been "Peace at home, peace abroad." In 1987, Ankara applied for membership in the EU.

It has been 34 years since Turkey's application for EU membership. During this period, EU membership has doubled, and one (UK) has left the Union. What is the latest status of Turkish accession negotiations? Table 8.3 summarizes the painfully slow, or rather lack of, progress, the key causal factor, as explained above, being religious politics. Technically, only 33 of 35 chapters of the European Law, *Acquis*

TABLE 8.3 Latest Status of Turkey Accession Negotiations

Total chapters necessary for complete accession	33 out of 35
Completed to date	1
Opened	16
Not to be opened (GC Veto)	8

Source: https://en.wikipedia.org/wiki/Accession_of_Turkey_to_the_European_Union, accessed on 20 April 2021

Communautaire, one has successfully been opened and closed, 16 have been open, and a further 8 are subject to Greek veto.

Theoretically, there is no better way to settle Greek-Turkish disputes, especially Cyprus, than to have all three countries as members in the EU. This point has been repeatedly stated by numerous observers, including Greek academics (Loizides, 2007; Ker-Lindsay, 2007; Tocci, 2007). Within the EU there are several examples of membership facilitating conflict resolution, including the Franco-German rapprochement. In the case of Spain and Portugal, both emerging from a fascist legacy at the time of admission, it was argued that membership would enhance and strengthen their democratic transition. The same argument was used in 2004, at the time of the Union's expansion into eastern Europe, in the admission of former Soviet satellites, especially Bulgaria and Romania, which were well behind Turkey in economic and political institutions and development. A recent Carnegie Europe evaluation (Pierini, 2019) has underscored the importance of Turkey-EU relations, highlighting "five dimensions – economics, domestic politics, foreign policy, defense policy and the rule of law," which "paint a challenging picture" to managing a difficult relationship.

At the end of 2021, it is evident that Turkish membership in the EU is not an achievable target; Ankara should simply accept the reality and walk away. There are alternatives to membership to develop an honest and realistic EU-Turkey relationship. One such formula might be a "privileged relationship," a special, mutually acceptable partnership in all, except the name. As Weber (2018) argued, such a strategy should be "based on honesty about long-term goal: EU membership is not an option for Turkey." Turkey is too important a country in terms of European security, increasingly in energy diversification (Sartori, ibid., 373–393), refugee management (Kaya, ibid., 347–272), and most recently, a new Cold War, to be totally dismissed. In future, a "cooperative relationship" as proposed in a recent book (ibid., 397–432) is perhaps the most feasible prospect.

In relation to Greek-Turkish maritime dispute or in the case of Cyprus, honest, frank policy-making in Brussels would guarantee avoidance of war between Greece and Turkey. De-escalation with meaningful incentives to both sides would be a rational way of achieving peaceful conflict resolution outcomes. Maritime resources in disputed waters could be shared. Designing and implementing sharing formulae should not be short term and opportunistic. Rather it should be long term and stable, a new Ankara Protocol, with a clear roadmap and a clear destination, mutually determined. The fact is that neither Turkey nor the EU can afford to dismiss each other. The relationship is too deep-rooted and multidimensional for a total break. European and Turkish leaders, irrespective of political persuasions, are condemned to comanage a challenging relationship. A settlement in Cyprus would help stabilize Greek-Turkish relations, with the EU facilitating the UN efforts.

Energy Cooperation on the SRE

Turkey is the gateway to Europe in the SRE, especially in energy security. In cooperation with Azerbaijan, a new Southern Energy Corridor (SEC) is emerging for European energy security (Yorucu and Mehmet, 2018). In October 2011, Turkey and Azerbaijan have signed an agreement on gas prices and delivery from the Shah Deniz sources, thereby opening a new chapter in energy cooperation on the Silk Route Economy (SRE), discussed in Chapter 7. Turkey is set become a regional energy hub, especially because of the war in Ukraine. Now that TANAP is operational, the Caspian Basin is rapidly developing as the most feasible SEC for European energy security. Ankara is the key in the diversification plans for several reasons. TANAP is now linked with TAP, and this pipeline will, in the next decade, be linked to, or supplemented with, Turkish Stream across the Black Sea as well as Middle East sources to the south and Trans Caspian sources along the SRE. Turkmenistan and Central Asian Turkic republic, rich in energy resources, know little about European energy markets. Turkey is in a critical position, not only as the Western end of the SRE, but as an energy transit country with cultural links to the Turkic countries. China's rapid emergence, and specifically the BRI, has encouraged rethinking of Western foreign policy objectives. The EU, For example, is formulating a Global Gateway strategy to counter Chinese influence globally. Under this strategy, Brussel would be better placed to stand up to China — whether on its human rights violations (in Tibet, Uyghur Turks or Taiwan) or pursuing value-based trade relationship. This is a potentially promising development as it may lead in future to a less exploitative trading system and a more sustainable world order (Lau and Cokelaere, 2021).

Conclusion

The EU is not a single body. Politically, it can be viewed as a federation of 27 sovereign nations who voluntarily have agreed to surrender a certain degree of their sovereignty for economic gains and political solidarity. Institutionally, it consists of a European Council, Commission atop a huge bureaucracy acting as its executive arm, and parliament, each one often acting independently from one another. In addition, there is term presidency of six months when each one of the member countries assume a leadership role for the term. During the French EU presidency, covering the first half of 2022, for example, president Macron advocated a neo-liberal slogan emphasizing pro-business, pro-market reforms (Cann, and Petitjean,

2022) which ultimately may empower more the corporations in the global market-place than the European citizens. Externally, the future of the EU may well be determined by the outcome of security threats from the East, centered in the war in Ukraine. At this point, the war seems unlikely to spread into neighboring countries, but in future such a threat cannot be dismissed.

Looking into the future, this study suggests a four-stage strategy to put the EU-Turkey relationship on an honest and healthy footing: (1) the Greek-Turkish equilibrium to be restored, (2) trade, economic, and political relations to be normalized, (3) regional and humanitarian issues cooperatively tackled, and (4) finally, an interfaith dialogue may be initiated for better Muslim-Christian relations.

To elaborate briefly, first and foremost, the Greek-Turkish equilibrium must be restored. It was disturbed when Greece in 1981 became member, and totally derailed in 2004 when a divided Cyprus was admitted. An equilibrium in Greek-Turkish relationship is a vital first step toward an honest and healthy relationship between Brussels and Ankara. Within this equilibrium, the Aegean and Cyprus disputes should be solved peacefully, with UN mediation supported by Brussels, in a manner acceptable to the parties. The Brussels politicians have an obligation to resolve these disputes, arising from promises made in the past to both Ankara and the Turkish Cypriots.

Second, once the Greek obstacles are removed, trade and economic relations, including European energy security, can be taken up. The starting point would be updating the Custom Union Agreement, now much outdated. In this package, visa liberalization for Turkish citizens may take place. In return, Turkey must reform its human rights and rule of law legislation in line with EU norms, including granting democratic rights to the Kurds.

Third, the war-torn neighboring countries like Syria and Iraq, and others like Libya, Palestine, Yemen, and Afghanistan, need to be handled within a comprehensive humanitarian program. These Muslim countries need a non-imperialistic "hand" to craft any feasible settlement, and Turkey is historically and culturally well suited for this partnership role.

Finally, the chaos in the Muslim world is the direct result of Western imperialism, as documented in this study. No less than a South Africa style Truth and Reconciliation process is required to heal the wounds in Palestine, Algeria, and the Middle East. Turkey may not have all the essential credentials for this momentous challenge, but, with its century-old secularization experience, it is well qualified for the job.

References

Adams, Mark, 2012, *Turn Right at Machu Picchu: Rediscovering the Lost City One Step at a Time*, New York: First Plume Printing.

Akyol, M., 2011, *Islam without Extremes: A Muslim Case for Liberty*, New York: Norton.

Anderson, P., 2020, "The European Coup", *London Review of Books*, Vol. 42, No. 24, 17 December.

Aydin, M. and Ifantis, K., 2004, *Turkish-Greek Relations: The Security Dilemma in the Aegean*, London: Routledge.

Bradford, E., 1961, *The Great Siege, Malta 1565*, London: Penguin.

Cann, V. and Petitjean, O., 2022, Macron Wants EU 'Sovereignty'—but for Whom? https://socialeurope.eu/macron-wants-eu-sovereignty-but-for-whom, accessed on 9 Jan. 2022.

Dodd, C.H., 1998, *The Cyprus Imbroglio*. Huntingdon, Cambridgeshire: The Eothen Press.

Ferguson, Niall, 2009, *The Ascent of Money, A Financial History of the World*, New York: Penguin.

Gibbon, Edward, 1980, *The Decline and Fall of the Roman Empire: An Abridgement by D.M. Low*, New York: Harcourt, Brace and Co.

Gurfinkel, M., 1997, Islam in France: The French Way of Life Is in Danger, www.meforum.org/337/islam-in-france-the-french-way-of-life-is-in, accessed on 20 August 2021.

Hindley, G., 2003, *The Crusades, Islam and Christianity in the Struggle for World Supremacy*, London: Robinson.

Huntington, Samuel P. 1996, *The Clash of Civilizations and the Remaking of World Order*. New York: Simon and Schuster.

Jewish Virtual Library, 2021, Holocaust Restitution: German Reparations, www.jewishvirtuallibrary.org/german-holocaust-reparations, accessed on 21 August 2021.

Keridis, D. and Triantaphyllou, D., 2001, *Greek-Turkish Relations in the Era of Globalization*, Herndon, Virginia: Brassy's.

Ker-Lindsay, J. 2007, *The European Union as a Catalyst for Conflict Resolution: Lessons from Cyprus on the Limits of Conditionality. Working paper Series No. 1, Helen Bamber Centre for the Study of Rights and Conflicts*. London: Kingston University.

Larsen, R.E., 2010, The Danish Cartoon Affair, www.counterpunch.org/2010/09/24/the-danish-cartoon-affair/, accessed on 5 Nov. 2021.

Lau, S. and H. Cokelaere, 2021, EU Launches 'Global Gateway' to Counter China's Belt and Road, www.politico.eu/article/eu-launches-global-gateway-to-counter-chinas-belt-and-road/, accessed on 24 Dec. 2021.

Loizides, N.G., 2007, "Ethnic Nationalism and Adaptation in Cyprus", *International Studies Perspectives*, Vol. 8, No. 2, 172–189. https://doi.org/10.1111/j.1528-3585.2007.00279.x

Mehmet, Ozay, 1995, *Westernizing the Third World, The Eurocentricity of Economic Development Theories*, 2nd ed., London: Routledge.

Mehmet, Ozay and Yorucu, Vedat, 2020, *Modern Geopolitics of Eastern Mediterranean Hydrocarbons in an Age of Energy Transformation*. Switzerland: Springer International Publishing AG.

Mendez, Errol and Ozay Mehmet, 2000, *Global Governance, Economy and Law; Waiting for Justice*, London: Routledge.

Özal, Turgut, 1991, *Turkey in Europe*, Nicosia, North Cyprus: K. Rustem & Brother.

Pazarci, H., 2020, *Uluslararası Hukuk*, 19th ed, Ankara: Turhan Kitabevi.

Pierini, M., 2019, Options for the EU-Turkey Relationship, Carnegie Europe, 3 May, https://carnegieeurope.eu/2019/05/03/options-for-eu-turkey-relationship-pub-79061, accessed on 17 April 2021.

Ray, M., 2021, Geert Wilders: Dutch politician, www.britannica.com/biography/Geert-Wilders, accessed on 21 Oct. 2021.

Runciman, S., 1965, *The Fall of Constantinople 1453*, London: Cambridge University Press.

Secret Army, 2022, The Algerian Story 1961–1962: The End of the War, https://sites.google.com/a/oxy.edu/the-algerian-story/1961-1962-the-end-of-the-war, accessed on 29 April 2022.

Seville Map, 2022, The Seville Map that challenges Turkey, Greece, US and the EU, www.keeptalkinggreece.com/2020/09/22/seville-map-us-turkey-greece/, accessed on 3 May 2022.

Solomon, B., 2021, The Dutch East India Company was richer than Apple, Google and Facebook combined, https://dutchreview.com/culture/history/how-rich-was-the-dutch-east-india-company/, accessed on 13 Oct. 2021.

Straits Times, 2020, France's Charlie Hebdo republishes Muhammad cartoons for trial start, www.straitstimes.com/world/europe/frances-charlie-hebdo-republishes-mohammed-cartoons-for-trial-start, accessed on 5 Nov. 2021.

Stoye, J., 1964, *The Seige of Vienna*, London: Collins.

Tocci, N., 2007, *The EU and Conflict Resolution: Promoting Peace in the Backyard*. London: Routledge.

Weber, M., 2018, "EU-Turkey Relations Need an Honest New Start", *European View*, Vol. 17, No. 1, 52–57. https://journals.sagepub.com/doi/full/10.1177/1781685818765095, accessed 17 April 2021.

Wheatcroft, Andrew. 2008, *The Enemy at the Gate: Habsburgs, Ottomans, and the Battle for Europe*, New York: Basic Books.

Yavuz, H. and B. Balci, 2018, *Turkey's July 15th Coup and Why*, Salt Lake City: Utah University Press.

Yesilada, B., 1999, *The Worsening EU-Turkey Relations*. Portland: Portland State University, Political Science Department Publications. https://pdxscholar.library.pdx.edu/cgi/viewcontent.cgi?referer=https://ca.search.yahoo.com/&httpsredir=1&article=1030&context=polisci_fac, accessed on 17 April 2021.

Yesilada, B., 2017, *EU-Turkey Relations in the 21st Century*. New York: Routledge.

9

THE MUSLIM REFUGEE CRISIS AND MORAL FAILURE

A huge number of civilians in the Muslim Core are living in refugee camps as dispossessed and displaced persons, victims of conflict and war. During the Ottoman period, there were no refugee camps. While it is impossible to say who is worse off, the Palestinians are special in that they are virtually permanent, a people who lost their homeland to make way for another. Below, latest statistics, however imperfect, are assembled to give in summary a quantitative picture of victims of conflict in selected Muslim countries.

> **Palestine:** On the World Refugee Day, 20 June 2020, human rights defenders recalled that 5.6 million Palestinians survive as refugees in Jordan, Syria, Lebanon, Gaza, and the West Bank (Telesur, 2020). Further details will be provided in the following pages.
>
> **Yemen:** Before conflict, poverty affected half the population, about 29 people, before the crisis. Today, poverty impacts between 71% and 78% of the population creating increased homelessness and internally displaced persons. More than 80% of the population requires humanitarian assistance to have access to clean water, food, and health care. Children and women are among the most vulnerable to the crisis. Moreover, many international organizations, such as UNICEF, Oxfam, and the World Food Program, are helping these helpless Yemenis (Borgen project, 2020).
>
> **Jordan:** Already hosting 2.4 million refugees in 2011, Jordan experienced a further influx of 0.7 million displaced persons as of 2020, bringing the total refugee population to 3.1 million (Macrotrends, 2022).
>
> **Turkey:** Turkey has emerged as the largest host country for victims of violence in the region. Just in the case of the Syrian conflict, the number of registered refugees under temporary protection in Turkey as of 16 July 2020 was 3,600,710 (Refugee Association, 2020).

DOI: 10.4324/9781003268994-9

Iraq: The number of internally displaced persons in Iraq as of 31 December 2020 numbered 1.2 million. Internal displacements during the period 2008–2021 numbered a staggering 5.7 million (IDMC, 2021).

The above list is incomplete. Also, it must be remembered that exact numbers of victims of conflict are impossible owing to difficulty of counting and keeping records. The key fact, however, is that generations are growing up in refugee camps lacking normal human standards. Living off charity is demeaning, especially when the recipients are able-bodied and capable of earning their own living. Temporary aid, because of earthquakes, floods, or other forms of environmental damage, is normal, but when the victims of displacement, dispossession of a homeland, have no place to go but to live in a camp, then the aid system itself becomes questionable on ethical grounds. Where does responsibility lie for the permanence of dependency inflicted on the victims? Clearly, failed states bear the prime responsibility. However, what is the moral justification for creating permanent aid and care dependency? These are types of questions we discuss in this chapter. We use the "Lords of Poverty" paradigm (Hancock, 1994) to document what we have termed the Palestinian Refugee Model (PRM), a permanent aid and care system, which has been created to house and care for waves of new refugees. New generations of Palestinians and Arabs now live in camps. In the process, a new "Lords of Poverty" system has evolved, replicating PRM. Rich countries have all but closed their doors to Muslim victims for fear of Islamization. The victims themselves reject moving to most Muslim countries that are repressive and opportunities for making a new life are limited. Who wants to move to "failed states"? Providing aid and assistance, multilaterally or bilaterally, has now emerged as a new system to care for victims of failed states, war, and conflict.

Foreign aid has a long history with dubious motives, as pointed out in an early study of Somalia (Mehmet, 1971). There are two main categories of aid flows: multilateral and bilateral. The former aid is provided, typically via the UN system, such as food aid under the World Food Program, financed by member states. Bilateral aid is provided as part of a specific donor's foreign policy and it comes as tied aid, with conditions such as supporting the donor's military or foreign aid objectives. Examples of this include the American aid to Egypt to safeguard the Egyptian Israeli peace agreement. The case of Palestinians, however, is special as it represents a deliberate example of moral failure of Western imperialist powers who planned and executed the creation of Israel, and then faced with the exodus of Palestinians devised PRM, initially as a temporary measure.

The Vital Issue of Land in Palestine

Alongside the responsibility of failed Arab states, the Palestinian tragedy is a Western moral failure. Xenophobia, Islamophobia in rich countries, is erecting walls to keep Muslim refugees out. Well before the Syrian refugee crisis, however, the West had created a humanitarian industry to care for displaced and dispossessed Palestinians in refugee camps. These camps have been expanded to care for victims of civil wars and dictatorships in the Muslim Core. It amounts to nothing less than collective moral failure, on the part of Western and the Arab elites.

Land has been the vital, central issue of the Jewish-Palestinian conflict. It is useful to present a summary of this highly complex issue as a background to the more recent plight of Palestinian refugees. The Holy Land was sacred for the Ottoman Sultan who was also the Caliph and Custodian of Jerusalem, the third holiest city of Islam, after Mecca and Medina, the al-Aqsa Mosque being the holy place from where Mohammed ascended to Heaven.

As regard land ownership in Palestine, the Ottomans did not allow foreigners to purchase land until the Tanzimat reforms in mid-19th century. Three factors changed this policy: (1) mercantilist penetration into the Empire following Industrial Revolution, (2) the start of railways construction in the second half of the 19th century, and (3) the Jewish national awakening, led by the Zionist movement.

The advent of the Baghdad Railway, as it moved into construction beyond the Taurus Mountains, along the coast of Alexandretta, Lebanon, and through the Holy Land to Mecca, had a major impact on land tenure and ownership. In the large Çukurova plain in the Adana region, through which the railway passed, wealthy Armenians began speculating, purchasing land, and converting small holdings into plantations. The displaced Turkmen therefore flooded large towns like Adana and Mersin. Ottoman-Armenian relations turned bloody in the aftermath of the 1908 Constitutional Revolution in Istanbul when Young Turks and Armenian revolutionaries danced in the streets, celebrating the arrival of Liberty. In Adana, Armenian nationalists also poured into the streets in celebration, shouting insults to Turks. The reaction was fast and furious. In the racial mayhem, which followed, thousands of Armenians were massacred in vengeance killings. One English eyewitness puts the blame on Armenians, but also explained the deeper economic reasons behind the riots (Childs, 2017, 350–351).

In the Holy Land and Arabia, the Hejaz railway was furiously opposed by the Bedouin and other tribes whose source of livelihood, the annual caravan pilgrim trade to Mecca, was threatened. They sabotaged the railway and subsequently became willing actors in the Arab Revolt.

The Ottomans accepted Jews and Christians as "People of the Book" and granted them religious freedom and autonomy under the *millet* system. However, the Sultan's government opposed the idea of Jewish self-rule in Palestine. When Jews were massively persecuted in Russia in the mid-19th century, the Ottomans were sympathetic to Jewish immigration into the Empire, but not into Palestine. This policy did not change until the Ottoman defeat in 1918. Prior to WWI, the Ottoman government had decided to prohibit the sale of land in Palestine to Jews, even if they were Ottoman citizens. But the law was not strictly applied, and many cases of Jewish land purchases went through with such organizations as the Palestine Jewish Colonization Association, Palestinian Land Development Company, and, most significantly, the Jewish National Fund (JNF).

From the 1880s to the 1930s, most Jewish land purchases were made in the coastal plain, the Jezreel Valley, the Jordan Valley, and on a smaller scale in the Galilee. At the beginning, there was preference for cheap rural land without any tenants or population. In sparsely populated areas, the sandy soil type made the main agricultural activity, corn cultivation impossible. Beginning in the 1930s, most of the land was bought from landowners, which included non-Palestinian landowners, Palestinian landowners, churches, and foreign companies. Only a small fraction was purchased from fellaheen or Bedouin farmers. On 31 December 1944, about 44% of land was possessed by the JNF. By the time of the declaration of their statehood, Zionists had acquired almost half the land of Palestine.

Jewish nation-building in Palestine was a carefully executed plan, first with land acquisition, followed by a military and terrorist plan during the British mandate. In the first stage, the idea of a Jewish Homeland emerged through visionaries like Theodore Herzl, but the idea was put into practical implementation by financiers like the Rothschilds and American Jewry who funded not only large-scale land purchases, but scientific research to develop new crops, introduce pest control, and carry out agricultural experiment for the most suitable land use methods, pioneered by agronomist Aaronsohn (Anderson, 2013, 51 and 133–4). While the British administration of the mandate held some sympathy for the Arabs, it was feeble compared with the support they extended to the Jewish national movement, especially when the latter became more aggressive, using all means possible, including terrorism, to achieve their goal of a homeland.

The British Mandate and the Bloody Way to Partition

In the final stages of the British mandate, there was a clear military operation to expel Palestinians from their homes and villages by force. A "Jewish Settlement Force" was created, some 20,000 strong, and terrorism and terrorist operations were organized and carried out, not only against Palestinians but also against the British. In the last year of the mandate, the kill ratio was four British officers for every Jewish terrorist. David Ben-Gurion himself plotted these terrorist attacks in his home, assisted by a secret group called the Consultancy (Plan Dalet, 1948).

Hagenah, Irgun, and Stern systematically operated as terrorist attacks in cafes and urban centers, but even more brutally, there were massacres and attacks against Palestinian villages. Thirty-four massacres were documented by Zionist historian Benny Morris to have occurred within a few months: Al-Abbasiyya, Beit Daras, Bir Al-Saba', Al-Kabri, Haifa, Qisarya. These attacks were part of Plan Dalet. In 1948, half the Palestinian villages were destroyed, an estimated 13,000 killed, and 737,166 forcibly evicted from their homes and land.

In November 1947, the UN adopted Resolution 181 partitioning Palestine, the USA pressuring countries to ensure its passage. Arabs rejected it and Arab-Israeli fighting ensued. After ten months of fighting, combined Arab forces from Egypt, Syria, and Transjordan; Israel controlled the area recommended in Resolution 181 plus almost 60% of the Arab state proposed in the earlier partition plan, which included Jaffa, Lydda and Ramle area, Galilee, West Jerusalem, and parts of the Negev. The Egyptian military took control of the Gaza Strip, while Transjordan annexed the remaining mandate areas. Some 700,000 Palestinians became refugees (Nakba, 2016). The Palestinian refugee crisis escalated in the Six-Day War, 1967 when Israel easily overcame the ill-prepared Arab forces. The West Bank and Gaza Strip were occupied, and another wave of Palestinian refugees were moved into camps in surrounding countries including Jordan, Syria, and Egypt. The West, in particular the USA, is responsible for the Palestinian tragedy, but equally the Arab unpreparedness and disunity to defend Palestinian rights on the battlefield must be acknowledged. Once the Ottomans were gone, Palestinians were dispossessed and went into permanent life on refugee camps to make room for a Jewish Homeland. The dispossession has been shameful. No charity can extinguish the moral wrong that has been inflicted on the Palestinian people. The Palestinian refugee camp became the model for the new generations of victims of war and conflict in the Arab Core.

A New Breed of "Lords of Poverty"

In 1994, Hancock wrote *The Lords of Poverty: The Power, Prestige, and Corruption of the International Aid*, a book critical of how the foreign aid system works, who it benefits, and what impacts it generates. He documented aid's negative impact on the environment and lives of target groups, and the lavish lifestyles in a vast international "aristocracy of mercy" (Hancock, 1994). Now, in the Arab Core, a new system of caring for Muslim refugees, displaced, and homeless people herded into camps. The worst is that the Palestinian tragedy has been repeated time and again.

Who exactly are the "Lords of Poverty"? They are international personnel, typically from rich countries, working in the new system designed to look after refugees. As in the Palestinian case, they are supported by area refugees, but the system is international, supervising and controlling refugee camps. They police borders and administer programs, funded from charitable organizations, expected to deliver benefit to the victims of war and conflict. By far the greatest percentage of this new personnel are honest and dedicated caregivers. But there are, amid this ever-growing system, some who abuse the system: They travel first-class, stay in five-star hotels, eat at gourmet restaurants, live on expense accounts, all paid for by funds earmarked for refugees or migrants.

We now examine in greater detail how the Palestinians have become a nation of refugees, generation after generation, living under the care of charitable organizations. The Palestinian problem was at first recognized as a refugee problem. It was not until 1974 that their right of return was acknowledged under international law (Siddiqui, 2003). By then it was too late; two wars had been fought over Palestine (the first in 1948 and the second one in 1967) and PRM was no longer "temporary." Indeed, the model has been universalized, extended to the Muslim Core and beyond to Africa and Asia. It is instructive to detail the principal features of PRM.

Palestine: A Nation of Refugees

Palestinians have been the classic case of a people dispossessed of their homeland to make room for another. In the post-Ottoman era, the Palestinians have become a nation dispossessed, dependent on charity, insecure, generations growing without hope. Nothing demonstrates more clearly the decline in the Arab world since the end of Ottomans. Palestinians are a nation of refugees; a new care industry has now been created to manage supply and distribution of basic human needs of these victims of conflict. The new care industry is huge, consisting of multinational food agencies (World Food Organization), disposing surplus food from Western sources, and charitable nongovernment organizations, including CARE, OXFAM, and countless missionary and aid agencies. It amounts to total abdication of moral responsibility, reflecting the fact that the unwanted Muslims are better placed in camps than allowed in Europe, the USA, or the First World. The Arab elite is quite comfortable with this. Personnel working in these organizations carry no moral blame. They are professionals and technicians delivering much-needed care and life-giving support. What is objectionable is the systemic victimization of innocent persons, subjected to violence, eviction, or other forms of atrocity.

The UNRWA System: UNRWA was created in December 1949 as an agency by the UN General Assembly, which earlier had voted for the creation of Israel. Its mandate was to provide humanitarian aid to the displaced and dispossessed Palestinians, in effect making them "wards" of the General Assembly on behalf of the international community. It was meant to be temporary, hoping to resettle the Palestinian refugees either by repatriation or reintegration. During the early years, from 1949 to 1960, UNRWA followed a declared policy of "reintegration" of Palestinian refugees into the normal life of the Middle East outside Israel.

The UNRWA group of refugees number 5 million or more, as generations pass from one to the next. Technically, refugee status cannot be passed from one generation to the next, but the UNRWA system is unique. Almost all the original refugees are no longer alive today. The system has become permanent, and Palestinians have become a nation of refugees. The Palestinian problem remains unresolved. It is an international moral failure on a massive scale. The vast majority of UNRWA refugees are descendants of original refugees, grandchildren and great grandchildren born in Jordan, the West Bank, Gaza, Lebanon, Syria, and elsewhere – not in pre-1948 Palestine. Unless something drastic happens, projections by the United Nations High Commission for Refugees, by 2030, UNRWA's refugee list will increase to 8.5 million (Rosen, 2012).

In 1950, the number of Palestinian refugee population, victims of the 1948 conflict, was estimated at 0.9 million. By 2018, it exploded to at least 5 million or higher. This is the population registered under UNRWA, the UN Work, and Relief Agency created, even Israel supporting it, right after the Arab-Israeli conflict to care for Palestinians who lost their homes and property, becoming homeless, stateless. At the beginning, UNRWA's aims were uncertain: temporary relief with the expectation of return or resettlement somewhere away from Palestine. Its camps were established with the permission of host countries, but UNRWA provided no police or protection beyond aid. The 1967 war further added to the Palestinian crisis, located in occupied territories and neighboring countries (Palestinian Central Bureau of Statistics, 2019).

Several kinds of camps exist, 58 "official" under UNRWA, and a further 10 unofficial, under a variety of conditions. Being stateless, statistics are no more than estimates. To be eligible for UNRWA aid, a Palestinian must be registered with proper documentation. These camps, with approval of host countries, after some seven decades, cannot be considered "temporary," intended for resettlement. High birthrates have created an expanding nation of refugees, receiving minimal levels of shelter, education, and other basic needs. New generations grow up under abysmal conditions, stateless, without hope of ever returning to their homeland. It is a system that inevitably breeds terrorism and violence.

Over the last 70 years, UNRWA has developed into a large parastatal organization, its most revealing redeeming feature being the fact that it is 99% Palestinian-run. But the system is nothing else than a grand dependency system that enables Israel to prosper, while the camps have no hope of evolving as civil society. Critics have accused them of radicalizing youth. Funded by voluntary international contributions, mostly from the West. UNRWA adopted its own definition of who is a Palestinian refugee: "persons whose regular place of residence was Palestine during the period 1 June 1946 to 15 May 1948, and who lost both home and means of livelihood because of the 1948 conflict. "Persons without documentation could not be registered. But even this restrictive definition became redundant when the Six-Day War of 1967 added a new wave of Palestinian refugees who did not fit into the earlier definition. In the end, beginning in 1991, the UN General Assembly has started to adopt an annual resolution allowing the 1967 refugees to come under the UNRWA mandate. UNRWA's "mandate" is not a single document but the sum of all relevant resolutions and requests of the General Assembly, testifying to its temporary or transitory foundation. While focused on Palestine refugees, UNRWA also extends its services to persons displaced by subsequent hostilities. As a result, several categories of persons have long been registered as eligible to receive UNRWA services although not "Palestine refugees." Most notably, the descendants of Palestine refugee males, including adopted children, are also eligible for registration as refugees. In effect, the UNRWA system has become a permanent aid organization, a unique, quasi-state organization.

In 2020, UNRWA had an Italian head and provided aid to some 1.5 million registered refugees, covering only the 1948 refugees, with a total expenditure of US $1.1 billion, a staff of almost 29,000, currently 90% being area refugees, and 10% being non-area refugees (UNRWA, 2020, 228 for staff data and 225 for expenditure). Funding has come principally from the USA, EU, and other European countries, which collectively account for about two-thirds of the total expenditure. Political considerations heavily influence these donations. In 2018, the Trump administration stopped funding owing to Trump's strong backing for Israel; they were resumed in 2021 after his defeat. By comparison to Western donors, the donations coming from oil-rich Arab countries have been miniscule relative to the size of the problem (UNRWA, 2022).

Palestinians are unique as a people to suffer loss of a homeland, displacement, and dispossession. They have been forced out to make room for another people in search of their homeland. Offsetting one wrong with another is no way of settling refugee problems. The worst aspect is that, in the context of the global refugee problem, there seems to be no end in sight; the problem, in fact, is getting worse owing to the American politics and the changing realities on the ground.

Edward Said, the literary giant, a child of Palestine, has an idea on why the West seems unconcerned about the dismal condition of the Palestinian refugees: "… no person academically involved with the Near East – no Orientalist, that is – has ever in the United States culturally and politically identified himself wholeheartedly with the Arabs …", for fear of discrediting political and economic interest (Said, 1979, 27). In comparison with Zionism, which had influential friends like Balfour and Truman who went to bat for the Zionists, Palestinians had no political sponsors, no literary or religious champions, or financiers like the Rothschilds. To put it differently, whereas the Jews were familiar from the Old Testament, the Arabs and Palestinian are exotic or alien, certainly outside the Judean-Christian family.

While one can argue the merit of Said's viewpoint, the fact is that the same indifference is repeated time and again in every case of the countries in the Muslim Core. Yes, there are food aid programs, humanitarian aid, and a huge array of multilateral and bilateral aid channels, but in each case, there is the self-interest of the West. Self-interest is most visible in corporate relations, as for example, the selective willingness of the USA and Western arms and weapons manufacturers to sell means of warfare to Muslim countries. Arms trading is a hugely profitable industry with a readymade huge market in the conflict-ridden Arab Core.

In the war against terror, the USA has taken the lead in the aftermath of the 9/11 Twin Tower attack by Al Qaeda. In the United States, there are some 3.3 million Muslims, barely 1% of the population, compared with 4.2 million who say they are Jewish by religion. There is, however, a huge difference between the two groups in terms of political power, financial clout, and influence in the news media. It was remarkably "easy" to brand all Muslims as terrorists or terrorist supporters. President Bush initially described the American response as "a Crusade," but quickly corrected himself. However, his initial response was surely accurate, reflecting the general sentiment in the West on relations between the Muslim and Christian worlds.

Edward Said was writing almost half a century ago. Today, at the end of 2021 are Western attitudes different? Better? More likely, they are worse. The desperate scenes at the Kabul airport in 2021 when, finally, the American-led coalition withdrew from Afghanistan testify that: (1) Whenever there is US invasion, chaos follows, and (2) the Afghan people are worse off, like the people of Iraq, Palestinians, and elsewhere in the Muslim world. At most, the departing Americans have helped those Afghanis who assisted with the invasion and occupation, but the country has been left to the Taliban who now will impose Islamic rule. The wishes of the ordinary people, as always, are ignored, especially the condition of women. While Afghanistan government funds are sequestered, and even the World Bank refuses to aid, mass starvation is a real threat as major powers decline working with the Taliban.

In October 2021, the EU announced a $1 billion fund for humanitarian aid in Afghanistan (Aljazeera, 2021). This fund is conditional upon the creation of a new European class of caregivers in the country, another case of "Lords of Poverty." It is a case of self-interest: International intervention, on humanitarian ground, in this case will be controlled by Europeans. Indifference is no option as the country would sink into anarchy and create a huge refugee problem regionally and internationally. From a systemic point of view, however, the EU is essentially creating jobs for Europeans, or European charitable organizations in yet another case of a failed Muslim state. Another Muslim nation may go the same way as the Palestinians as a nation of refugee living in camps. Once more, the people of Afghanistan have been displaced or made homeless in their homeland, the direct result of American and Western failure in the country, in the aftermath of a futile invasion. In the wake of the disorderly and sudden US pullout, followed by Taliban takeover, Afghanistan has become the latest case of a war-torn Muslim country, likely to be placed under the care of Western-aid personnel.

Afghanistan is a war-torn country, first invaded by Russia (strictly invited by the Communist government then in power), in recent times, and then the US-led Western coalition. The coalition's objectives were unclear from the outset, especially as Al Qaeda was long ago defeated, its leader Osama bin Laden was ambushed and killed on 2 May 2011 in Pakistan, which protested the illegal entry of the US military into its territory. As for domestic geopolitical dynamics, Afghanistan, like Middle East countries, toyed with alternative ideologies, first allying itself with Moscow and then falling under American influence. It is a multiethnic, multilinguistic country in which national unity has been an elusive target. The Taliban initially used brutal force to enforce discipline according to Islamic law, but most recently it has promised equal treatment of everyone. However, the international community has been reluctant to grant recognition. The EU initiative is a tentative experiment.

From a moral perspective, neither the Soviets nor the NATO alliance has been able to solve the country's deep-seated, multiethnic problems. Historically, Afghanistan has always been a frontier society, a largely lawless land with many tribes and linguistic groups earning a living from caravans to modern trucking as a transit country on the Trans Asian route. Illegal poppy cultivation and arms dealing have mushroomed because of successive wars since the 1970s.

The future is bleak indeed. Taliban is unlikely to succeed in stabilizing the country. It may not even be able to win the necessary recognition by the international community, essential precondition for ensuring regular supplies of food, medicine, and normal life. The petrol-rich Muslim Core is also implicated: Just as in the Palestinian case, the people of Afghanistan should be helped, but regimes like the House of Saud are too dependent on the USA.

The "Great Game" in the Middle East

The phrase "Great Game' was invented by Rudyard Kipling in his novel, *Kim*, the captivating story of an Anglo-Indian boy and his Afghan mentor foiling Russian designs along the Indian highways. It was a metaphor to describe the First Afghan War, the British imperial expansion beyond the Hindu Kush into tribal Afghanistan. In Victorian England, the diplomatic game centered on protecting the declining Ottoman Empire against an expansionist Tsarist Russia. In the post-Victorian age, the metaphor was carried forward by European rivalries carving up foreign territories for power and wealth. Finally, in the pre-WWI period, with the onset of the Automobile Age, when oil politics emerged as a key strategic objective, the new "Great Game" was redefined as the struggle for the vast, oil-rich lands of the Ottomans.

The moral consequences of the "Great Game" in the making of the modern Middle East has been recognized by historians and observers widely, from Fromkin (1989) to contemporary historians reviewed in Chapter 3. Of the authors considered here, Hardy (2017) has likely gone the furthest in acknowledging the fact that

> the West is deeply implicated in the region's failure. With reckless and ill-planned interventions, its indulgence of autocratic leaders, its double talk about democracy and human rights, it has contributed in no small measure to the instability of the region.
>
> *205*

Reparations

For several reasons, Europe, the USA, and the West generally will not shoulder a fair burden for the care of today's global refugees. However, slavery and imperialism are historical facts that are undeniable. They have enabled the rich countries to reach the level of prosperity they now enjoy. For global equity, they must bear the cost of refugee crisis in the world. In brief, four reasons come to mind that justify reparations in lieu of aid or for refusing to admit refugees and economic migrant into these rich countries.

1. Slave trade was immoral. It mercilessly destroyed indigenous cultures in Africa and elsewhere, and it is morally equivalent to the Nazi Holocaust for which Germany paid Israel reparations.
2. Imperialism: From the "discovery" of the "new world" on Europe colonized and exploited Africa, Asia, and Latin America. Slave trade, Aztec gold are examples. Europe acquired its prosperity through imperialism: The English Slave traders, the Dutch in Indonesia, French in North Africa, and the Sahel, the Belgian, Danish planters in Central and East Africa systematically impoverished their colonies. Now, refusing refugees and economic migrants is morally unjustified. The Europeans were in colonies; but colonial people are not welcome

in Europe. If Europeans wish to keep "pure," "Christian," or whatever, at least they should bear the financial burden of keeping the unfortunate victims of wars and conflict in host countries.

3. No More Aid: Postwar Marshall Plan type of aid and technical assistance to developing countries is no more. After 9/11, foreign aid has been replaced by military interventions destabilizing fragile countries, producing refugees and economic migrants. Rather than aid, reparations might be paid for the care of today's refugees and economic migrants to keep them in their own original homelands, or if that is unfeasible, in hosting countries.

4. Unequal Trade: Today neo-imperialism continues in the form of unequal commodity trade, controlled by monopoly corporations. Bananas, coffee, and other tropical commodities are traded at unfair trade practices that continue to enrich prosperous countries. These countries are magnets in an age of global injustice.

5. Rich countries must accept their historic obligation and pay reparations for past exploitation. It is morally equivalent to expecting poor countries to honor foreign debts. No payment to failed states are envisaged. A fair share of reparations payment should go to solving the Palestinian conflict, following the German precedent. Reparations, as part of solution to the Palestinian conflict, has been discussed in a recent book (Saaty et al., 2021, 129–157). The existing situation of Palestinians is tragic and unsustainable. For Palestinians the conditions are miserable; for Israel they are increasingly shameful. The Human Rights Watch recently found evidence of state crimes against the Palestinians in Israel and the occupied territories and East Jerusalem, amounting to the crimes against humanity of apartheid and persecution (Human Rights Watch, 2022). The report, however, like previous ones, has been ignored. Amnesty International has also reported in similar vein (Amnesty International, 2022).

6. Solving the Palestinian conflict is the key to peace in the Middle East. Whether in the end, a two-state, or a binational, one-state solution (Abunimah, 2006) is reached is difficult to predict. Abunimah's idea for a unified state for all Palestinians and Israelis has recently found support by Peter Beinart who argues for a state in which Jews and Palestinians have "equal rights" (Beinart, 2020). But these are voices in the dark, for even Ilan Pappe (2007), a historian most critical of Israel, concludes that the Palestinians "can never be part of the Zionist state and space …" (ibid., 261). It is worth remembering that in the nearby Cyprus binational statehood has failed, as discussed later in the chapter.

The refugee crisis management must go beyond maintenance. Creating new camps and simply maintaining them is no solution to the global refugee challenge. Huge amounts of funds are required to find innovative, permanent solutions as part of creating a more just and humane world order. A good part of reparations may be channeled into creating such a new world.

The Global Refugee Challenge: The Palestinian Model Is Globalized

The UN High Commission for Refugees (UNHCR) was established in 1950 to aid and protect refugees. In the last decade, the refugee numbers have exploded, the global total number of refugees more than doubled to 89.9 million, 22.1 million under UNHCR mandate (UNHCR, 2022). The figure is rising by the year. By far the biggest groups are internally displaced persons due to civil war and persecution. While Venezuela, Latin and Central America, and African countries are recent major cases, the endless conflict in the Muslim world including such cases as Myanmar, Afghanistan, and the African continent from Somalia to the western end of the Sahel are particularly significant as it seems to follow the Palestinian model. It is not far-fetched to say that the UNRWA model is now globalized. More and more Muslim victims of war and conflict are herded into camps supervised by international staff. In 2011, UNHCR's field staff numbered 6.696 (UNHCR, 2011). In the next decade, the number had increased almost threefold to 18,879, operating in 137 countries (UNHCR, 2022).

Syria, for the tenth year, topped the list of refugee-producing countries and several Muslim-majority countries, conflict-plagued, were "hotspots": Afghanistan, Somalia, the African Sahel, Yemen, Sudan, and South Sudan. Not all refugee camps are solely humanitarian projects. In Northern Iraq, camps have been used by terrorist organizations, from PKK to Al Qaeda and ISIL. It is all a sad story of US-led invasion, CIA plots paving the path to Islamic terror.

The Charity Business

Care of victims of conflict and persecution is big. Beyond the multilateral aid organizations in the UN system, and foreign aid provided bilaterally to further the donor's foreign and military objectives, there are huge numbers of western care-giving organizations, including missionary and private. The charity business is as old as colonization. In other sections in this study, we have referred to missionaries working with Conquistadors in search of Mayan and Aztec gold. In more recent times, funds raised by private donations and campaigns are not always used in legitimate care and aid of the victims of war and conflict. Caregivers, going abroad on charitable missions, may sometime have hidden objectives.

Passion and zeal to proselytize the "heathen," to convert the native people, has been so controversial that none other than the Pope has had to formally apologize to the Canadian First Nations for the huge pain caused by Catholic missionaries in the notorious Residential School System (CBC, 2022). In Africa, Bishop Desmond Tutu succinctly put the issue: "When the missionaries came to Africa, they had the Bible, and we had the land. They said: 'Let us pray.' We closed their eyes. When we opened them, we had the bible, and they had the land" (quoted in Sood, 2007, 70).

Conditional care, given to poor communities as part of organized efforts to convert them to Christianity, is objectionable. In Muslim countries, missionaries have been attacked and killed, and governments have had to intervene, whenever pros-elytizing activities have gone beyond what can be considered legitimate caregiving (OpIndia, 2022). In Uganda, where there is a long history of Christian missionary activity, confrontation with Islam has sometimes led to bloody conflicts, even mas-sacre (Ward, n.d.). A notorious case is the Catholic missionaries who have been involved in the Rwandan Genocide (Manchester Guardian, 2016).

Care for victims of conflict and persecution is also provided by private organizations, such as CARE, OXFAM, and a myriad of others. In Cambodia, following the Khmer Rouge genocide, the country was literally invaded by Western charitable NGOs, competing with one another in a general climate of weak political environment (Mehmet, 1997). In some cases, transparency is a serious issue as private donations may be misallocated, or even channeled into dubious uses. Some Muslim aid NGOs have been accused of diverting funds into terrorist activities (Tomlinson, 2021).

The Brutal Saddam Regime, American Invasion, and the Rise of Terrorism

In 1988, Saddam Hussein and his cousin "Chemical Ali" used chemical weapons against the Kurds of Northern Iraq. Thousands of Kurdish refugees fled to Turkey. The use of chemical weapons created the myth that the Saddam regime possessed weapons of mass destruction. In the Iraq–Iran war, the USA supported Saddam. After the first invasion of Iraq, Washington established the no-fly zone in Northern Iraq, creating the autonomous Kurdish Regional Government (KRG). The PKK, the Marxist–Leninist organization, recognized as a terrorist group internationally, took advantage and established military camps for cross-border attacks against the Turkish military.

The second, and much larger, invasion of Iraq took place in 2003 justified initially with the nonexistent weapons of mass destruction. The invasion was ambiguous from the start. Partly seeking weapons of mass destruction (WMD), and revenge for the attack on the World Trade Center on 11 September 11 2001, later shifting to regime change and end a brutal dictatorship, it even had wishful hopes of bringing democracy to Iraq (New York Times, 2005). In fact, invasion was all about securing the Middle East oil supply. The priority of Pentagon under Secretary Rumsfeld, acting together with Vice-President Cheney was to save the oil fields; Saddam responded by setting the fields on fire. It made little difference. Cheney personally profited hugely; he was the Chief Executive Officer of weapon producing firm Haliburton, the stock of which jumped fivefold.

Earlier, with American support during his disastrous war against Iran, Saddam had turned Iraq into a full-fledged police state, a brutal military dictatorship. In 1960, health, as a percentage of GNP, represented 1% of public expenditure, edu-cation 5.8%, and military 7.3%. By 1990, health's share had declined to 0.8%, edu-cation to 5.1%, while the military share skyrocketed to about a third of total public spending (Ismael and Ismael, 2015, 16).

American invasion was a catastrophe for Iraq. "The dethroning of Saddam Hussein from power was comparatively an easier task than the construction of a democratic and federal post-Saddam Iraq" (Pattanayak, 2005). In the colonial spirit of "divide and rule," attempts were made to split the country into three regions among its Kurds, Sunni, and Shi'a population, but it bore no results because it was a top-down artificial project dependent on the American military. Successive governments failed for the same reason. Post-Saddam Iraq, under Americans, suffered massively when, for example, the head of the Provisional Coalition Authority, Paul Bremmer, cut the gasoline, electricity, and fertilizer subsidies because he had come to Iraq "to build not just a democracy but a free market" (Ismail and Ismail, 2015, 63). The damage of the US invasion was massive, not only in human terms, described as "collateral damage," but in cultural terms as well. "The systematic destruction of … Iraq's cultural heritage and infrastructure" was vast. "The significance of looting and destruction of Iraq's cultural symbols cannot be overstated" (Ismael and Ismael, 2015, 20).

The real mastermind behind the invasion of Iraq in March 2003 was Vice President Cheney who took advantage of President George W. Bush's weakness and created, together with the Defense Secretary Rumsfeld, the myth of WMD to justify the invasion. The invasion plan, originally from Turkey into Northern Iraq, was rejected by the Turkish parliament, but went ahead from Kuwait with the support of Saudi Arabia and Gulf States.

The Obama administration in 2011 decided to "leave" Iraq, meaning scaling down the invasion. It came after a US massacre of civilians in downtown Baghdad, and the Iraqi refusal to legitimize US mercenaries, exempt from Iraqi criminal law. The decision was catastrophic not only for Iraq, but the entire region. Suddenly the Islamic State of Iraq and the Levant emerged (ISIL). It acquired the massive store of military equipment left behind by the American forces. ISIL quickly run over much of Northern Iraq, announcing a Caliphate in Mosul, and capturing the oil-rich regions of the Syria-Iraq border. ISIL's chief weapon was brutality, beheading its enemies, carrying out genocide against Yazidis. It was not until 2017 that the US-led coalition was able to defeat ISIL. By then, the Syrian civil war had erupted as people finally revolted against tyranny and oppression. The Syrian Kurds, especially those in the Kobani region, organized as PYD, an extension of PKK, had emerged as a partner of the Pentagon in the fight against ISIL, much to the disapproval of Ankara. In the end, during the Trump administration, the USA decided to withdraw its military presence in Syria, leaving their Kurdish partners feeling betrayed.

The Americans left behind some 20 camps housing more than 3 million Iraqi refugees and displaced persons within the country and another 260,000 have been forced to flee to neighboring countries. The worst hit is the Kurdish region in Northern Iraq. In 2017, the Iraqi authorities closed these camps and sent the residents back to their homes. But instability in the country and region did not end.

The Syrian Refugee Crisis

The Ottoman birth took place in Syria, and last nail on its coffin was hammered in Damascus in 1918. Syrians had suffered imperialist rule after WWI, followed by misrule ever since. This is not the place to repeat the origins or the politics of the Syrian civil war. Rather, our focus here is to explore the humanitarian crisis and the moral failure in this case.

Arguably the worst case of modern Islamic state failure began in 2011, at the height of the ill-fated democratic experiment known as the Arab Spring. People of great cultural and linguistic diversity revolted against the oppressive Assad regime, but their revolt has ushered in a decade of untold loss and misery, which continues to this day. During this agonizing decade, more than half the pre-civil war Syrian population of 22 million have been internally displaced, more than a million died, and millions became refugees flooding into neighboring countries forced to live in camps. In response, a huge international effort has emerged to provide humanitarian aid to the victims of this unfortunate war-torn country. An astonishing range of charitable NGOs, multilateral, and bilateral aid givers have moved in to fill the vacuum created by state failure. Although there is a UN agency to coordinate the operations of aid and humanitarian agencies (OCHA, 2021), it is impossible to document reliably the cost, finance, and the number of staff providing care for Syrian victims of conflict. Where the state has failed in responsibility to its citizens, a large-scale aid bureaucracy has emerged delivering food, shelter, and other basic needs. Families suffering food insecurity, children lacking education, all victims facing an uncertain future while international actors pursue diverse geopolitical interests. A new humanitarian aid system has evolved, paralleling the Palestinian case reviewed earlier. Political failure to bring peace and stability in Syria runs the risk of yet another Palestinian-like impasse.

The Politics of Humanitarian Aid: The proliferation of aid organizations in war-torn Syria has created not only a large caregiving bureaucracy, it has also led to rivalries and competing ideologies. At one point, no less than 73 NGOs felt the need to make a joint declaration to condemn UN aid organizations based on Damascus for using aid delivery as a political tool, supporting the Assad regime (NGOs, 2016).

In a war-torn environment, aid organizations need to be neutral, focused on helping victims of war, and avoiding activities, specifically in food delivery, that would change the course of the war. In 2013, Médecins Sans Frontieres (MSF) released a statement condemning what they called an imbalanced distribution of aid. The MSF argued that areas under government control received nearly all international aid, while opposition-held zones receive only a tiny share. This kind of aid empowered the Assad regime.

Subsequently, the UN Security Council authorized the delivery of humanitarian assistance across the Turkish and Jordanian borders to ensure delivery of aid to parts of Syria controlled by opposition groups. An accountable humanitarianism is essential. Aid providers cannot hold preferences in military or political terms. In a state of civil war, how aid is delivered, who receives, and who doesn't play a role in determining military outcomes? An accountable humanitarianism must always be transparent, and aid organizations must openly justify their aid decisions to the global community.

Syrian Refugee Exodus: Europe now hosts more than 1 million Syrians, 60% in Germany. Initially, the Merkel government showed great hospitality accepting Syrian refugees, in part in search of cheap labor, but in due course, Syrians faced growing Islamophobia in Europe, Denmark becoming the first European country to stop officially accepting them. Syria is by no means the only source of refugee-producing Muslim country. Waves of refugees from Afghanistan, Yemen, Iraq, and Libya are risking their lives in unsafe journeys, some drowning in the sea, to escape oppression, persecution, or dispossession at their homeland. Greece, on the eastern border of the EU, has herded the Muslim into islands such as Lesbos, where feelings of abandonment finally erupted into a huge fire in June 2020 (Guardian, 2021).

A Successful Refugee Camp: Before the modern boundaries were imposed by European powers, Gaziantep (then Antep) and Aleppo were linked by trade networks. Family ties across the Turkish border were normal. When the Syrian civil war broke out, thousands of refugees sought asylum in Turkey. One of the most successful refugee camps was Nicip2, a container temporary city with clean streets, schools, and mosque, became a "best practice" model (Anitakomuves, 2016), until the Turkish government decided to close the refugee camps down in 2018 and repatriate these Syrians back to their homeland (Hurriyet Daily News, 2018).

Refugee camps cannot become permanent. In the end, refugees must either return to their homeland, or, as economic migrants, move to a new country willing to host them. In the case of Nicip2, the Turkish government's decision to close it, and several others along the Syrian border, was due to two reasons. First, the high cost became a budgetary burden on Turkey. The EU-Turkey refugee deal in 2015, under which Brussel had promised billions of financial support to Ankara, did not materialize; Turkey spent as much as $40 billion from its own resources as the country emerged as the largest refugee-hosting nation in the world. Second, and more politically, the Erdogan government pursued its own policy objectives for solving the Syrian conflict. Part of that solution, according to Ankara, was relocation of Syrians back to their homeland.

International Moral Failure, The Next 50 Years

Every refugee case is an indicator of state failure, but those in the Middle East are unique since they are the direct result of Western imperialism imposed at the time of WWI. The map of the Middle East, as we have seen earlier, was drawn by victorious imperial powers at the end of WWI with the interest of those powers overriding the welfare of the local populations. In Syria, Iraq, and elsewhere local populations rose in rebellion right after the fall of the Ottomans, and the start of trusteeship regimes. The invasion of Iraq by the Bush–Blair coalition was no more than a continuation of the imperialist control of the Middle East. It has destabilized the entire region, costing millions of innocent lives, and unmeasurable collateral damage.

Israel has been created by direct displacement of Palestinians. Generations of refugees are growing up in camps with no future except camp life under the care of charitable organizations. If this is the best, the prosperous nations, responsible for world order since 1914, can provide, then humanity is condemned to repeated cases of massive moral failure.

The Syrian refugee crisis in the Middle East is the largest case of international ethical failure. Europe has not only turned a blind eye, but it has also resorted to building walls to keep out the Muslims from flooding in. Neighboring countries like Turkey, Lebanon, and Jordan, by necessity, have become dumping grounds, accepting a second Palestine, in effect sheltering international indifference to Muslim suffering. Turkey fighting a long war against the PKK, had its own interest in Syria, but lack of a Syrian settlement is, first and foremost a moral failure, a product of the ill-conceived invasion of Iraq with no prior understanding of the complexity of the task.

Who carries the principal moral burden of state failure in Syria and elsewhere in the Arab world? In this study, two actors are identified: imperialists and their collaborating Arab elites. The European imperialists who planned destruction and partition of the Ottoman Empire must be regarded as the primary actors responsible: drawers of lines in the sand, creators of artificial countries through deceit and lies; neo-imperialists, including in the most recent two decades, American invasions, regime change, pursuit of oil wealth, sacrificing in the process the welfare of the grassroots. Collaborating Arab elites, in particular dynasties and military dictatorships, carry no less moral blame. In the case of Palestine, the Nazi war criminals, who carried out the Holocaust, bear a special responsibility, which, to its credit, Germany has shouldered, but it unreservedly supports Israel. But equally, the loss and suffering inflicted on the Palestinians cannot be ignored by crowding them into refugee camps. The USA, which led the creation of Israel, owes a huge moral debt to the Palestinians; the debt has been magnified during Trump's administration by further trampling the rights of Palestinian people to satisfy the Zionist aspirations.

The American invasion of Iraq has destabilized the entire region, transplanting religious and messianic terrorism, even though it might have been unintentional. The modern Middle East is a huge moral failure for the West. Perhaps, it would be too much to expect that, any time soon, geopolitics will change, and Western leaders will adopt a more equitable policy in the Middle East. Oil politics, and specifically the interests of dynastic families controlling oil fields, are shaped by Western powers and this status quo may be around for as long as the age of fossil fuels lasts. However, it is evident that a new world, cleaner and greener, is emerging and the age of fossil fuels is slowly ending. The next 50 years will be crucial: While long-term scenarios are difficult to predict, a post-fossil fuel world is almost certain to emerge. In the transition, two major options are available for a saner, just world order.

One is the Western capability in finding ways and means to help democratize the Arab Core, starting with an equitable settlement of the Palestinian conflict. The Arab Spring has demonstrated the impossibility of quick solutions. The failures of the USA in Iraq, Syria, and Afghanistan are ample proof of outsiders' limitations, especially in terms of attempting to impose solutions from outside, including regime change. Democratic development is a long-term project, requiring huge investments in social capital formation, institution-building, and civil society reforms; it must start from below, the grassroots. Sadly, no short-term solutions to the crisis of the Arab Core are seen.

The other option, a non-Western one, is also feasible. This is the subject of Chapter 10.

References

Abunimah, Ali, 2006, *One Country, A Bold Proposal to End the Israeli-Palestinian Impasse*, New York: Metropolitan Books.

Aljazeera, 2021, EU Announces 1bn Euro Aid Package for Afghanistan, www.aljazeera.com/news/2021/10/12/eu-announces-1-15bn-aid-package-for-afghanistan, accessed on 13 Oct. 2021.

Amnesty International, 2022, Israel's Apartheid Against Palestinians: A Cruel System of Domination and a Crime Against Humanity, www.amnesty.org/en/latest/news/2022/02/israels-apartheid-against-palestinians-a-cruel-system-of-domination-and-a-crime-against-humanity/, accessed on 28 April 2022.

Anitakomuves, 2016, Refugee Kids of the Nizip-2 Camp in Turkey, https://anitakomuves.com/2016/03/21/refugee-kids-of-the-nizip-2-camp-in-turkey/comment-page-1/, accessed on 17 August/2021.

Beinart, Peter, 2020, Opinion: Bringing Democracy To Iraq, www.nytimes.com/2020/07/08/opinion/israel-annexation-two-state-solution.html, accessed on 4 Jan. 2022.

Borgen Project, 2020, 6 Facts About Homelessness in Yemen, https://borgenproject.org/homelessness-in-yemen/, accessed on 24 May 2021.

CBC, 2022, Pope Francis Apologizes to Indigenous Delegates for 'Deplorable' Abuses at Residential Schools, www.cbc.ca/news/politics/pope-francis-responds-indigenous-delegations-final-meeting-1.6404344, accessed on 19 July 2022.

Childs, W.J., 2017, *Across Asia Minor on Foot*, 2nd ed., Edinburgh and London: William Blackwood and Sons.

Fromkin, David, 1989, *A Peace to End All Peace, the Fall of the Ottoman Empire and the Creation of the Modern Middle East*, New York: Avon Books.

Guardian, 2021, Jailing of Afghans for Lesbos Migrant Camp Fire a 'Parody of Justice', www.theguardian.com/world/2021/jun/13/jailing-afghans-for-lesbos-moria-migrant-camp-fire-parody-of-justice, accessed on 17 Sept. 2021.

Hancock, 1994, *The Lords of Poverty: The Power, Prestige, and Corruption of the International Aid*, New York: Atlantic Monthly Press.

Hardy, Roger, 2017, *The Poisoned Well, Empire and Its Legacy in the Middle East*, New York: Oxford University Press.

Human Rights Watch, 2022, Israel and Palestine: Events of 2021, www.hrw.org/world-report/2022/country-chapters/israel/palestine,. accessed on 28 April 2022.

Hurriyet Daily News, 2018, Turkey to relocate Syrian refugees to camps on border, www.hurriyetdailynews.com/turkey-to-relocate-syrian-refugees-to-camps-on-border-135353, accessed on 17 August 2021.

IDMC, 2021, www.internal-displacement.org/countries/iraq, accessed on 18 July 2022.

Ismael, Tareq and Jacqueline Ismael, 2015, *Iraq in the Twentieth Century: Regime Change and the Making of a Failed State*, London: Routledge.

Macrotrends, 2022, Jordan Refugee Statistics 1960–2022, www.macrotrends.net/countries/JOR/jordan/refugee-statistics, accessed on 18 July 2022.

Manchester Guardian, 2016, Rwanda Genocide: Catholic Church Sorry for Role of Priests and Nuns in Killings, www.theguardian.com/world/2016/nov/21/rwanda-genocide-catholic-church-sorry-for-role-of-priests-and-nuns-in-killings, accessed on 19 July 2022.

Mehmet, Ozay, 1997, "Development in a Wartorn Society: What Next in Cambodia", *Third World Quarterly*, Vol. 18, 673–686.

Mehmet, Ozay, 1971, "Effectiveness of Foreign Aid: The Case of Somalia", *Journal of Modern African Studies*, Vol. 9, No. 1.

Nakba, 2016, www.centuryassociation.org/26-articles/islamic-history-and-personalities/2680-1948-over-700-000-palestinians-become-refugees-in-the-nakba, accessed on 27 April 2022.

New York Times, 2005, www.nytimes.com/2005/08/07/opinion/bringing-democracy-to-iraq-567418.html, accessed on 18 August 2021.

NGOs, 2016, UN Position Paper final, www.sams-usa.net/wp-content/uploads/2016/09/UN-Position-Paper-final-2.pdf, accessed on 17 Sept. 2021.

OCHA, 2021, United Nations Office for the Coordination of Humanitarian Affairs-UNOCHA Syria Hub, http://ocha-sy.org/index.htm, accessed on 17 August 2021.

OpIndia, 2022, Hindu Refugees from Pakistan Say that Christian Missionaries are Active in the Majnu ka Tilla Camp, www.opindia.com/2021/11/majnu-ka-tila-hindu-refugees-forced-thumb-impressions-basic-supplies-christian-missionaries-conversion/, accessed on 19 July 2022.

Palestinian Central Bureau of Statistics. 2019, Palestinian Central Bureau of Statistics (PCBS): The International Day of Refugees 2019, www.badil.org/phocadownloadpap/Statistics/(PCBS)The-International-Day-of-Refugees-2019-eng.pdf, accessed on 27 April 2022.

Pappe, Ilan, 2007, *The Ethnic Cleansing of Palestine*, London: Oneworld Publications.

Pattanayak, S., 2005, "Regime Change in Iraq and Challenges of Political Reconstruction", *Strategic Analysis*, Vol. 29, No. 4.

Plan Dalet, 1948, LEST WE FORGET – Palestine and the Nakba, www.1948.org.uk/plan-dalet-and-the-nakba, accessed on 27 Sept. 2021.

Refugee Association, 2020, Numbers of Syrians in Turkey July 2020, https://multeciler.org.tr/eng/numbers-of-syrians-in-turkey-july-2020/, accessed on 24 May 2021.

Rosen, S., 2012. Why a Special Issue on UNRWA? www.meforum.org/3344/unrwa-special, accessed on 15 Nov. 2021.

Saaty, Thomas L., H.J. Zoffer, Luis G. Vargas, Amos Guiora, 2021, *Overcoming the Retributive Nature of the Israeli-Palestinian Conflict*, Switzerland: Palgrave-Springer Link.

Siddiqui, H., 2003, The Right of Return of the Palestinian People, https://mediamonitors.net/the-right-of-return-of-the-palestinian-people/, accessed on 27 April 2022.

Sood, S.V., 2007, *Victoria's Tin Dragon; A Railway that Built a Nation*, Cambridge: Vanguard Press.

Telesur, 2020, At Least 5.6 Million Palestinians Live in Refugee Camps, www.telesurenglish.net/news/At-Least-5.6-Million-Palestinians-Live-in-Refugee-Camps-20200620-0003.html, accessed on 24 May 2021.

Tomlinson, C., 2021, Germany Bans Islamic NGO after Accusations of Terrorism Funding, www.breitbart.com/europe/2021/05/07/germany-bans-islamic-ngo-after-accusations-of-terrorism-funding/, accessed on 19 August 2022.

UNHCR, 2011, UNHCR Annual Report, www.unhcr.or.th/sites/default/files/UNHCR_Annual%20Report%202011_English.pdf, accessed on 16 August 2021.

UNHCR, 2022, Figures at a Glance, www.unhcr.org/figures-at-a-glance.html%20, accessed on 18 July 2022.

UNRWA, 2020, Annual Operational Report 2020, www.unrwa.org/sites/default/files/content/resources/2020_aor_eng.pdf, accessed on 15 August 2021.

UNRWA, 2022, Funding Trends, www.unrwa.org/how-you-can-help/government-partners/funding-trends, accessed on 18 July 2022.

Ward, K., n.d. A History of Christianity in Uganda, https://dacb.org/histories/uganda-history-christianity/, accessed on 19 July 2022.

10

WHY THE ARAB WORLD NEVER PRODUCED A DEMOCRATIC LEADER?

A few months before he was assassinated, Jamal Khashoggi gave a speech stating that the Arab world was moving toward the idea of the benevolent autocrat, the just dictator. He was the keynote speaker at the University of Denver and the Center for the study of Islam and Democracy (al Aiwah, 2018). He argued that, although most of the Arab people, from Tunisia to Cairo and all over the Arab world, wanted democracy as manifested in the Arab Spring, the traditional leaders wanted nothing to do with democracy. They wanted a benevolent autocrat, a just dictator. He cited, favorably, the Crown Prince Mohammed bin Salman and his reforms. Yet, Khashoggi was killed by Saudi agents, under the direction of the Crown Prince, inside the Saudi consulate in Istanbul on 2 October 2018. It is doubtful that the House of Saud will outlast the age of fossil fuel. For one thing, the Crown Prince does not have the charisma and popularity and his reforms are a top-down process.

Conflicts, Civil Wars, a Natural State: Al-Ghazzali's Ideal State[1]

Yemen, Sudan, Somalia, Lebanon, Iraq, Syria, Libya: The list covers a number of Arab countries. Virtually everywhere in the Arab world there is no room for freedom of expression; disputes erupt into violence and brutality; regime change is by coups and bloodshed. Acquisition of power is through gun fire. Social capital is scarce. Conflict began upon the death of the Prophet. According to the dominant Sunni branch of Islam, Mohammed left no successor, but the Shi'a believe that he, in fact, had selected Ali as his successor, but Ali's enemies prevented his rightful elevation until the last of the Rightful Caliphs (Esposito, 1988, 41–44).

At the deepest, emotional level, it is all tribal, feuding among kinsfolks. The Arab nation is a collection of tribes, and first loyalty is always to the tribal elders, family, or clan. In Pre-Islamic Arabia, virtue meant courage in defending honor, as

DOI: 10.4324/9781003268994-10

for example, the tribe's honor. The tradition of settling feuds, whether over grazing lands as in a nomadic society, debt settlement, or boundary disputes in modern times, is not by recourse to some judicial tribunal, it is via fighting, the winner proven right. The Prophet was a glorious ruler, a brilliant commander and *Jihad* was the path to social justice; Allah's will revealed. From the Golden Age of Islam to the current toxic, Pandemic world, there has always been a huge chasm between the ideal and the actual.

Al-Ghazzali's Ideal State

Avoiding chaos was the principal aim of Abu Hamid Muhammad al-Ghazzali, the great medieval scholar who was born and died in the city of Tus in Khurassan, Persia (1058–1111). Conflict avoidance meant submission to the monarch. For Ghazzali, it was far better to submit to the ruler than risk civil war and chaos.

Al-Ghazzali lived in a period of turbulence when the Abbasid dynasty in Baghdad was in decline; chaos ruled everywhere. As a scholar, he set out to define the prerequisites of good governance, making regime stability and submission to a monarch central in his theory. For Ghazzali, regime stability is sacred, because instability leads to chaos and anarchy, which must be avoided at all costs. The individual must submit to the ruler; Ghazzali wrote centuries before Hobbes penned his Leviathan.

Of course, Ghazzali's ruler (a monarch) is an ideal king: a wise and virtuous man, guided only by social justice, delivering nothing but good governance to his subjects in return for their undivided submission. There are no social or political checks and balances in Ghazzali's ideal state. The ruler is only answerable to Allah to bring prosperity and development through justice and equitable rule. In his duties, the ideal ruler seeks and is guided by philosophers and wise men, like al-Ghazzali himself. But there are no parliaments and opposition voices, no agora for critical opinion, no tribunals for dispute settlement. The ruler's judgement is final and absolute.

In the ideal *Dawlat*, (state), wisdom is supreme, *ad'l* (social justice) is a divine gift. In such a state, there is no tension between state and individual; the wise ruler does not have an iota of Machiavellian opportunism. Society is harmonious; no state of natural warfare can exist because man, by nature, is good, created by Allah, without sin or fault. Man is not a "noble savage" as in Rousseau living, in Hobbes' state of nature life is solitary, poor, nasty, brutish, and short.

Al-Ghazzali's theory of the ideal state is summed up in the following:

> *The religion depends on the monarchy,*
> *The monarchy on the army,*
> *The army on supplies,*
> *Supplies on prosperity, and*
> *Prosperity on justice.*

Al-Ghazzali influenced Ibn Khaldun (1392–1406), arguably the greatest Muslim historian, who coined the Circle of Equity:

> There can be no royal authority without the military,
> There can be no military without wealth,
> Justice preserves the subjects' loyalty to the sovereign,
> Justice requires harmony in the world,
> The world is a garden, its walls are the state,
> The Holy Law [Shari 'at] orders the state
> There is no support for the Shari 'at except through royal authority.

Ghazzali and Khaldun were the last of the great scholars who wrote on the ideal Muslim state. The decline of the Abbasid dynasty that Ghazzali witnessed in his life resulted in the "Closing of the Gate of Ijtihad" (II&D, 1990: 60). While the Muslim education, in traditional *madrassa*, consisted of memorizing the Quran, the myth became reality and the Arab tradition emerged as the norm, symbolized by monarchy, or one-man rule, to whom obedience is obligatory. However, from a terrorist's perspective, the teachings "justified" rebellion against an unjust ruler.

The Current Arab Leadership Dilemma

Every Arab leader believes he is virtuous and assumes power with the loftiest promises and declarations of intent to create an ideal state not much different than al-Ghazzali's. The reality, however, is far from ideal. The Arab personality, always nostalgic and emotional, is easily carried away with flowery promises, when things turn ugly, as in Nasser's Egypt after the humiliation of the Six-Day War, gloom takes over and tragic consequences follow; another leader appears … … in revolutions, coups, and civil wars. This pattern is repeated time and again.

The inability of Syrians to get rid of Assad and fend off extreme Jihadism in the form of ISIS is a telling example of dictatorship and state failure. State violence is a powerful tool to eliminate dissent and force submission. Non-state actors confronting a dictatorship may be able to topple a brutal regime, but once in power, as in the case of Taliban in Afghanistan in 2021, they then rely on force to stay in power. Such non-state actors have no chance of ever turning themselves into a democratic force, willingly giving up power to an opponent.

The Ottomans, during the four centuries of ruling the Arab Core, were by no means democratic. They were, like the Romans, administrators, with a keen sense of Islamic law, conquering "to subdue the infidel world, the *darülharb*" (Inalcik, 1973, 7). They had built institutions and developed a system of administration. Ottomans were great record-keepers, essential for any successful administration. Tax records, land titles, demographic statistics, guidelines for trade regulation, and a myriad other data were what enabled the Ottoman state to function. Dynastic or military regimes have followed the Ottomans with one cardinal objective: to sustain themselves in power. State formation with accounts and record-keeping were minimal or casual.

No Arab country has been able to replace and better the Ottoman heritage to evolve into sustainable nationhood.

Saddam Hussein, a Brutal Arab Dictator

The typical way of rising to the top in the Arab world, for one not born at the top, is a career in the military and, at the right time, making a successful coup. The rise and fall of Saddam Hussein are typical of military dictatorships representing Arab a "failed state" (Ismail and Ismael, 2015). Hussein was born in April 1937 to a poor family in a village near Tikrit, north of Baghdad. He was a radical revolutionary in his youth, in Baghdad in the 1950s, when he joined the new Ba'ath or Renewal Party, a socialist party that aimed at unifying the Arab world. In 1959, he took part in an assassination attempt on Iraqi leader General Abd-al-Karim Qasim (see Chapter 5), who had overthrown the British-installed monarchy the year before. The assassination attempt failed, and Saddam escaped to Cairo. He returned in 1964; he quickly rose in the Ba'ath Party, but soon he was put in jail due to ideological differences. When al-Bakr became president in yet another coup in 1968, he made Hussein his vice president.

In 1979, with "help from the US" Saddam Hussein "assumed the presidency," staging a palace coup by forcing the ailing al-Bakr to resign for health reasons. Hussein seized power and immediately announced that his rule would be absolute; he established "a totalitarian regime in Iraq through control of a command economy, the subordination of the army, and other sources of state coercion, including total control of the media and other vehicles of communication" (Ismael and Ismael, 2015, 15). He orchestrated a cult of personality around himself, declaring that he was "the Great Uncle," a sort of Iraqi version of Mao. The same year he took power; the Islamic revolution in neighboring Iran swept the US-backed Shah from power and replaced him with the radical regime of Ayatollah Ruhollah Khomeini. Relations between the two neighbors soured. The next year, in September 1980, Iraq invaded Iran, sparking a costly eight-year war that impoverished the country.

The next decade witnessed rising oil prices and increased government revenues. Iraq's economy grew and a period of socioeconomic reform was launched. Literacy soared under a compulsory reading program, earning Hussein an award from UNESCO, the UN's Educational, Scientific, and Cultural Organization. The country's public-health system became a model in the Middle East. Iraq's standard of living rose. Iraq was a model of socialist development in the Arab world. In the mid-1970s, Saddam, as chief of the Ba'ath party's intelligence services, was the country's de facto leader. However, several internal factors threatened the country's stability, oil politics, the sectarian tensions between the Sunni and the Shi'a communities. Relations with the Iraqi Kurds nose-dived over division of oil revenues and political rivalries. In this environment, Iraq's conflict with the neighboring Iran erupted into a full-scale war, due to border disputes over the Shatt al-Arab waterway. The war was very costly, in human and financial terms, squandering oil wealth in both countries.

But Hussein's fortunes rose in the West because the Americans believed he could resist Tehran's Islamic revolution from spreading into the region. The United States and Britain turned a blind eye to Hussein's war crimes, such as gassing Iraqi Kurds and Iranian soldiers. In the war, the Kurdish separatists accepted Iranian arms and money and began to attack Iraqi forces. In retaliation, Saddam used chemical weapons not only against soldiers, but civilians in the village of Halabja, a Kurdish town occupied by Iranian forces at the time. Over 3,000 Kurdish civilians died as a result (Abdulrazak, 2017). It was not only the Kurds, Marsh Arabs in Southern Iraq were also target of his brutality. The marshlands were drained and the traditional way of life of the people destroyed.

The war with Iran was a disaster, both militarily as well as in human cost. Hundreds of thousands of soldiers and civilians were killed on both sides. But the worst was to follow. Saddam suddenly ended the Iran war, and in 1990 invaded Kuwait claiming it was historically part of Iraq. It appears that Saddam was misled in his adventurous plans over Kuwait. April Glaspie, the US ambassador in Baghdad had spent two hours with Saddam on 25 July 1990, a week before the invasion. While no warning was given to him that the invasion would be opposed, at the same time Saddam was quite ambiguous about his own plans (Cockburn, 2011).

Iraq was roundly defeated in the first Gulf War, when a US-led coalition evicted Iraqi forces. More than 1 million people lost their lives – through wars, ethnic cleansing, or simply by his efforts to get rid of opponents, internal and external. Saddam was a tragic figure, a victim of self-delusion. He believed in his own greatness. His ambition was to be the great Arab leader, outrivaling Abdul Nasser, perhaps becoming a modern-day Saladin who had defeated the crusaders. In the end, he destroyed his regime and Iraq, his actions attracting a new imperialist invasion, and bringing nothing but a huge loss and misery to millions.

Nasserism and Modern Arab Ideology

In modern times, the case of Gamal Abdul Nasser is the protype of Arab military coup d'états. It demonstrates the futility of military coups and political assassinations to achieve power. A revolutionary group of military Free Officers led by General Naguib seized power on 23 July 1952, ousting the decrepit rule of King Farouq who went into exile. It soon became apparent that the real power was in Nasser's hands. His coup launched a brand-new era in Egypt, and a highly promising one: "It was the first time Egypt had been ruled by Egyptians since the days of the Pharaohs" (Hardy, 2017, 139).

Nasser began by ousting the old aristocratic (Ottoman) elite, replacing it with a new regime and began a series of sweeping reforms in health, education, and the economy. At the same time, typical of Arab military regimes, he crushed all dissent, the communists on the left, and the Muslim Brotherhood on the Islamic front. Britain was still the master in the region and had 80,000 troops in the Canal zone. Nasser, the pragmatist, in 1953, let the Sudanese decide whether they wanted union with Egypt or full independence. The Sudanese opted for independence. In his relations with Britain, the key was the Canal. Israel had not yet established a special relationship with the USA. Nasser's "great drama" occurred in 1956 when he seized the Canal and was attacked in a last desperate gunboat diplomacy by the combined forces of Britain, France, and Israel.

Nasser, in the meantime, had turned into a leading voice in the Non-Aligned Movement, with Nehru, Mao, and Tito. He turned to the Soviet Union for arms and support against imperialism. Moscow responded positively, including financing of the construction of the Aswan Dam. Nasser had hoped to nationalize the Canal and use the $100 million annual revenue from it to finance the Dam. Eden, replacing Churchill as Prime Minister was furious and he, together in secret with Israel and France, met in Sevres, on the outskirts of Paris and "hatched" (Hardy, 2017, 142) the joint attack on Nasser's Egypt. On 31 October the British and French warplanes, from Cyprus, attacked the Egyptian airfields with active Israeli support. An international uproar followed and within a week the attackers were forced to pull back and accept an UN-mandated ceasefire. The United States took the lead in what turned into a defeat for the Anglo-French imperialists acting in concert with Israel. It "marked the demise of empire" (ibid., 143). Eden fell from power. Nasser became a national hero, not only in Egypt but in the Arab world.

Now, a typical Arab leader had emerged: charismatic, populist, and an orator who could move the masses into his will. Nasser became the model for the rest of the Arab world. The military dictator kept inventing grand plans, one after the other. He forged Arab Union with Syria, hoping to turn it into a march of Pan-Arab unity, toyed with Ba'ath socialism as "Arab socialism," which had been "adopted without any preparation for it" (Khadduri, 1969, 248). Iraq was expected to join in, thus Arab reinforcing Arab unity. In fact, however, the mystique of Nasser was unfortunate because Iraq is a country rich in natural resources, but deficient in human resources. Had a domestic development plan been chosen instead, giving top priority on human resource development, nation-building would have been far more successful.

In the end, Nasser took the country and the Arab world into the disastrous Six-Day War, 1967 (Fisher, 1979, 693–695), for which neither Egypt nor other Arab countries were prepared. After a theatrical resignation, he managed to hang onto power, courted the Soviet Union. Palestinians paid the heaviest price of his folly. To his credit, before his death, Nasser managed to avert a military confrontation between the Palestinian Resistance Movement and the Jordanian army. When he died in 1970, his legacy was anything but that of a modernizing, democratic leader (Choueiri, 2000, 207). While Egypt experienced cultural progress, he left behind the model of military coups and takeovers as the most effective way of regime change in Egypt. His successor, Anwar Sadat, was assassinated for visiting Jerusalem and making peace with Israel, a deal which remarkably is still in force.

Arabia and the House of Saud

The vast desert Kingdom of Saudi Arabia is not a nation, but a land of tribes, in which tribal identity and loyalty reign supreme. The House of Saud is the ruling tribe, composed of nearly 7,000 families, but the core power rests with some 200 members of the ruling King's family. They exert power in the form of political, financial, and religious control. Obsessed with wealth, the regime has gone to the extent of building five- and six-star Western franchise hotels around the Kaaba, the most sacred monument in Islam, the object of annual pilgrimage. The royal family lives off coupon-clipping and interest, officially banned in Islam. From ancient times till the Ottoman project of constructing the Hejaz railway, the tribes and nomads of Arabia earned their living from caravan trade, handling the annual pilgrimage to Mecca. A major motive for their willingness to join Lawrence's Arab Revolt was the fact that the railway threatened their lucrative pilgrimage trade.

Interfamily and tribal feuds have always dominated life in Arabian desert. Palace coup in the House of Saud was nothing unusual. On 25 March 1975, one of the strangest assassinations occurred. King Faisal and his oil minister Sheik Zaki Yamani were welcoming a visiting delegation of Kuwaiti officials. Then the bloody palace coup was staged by two brothers of the King: Crown Prince Khalid and Prince Fahd. Right in front of TV cameras, a nephew, Faisal bin Musiad Abdulaziz, rushed forward, pulled his revolver, and fired three rounds, murdering the 70-year King in broad daylight. Crown Prince Khalid quickly and quietly succeeded his brother, while another brother, Prince Fahd, exercised real power behind the scenes. The Kissinger diplomacy, busy at the time staging a strategic shift from Tehran to Riyadh, received no more than a temporary setback; the American abandonment of the Shah in favor of the House of Saud continued undisturbed (Cooper, 2011, 246–247). Plotting assassinations in the House of Saud did not end in 1975; it resumed with the Khashoggi murder in Istanbul in 1918, implicating the Crown Prince Mohammed bin Salman (ndtv, 2021); the culprit openly sheltered by the Trump administration.

Earlier in WWI period, the British had taken full advantage of the Saud dynastic rivalries. Then, it was the rivalry between the Arabian Saud and the Hijaz Husseini families, both claiming direct lineage to the Prophet. The former was the big winner. The Husseini dynasty, however, ended as a secondary beneficiary in the carving of the former Ottoman lands. In March 1921, Abdullah, the Hashemite Husseini family in Hijaz, almost accidentally, met in Jerusalem Churchill's men and was made King of the "little" Kingdom of Transjordan (Hardy, 2017, 87). His son, Feisal, became the King of Iraq, but these "Arab provinces" were perceived merely as consolation prize for Abdullah who had aspired to become the King of Arabs. Lawrence describes in full detail, in his *Revolt in the Desert* (1927), the bombing raids he organized of the railway and bridges, always after the customary tribal feasting (Chapters 9, 10).

One common thing, which brought the British agent and the Arab tribes in revolt, was the enmity of the Turks. The last Ottoman Governor Djemal in Damascus had been a brutal dictator, using extreme measures to punish the cream of the Arab national movement. Many Arab officers and soldiers in the Ottoman armies deserted, joining the revolt led by Lawrence, their intimate knowledge of

Ottoman commanders and plans proving vital intelligence. In his *Seven Pillars of Wisdom* (1926), Lawrence admits his role as a double agent, agonizes over serving two "masters" each with different aims, in conflict with one another. On the one hand, he was an agent of Allenby and his commanders, on the other he was "advisor" to Feisal, Abdullah's son, because as Lawrence confesses, "in the last resort" he sacrificed the Arabs for the Allied victory (ibid., 394–395).

The rise of the House of Saud is tied to Muhammad ibn Abd al-Wahhab, a mystique who arrived in Diriyah in 1744 where he and Muhammad ibn Saud swore an allegiance in which they promised to work together to establish a regime run according to a "pure" version of Islamic principles. The al-Saud tribe's control extended over the central and eastern Arabian Peninsula of Nejd. The nobility tribe of al-Hashim, a clan of the Quraish to which Prophet Muhammad belonged, controlled the western Arabian area of Hijaz, which extended from Jeddah and Mecca in the south to Yanbo and Medina in the central areas and Tabuk near the Jordanian border in the north. After WWI, ibn Saud of Nejd annexed the Hejaz area in 1925 from the Sharif of Mecca Hussein bin Ali and formed Saudi Arabia. Bin Ali's son Abdullah I, who had collaborated with the British against the Ottomans, was "rewarded," becoming the King of Jordan and the other son Faisal became the King of Iraq, all under British tutelage.

In ancient Arabia, the principal trade route extended from the Red Sea from the northern biblical lands to Yathrib (Medina), Mecca and Sanaa (Yemen) on the Indian Ocean. Mecca was a central point and a crossroad, serving as the trade and pilgrimage center for caravans and a watering station from the zam-zam well. The most powerful tribe in Mecca was the Quraysh who were custodian of the deity, such as the goddesses al-manat, al-uzza, and al-lat, the patron goddess of Mecca revered by all visiting the Kaaba. The advent of Islam eliminated the systemic corruption of the ruling families and instituted a system suggestive of social democracy. Slaves were granted freedom; women were given certain rights and governance was to be based on God-given texts. Jews and minorities were recognized and given rights under the Constitution of Medina (II&D, 1990, chapter 3). This period, the Islamic ideal, is known as the rule of the Rightly guided Caliphs (ibid.,1990, 10–11).

Saudi Arabia has been the voice of conservatism in the Arab world, especially after its emergence as a regional power after 1973, with the meteoric rise of oil prices. It has opposed any democratic system of government, preferring its own tribal top-down "patronage system" (Choueiri, 2000, 173). As well, the House of Saud has opposed radical schemes of Pan-Arabism, defended the Sykes-Picot countries, and chose to rely instead on Western powers like Britain and the USA (ibid., 100). The Khashoggi murder reference at the beginning of this chapter needs to be understood within this historical context.

The House of Saud, however, is vulnerable. Dissent within the dynasty is explosive and contains the seeds of its own destruction, as illustrated in the case of Osama bin Laden.

The Rise of Al Qaeda, ISIL Terrorism

Finally, the House of Saud imploded with the rise of Osama bin Laden, the founder of Al Qaeda. Originally from Yemen, Osama became self-made billionaire, in charge of major construction projects for the royal family. Bin Laden became a close family partner. When the Soviet Union invaded Afghanistan in 1979, bin Laden viewed the invasion as an act of aggression against Islam, began traveling to meet Taliban leaders and raise funds for the resistance with CIA involvement.

In 1989, following the Soviet withdrawal from Afghanistan, bin Laden returned to Saudi Arabia, where he was initially welcomed as a hero, but he soon came to be regarded by the government as a radical and a potential threat. In Riyadh, bin Laden directly observed corruption in the highest Saud house and developed connections with the Texan oil interests (Texas Observer, 2001). In 1991, he left Saudi Arabia for Sudan, where he launched a violent struggle against the US dominance in the Muslim world. In 1996, Sudan, bowing to foreign pressure, expelled bin Laden, and he returned to Afghanistan, joining the ruling Taliban militia. He then declared a *Jihad* against the United States, for looting the natural resources of the Muslim world, occupying the holy sites of Islam, and supporting governments servile to US interests in the Middle East. He was by then committed to an agenda of global terrorism to dismantle the existing world order and establish a single Islamic state. On 11 September 2001, bin Laden masterminded the Twin Tower attacks in the World Trade Center, New York. This resulted in yet another wave of Western invasion of the Islamic lands, first the US-led intervention in Afghanistan, then the invasion of Arab Core itself, ostensibly for regime change and democratic transition, but in fact to secure oil fields and supplies. This was nothing else than neo-imperialism. ISIL terrorism emerged "with the erasure of state authority" because of US policies in the region (Ismael and Ismael, 2015, 222). The combination of Western imperialist invasion and Islamic terrorism took the Islamic Core hostage. But there was a short period in 2010, known as the Arab Spring, when the winds of democracy blew in the Arab world, and the hope and impatience of the youth with the tyranny of oppressive leaders, once more, reigned in the main squares of the Middle East.

A leading Sunni cleric, Yusuf al Qaradawi, ardent supporter of the short-lived elected Morsi regime, argued passionately that Islam and Democracy are perfectly compatible (Qaradawi 1997). According to Qaradawi, under "democracy people choose who rules over them" (232) and the "essence of democracy is in accord with the essence of Islam" (233).

Soon, however, the Arab Spring turned out to be a false start, an opportunity lost; the tyrannical leaders again prevailed. Khashoggi, a lone democratic voice, paid the ultimate price for speaking the truth. In the Arab world, the powerful leaders won, the people lost. In this environment, the ideal academic or public commentator is, following al-Ghazzali's example, one who recommends submission to the leadership. Advocating democracy or progressive reform is tantamount to radicalizing society, resulting, as in Khashoggi's case, ultimate punishment. Qaradawi fled Egypt after the military coup deposed Morsi and died in exile in Qatar in 2022.

The Profile of an Islamic Terrorist: Abu Bakr al-Baghdadi

In contrast to military leaders who rise to the top with coups and assassinations, in the Arab Core, where there is no room for dissent in the political space, there is one more avenue for emerging as a leader: as a messianic terrorist. Such is the case of Abu Bakr al-Baghdadi, leader of ISIL and self-declared Caliph of the Sunni world.

This reclusive leader only appeared in public once, but after he declared himself leader of the Islamic State in June 2014, he became the most feared terrorist leader in the world. Born Ibrahim Awad Ibrahim al-Badri al-Samarra in 1971 in Samarra, Iraq, he grew up in a devout, lower-middle-class family that claimed to be able to trace its lineage back to the Prophet Muhammad.

He taught the Quran as a teenager to the neighborhood's children and went on to preach at the local mosque. At Baghdad university, he earned a PhD in Islamic Studies and joined the Muslim Brotherhood. He soon proved too radical for the Brotherhood and, following the US-led invasion of Iraq in 2003, found his own militant group, Jaish Ahl al-Sunnah wal-Jamaah, the Army of the Sunni People. In February 2004, he was arrested by US forces in Fallujah and spent four years in the Camp Bucca prison in Southern Iraq, where he met many former Baathists who later joined his movement. He was released when the camp shut down in 2009. He joined the sectarian war between Iraq's Sunni and Shi'ite and eventually joined Al Qaida, pledging allegiance to Osama bin Laden.

He emerged as leader of the movement in 2010 owing to his ruthless and brutal strategy. He then merged with the Nusra Front to fight against the Assad regime in Syria. He achieved fame with his most rigid interpretations of Sharia and his brutal executions of captives, beheading anyone deemed an apostate. He targeted the ancient minority community in the region, the Yazidis, who never forgave his atrocities (Talabi, 2019).

By the end of year, Baghdadi had taken control of the Iraqi city of Fallujah and six months later seized the northern city of Mosul where he declared his Caliphate in the only TV appearance. At that time, he was at the height of his power, thanks to the control of the oil fields of eastern Syria. Finally, he was killed by US forces in October 2019 when Trump announced control of these oil fields and went along with a Turkish incursion to clear the area of PKK-PYD terrorists (Borger, 2019).

The Question of Incompatibility

The general belief that Islam is incompatible with democracy, which requires public consultation and consent in governance, is incorrect. Both in the Qur'an and the practice of the Prophet himself, there are democratic requirements in Islam. Thus, Surah 42, called "Counsel," lays emphasis on shura' (consultation) (42:38). Allah required the Prophet to consult his people in worldly matters and Muslims are required to consult each other in their secular matters. The Qur'anic text not only endorses the concept of popular consultation, but condemns "those who oppress mankind", that is, dictators or authoritarian rulers (42:42). The Prophet himself regularly consulted the Bedouin tribes, the most independent-minded people in the Arabian desert.

On the other hand, the Surah 4 on women and verse 4:59 seem to justify obedience to any kind of authority, whether a monarch or a caliph or a military dictator. Even the great al-Ghazzali went along with this interpretation, as we saw earlier. However, the Qur'an must be read as a whole, integral message from the Creator. On this basis, the verse 4:59 must be read together with 42:38. An authority must be legitimate and properly constituted. A believer must submit to properly and democratically constituted authority.

It is also necessary to observe the status and role of the *Ulema* (religious leaders) on this question. As part of the ruling class, the *Ulema* are typically co-opted, functioning as mouthpieces of the rulers, and one sees this today in most of the Islamic countries. The 'Ulama in Saudi Arabia are very much part of monarchical power structure and legitimize everything the Saudi rulers do.

Finally, note must be taken of the negative role of imperialism and foreign invasion. The United States and Western interests often coincide with those of dynastic and military dictatorships and authoritarian rulers. In the Islamic Core, people want freedom, as the Arab Spring has shown, but, in the end, dictators and oppressors win, and people lose because powerful vested interests, both internal and external, which do not permit democracy, to be established.

A Tunisian Exception: Habib Bourguiba?

The Tunisian leader, Habib Bourguiba, was a great modernizer, in his early years, perhaps the closest Arab leader to Atatürk. He led Tunisia to independence and then served as president of Tunisia from 1957 to 1987. Bourguiba became authoritarian in later years, acquiring the title president for life in 1975. In November 1987, at age 84, he was ousted by his new prime minister, Zine el-Abidine ben Ali, who declared that the president was too senile to govern. He died at 96, a broken man, a common enough fate in the Arab world (Pace, 2000).

In the early years, Bourguiba was a modernizing reformer. He pushed economic, social, and educational development. Per capita income and literacy soared. Tunisia evolved into one of the most politically tolerant Arab countries and was a showcase for development. Like Atatürk, he used his power to achieve gender equality. He enacted a "code of personal status" that granted women's rights, overriding the customary Sharia laws. Polygamy was outlawed and marriage was redefined as a voluntary contract between the wife and the husband. No longer was marriage an alliance of families. A minimum age was set for marriage and the consent of the bride was made legally mandatory. Thus, the traditional practice of selling young girls was outlawed.

Bourguiba also attempted reforms to improve the primitive living conditions of his country's seminomadic tribesmen. He was himself a product of urban society. He was born on 3 August 1903, in Monastir, the ancient port in the east, the youngest of eight children in a family of low-ranking civil servants. He went to school in Tunis, and an older brother provided the money for him to go to Paris in 1924 to study law, political science, and French literature. He was greatly influenced by French secularism, married a French woman, many years his senior.

In later years, he lost much of his influence, and public appreciation of his accomplishments was affected by disillusionment over high prices, low wages, and high unemployment. Confidence in his stewardship was shaken, often marred by rigged elections. In his final years in power, Bourguiba faced Islamic militants, and he was removed from office, after he ordered retrials and death sentences for several of them. His Prime Minister ben Ali and others feared the country was facing a civil war.

On foreign policy he differed from typical Arab leaders, advocating moderation toward Israel. But when the militants of the Palestine Liberation Organization (PLO) left West Beirut in 1982 after an Israeli invasion, Tunisia admitted 1,100 militants, who arrived to a tumultuous welcoming, led by Bourguiba from the dock. The PLO then set up its headquarters in Tunis.

One of the reasons why the Arab Spring started in Tunisia was the fact that the country has strong similarities with Turkey. Thanks to Bourguiba's reforms, Tunisia had generations growing up like Turkish people: secular, well-educated, and with women enjoying equal rights to men (Yazdani, 2008).

The example of Bourguiba is significant as it illustrates both the possibilities and the obstacles facing an Arab leader in modernizing societies in the Arab Core. He was certainly a modernizer, and a champion of gender equality, but his democratic credentials were dubious at best. At the height of his power, when asked about what the Bourguiba "system" was, he arrogantly replied, "I am the system" (Global Security, 2011).

His behavior in old age was anything but democratic. In the end, one is obliged to conclude that he was an exceptional leader, who managed to establish a democratic foundation in his country, even though the building never managed to go beyond foundation; in the end, the foundation, unnurtured, did not endure.

Note

1 For an expanded discussion of Ghazzali, see the author's, "Al-Ghazzali on Social Justice: Guidelines for a New World Order from a Medieval Scholar", International Journal of Social Economics, Vol. 24, No. 11, 1997, 1203–1218.

References

Abdulrazak, T., 2017, The Gassing of the Kurds at Halabja, www.middleeastmonitor.com/20170316-the-gassing-of-the-kurds-at-halabja/, accessed on 1 Oct. 2021.

al Aiwah, 2018, Jamal Khashoggi: Why the Arab World Needs Democracy Now, https://alaiwah.wordpress.com/2018/11/17/jamal-khashoggi-why-the-arab-world-needs-democracy-now/, accessed on 28 Oct. 2020.

Borger, J., 2019, US Deploying More Troops Around Syria Oil Fields After Killing of Isis Leader, www.theguardian.com/us-news/2019/oct/28/syria-us-troops-oil-fields-isis, accessed on 28 Oct. 2021.

Choueiri, Youssef M., 2000, *Arab Nationalism: A History*, Malden: Blackwell Publishing.

Cockburn, T., 2011, Did the US Really Give Saddam Fake OK to Invade Kuwait? www. counterpunch.org/2011/01/05/did-the-us-really-give-saddam-fake-ok-to-invade-kuw ait/, accessed on 1 Oct. 2021.

Cooper, Andrew Scott, 2011, *The Oil Kings: How the US, Iran, and Saudi Arabia Changed the Balance of Power in the Middle East*, New York: Simon & Shuster.

Esposito, John L., 1988, *Islam: The Straight Path*, New York: Oxford University Press.

Fisher, Sidney N., 1979, *The Middle East: A History*, 3rd ed., New York: Alfred A Knopf.

Global Security, 2011, Habib Bourguiba, www.globalsecurity.org/military/world/tunisia/ bourguiba.htm, accessed on 19 July 2022.

Hardy, Roger, 2017, *The Poisoned Well: Empire and Its Legacy in the Middle East*, New York: Oxford University Press.

Inalcik, Halil, 1973, *The Ottoman Empire: The Classical Age, 1300–1600*, London: Phoenix.

Ismael, Tareq and Jacqueline Ismail, 2015, *Iraq in the Twenty-First Century: Regime Change and the Making of a Failed State*, London: Routledge.

Kashoggi, Jamal, 2018, Jamal Khashoggi: What the Arab World Needs Most is Free Expression, www.washingtonpost.com/opinions/global-opinions/jamal-khashoggi-what-the-arab- world-needs-most-is-free-expression/2018/10/17/adfc8c44-d21d-11e8-8c22-fa2ef74 bd6d6_story.html, accessed on 22 Feb. 2022.

Khadduri, Majid, 1969, *Republican Iraq: A Study in Iraqi Politics since the Revolution of 1958*, London: Oxford University Press.

Lawrence, T.E., 1926, *Seven Pillars of Wisdom: A Triumph*, Harmondsworth, Middlesex: Penguin Books.

Lawrence, T.E., 1927, *Revolt in the Desert*, London: Jonathan Cape.

Mehmet, Ozay, 1990, (II&D), *Islamic Identity and Development: Studies of the Islamic Periphery*, London: Routledge.

ndtv, 2021, Saudi Crown Prince Implicated in Khashoggi Murder, US Finds: Report, www. ndtv.com/world-news/saudi-crown-prince-implicated-in-jamal-khashoggi-murder-us- finds-report-2378944, accessed on 20 August 2021.

Pace, E., 2000, Habib Bourguiba, Independence Champion and President of Tunisia, Dies at 96, www.nytimes.com/2000/04/07/world/habib-bourguiba-independence-champion- and-president-of-tunisia-dies-at-96.html, accessed on 2 Nov. 2021.

Qaradawi. Yusuf, 1997, Yusuf al-Qaradawi on Democracy, https://www.academia.edu/38175 408/Yusuf_al_Qaradawi_on_Democracy... accessed on 26 Sep. 2022.

Talabi, R., 2019, For Yazidis, Death of Islamic State Leader al-Baghdadi Doesn't Feel like Justice Yet, www.theglobeandmail.com/world/article-for-yazidis-death-of-islamic-state- leader-al-baghdadi-doesnt-feel/, accessed on 28 Nov. 2021.

Texas Observer, 2001, Andrew Wheat: The Bush-bin Laden Connection, www.texasobserver. org/480-andrew-wheat-the-bush-bin-laden-connection/, accessed on 20 August 2021.

Yazdani, I., 2008, Atatürk Was Inspiration for Founder of Tunisia, Habib Bourguiba: Safwan Masri, https://globalcenters.columbia.edu/news/ataturk-was-inspiration-founder-tuni sia-habib-bourguiba-safwan-masri, accessed on 29 April 2022.

11

DEMOCRACY, ARABS, AND ISLAMIC REVIVAL

Liberal democracy, with rule of law, human rights protected under a constitution, and free institutions, including an elected parliament and free press, have been the ideal of modern governance, at least in the so-called "free world." That world is primarily a Christian-White world, shaped by capitalism. The age of liberty and aggressive capitalism was built by the ideas of such 19th-century political philosophers as John Stuart Mill who advocated a new brand of globalization as "free trade," but, in fact, it gave rise to a Eurocentric system (Mehmet, 1999, 35–37). In the post WWII period, the torch of liberty was carried on by such Chicago economists as von Hayek and Milton Friedman. The age of liberty may now be phasing out under the force of a new wave of globalization from the East. In the Cold War era, it faced a threat from Communism, but now China is the new threat; a new world order may be just around the corner.

The Muslim world evolved on a different political path. The wonderful example of the man-made Islamic social contract, the Constitution of Medina, for social and political governance in this world (II&D, 53–55) was, in the hands of successors to the Prophet, abandoned in favor of an absolute One-Man rule. Whenever wise and enlightened monarchs ruled, as in the example of the Four Righteous Caliphs (II&D, 11), Islamic society progressed; more often, however, it regressed into tyranny and chaos. The post-Ottoman period in the Islamic Core has been particularly brutal, as documented in this study.

In the aftermath of the COVID-19 Pandemic, a new world order seems to be emerging. In the new age, equality, rather than liberty, may then be the leading principle. Now, even a daring proposal such as a global universal basic income is on the agenda for a more just and equal world order. Capitalism was built on unequal income distribution, reflecting the classical belief that only the rich save to finance investment for growth. If, as is almost certain, the post-Pandemic world will be an "Asian 21st Century" (Mahbubani, 2022), it is most likely that the new world order

DOI: 10.4324/9781003268994-11

emerging will reflect more equality and less liberty. A more equal distribution of incomes in the emerging world order is a positive step for global peace and security. This may mean less personal liberty and free markets as originally advocated by the prophets of liberalism and free enterprise system like Hayek and Friedman, but also less conflict as the world moves beyond fossil fuels toward a green, sustainable ecology.

At the beginning of 2022 when this monograph was completed, the Pandemic-ridden world was in a sorry state. Fears of new virus variants on the one hand, and worsening relations between Moscow, and on the other hand, the dispute between NATO, finally exploding into Russian invasion of Ukraine and the bloody war that followed, all indicate a troubled world. Humanity and the European project itself face an uncertain future. One thing that is almost certain, a major conclusion of this study on the making of the Middle East at the end of WWI, is the fundamental importance of an ethical basis for a world order. When, lies, deceit dominate geopolitics, and betrayal of people is tolerated, the result is not a peaceful, sustainable world; it is the gateway to instability and chaos.

Where does the Arab Core fit in the emerging new world order? Is democracy relevant for the Muslim world? Perhaps Arabs, speaking Arabic and professing Islam, require a different system of governance, a homegrown one, especially in these days when Western democracy itself is facing critical questioning. In the past century, however, since the end of the Ottoman Empire, the Arab world has made little progress, if any, creating lasting and peaceful homegrown institutions of government. This is the dilemma facing the Arab Core, and to which this chapter is addressed. It is organized in two parts: the first focused on global democracy and the second on the Arab world.

Is Democracy Dying?

Richard Falk (2021) has made apt, criminal link between the Vietnam and Middle East wars, arguing that the USA failed to learn important lessons from the first and, as a result, the same moral failure escalated into war criminality. Judging wars abroad as criminal is appropriate as it connects moral failure to legal culpability and reparations, discussed in Chapter 10; it also marks, in terms of domestic American politics, the high-water mark in liberal democracy.

Morally, America never recovered from the Vietnam failure. Nixon's resignation led to Thatcher–Regan style of authoritarian leadership. Deeper causal factors at work must also be noted undermining capitalism upon which Western democracies have been built. With Vietnam, the industrial-military complex grew bigger and stronger; the process has had a worsening impact on income inequality as the financial elite at the top have monopolized much of the gains of technical progress, not just in banking and finance, but in all sectors of the economy. Bill Gates, George Soros, Warren Buffet, and the likes, atop the financial elite, have derived the lion's share of these gains. On the other hand, working classes have regressed. In the labor market, casualization and informalization have wiped out job security. In the USA, no less than a quarter of the working population depend on food stamps to make ends meet. This is a huge subsidy to corporations. It is but one example of how politics have been captured by big corporations. The heavy-hand of the industrial-military complex in American politics is well-known (Powers, 2022). For some time now, public confidence in the democratic institutions has been eroding, the rise of China perceived increasingly a threat. It is a sad reflection of how the age of liberal democracy is being undermined by forces from within the system, as it becomes increasingly illiberal and authoritarian. Thinking beyond neoliberalism has now emerged as a serious academic topic for a post-Pandemic world, with innovative paradigms and proposals for a more equal world (Harris and Aceroglu, 2021), including a system of global minimum income to combat global income inequality (ibid., Nwogbo, 2021, 79–94 in Harris and Acemoglu, eds., op.cit.).

The rise of China may reflect this global shift. Arguably two forces are working to undermine liberal democracy: (1) Moral decay of such key organizations as the EU supposedly custodians and champions of liberal democratic values and (2) the rise of illiberal politics.

Moral Decay in Liberal Democracies, the Crisis of Capitalism

Trump's election in 2016 was a turning point, a victory of illiberal politics. The "angry American voter" changed the American democracy (Tolchin, 2019). Trump's victory over Hillary Clinton was a victory of the angry American voters. Clinton, the favorite until the last week of the campaign, squandered her chances for several reasons, but the Benghazi killings of four American diplomats, including the Ambassador, by Islamic terrorists when she was the State Secretary played a major role. Clinton lost the Public Relations war, appeared weak and unable to protect American diplomats (Reid, 2018).

All American presidents from Bush senior on have taken a strong anti-Islam stand, but none more so than Trump. Hate crimes against Muslims exploded as part of the general atmosphere of racism, police brutality, and systemic violence in the USA, where carrying guns is considered an act of individual liberty, similar (in an ironic way) to the Bedouin custom. White supremacists, Southern ultraright groups, and messianic networks all converged, finally bursting into the violent attack on the Capitol Hill on 6 January 2021. Trump pressured his own vice president, in his capacity as Speaker of the Senate, to declare him winner of the election. The USA has never been more divided since the Civil War.

Recognizing Jerusalem as the Jewish capital, Golan Heights as part of Israel, and cutting aid to Palestinians, and his ban on Muslim travels to the USA, are examples of Trump's clear hostility toward Islam. Being anti-Islam is not, necessarily, antiliberal or antidemocratic. His failure to win a second term in office was, for him and his supporters, a "stolen election." The ultimate demonstration of illiberalism was the insurrection on 6 January 2021 when a pro-Trump mob raided the Congress, briefly occupying the citadel of American democracy and attempting to violently force the lawmakers to keep Trump in power against the will of the American people. Trump's acquittal in the second impeachment trial in the Senate, however, represented the depth of polarization of America, the strength of the illiberal movement. It is not a monolithic movement with a single personality or ideology, but rather a diversity of interests, ranging from Jewish/Zionist groups, Christian fundamentalists to anti-immigration groups.

What happens in future will depend, significantly, on the ability of Joe Biden to reunify a highly fractured country, healing the wounds of racist policies and policing, and on how quickly and effectively the economy recovers. The racial divide is so entrenched in the USA that it is very doubtful that an aging president, whose election is still disputed by a significant section of the American public, will ever heal the deep wounds created during the Trump years. The sad fact is that Trump represented widespread anger in US mass opinion that the Washington establishment is corrupt, run by corporate interests, that it cannot listen, let alone respond to, the needs of mainstream American voters, a view strangely shared by both the left and right spectrum in American politics. The *Black Lives Matter* and similar movements that erupted after the George Floyd murder in Minnesota on 25 May 2020, in the middle of a Pandemic, have exposed the true nature of America: a country, built by European pilgrims and slave owners escaping a Europe torn by religious wars and persecution, prospered on slavery and free land acquired by genocide against the indigenous American natives. It is doubtful that slogans like "America First," "Making America Great Again" can ever restore democracy. The labor market trends, briefly mentioned earlier, reflect decay of the democratic-capitalist system from within.

The EU Case: The rejection of Muslim-majority Turkey into the EU, pri-marily to preserve the Christian heritage of Europe, is rejection of the ideal of a globalized democratic world, cutting across different faiths and cultures. In an earlier era, the EU presented itself as a Union of Values, a voice for free institutions, and four freedoms, free movement of people, of capital and technology, as well as free expression of ideas and beliefs. Thus, Spain and Portugal, with their fascist legacies, and later Greece, fresh from military dictatorship, were admitted to membership precisely to promote democratic values and institutions. The German unification was likewise heralded at the time of Glasnost, when some observers talked of the "end of history" and the triumph of liberal democracy (Fukuyama, 1989). That was a premature judgement at best, misleading and self-congratulatory. It ignored the deep-rooted racism in Western societies that was soon to erupt into Islamophobia in Europe and race riots in the USA. At its triumphant moment of Western liberal democracy, several European countries like Yugoslavia and Czechoslovakia broke up on ethnic lines, but mysteriously Germans, who were themselves reunited in the face of this neoliberal trend, other powerful voices patched up these ethnic eruptions and kept all components within the Christian Club, the European Union. No such accommodation took place in the case of the Cyprus dispute because the border in divided Cyprus became an extension of the Christian-Muslim frontier in the Balkans. In the case of Kosovo in the Balkans, an uneasy accommodation was achieved.

In 2004, at Athens, no less than nine former Soviet satellite countries (Czechoslovakia, Slovakia, Latvia, Estonia, Slovenia, Hungary, Poland, Romania, and Bulgaria) were admitted in one single "enlargement" round. Similarly, NATO expanded eastward. The EU's Copenhagen Criteria (rule of law, free press, human freedoms, etc.), normally expect from new members, were in this enlargement abandoned. In addition, as we have seen in Chapter 8, faced with a Greek veto, Germany, and key members, agreed to admit Greek Cyprus as member, completely ignoring the 1960 Cyprus Constitution and the rights of Muslim Turkish population of the island embedded in that Constitution.

Did the enlargement bring liberal democracy to new members since? Authoritarian rule in such countries as Hungary and Poland have emerged to the point that the EU Council have had to take disciplinary action (Newsbreak, 2022). Turkey, which applied for membership in 1987, has been held up and is unlikely ever to be accepted as a member, chiefly because it is a Muslim country, one which has had a troubled historical relationship with Europe. Xenophobia reigns high in European politics and popular misconceptions, including fear-based politics, will not disappear. Sadly, it seems that the age of liberal democracy may be ending, while illiberal politics are on a rising trend.

The Evolution of Arab Nationalism

It is possible to push an analysis of the origins of Arab nationalism to medieval or even earlier times, as far back as the Pharaohs (Choueiri, 2000, 25) especially in terms of "cultural Arabism (that is) … Arabic civilization as a glorious golden age" (66). That would, however, be a romantic exercise. It is more fruitful to stick to the more recent history. Emotionalism has been an integral part of Arab nationalism. Thus, when Nasser led an unprepared army to the greatest modern defeat in the first few hours of the Six-Day War on 9 June 1967, the leader took the only honorable step available; he took responsibility and resigned in a passionate speech to the Arab nation over the radio and television. Nasser's decision

> stunned the Arab world at large. Millions of Egyptians responded by pouring into the streets in spontaneous demonstrations calling on their president to stay in office. *It was as if the military defeat had given the ordinary civilian population to assert its own national defiance.* [italics added] (207)

Realism was buried in the sands of the Sinai desert.

Nation-building requires realism, ability to evaluate facts as they are, and a national leader must always act within the limits of what is achievable. Passion and ability to whip up public emotions on radio and TV may be an act of showmanship, but these cannot be substitute for total dedication and self-reliance in the struggle for liberation.

Before WWI, in the second half of the 19th century, Arab nationalism was led by Western educational institutions. Taking advantage of the Tanzimat reforms (Lewis,

1961, chapter IV) and the governorship of the liberally minded Midhat Pasha (an exiled leader of Tanzimat), France, Russia, Germany, Italy, and American missionaries and educationalists opened schools in Syria and Lebanon, but each country pursuing its own interest, in this case spread of a specific kind of cultural influence. In the words of Antonius, the following was the pattern:

> The French Government, anxious to strengthen their influence, subsidized the French ecclesiastical missions; and these, entering into an alliance with the Maronite and Melchite clergy, strove to give their rising generation an *education which, although well enough in itself, aimed also at shaping their minds in a French mould and turning their outlook and their mental allegiance towards France.* [italics added]
>
> *Antonius, 1939, 92*

Antonius identified three distinct periods in the evolution of Arab Awakening: The Infant Movement, 1868–1908, the Young Turks period, 1908–1914, and WWI period.

The first leaders of the Arab National Movement, which Antonius traced back to 1875, were five, all Christians, educated at the Syrian Protestant College in Beirut. They formed a secret society, writing and distributing anonymous placards in streets (ibid., 79). Later, acting out of necessity, they included Arab and Druze members. True, this was a period of Hamidian censorship and repression, from which all suffered, Turks no less than the Arabs and Christian minorities in the Empire. In fact, Midhat, the governor, like the Mehmet Ali in Egypt, aspired to carving out his own state in Syria and so he was sympathetic to the infant Arab national movement. The fact is that there was no "*Arab Awakening*" evolving out of the grassroots, driven by popular demand for self-rule. Nation-building, a new European invention, was still an idea for the future.

During the final years of the Ottoman Empire, when the Young Turks regime was in control, Arab deputies in the Ottoman parliament, aspired to some form of decentralization or autonomy within the multiethnic Empire (Ahmad, 1969), an idea not entirely opposed by the dominant Committee of Union and Progress (CUP). However, there was no clear consensus on Ottomanism and the Arabs' place in it. The CUP leadership favored centralization. But the CUP, as a movement, was too inexperienced both in running a government and a big multinational Empire. From the beginning of its power, it lacked a coherent program, owing to infighting (Aksakal, 2008, 58–60).

One issue that divided the Turkish and Arab deputies was the status of Arabic in the Empire. The more patriotic deputies wanted Turkish in place of Arabic, the language of the Quran, but opponents regarded this anti-Islamic as well as anti-Arab (Ahmad, 124–125). Education reform was another contentious issue, the CUP reformists arguing for modern education "to bring Islam in line with the modern world in order to save it from decay" (ibid., 130), a view which most Arabs found hostile. The imperial powers took advantage of disunity in the Turkish capital, exploiting the weaknesses of both the CUP and the Arabs. For example, the British Ambassador Mallet took an active role in Turkish-Arab affairs, passing intelligence about Arab "conspiracies" and "insurrections," undermining any possible Turkish-Arab accord (127–128). In the larger picture, all Allied representatives, especially the Russian, French, and English, in the Sultan's capital teamed up when it became clear that neutrality in the coming European war was not an option for the Ottomans who, finally, were lured into the German camp.

In the interwar years, the Arab world was a vast land under occupation by imperial powers. At the beginning, the Arab leadership was full of high hopes. With Ottomans gone, the Arab leaders convened in Damascus on 2 June 1919 and adopted several key resolutions, with incredible naivety and contradictions. On the one hand, a petition submitted to the Inter-Allied Commission, demanding "absolute political independence for Syria" (Antonius, 1939, 440), but, on the other hand, they demanded an American mandate, rejecting the British and French colonialism. "… in the belief that the American nation is devoid of colonial ambitions, and it has no political designs on our country" (441). The term "our country (Syria)" was defined as a huge area extending from the Taurus mountains in the north to the Hejaz border, below Aqaba in the south, from the Euphrates in the east to the Mediterranean in the west. It included not only Lebanon but Palestine as well.

These Arab leaders, believing in Wilsonian principles, were totally ignorant of the scientific and agricultural activities of the American Zionists, using American money and technology, busily building the foundation of a future Israel in the Holy Land at time (Anderson, 2013: 11–15). Their earlier pleas at the Peace Conference rejected, they naively turned to America for funds and technical aid, arguing that "the Arab inhabitants of Syria are not less fitted or gifted than … the Bulgarians, Serbs, Greeks and Romanians" (Article 3). In the same breath, however, they sought American "assistance in the technical and economic fields … on the understanding that the duration of such assistance shall not exceed twenty years" (Article 4).

They got nowhere. Wilson was not ready to challenge the Allies. His 19 Points were no more than a huge public relations stunt. Betrayed, Arab nationalism took the form of a resistance movement, organizing rebellions against the French in Syria and the English in Iraq. The ruling dynasties in Iraq, Saudi Arabia, and Jordan were little more than English puppets. In the words of Sir Andrew Ryan, *The Last of the Dragomans* in Istanbul, and subsequently a faithful colonial advisor in the Saudi royal court: The Saudi King knew "that British friendship was a condition of his survival" (Ryan, 1951, 278). As for the French, Edward Said put it best: "If France was to continue to prevent 'le retour de l'Islam,' it had better take hold of the Orient" (Said, 1979, 225), a view repeated time and again, because of WWI "Asiatic Turkey" was ready for "dismemberment" (223). This is how Paris politicians saw, Lebanon, Syria, Algeria, and the Muslim Middle East, Osman's loot ready for the picking!

After WWII, Pan-Arab nationalism took a revolutionary turn, driven by radical ideology (Khadduri, 1969, 2). No clear ideology existed, alternatives of socialism, capitalism generally ill-suited to the Arab national development. Ambitious projects like Pan-Arabism failed to take root. One language and a common Islam proved insufficient to overcome local customs and loyalties, so deep-rooted in the vast areas from Morocco to Saudi Arabia. Cult of personality, notably after Gamal Abdul Nasser's success at the Suez in 1956, led an experiment on a more reduced scale, as in the Union of Egypt and Syria. The experiment was born in discord, its leaders condemning Qasim of Iraq for not joining the Union and preventing "the procession of Arabism" (204). A competing Federation of Jordan and Iraq was roundly criticized as a cheap way of strengthening the Hashemite dynasty (24). As we have seen in this study, the existing Arab states, originally drawn as lines in the sand by Sykes-Picot, were artificial, lacking national cohesion and identity, and since the end of the Ottomans, they failed to make much progress in developing such a national identity.

Radical, revolutionary ideology has been manifested in the Ba'ath party, but the movement has evolved into military dictatorship, brutal in the extreme, such as the Assad regime in Syria and the Saddam Hussein in Iraq, Elsewhere, dynastic families, dependent on imperial powers, have ruled, intolerant of dissent and personal freedoms. Generally, identity search (who is an Arab? What are the Arab ideals or goals? Will the ruled consent?) has not figured as critical question.

Voices in the Dark

It is difficult to find studies of post-Ottoman Arab nationalism focused on identity and national development. There are, to be sure, case studies of countries on important figures and historical works of a general nature or on economic development, or on significant events such as the Crusades. However, one is hard-pressed to find scholarly studies of who is an Arab. What are the Arab aspirations? Where are the boundaries of an Arab homeland? Antonius, examined earlier, is useful on the early years, but sadly his example has not been followed. More recent scholarship has focused on the humiliating defeat in the Six-Day War, which, at first, was described as a "setback" (Choueiri, 2000, 207). Bassam Tibbi (1981) is useful on the rise of competing political ideology, including Islam, after the Six-Day War. By contrast, there are all kinds of studies by Westerners, as outsiders looking in, portraying generally a negative image of Arab identity and nation-building. Below we examine a couple of voices in the dark, studies of exceptionalism, Edward Said and Arnold Toynbee, in the post-Ottoman era.

Orientalism: Perhaps Edward Said's justly celebrated work, *Orientalism* (1979), is one of the closest expositions of modern Arab national identity. It is full of anguish, an angry voice directed at the Western literary icons, paving the way for the Palestinian dispossession. The result is that, following the end of the Ottomans, Zionism won, and Palestinians lost a homeland, and there has been much betrayal since the Ottomans. The lost homeland in Palestine, a small part of where the Arab lived, is what motivated Said to take on his literary deconstruction, a passionate, personal experience: It was "disheartening" (27) he states, a protest acquired as an Arab Palestinian living in the West, particularly in America.

Said is especially candid on orientalist presentation (or misrepresentation) of Islam. He notes perceptively that orientalists produce books and articles "in a market." As in any market, there are buyers, sellers, and commodity exchange. When orientalists claim expertise on Islam or the Middle East, they are "covering" these topics in the most superficial manner. These experts are speaking and plying their products to Westerners. "Islam, if it is 'Islam' that is being studied, is not an interlocutor, but in a sense a commodity" (Said, 1981, 142). Islam is simply just another commodity. For Said, this is "institutional bad faith." He is especially critical of the academic community in this commodification of Islam, displaying bad faith because all too often the academic community realizes what it is doing: The academic expert in this case is delivering intellectual product in a market where the buyers are only interested in confirming their own perceptions, the interest of America or the West.

Historically, the Western academic has followed a military leader's footpath. Thus, when Napoleon invaded Egypt in 1798 or when France occupied Algeria in 1830, French academics suddenly "discovered" Egypt or Algeria (24–25). French institutions were established to study these countries and their people and cultures. Colonization followed, based on the works of experts. Orientalist scholarship served home country interests, providing indispensable intelligence for the colonial administration. From Richard Burton and Speke and countless other "discoverers" and "experts," a flood of valuable scholarship was produced, but "Islam was never welcome in Europe" (12–13). But exceptions do exist. One leading case is the Toynbee controversy summarized below.

The Arnold Toynbee Controversy: Said's was not the first voice of protest at the European bias against the Muslim world. It is instructive to briefly examine another leading voice of disapproval of the methodology generally used to portray a "parochial," Eurocentric image of non-European societies in the West, Arnold Toynbee. Toynbee was not an Arab specialist. He was a contemporary of Lawrence, Bell, Philby, and other team members, knew them from college, but stood apart from them. An internationalist by upbringing, Toynbee was well versed in other civilizations, and he understood the world was much larger than Christian Europe, consisting of "the Chinese and the Japanese, the Hindus and the Muslims" and predicted "a future world which will be neither a Western nor non-Western but will inherit all cultures in a single crucible" (Toynbee, 1948, 90). In his professional career, his expertise was in the field of Greek-Turkish relations, which Toynbee insisted on seeing in a new light. His independence of mind got him into trouble.

The climax in Toynbee's career was the Korais Chair controversy. This was an endowment in the King's College London, financed secretly by Greek shipping magnates, in Byzantine and Modern Greek studies. It was awarded to the young and promising Toynbee in 1920. He had stellar qualifications and most recently he had worked assisting Lord Byrce, a well-known jurist, who was also a passionate defender of the cause of the Ottoman Armenians. Together, Byrce and Toynbee had worked for the British government to produce a Blue Book on the recent treatment of the Armenians by the Ottoman government. A few years later, Toynbee wrote in his celebrated study, *The Western Question in Greece and Turkey, a Study in the Contact of Civilisations* (1922), that the Blue Book was "published and distributed as war propaganda" (50).

Soon after his appointment to the Korais Chair, Toynbee was recruited by the editor of the Manchester Guardian, C.P. Snow, to travel to Asia Minor to cover the Turkish War of Independence. He duly started his mission in Athens, and he expected to be a witness to the rebirth of a new Byzantium empire, as provided under the terms of the Treaty of Sevres. What he saw was shocking. He started sending back to Snow "telegrams describing atrocities that were being committed by the Greek Army against the Turkish population" (Toynbee, 1967, 230). Manchester Guardian was the leading voice of Liberalism. However, the readers, found Toynbee's dispatches unlike the "Gladstonian orthodoxy" praising Hellenism against the "unspeakable Turk." Complaints flooded to the newspaper. Editor Snow, stood by his principles, kept on publishing Toynbee's shocking reports of Greek soldiers running amok, killing, at random, Turkish civilians, torching entire towns and villages. Readers questioned whether Toynbee was reporting the truth. Snow did not relent, but the academic masters of King's College did. Upon complaints by the Greek shipping sponsors of the Chair, Toynbee's appointment was cancelled (Clogg, 1986). Academic freedom then was a commodity for sale and Toynbee became the sacrificial lamb. When it came to Greek-Turkish relations, orthodoxy required that truth must be abandoned. In a case of conflict between Greeks and Turks, there should be no question of Western orthodoxy supporting the Greeks. Similarly, in the Arab-Israeli conflict, or indeed in general Muslim-Christian relations, it is the norm to dismiss the Arabs and Muslims as uncivilized, barbaric, and unworthy of Western support or sympathy.

Edward Said lived much later than Arnold Toynbee. When the latter covered the Greek-Turkish war, Israel did not exist. But faithful to his principles of always seeking truth and fairness, Toynbee had much in common with Said. In the 1920s, he distanced himself from Zionism and Zionist friends in the British government. He personally knew key persons in Arab affairs like Hogarth, Lawrence, and Gertrude Bell, but he steadfastly voiced his concern for Palestinian Arabs. He would have endorsed Said's opinion of Bell who, on a visit to "liberated" Damascus, rejoices:

> I believe the fact of my being English is a great help … We have come up in the world since five years ago. … my impression is that the vigorous policy of Lord Curzon in the Persian Gulf and on the Indian frontier stands for a great deal more. No one who does not know the East can realize how it all hangs together. It is scarcely an exaggeration to say that if the English mission had been turned back from the gates of Kabul, the English tourist would be frowned upon in the streets of Damascus.
>
> *Said, 1979, 229*

Lawrence, as Bell, admires the "primitive simplicity" of the Arab: "… the Arab seems to Lawrence to have *exhausted* himself … The enormous age of Arab civilization has thus served to refine the Arab down to his quintessential attributes, and to tire him out morally in the process" (230). Said, in agony, is forced to conclude: "What we are left with is Bell's Arab: centuries of experience and no wisdom" (230). It was up to the White Man to rule and civilize the Arab. This is the opinion of someone (Bell) who had so much impact on the creation of Arab countries under the Sykes-Picot Agreement. For Said, historians like Bernard Lewis played an enabling role in the process: Zionists got their homeland; the Arabs were placed under tutelage.

However, even Said does not go far enough. He fails, as do most Arab nationalists, to ask some troubling, self-critical questions: Why did the Arab world fail to produce its own Ataturk, a truly honest leader, not only brilliant on the battlefield, but a world-class statesman, with total commitment to creating a modern, democratic nation out of the ashes of a glorious medieval, feudal heritage?

Indeed, the legacy is worse and more troubling questions must be faced. Theodore Herzl, an Austrian Jew who became a dedicated Zionist after the Dreyfus case, and wrote the *Jewish State* in 1896 (Ben Gurion, 2022), visited the Ottoman Sultan Hamid and offered huge sums of cash in return for his permission to permit Jewish settlement in the Holy Land by land purchase. The offer was summarily dismissed as an attempted bribe. Even with a background of fiscal insolvency, the Sultan-Calif stuck to his own true values: As a devout Muslim, he could not betray his sense of duty, he must protect the Holy Land. In this respect, Sultan Hamid was not only honorable, but he was also trying, in vain, to protect his Arab subjects. Meanwhile, the landed aristocracy in Palestine chose to sell large tracts of land to the Jewish National Fund (JNF, 2022).

Arab Spring: A Failed Young Turk Revolution, a Century Later?

Arab spring was a replication of the Young Turk revolution in the Ottoman capital in 1908 (Lewis, 1961, chapter VII). In both cases, the short-lived age of liberty ended in repressive counterrevolution led by religious fanatics and fundamentalists, ultimately paving the way for the return of dictatorship. As in Istanbul in 1908, the movement for liberty and freedom in Arab capitals had military support, more tacit in the Arab case than actual as the case in the Young Turks' case. But the crowds in Tahrir Square and in other Arab capitals would not have succeeded in toppling long-ruling dictators without the green light from the military who preferred to stay, for a time, on the sidelines.

In both cases, the liberty experiment brought out into the open diverse minorities and fringe groups, all lacking experience in the running of a successful government. In the Ottoman case, the Young Turks were actively joined by ethnic minorities, Armenian, Jews, and Arabs, as well as supporters in Europe. They all joined in celebrating the end of the long Hamidian dictatorship, falsely believing that the transition to the age of equality and justice was now within reach.

Three communities in particular – Arabs, Armenians, and Jews – had their own, conflicting agendas. They aspired to some sort of self-government or autonomy. Little heed was paid to the centralizing aspirations of the dominant leadership, the

Committee of Union and Progress (*İttihat ve Terakki Cemiyeti*) or CUP. Initially, the Armenian political activists, such as members of the Armenian Revolutionary Federation, were in alliance with the Young Turk leadership and had taken an active part in the changeover of power. The Jewish *millet*, especially its younger nationalist generation, expected freedom for Zionism and hoped the age of liberty would facilitate increasing Jewish settlement in Palestine, leading ultimately to some form of political autonomy. The Arab elite was openly hostile toward the Young Turks, but Arab Christians, leaders of the nascent Arab nationalist movement in places like Damascus and Mount Lebanon, already enjoying a large measure of self-government from the Ottoman center, aspired to greater decentralization and more use of the Arabic language.

The Young Turks themselves were unclear in their objectives. Romantically, they were attached to the ideals of the French revolution, but, deep in their soul, they were Turkish nationalists. They wanted a modernized Turkey as a Turkish homeland, first and foremost. Equality between the Turks and minorities was not something embraced by the CUP leadership. The CUP press published articles propagating the idea of "Turkey for the Turks."

Within a year, a counterrevolution led by religious fanatics, supported by the palace guards, took place on 13 April 1909 demanding introduction of Şeriat, the Koranic Law (Ahmad, 1969, 36). The inept CUP, caught unawares, was temporarily out, but not out. Within months, revolutionary officers marched in from the CUP stronghold in Salonica. The despot Abul Hamid was forced to abdicate in favor of his brother Mehmet Reşat. The reins of power now belonged to the CUP triumverate of Enver, Talat and Djemal, which ruled to the bitter end and dissolution of the Ottoman Empire.

Arab Spring was largely a grassroots movement, but, like the CUP, it had top-down characteristics. The Nasserite and Ba'athist regimes in Egypt, Syria, or Libya, in true Young Turk tradition, promised national modernization, and the ideology of liberalism, that had shaped the Arab revolutionary minds. In the Arab capitals in 2011–12, after the dust of public demonstration settled down, the only organized group ready to move in to take power, was the Islamic movement. The Egyptian Islamic Brotherhood which brought in the Mohamed Morsi regime was nothing else than the culmination of decades of preparation by Islamists for political action. Morsi, once elected, wasted no time revealing his intolerance. Here too, there is a historical parallel to the Young Turks' failure in 1908. Within a year, a counter-revolution was staged, and standard form of dictatorship and military rule returned with the coup of the El Sisi regime in Cairo.

Ba'athism and the Question of Legitimacy

Modern Arab nationalism has oscillated between the nationalism of the Arabs as a whole and state-based nationalism. This has given rise to tension between pan-Arab and state-based nationalism, with apparent shifts, like desert winds, alternating between both forms, further complications arising from questions of region-based legitimacy as in Wahhabism or Berber nationalism in the Maghreb covering Algeria to Morocco (Ben Forstag, 2022). As a result, ambiguity surrounds the fundamental question of who exactly an Arab is. Nasserism, as a cult of personality, dominant during Gemayel Nassir's life, was a secular ideology, aspiring to modernize the Arab societies regardless of political boundaries imposed by imperial power.

In 1953, the principles of Nasserism were defined as: (1) the liquidation of imperialism, (2) the abolition of feudalism, (3) an end to monopolies and of the domination of capital over government, (4) the building of a strong army, (5) the achievement of social justice, and (6) the establishment of a healthy democratic life (Choueiri, 2000, 182). It was bold, comprehensive, and daring. First, a national land reform was launched to end feudalism, but soon the regime realized the importance of finance to carry out land redistribution. It therefore attempted to nationalize the Suez Canal, terminating the British military base in the Canal Zone. It led to the Israel-France-Britain attack of 26 October 1956, one of the last gunboat showdowns in modern times; the attack ended British imperialism. The USA was kept in the dark, and President Eisenhower was furious. It opened the door to American involvement in the Middle East and, in a geopolitical sense, raised Nasser's prestige in the Arab world. He then turned socialist, pursing higher and more ambitious aims. Ba'athism, originating in Syria in 1947 as a peasant movement, evolved as Arab socialism, borrowing heavily, at the leader's choice, from Western Marxist ideology. It aspired to state-controlled enterprises and increased dependency on the USSR. Both lacked national authenticity, representing top-down rather than bottom-up social grounding (despite its origin as a peasants' movement) and, as a result, failed to overcome questions of legitimacy. Nasser overextended his resources and overplayed his hand. After the humiliating defeat in the Six-Day War in 1969, these movements declined, while political Islam gained popularity (Tibbi, 1997).

However, neither Islam, as a common religion, nor Arabic, as a unifying language, has proved decisive in defining Arab identity and nationalism. In the late 19th century, Islamic thinkers like Muhammad Abdu and Jamal al-Afghani extensively discussed Pan-Islam (II&D, 1990, 72–73) under the Ottoman Sultan-Caliph, but WWI, specifically the Arab Revolt, exposed the emptiness of this ideology, giving nationalism a big boost, empowering national leaders like Mustafa Kemal Ataturk, Ali Jinnah, and Sukarno (73 and Part Three). These voices, however, were in the Islamic periphery. Even though they shaped nation-building in Turkey, Pakistan, Malaysia, and Indonesia, they failed to have much of an impact in the Arab Core.

In the Arab Middle East, dynastic rulers and military dictatorship emerged in charge of nation-building. Nationalism has taken a local manifestation, and economic and social development has been strictly defined in a top-down manner depending on the whims and fancies of the local ruling leadership. Similarly, questions of legitimacy and accountability have remained at the mercy of these leaders.

Is Arab Democracy an Impossible Dream?

In its classical Greek definition, democracy is direct rule of the people, with a floating majority determining public policy. In this definition, three criteria stand out: (1) direct rule, (2) a homogeneous people, and (3) an open or free debate. Direct rule requires in a democratic state means informed participation by citizens, voting in free and fair elections. This is open society with free expression of ideas, free press to ensure that in elections voting is based on full and up-to-date information, with legal guarantee of transparency and freedom of access to public information. In closed societies, voters are herded by religious, military, or dynastic leadership into bloc voting without accurate and up-to-date information.

"People" mean a group of generally like-minded entity, typically speaking the same language, with shared customs and cultural heritage, living in a shared homeland. In multiethnic countries, such as the Canadian federalism, there is always a risk of breakup; much goodwill and plenty of federal fiscal transfers are used to ensure that voters can change their voting from one election to the next, so that there is peaceful transfer of power based on free election results.

In the Arab world, indeed in much of the world, these three conditions rarely hold. Take for example small state such as Lebanon. Prior to the Six-Day War in 1967, it was a success story, Beirut being the Paris of the Middle East. Lebanese politics were elite-managed but "sectarian" (Sallolukh, et al., 2015). Religious leaders, as in Ottoman times, ruled religious communities. Population statistics determined power sharing. The last Census was the one held in 1944, when Lebanon was a French protectorate. In the 1970s, in the aftermath of Palestinian refugee influx, the old power-sharing system became dysfunctional. The country descended into civil war and Lebanese politics never recovered. The Syrian civil war was the last nail on the Lebanese coffin with a huge influx of refugees. The country became another "failed state" in the Arab world, torn from within due to political corruption.

Lebanon is not alone as a small country in the Arab world. There are numerous small states in the Gulf, Kuwait, UAR, Qatar, Oman, all rich in hydrocarbons, and all remnants of British imperialism. With huge oil revenue, these small emirates, followed the lead of big dynastic powers like Saudi Arabia, opting for large-scale imports of technical and professional manpower as well as manual workers (as domestic servants), so much so that in some cases, the actual demographics, these imported workers outnumber native citizens. Table 11.1 gives a summary of the latest demographic statistics.

In Qatar and UAR, nine or eight residents out of ten are foreign nationals. The proportions are somewhat less in Kuwait and Bahrain. And in the case of Saudi Arabia, the proportion is about a third. In the light of these demographic facts, it is not an idle question to ask whether or not democracy, as defined earlier, is possible in these Arab countries.

The case of Saudi Arabia is different from others in Table 11.1. It is a large country in territory and with a population of more than 30 million. In these regard, it is a country closer to Iran, another large country in the Islamic (not in the Arab)

TABLE 11.1 FOREIGN NATIONALS IN GULF STATES

	Date	Total population	% Foreign nationals
Bahrain	Mid-2014	1.3	52
Kuwait	31 March 2016	4.3	69.4
Oman	April 2016	4.4	45.4
Qatar	April 2015	2.4	89.9
UAR	Mid-2010	8.3	88.5
S. Arabia	Mid-2014	30.8	32.7

Source: National Institutes of Statistics, latest year or period available as of 20 April 2016.https://gulfmi
gration.org/gcc-total-population-percentage-nationals-foreign-nationals-gcc-countries-national-statist
ics-2010-2016-numbers/, accessed on 21 August 2021.

Core. In one more respect there is a significant commonality between Iran and
Saudi Arabia: Both are religious regimes. Although politically rivals, one is Sunni
and the other Shi'a, direct democracy within the existing system would likely result
in herd voting as in closed, or "not free" societies (see above Table 2.2). Elsewhere
in the Arab Core, Egypt, Syria, and Iraq, there are military dictatorships with effectively one-party elections. In the countries of the Maghreb, Morocco is a dynastic
Kingdom as is Saudi Arabia; Tunisia (the home of Arab Spring) and Algeria are what
may be termed authoritarian rule.

Civil Society

During the 1990s, many researchers took inspiration from the burgeoning Western
scholarship on civil society, which saw voluntary associations and social capital as
the hallmarks of a healthy democracy. This trend echoed in the Arab Core, leading
researchers to view positively non-state actors, such as Islamist charities, service
providers, trade unions, student committees, and human rights NGOs (Choueiri,
2000, Epilogue). Perhaps, according to this train of thought, civil society organizations
could become the vanguard of a new democratic revolution in the Middle East.
Suddenly the Arab Spring in 2011 became the living proof. As discussed earlier, it
unfolded and popular insurrections toppled long-serving autocrats in Tunisia, Egypt,
Libya, and Yemen; optimists began to hope that the pendulum now was starting to
swing from the state back to society as the arbiter of democratic change, but some
argue that the movement was funded, recruited, and guided from Western intelligence (Smith, 2019). Arabists trumpeting the democratic potential of civil society
were aboard this new trend, using language more guarded than their predecessors
but brimming with no less optimism regarding the ability of civic organizations to
lead liberal democratic change. It was all premature; hope was replaced by despair.

Is Arab civil society dead after the Arab Spring? A few examples would be sufficient to reach a negative conclusion. In Syria and Yemen, civil wars have killed any
NGO sector, except for humanitarian aid organizations. In Egypt, under the new
autocracy of the Sisi regime, many NGOs have been co-opted by the government

to qualify for funding, or even to get registered, in the process of losing their independence. In general, Arab civil society has been much weakened. There are a few exceptions such as Jordan, Kuwait, and Morocco. In Jordan, citizens still have the theoretical right to organize everything from women's rights groups to political clubs, but a convoluted set of antiterror laws makes any kind of bold public expression liable to prosecution. Elsewhere the situation evokes little hope.

Is It Possible to Have Democracy in the Arab World?

In the short run, it is difficult to be hopeful. History is bitter. Arab independence came first under imperialist protection; it did not lead to freedom. It brought in Western neo-imperialism. Dynastic rule has been in direct control from London, Paris, or Washington. Freedom and democracy were never given a chance because top priority was oil wealth pursued by imperialists. Where dynastic rule did not survive, Arab countries fell to military dictatorship and authoritarian regimes. Civil war, proxy wars, assassinations, and repressive regimes followed one another. Arab nation-building rested on ideology imported from the West; some experimented with socialism. Islamism, mixing Islam with politics, has also been a major factor behind state power (Nasr, 2001). The resulting combination has been dangerous and costly leading, case after case, to failed States (Chomsky, 2006).

As Chomsky points out "failed states" come in a variety of forms: outlaw states, illegal, and so on. In all cases, however, there is an underlying characteristic, namely power grab, and abuse of power. In the case of the failed Arab states in the Middle East, often external powers have been complicit, European imperialists before WWII, and the USA since then. The CIA, as we have seen, was a major actor in Mosaddeq's fall in Iran, more recently in the Arab-Israeli conflict, but elsewhere, from Lebanon in 1985 to the invasion of Iraq in 2004 and in the descend into regional chaos ever since. For the USA, "democracy promotion" (171–173) has always been hypocritical, conditional on the fact that America's own interest trumps all else. Thus, Arafat, when alive, was regarded as "obstacle" to peace, but his death in November 2004 altered nothing.

It is, of course, futile to expect democratic development, like manna, to fall come from outside, it must evolve from the grassroots to upward. In the Arab world, no such foundation existed; the Arab soil was never fertile for democratic nation-building. A couple of illustrative cases can be given. The Morsi regime in Egypt, during the short-lived Arab Spring, was a democratic experiment which failed miserably. The democratic transition was taken over by the Muslim Brotherhood, which soon started acting like a single party, intolerant of other views and parties, in short, "it failed to make a national coalition" (Atwana and Othman, 2015).

In a functioning democracy, there must be several parties competing for power to ensure peaceful transfer of power at the end of free elections, it is essential that there is national consensus to respect opposition parties. The Egyptian Mohamed Morsi case demonstrated the opposite: Morsi increasingly became intolerant and doctrinaire, sowing the seeds of his own demise. The Morsi regime was founded on religious politics. It will not work. Lebanon is a living proof of the failure of a sectarian system. It was multiparty system, but it is a sectarian system in which power sharing is elitist, based on ethnic and religious divisions within both the Christian and Muslim populations. Lebanon's multireligious communities, made up of Maronites, other Christians, Druze, Sunni, and Shia, including the powerful Iran-backed Hezbollah, can no longer function as a democratic system. It is clientelism that empowers self-serving community leaders and promotes corruption. An additional challenge is that the boundaries of the current population is unknown as it is heavily inflated by refugees from Syria as well as Palestinians displaced by Israeli wars.

In contrast, it is evident that the Ottoman multiculturalism was better suited, allowing different religious and ethnic communities, *millets*, of Muslims, Jews, Christians, and a myriad of ethnic groups in the Empire to coexist with mutual respect, living in tolerance, peace, and security. The Sultan's government, to varying degrees, provided peace and security in return for taxes and other obligations. Mutual respect came from custom and tradition. The system, though far from perfect, fitted very well the polyglot world of the Middle East.

What did the Middle East lose with the Ottomans gone? *Multiculturalism.* The region still needs it, as does the ethnically diverse world. When the "Sick Man" finally died, so did multiculturalism and tolerance in his empire. Intolerance took over. A millennium of good relations between Turks and Armenians [known in Ottoman Empire as the *Sadık Millet*, the loyal community] suddenly burst into an ethno-religious inferno provoked by imperialist powers, the Tsarist Russia in particular. Similarly, colonial Divide and Rule fragmented the Ottoman Arab *millet* and opened the floodgates of the Arab-Jewish conflict, producing wars and millions of displaced and disposed Palestinians. Generations are now growing in refugee camps, dispersed all over the Middle East, breeding ground for terror and continued warfare as in Gaza.

Self-Reliance, Social Capital, and Institution-Building for a New SRE

In the post-Ottoman period, the Arab countries have experimented with numerous models and paradigms, none of which have worked because these were based on imported ideologies or regimes have depended on foreign powers, not on the consent of the ruled. The map and boundaries drawn by Sykes and Picot are no longer tenable. Imperialists, including neo-imperialists, have always been after oil, as Chomsky and others have explained. There is no substitute for endogenous development for nation-building. It is a long-term process, starting with rule of law and free press to allow free ideas to flourish. Social capital, building trust, sharing, and cooperating with one another, accumulates like human capital, only through deliberate public investment.

The best option for the Arab Core oil-producing countries is the long-term evolution of the Silk Route Economy (SRE). Rebuilding a new Muslim world, modelled on what existed at the time of Marco Polo, is now feasible. This amounts to looking East, especially Central Asia, but it is more likely to lead to sustainable development than any Western model. A new age of equality may evolve, one which would be more in accord with the ideal Islamic social contract than the Western liberal democratic model.

There are now clear signs that the Western liberal democracy is slowly dying. A new China is emerging. But China is primarily interested in infrastructural megaprojects. It is a one-party dictatorship, not a democratic model. A Chinese-led SRE, by itself, is not likely to bring much benefit; oil-producing countries must be ready to invest to make SRE a truly new, more humane world. The Central Asian Turkic republics are rich in resources. Development of these resources may attract Western multinational companies (MNCs) with their pools of investment and skills. They should not be allowed to replicate a new wave of neo-imperialism. Oil producers in the Arab Core need to realize that oil neo-imperialism is unsustainable. MNCs in the SRE must be taxed properly and fairly to generate revenue for sustainable development.

Central Asian republics have been devastated by years of Communist rule. To achieve sustainable development, they need huge investments to develop their human resources, build social capital, institutions, and define their place in the new world. Oil-rich countries in the Middle East have a stake in this new world, and they must invest. It all starts at home, however, with institution-building.

Civil society institutions require first social capital formation, investment in human resource development. Schooling based on modern curriculum and skill development to develop technical know-how is essential. Importing skilled and manual workers may bring quick development and high-rise towers, but when basic human freedoms are curtailed by oppressive regimes interested in self-perpetuation, it does not lead to sustainable development, only to showpieces. If models are required for sustainable development, the tiny case of the Turkish Republic North may serve this purpose.

Freedom under Embargoes: The Case of North Cyprus

Greeks and their friends in the West view North Cyprus as a product of Turkish military operation in 1974, calling it "invasion." Why did this case succeed whereas, as we have seen in this study, all other cases of invasion in the Middle East, have failed? The short answer is that Turkey enjoys the support of most of the population in the North.

The case of North Cyprus is special and unique, as highlighted in Table 2.2. Its status is ranked as the only "free" among the countries listed. In this remarkable case, freedom was achieved under embargoes imposed by the internationally recognized all-Greek regime in South Cyprus. The Turkish Republic of North Cyprus (TRNC), established in 1983, is recognized only by Turkey, recognition being withheld by European and Western powers, especially the permanent members of the UN Security Council, in deference to the wishes of Greece. Greeks are in the Christian West, the Muslim Turks are not. This case is important and deserves elaboration as it sheds considerable light on what might constitute "freedom" in a Muslim-majority land and how it may be sustained.

Much credit for this belongs to the British rule because the island was "rented" from the Sultan in 1878 and the rental agreement provided for the protection of Islam and Muslim Turks on the island. This special obligation toward Turkey and the Turkish community on the island lasted from the beginning to the end of the colonial rule. The historian Sir Harry Luke (1921), for example, viewed one of the last Ottoman Prime Ministers, Kiamil Pasha of Cyprus, who was violently over-thrown by the Young Turks, "the greatest Cypriot since Zeno of Citium" (Luke, 1921, 210). Throughout the seven decades of British rule on the island, the colo-nial administration was always based on "two communities, Turkish and Greek." In the London Conference in 1960, when Independence was granted, sovereignty was transferred to both communities, with five signatures (two communities plus three Guarantors) on the 1960 Accords. The Turkish community on the island has retained the British system of judicial administration and a close attachment to the rule of law.

In 1963, the Makarios regime staged a bloody coup to oust the Turkish partner out of the Republic of Cyprus. This was followed in the summer of 1974 with a second coup by the Junta in Athens, which ousted Makarios as a first step toward annexing the island to Greece by declaring ENOSIS. The 1960 Constitution had a provision explicitly banning ENOSIS; it also empowered Turkey with a right of military intervention in case it happened. There is some evidence of CIA's prior knowledge of the Turkish intervention. The US Secretary of State, Kissinger, upset by the fascist Junta and the Makarios maneuvers with the Soviets, chose diplo-macy to save NATO. He authorized shuttle diplomacy. Acting in concert with Callaghan, the British PM, he proposed, rather vaguely, that Turks in Cyprus be granted more constitutional rights, "But Clerides (temporarily replacing Makarios) refused" (O'Malley and Ian Craig, 1999, 215).

After the Turkish intervention, the island was divided into a Turkish North and Greek Cypriot South. In 2004, the South rejected the UN Plan for a bizonal and biethnic federal republic, but, nevertheless, won membership and was accepted into the EU. Once the Europeans granted membership to the Greek Cypriots, they did a U-turn, breaking all previous undertakings to settle the Cyprus Problem. Everyone, even the top EU diplomats were furious, but it was all political expedi-ency. The Brussels politicians supported the Greeks fully to keep a Muslim Turkey outside the Union. An angry British mediator, David Hannay (2005), denounced the Greek Cypriot leadership:

> Let down by their leadership, they (the GCs) chose, just when they were on
> the point of entering the European Union, to demonstrate that they had not
> understood the first thing about the fundamental objectives of that Union.
> … What will happen now? Much will depend on the prospects for Turkish
> accession to the EU. … as the reality of Turkish accession comes closer, a

solution to the Cyprus problem will become a necessity ... if Turkey's candi-
dature stalls or is blocked, it is not easy to be so sanguine.

245–246

In 1983, frustrated by lack of progress in solving the Cyprus Problem, the North
declared its own independence. The Turkish Republic of Northern Cyprus (TRNC)
is a small country fighting to preserve their Turkish identity for over half a century.
It is as sustainable as the South (Mehmet, 2009); it received aid from Turkey, but the
South received even more aid from the EU. It shares the island with about 700,000
Greek Orthodox people, the majority of whom aspire to turning the island into a
Hellenic republic. The Turks of the island, around 0.6 million, are Muslim, but the
most significant character of the country is its secular character. Turks of Cyprus are
staunchly Kemalist, believing in the doctrine that religion is a private matter. There
is no compulsion in Islam. Each person is free to fast or worship Allah in a private
way. There is no punishment for not fasting during Ramadan, nor for not praying
five times a day. Political and civil rights are respected under laws that also ensure
gender equality, freedom of press, and rule of law. The judiciary is independent
and well-functioning. Secularism was introduced by Mustafa Kemal Ataturk, the
founder of modern Turkey, at the end of WWI when the Ottoman Empire was
defeated and dissolved (Mehmet, 1999,). Ataturk disestablished Islam, abolished the
Caliphate, replaced the Arabic alphabet with the Latin one, and pushed through
numerous laws modelled after universal standards. The idea was to make Turkey a
modern state.

Under President Recep Tayyib Erdogan, a comprehensive program of
Islamization is about the only wedge inserted between Turks of Cyprus and mainland Turkey. Turks of Cyprus are patriotic and identify strongly with Turkish nationalism. But their patriotism is secular; their understanding of Islam excludes *zulm*
(torture), and rejects *zalim* (oppressor), forcing people into obedience in the name
of Islam. Being Muslim is freely submitting to Allah and living an ethical life, along
the True Path, *sera 'til mustakim.*

Under the Turkish Republic, Kemalist ideology replaced *millet* (religious community) with *ulus*, ethnic nationalism. Kemal Ataturk redefined identity and put
the Turkish nation on the road to modernity. Turkish nationalism emerged late
in the Empire. Patriots like the feminist Halide Edip Adivar put forward Turkish
nationalism with passion and Mustafa Kemal's clear-cut vision transformed it into a
winning formula (Mehmet, 1990, chapter 6). It was sheer genius that Kemal went
beyond the French Revolutionary ideals and embraced *Laicism* (secularism) as the
anti-clericalist cornerstone of the Republic. For, only in a political space, freed
from the shackles of religion, could national development based on basic freedoms,
equality of all citizens, and rule of law take root. Now, Kemalism is under attack
by Erdogan's Islamism, but Kemalist ideology remains strongly imbedded in the
Turkish population, and it is strong enough to outlast Erdogan.

In the Muslim Middle East, no Kemalist transformation occurred, save for
a brief experiment under the reforming Shah in 1920s. Nation-building, a

long-term process of economic, social, cultural, and political development, requires social grounding, popular mobilization from grassroots up to the top. It requires institutions like multiparty system, free press, and rule of law, guaranteeing freedom of expression and belief. Virtually all the oil-rich Arab countries lack these institutions, their development being dependent more on guestworkers from the East and professionals from the West, rather than on their own human resources; women remain subjected to patriarchy. Human development is at best a long-term dream. Arab Core countries would do well by embarking on the long-term process of democratic transition and sustainable development by recognition of the TRNC. This would be an act of independence, standing against Western neo-imperialism and voting for the fact that freedom is possible in the Islamic world.

References

Ahmad, Feroz, 1969, *The Young Turks: The Committee of Union and Progress in Turkish Politics, 1908–1914*, Columbia: Columbia University Press.

Aksakal, Mustafa, 2008, *The Ottoman Road to War in 1914, The Ottoman Empire and the First World War*, Cambridge: Cambridge University Press.

Antonius, George, 1939, *The Arab Awakening: The Story of the Arab National Movement*, Allegro Editions, USA.

Atwana, Ahmad A.M. and Muhammad R. Othman. 2015, "Obstacle Faced the Democratic Transition in Egypt in Muhammed Morsi Era", *Procedia – Social and Behavioral Sciences*, Vol. 172, 540–547.

Ben Forstag, 2022, Berber Identity and the Crisis of Algerian Nationalism, https://auisland ora.wrlc.org/islandora/object/jisv18n1%3A3/datastream/PDF/view, accessed on 15 Sept. 2021.

Ben Gurion, David., 2022, www.britannica.com/biography/Theodor-Herzl, accessed on 30 August 2021.

Chomsky, Noam, 2006, *Failed States: The Abuse of Power and the Assault on Democracy*, New York: Metropolitan Books.

Choueiri, Youssef, 2000, *Arab Nationalism: A History*, Maldon: Blackwell Publishing.

Clogg, Richard, 1986, Politics and the Academy, www.taylorfrancis.com/books/mono/ 10.4324/9781315035161/politics-academy-richard-clogg, accessed on 29 April 2022.

Falk, Richard, 2021, " 9/12: Reacting to Crime by War(s): International and Internal Impacts of 9/11", *Journal of Contemporary Iraq & the Arab World*, Vol. 15, No. 3, 1 September.

Fukuyama, F., 1898, "The End of History?", *The National Interest*, Summer.

Hannay, David., 2005, *Cyprus: The Search for a Solution*, New York: I.B. Tauris.

Harris and Aceroglu, eds., 2021, *Thinking beyond Neo Liberalism*, Switzerland: Palgrave-Springer Link.

Ismael, Tareq and Jacqueline Ismael, 2015, *Iraq in the Twenty-First Century, Regime Change and the Making of a Failed State*, New York: Routledge.

JNF, 2022, Jewish National Fund USA, www.jnf.org/our-history, accessed on 29 April 2022.

Khadduri, Majid, 1969, *Republican Iraq: A Study in Iraqi Politics since the Revolution of 1958*, London: Oxford University Press.

Lewis, Bernard, 1961, *The Emergence of Modern Turkey*, London: Oxford University Press.

Luke, Sir Harry, 1921, *Cyprus under the Turks, 1571–1878*, London: C. Hurst and Co.

Mahbubani, Kishore, 2022, *The Asian Century*, Singapore: Springer.

Mehmet, Ozay, 1990, *Islamic Identity and Development: Studies of the Islamic Periphery*, London: Routledge.

Mehmet, Ozay, 2009, *Sustainability of Microstates: The Case of North Cyprus*, Salt Lake City: University of Utah Press.

Nasr, Seyyed Vali Reza, 2001, *Islamic Leviathan: Islam and the Making of State Power*, New York: Oxford University Press.

Newsbreak, 2022, European Commission Takes Legal Action Against Hungary, Poland for LGBT policies, www.newsbreak.com/news/2311243407271/euopean-commission-takes-legal-action-against-hungary-poland-for-lgbt-policies, accessed on 31 August 2021.

O'Malley, Brendan and Ian Craig, 1999, *The Cyprus Conspiracy and the Turkish Invasion*, New York: I.B. Tauris.

Powers, John, 2022, The U.S. Military-Industrial Complex: The True Victors of War, www.carolinapoliticalreview.org/editorial-content/2022/3/7/the-us-military-industrial-complex-the-true-victors-of-war, accessed on 3 May 2022.

Reid, P., 2018, Final Benghazi Report Reveals Hillary Clinton's Failure To Competently Realize Risks, https://americanmilitarynews.com/2016/06/final-benghazi-report-reveals-hillary-clintons-failure-to-competently-realize-risks/, accessed on 31 August 2021.

Ryan, Andrew, 1951, *The Last of the Dragomans*, London: Geoffrey Bles.

Said, Edward, 1979, *Orientalism*, New York: Vintage Books.

Sallolukh, et al., 2015, *The Politics of Sectarianism in Post-War Lebanon*, London: Pluto Press.

Smith, Marcie, 2019, "Change Agent: Gene Sharp's Neoliberal Nonviolence (Part One)", May 10. https://nonsite.org/change-agent-gene-sharps-neoliberal-nonviolence-part-one/

Tibbi, Bassam, 1981, *Arab Nationalism: A Critical Enquiry* (Translated and Edited by Marion Farouk Stuglett and Peter Sluglett), London: Macmillan Press.

Tolchin, Susan, 2019, *The Angry American: How Voter Rage is changing the Nation*, New York: Routledge.

Toynbee, Arnold, 1922, *The Western Question in Greece and Turkey: A Study in the Contact of Civilisations*, New York: Howard Fertig.

Toynbee, Arnold, 1948, *Civilization on Trial*, London: Oxford University Press.

Toynbee, Arnold, 1967, *Acquaintances*, London: Oxford University Press.

12

A SUMMING UP

In our Pandemic-ridden world, racism and xenophobia, including Islamophobia, are rampant.

Dar'ul Islam is in deep crisis: Terrorism has taken Islam hostage, while in several countries, military or dynastic regimes oppress people. Civil wars are creating waves of refugees who are being herded into camps in care of a new system of care-providers, an industry of permanent humanitarian aid. At the end of the day, Muslim victims are wards of American-led neo-imperialist interests.

In this environment, it is difficult to be optimistic about prospects of Islamic unity and progress. After the fall of the Ottomans, nation-states became fashionable, and nationalism has emerged as the modern ideology for determining identity and national development. The analysis in this study supports the following major findings:

1. Oil has been a curse for the Arabs. It directly led to the demise of the Ottoman Empire and partition of the Arab lands. Islamic unity has never recovered from this imperialist plan, which included the creation of Israel. The Zionist prevailed because they were well prepared to seize the diplomatic opportunity given to them by the British government, starting with the Balfour Declaration. Afterward, the United States under Truman facilitated the birth of Israel. Beyond diplomacy, the Zionists were highly successful in nation-building on the battlefield and in institution-building in peace. Through agricultural development they made the desert bloom; they utilized modern technology to feed and house immigrants and settlers escaping persecution and genocide in the West. That is an impressive achievement, which cannot be denied.

2. By contrast, the Arabs have contributed to Israeli nation-building not only by selling land to Zionists, starting this process in the Ottoman times, but also by entering into wars they had no chance of winning. In the WWI, the

DOI: 10.4324/9781003268994-12

Arabs were duped with lies and deceit, known as the Sykes–Picot Agreement. Since WWI, dynasties have relied on neo-imperialists to ward off military dictators or messianic false prophets promising a new Islamic Golden Age but delivering only human suffering. To this day, Arab disunity and weakness have facilitated empowerment of Israel. Except for limited diplomatic victories at the UN General Assembly, Palestinians and Arabs have lost ground. The future looks grim.

3. The USA has staunchly supported Israel from its inception at the UN in 1947–1948. American hegemony in the Middle East has continued, aided, and abetted by dynastic and military regimes dependent on American support and protection for their own survival. This dependence has generated huge losses of people's life and security. Through several invasions and regime change, America has continued to get the oil, while Israel has expanded, and Palestinians and more recent refugees have been pushed into permanent life in camps.

4. These outcomes, like bitter pills, must be swallowed, pride put aside, and the hard truth must be faced realistically. There is no shortcut to nation-building and identity formation in the modern world. Medieval prescriptions will no longer do. Modern institutions take time to build. Social capital is costly. Massive investment is required in sustainable economic and social develop-ment. Such development must be endogenous, home-based, and authentic, based on popular consent, bottom up. The grassroots must quickly witness and enjoy the benefits of modern education, skill development, health, and other basic human needs. There must be accountability between the rulers and the subjects.

5. Secularism, as defined and implemented in Kemalist Turkey in 1920s, is a valid formula today. The tiny example of Turkish Cyprus is significant. Freedom requires separation of Islam and politics. A way must be found for the Arab Core to develop secular politics and regimes.

What are the prospects ahead? In the short run, no escape from the current chaos and global mismanagement can be foreseen. Only a glimmer of hope exists in the long run through the newly emerging Silk Route Economy (SRE). Below we highlight some key conclusions emerging from this study.

No Caliphate

The proposal at the end of II&D was well-intentioned, but, in view of prevailing Islamic disunity, it is an impractical idea. It is tempting to think that problems confronting the Muslim world should be remedied by Muslim leaders. Unfortunately, that is wishful thinking. Much of the chaos in the Muslim Core stems from for-eign invasion. As we have seen, the map of the modern Middle East was drawn by European imperialist powers at the fall of the Ottomans.

The House of Saud bears special responsibility. It is far from being a model of leadership in the Muslim world. It is a fundamentalist regime created out of a conspiracy in partnership with imperialists and is sustained by the biggest hegemon in the world, which has invaded and destabilized the Muslim Core. As the wealthiest Muslim country, it has one of highest ratio of military spending in the world (Global Economy, 2021). It has launched a bloody attack on a neighboring Muslim country, creating one of the biggest humanitarian crises in the world, and it has exported terrorism abroad. Instead of acting as a unifying force, an example of peace and compassion, befitting the host of the Holy Cities of the Hejaz, the Saud dynasty has been a source of discord and violence, exporting fundamentalism, itself one of the most repressive regimes in the world.

Western Guilt and Responsibility

Of course, the seeds of the current chaos were sewn at the end of WWI by invading powers in pursuit of oil. Countries built on lies and deceit become inevitably failed states. The West must accept its moral responsibility for the conspiracy to dismantle and partition the Ottoman Empire at the dawn of the Oil Age. Yes, "the Sick Man of Europe" was badly governed by the inept Young Turks, but the creation of artificial Arab countries behind arbitrary lines in the sand, based on deceit and greed, is the fundamental reason for persistent war and conflict in the Middle East, including the Palestinian problem. Almost all these countries have shown to be unsustainable, leading to oppressive dictatorships and civil wars. The waves of refugees that have been created from 1948 to the present time is truly an international challenge, a failure of the League of Nations and the UN included. Justice would demand that it should be tackled globally with goodwill, starting with reparations to be utilized for genuine nation-building. In future, new Crusades or Interfaith Wars, must be avoided. Waiting for justice, however, may be a long wait!

The Western quest for oil has been the chief source of the crisis in the Muslim Core. The evidence presented in this study, from the Sykes-Picot Agreement to the invasion of Iraq, the West is deeply implicated in the problems of the Middle East. The dispossession of Palestinians, the waves of refugees from the Arab-Israeli conflicts from 1948, the fall of Mosaddeq, the Suez Canal crisis of 1956, the fall of Saddam Hussein of Iraq, the attack on Qaddafi, the Syrian civil war, and, most recently, the abrupt US exit from Afghanistan are all cases of Western invasion and failed states. They are reminders of the collective responsibility, which awaits to be faced to fix the problems if we are to avoid future clash of civilizations. However, the help from the West in solving Muslim problems must be minimal. The primary responsibility must rest on Muslim countries, the leadership, and the people, however challenging the task. Democratic transition can never be imported. Outsiders can help, but under the best possible conditions, this help is limited; foreign powers always have their own interests. In the world at large, there are tremendous challenges of inequality and racism. Building a safe, secure, and democratic society must always be an endogenous process, a long-term process which starts with sustained development.

In sustained development, the welfare of the people comes first, but people's well-being must rest on clean environment, healthy living with dignity and tolerance. Our world is multinational with many religions, cultures, and civilizations. But humanity is ultimately One Family aspiring for peace, security, and well-being. Aggressive capitalism, the product of mercantilism and imperialism, as this study has shown, has divided humanity into haves and have-nots. It has set people and nations apart in an adversarial, hostile relationship. Now, humanity faces an environmental catastrophe. Global warming and desertification are real challenges. If not tackled globally, in partnership and solidarity, we may all perish. Aggressive capitalism must be replaced by global goodwill to build a just and humane world.

In our post-Pandemic world, as shown in Chapter 7, there are clear signs of China overtaking the USA; the West is no longer the global economic dynamo. Liberal democracy is weakening, and illiberal regimes are rising everywhere. China, no less than the Western mercantilist powers, is pursuing its own national interest. At most, Western guilt will finance the new charitable system caring for Palestinians and other Muslim refugees in camps. If they wish to ensure a sustainable future, the Muslim countries in the Arab Core still enjoying unprecedented oil wealth must invest in a Muslim future. Neither China nor the West will do that. Only Muslims can solve Islam's crisis.

A Cleaner, Sustainable World

Energy transformation, transition to a greener world, energized by renewable energy, has become a global trend, unstoppable, and accelerating. The speed of transformation to clean energy will not derail the transition to net-zero by 2050 at the latest. COP26 is providing the roadmap and an opportunity to redefine green energy and renewables. Oil and gas companies have reduced capital spending on fossil fuel projects and are shifting to alternatives. Qatar and Russia are building huge new gas liquefaction facilities that can provide some of the cheapest LNG in the world. COP26 and the growing climate change pressure by activists, and financial institutions, is accelerating decarbonization. Oil producers in the Islamic Core must shift to a greener and sustainable world.

The Prospects of SRE

Equally important is the transition to a more humane and just world. This is possible, but if the West continues to refuse its moral responsibility, China may rise to the occasion. This is a long-term prospect, most likely in the context of a new SRE creating prosperity for Muslim masses long shut out of the benefits of Western capitalism. So far, the China-led SRE initiatives have been primarily infrastructural. A transcontinental railroad, linking Beijing to Istanbul is now operational, and new highways, pipelines, and mega-infrastructural projects are opening new markets and trade opportunities (Frankopan, 2015, 2018).

However, infrastructural investments and projects are not enough. Massive investment is required for human development as defined by the UN Development Program. It aims at: "… expanding the richness of human life, rather than simply the richness of the economy in which human beings live. It is an approach that is focused on people and their opportunities and choices" (UNDP, 2021).

Toward a Humane and Just World

Human development for a humane and just world cannot be created without deliberate action on the part of world leaders, including Muslim leaders. Imperialist leaders led the creation of the present Middle East, putting their own interest first. Oil politics took the center stage ever since the welfare of the ordinary people was pushed into the background. Leaders who created the modern Middle East in 1919 did the people of the region a great disservice. Many in the Middle East believed in the Wilsonian pledges, some of them blatantly contradictory. Admittedly, in 1919, imperialism was at its height and the Arabs were betrayed. This, however, is no excuse; America was always, always, pursuing an America First policy.

Ideally, humanity is one big Global Family, but a family waiting for justice. It faces a global challenge requiring huge investment of funds to build a just and humane world. In a post-Pandemic world, it is hoped that a new, global vision will emerge to build a safer, healthier, and peaceful world. A humane world order needs to be funded autonomously, not through charity or humanitarian aid. Refugees cannot stay in camps forever, while the rich are sheltered behind walls and barbed wires. There must be an international tax to finance social and economic development for the sustainable new world order. Multinational corporations, modern-day descendants of imperialism and colonization, must finally pay their fair share for the cheap oil, and developing country resources that have plundered since the age of Slavery and Mercantilism. International taxation, not charity or tied aid, is the formula to build a more humane and just world. Tolerance, learnt from the Ottomans, is the essential ingredient for the Jews, Christians, Muslims, Buddhist, Hindu, and the rest of Humanity to coexist in peace and dignity.

More realistically, however, it must be recognized that idealism, alone, is no solution. Muslim problems cannot be solved by simply imagining past glory or by appealing for help to others. It is futile to wait for justice from the West, China, or elsewhere. If a Muslim revival is going to happen, Muslim societies and leaders must meet the challenge in the present. Investing in the SRE, with a heavy emphasis on human development, offers the optimal long-term hope as the fossil fuel age draws to a close.

From the critical analysis in this study, a few key conclusions may briefly be highlighted.

First, Western imperialists have invaded the Islamic Core, repeatedly since WWI, drawing lines in the sand, creating artificial countries, displacing, and causing huge human loss and waves of refugees, but when it suits their interest, they go, abandoning "allies" of convenience, the latest case being Afghanistan. In the historical review, analyzed earlier, the United States has betrayed Iran, Iraq, the Kurds, Afghanistan, and, in time when the fossil fuel age ends, oil-seekers will surely do so in Saudi Arabia. In the meantime, much of the oil wealth of producing countries is being squandered in a variety of wars and conflicts at the expense of the welfare of the masses.

Second, state formation, when based on lies and deceit, does not lead to peace and stability built on popular consent. It leads to "failed states" ruled by dynastic or military regimes, oppressing people. Since the departure of the Ottomans, the condition of the Arab masses, in Palestine and elsewhere, has regressed; in several failed states, oppressive regimes, often aided and protected by Western powers, have turned on their own people.

Third, in much of the former Ottoman lands, Muslim values, shaped by Ottoman institutions and custom, still prevail, maybe not among the dynastic and military elites in power but certainly at the grassroots. Identity formation and nation-building have led to cul-de-sac; Islamic unity has led to competing ideologies, most recently, Islam becoming a hostage to terrorism.

Against these hard and bitter realities, our key conclusion is that, sadly, there seems to be no short-term escape from the deep chaos in the Arab and Muslim Core; only a glimmer of hope exists in the long run within the emerging SRE.

Conclusion

One source has estimated the total number of dead (soldiers and civilian) in WWI as 15.6 million, and a further 5.8 million direct civilian casualties (Brill, 2012). Since 1922, when the borders of the Middle East were drawn, the region has descended into permanent war and conflict. In the post-WWII, no less than four wars have been fought between the Arabs and Israel (1948, 1956, 1967, and 1973). In the last two decades alone, in the Muslim Core, deaths, displacement, and refugees due to war and conflict have been no less than 30 million (Table 2.4).

It may be fanciful to speculate the consequences if the Ottomans had stayed out of WWI. The discovery of oil would have gone ahead, for sure. The Turkish Petroleum Company was already a fact. A deal between London and Istanbul, a British-Ottoman alliance was possible had Grey and Asquith did not reject the peace offer from the Sultan's government in 1911 (Fromkin, 1989, 561). Even more likely, had Churchill in the summer of 1914 refrained from impounding the two Turkish warships, built, paid for, and ready for handing over in Newcastle, the Porte would not have succumbed to German pressure to enter the War.

At the onset of WWI, the Old Europe, the Allied Powers, and Tsarist Russia were united against the Ottomans; they succeeded in defeating the Sultan-Kaiser alliance, but it was unholy and unethical all around: the War itself destroyed the Tsar, giving birth to Communist Soviet Union. At Versailles, the Allied leaders, united in an aggressive capitalist spirit, imposed crushing reparations on a defeated Germany and thus paved the way for Hitler, Holocaust, and WWII. Regarding the Middle East, the Allies in 1914 "had little understanding of Islam" (Fromkin, 1989, 564);

they might have been "driven by what proved to be an unwarranted fear of jihad" (Rogan, 2015, 404), and there is no doubt that in Istanbul at the time, there was "a failure of leadership" (Aksakal, 2008, 194). The one issue, however, stands out tallest of all: The Jewish hopes had been raised "to such a pitch that non-fulfillment of the Zionist dream of a Jewish state in Palestine" (Antonius, 1939, 411) was unavoidable. It caused, not only the "the cruelty" of "dislodging or exterminating the nation in possession" (ibid., 412), on a wider scale, it led to imperial deceit, and dynastic betrayal of the Arab masses for whom not even Wilson was able to apply his principles of "consent" of the governed.

In the end, the new map of the Middle East was created, by lines drawn in accordance with the Sykes-Picot and Red Line Agreements, out of which the biggest winners were the Seven Sisters and the Armenian Gulbenkian. The welfare of the people was sacrificed for the sake of barrels of oil that had fueled the most lethal industrial-military complex the world has ever witnessed. Now, with the Ukrainian War raging, Europe and the world face an uncertain world. An SRE, as discussed in this study, seems now a closer prospect.

References

Aksakal, M., 2008, *The Ottoman Road to War in 1914, the Ottoman Empire and the First World War*, Cambridge: Cambridge University Press.

Antonius, G., 1939, *The Arab Awakening, The Story of the Arab National Movement*, USA: Allegro Editions.

Brill, 2012, *Brill's Encyclopedia of First World War*, Boston: Brill.

Frankopan, Peter, 2015, *The Silk Roads: A New History of the World*, New York: Vintage Books.

Frankopan, Peter, 2018, *The New Silk Roads: The New Asia and the Remaking of the World Order*, New York: Vintage Books.

Fromkin, D., 1989, *A Peace to End All Peace, the Fall of the Ottoman Empire and the Creation of the Modern Middle East*, New York: Avon Books.

Global Economy, 2021, Saudi Arabia: Military Spending, Percent of GDP, www.theglobaleconomy.com/Saudi-Arabia/mil_spend_gdp/, accessed on 8 Nov. 2021.

Rogan, E., 2015, *The Fall of the Ottomans, the Great War in the Middle East*, New York: Basic Books.

UNDP, 2021, Human Development Reports, http://hdr.undp.org/en/humandev, accessed on 29 May 2021.

13

POSTSCRIPT ON UKRAINE WAR

As the main writing of this book was completed, war broke out in Ukraine. The impact of this war on the emergence of a new world order is difficult to determine now. A few tentative observations may, however, be in order.

First and foremost, Putin was provoked by the Ukrainian failure to implement the 1914–1915 Minsk agreement granting autonomy to the eastern provinces. Former Chancellor Merkel smartly averted earlier war threats by diplomatic overtures to Putin; after her retirement a leadership vacuum in Europe could no longer avoid war. Now (as of July 2022), after a record hot summer, Europe may look forward to a freezing winter if Gazprom goes ahead with a threatened interruption of gas deliveries.

In terms of finance, the economic sanctions imposed on Russia in the West, initially caused a quick depreciation of the ruble in the wake of sanctions, but Putin's retaliation by insisting that gas exports be paid in ruble has offset this devaluation. Combined with the substitution of the costly American gas for Russian, there has been a significant decline in the Euro: dollar exchange, hitting parity in July 2022.

The Ukraine-Russia war may be seen as a proxy war between NATO/West versus an imperialist Russia. It represents a return to a new Cold War in which the real winners are the weapon dealers and producers, especially in the American military-industrial complex. The economic waste of war material in Ukraine has contributed to inflation in the West, reinforcing supply shortages caused by the COVID-19 Pandemic.

In geopolitical terms, Putin, and the West seem to have mismanaged this conflict. With smart leadership, the war could have been avoided. Putin's imperialist aims are untenable; he may yet pay a high price for his folly. On the other hand, the ultraright, including neo-Nazi extreme groups in Ukraine, should have been reined in and the persecution of the ethnic Russians in border provinces resolved in a manner satisfactory to Moscow. In the end, the map of the region may be revised

DOI: 10.4324/9781003268994-13

to allow a Russian corridor through Donbas to Crimea. However, Ukraine will not easily give up its territorial integrity.

The Ukrainian war will have far-reaching implications for global geopolitics. It may accelerate the emerging Silk Route Economy (SRE), as Russia looks increasingly to the East toward closer relations with China, India, Iran, and develop non-Western markets. In a trilateral meeting in Tehran on 19 July 2022, Putin, Erdogan, and Raisi announced the gradual phasing out of the US dollar in future energy and trade deals. The yuan may appreciate along with ruble. Energy markets are now generating inflation worldwide, and the Biden Administration may put more pressure on Saudi Arabia and the Gulf oil producers to increase production. In the short term, the US-Saudi-Israel relations, directed against Iran, may prevail, but this unholy alliance, including the frosty Biden-MBS relationship, is unsustainable given the widespread anti-American sentiment at the grassroots in the Muslim Core.

In humanitarian terms, it is sad that the Ukraine war has displaced over 4 million refugees, burdening not only neighboring countries in eastern Europe and beyond. However, the speed and open-arm accommodation in the EU and elsewhere in the West stands in sharp contrast to the plight of Syrian and Muslim refugees. Sad as the condition of the Ukrainian refugees is, sadder still is the ethical footing of the world order itself, discussed briefly at the end of this study. When the ethical foundations following the WWI were built of deceit and lies, as happened in the case of the Middle East, it is certain that war and conflict follow. There is a "lesson" here of the utmost significance as Humanity stands and awaits the emergence of a new world order.

INDEX